For Shinji
close frre
of the west

I an w[...]

1 June 97

BRITAIN & JAPAN
BIOGRAPHICAL PORTRAITS
VOLUME II

Anglo-Japanese gathering, London, mid-1930s
PICTURE COURTESY ITO YOSABURO

A note about the Editor

IAN NISH, who also edited Volume I and has contributed three essays to this volume, is Professor Emeritus of International History at the London School of Economics (University of London). He is one of the leading figures in Japanese Studies in Britain and has published widely, particularly with regard to the Anglo-Japanese Alliance and the foreign policy of the Great Powers. Most recently, he has published *Japan's Struggle with Internationalism: Japan, China and the League of Nations, 1931–3).*

He has held many distinguished posts, including President of the European Association of Japanese Studies; in 1991 he was decorated by the Japanese Government for his academic contributions to Anglo-Japanese relations. He is currently one of the vice-chairmen of the Japan Society of London.

Cover picture
This photograph illustrates the chapter on the Mutsu family (ch.11) and shows Count and Countess Mutsu in London in 1907 with the author, presently Ian Mutsu.

BRITAIN & JAPAN

Biographical Portraits

VOLUME II

Edited by

IAN NISH

JAPAN
LIBRARY

BRITAIN & JAPAN: BIOGRAPHICAL PORTRAITS
Volume II
Edited by Ian Nish

First published 1997 by
JAPAN LIBRARY

Japan Library is an imprint of Curzon Press Ltd
St John's Studios, Church Road, Richmond, Surrey TW9 2QA

ISBN 1–873410–62–X [Case]

British Library Cataloguing in Publication Data
A CIP entry for this book is available
from the British Library

Set in Bembo 12 on 12½ point
Typesetting by Bookman, Slough
Printed and bound in Great Britain by Bookcraft, Midsomer Norton, Avon

Table of Contents

List of Contributors

BEST, Antony   Lecturer in International History, London School of Economics. His most recent book is *Britain, Japan and Pearl Harbour: Avoiding war in East Asia, 1936–41* (Routledge, 1995)

BLACKER, Carmen   University lecturer in Japanese (retired), Cambridge University. Has published books and articles on Japanese religion and folklore.

BOYD, Julia   Has recently published *Hannah Riddell: An Englishwoman in Japan* (Tuttle, 1995)

BRITTON, Dorothy   Japan-born author, poet, composer. Her latest book is *The Silver Drum*, a translation of Princess Chichibu's memoirs (Global Oriental, 1996)

CHECKLAND, Olive   Fellow (Overseas), of the Fukuzawa Memorial Centre, Keio University, Tokyo. Her latest book is *Isabella Bird and 'a Woman's Right'* (June 1996)

CORTAZZI, Hugh   A former British Ambassador to Japan and Chairman of Council of the Japan Society, 1985–95; and author of various books about Japan including *The Japanese Achievement* (Sidgwick & Jackson, 1990)

GIFFARD, Sydney   A former British Ambassador to Japan and author of *Japan among the Powers, 1890–1990* (Yale, 1994)

GRAY, Robin   Deputy-Secretary with responsibility for international trade relations, Department of Trade and Industry (now retired)

HANAOKA, Sosuke   Former Director-General of International Trade Bureau, Ministry of International Trade and Industry (MITI) and Executive Vice-President, Osaka Gas. Currently President, Japan Bicycle Promotion Institute

HOARE, James   Senior Principal Research Officer, HM Diplomatic Service. Author of *Japan's Treaty Ports and Foreign Settlements* (Japan Library, 1994)

ION, Hamish   Professor of History, Royal Military College of Canada. Author of various studies including *The Cross and the Rising Sun* (2 vols.) (Wilfrid Laurier University Press)

MORITA, Yoshihiko   Director-General, Planning Office, Export-Import Bank of Japan (formerly London office)

MURRAY, Paul   Counsellor at the Irish Embassy, London. His publication, *A Fantastic Journey: The Life and Literature of Lafcadio Hearn* (Japan Library, 1993) was the winner of the 1995 Koizumi Yakumo Literary Prize in Japan. He is currently working on a biography of Bram Stoker.

MUTSU, Yonosuke Ian Journalist and film-maker. Founder-President of the International Motion Picture Co., Tokyo

NAKAMI, Mari   Professor of International Relations, Seisen University, Tokyo. Her latest article is 'Yanagi Muneyoshi to sono jidai I' in *Seisen Joshi Daigaku kenkyūjo kiyo*, XVII (1996)

NISH, Ian   Emeritus Professor of International History, London School of Economics. Author of *Japan's Struggle with Internationalism, 1931–3* (Kegan Paul, 1993)

OBA, Sadao   Former staff member of Mitsui & Co. First recipient of Japan Society award, 1994. Author of *The Japanese War* (Japan Library, 1995) and *Jawa haisen yokuryū nikki*, 1946–7 [Java internment diary]

TAMAKI, Norio   Keio University, Tokyo. His latest book is *Japanese Banking: a History, 1859–1959* (Cambridge, 1995)

YAMAMOTO, Yumiyo   M. Jur. (Oxford, BNC; Jardine scholar), Ll.B (Gakushuin). Currently legal officer at Bayer Ltd, Japan. Great-great-granddaughter of Masaru Inoue.

Preface

THE JAPAN SOCIETY has in two previous volumes published in 1991 and 1994 tried to interpret the relationship between Britain and Japan, not so much through governments and states as through individuals. In this third volume we have assembled 24 essays mainly about the lives of individual citizens and their reactions to Japan or Britain. These essays have been contributed by Japanese and British writers and have been arranged chronologically.

As before, much of the action is concentrated in Tokyo and London. The essay on British royal visits to Japan in the Meiji period (ch.6) shows the importance which Britain placed on its connections with the Japanese monarchy, while that on the Crown Prince's visit to Britain in 1921 (ch.15) shows the reciprocal interest which Japan had in fostering the relationship with the British royal family. Diplomats, because they reflect better than most the changing relations between two countries, have a prominent place in this volume: from the Meiji period Sir Rutherford Alcock (ch.1); Laurence Oliphant (ch.3); John Gubbins (ch.8); and Mutsu Hirokichi (ch.11), while Yoshida Shigeru, Shigemitsu Mamoru (chs.17–18) and Sir Vere Redman (ch.21) were distinguished figures who bridge the pre-war and post-war periods.

But we have tried to look beyond the national capitals. The two railway pioneers – Inoue Masaru (ch.2) and Edmund Morel (ch.4) – had to operate outside Tokyo – but not too far away! Sadao Oba in his article on Japanese businessmen in Britain writes not only of London but also of Japanese enterprises in Manchester (ch.19).

From the Victorian period onwards Britons have resided in 'rural Japan' and have shown a passion for travel in all parts of the

Japanese islands. And Britons have shown remarkable initiative in putting down roots in what may more appropriately be called 'provincial' Japan: Hannah Riddell in Kyushu (ch.9); Lafcadio Hearn in Matsue, Kumamoto as well as Tokyo (ch.10); John Robertson-Scott in Niigata and Tohoku (ch.12); Berners Cholmondeley in the Bonin islands (ch.13); Richard Ponsonby-Fane in Kyoto (ch.14); and Dr John Batchelor for half a century in Hokkaido (ch.16). Despite difficulties over access, transport and diet, these adventurous 'pioneers' accumulated a wide variety of experience of outlandish parts of Japan, probably more than the current generation can claim. And there was generally the protection of a British consular officer within accessible distance as James Hoare has recorded in his essay on the Japan Consular Service (ch.7).

Not only have we tried to present a broader geographical distribution of connections but we have tried to reflect the individualism – not to say eccentricity – of those who served in our two countries. Those like Robertson-Scott, Hearn and Ponsonby-Fane were strong non-conformist types and attracted an interesting circle of Japanese friends. Even Yoshida and Shigemitsu at the London embassy differed widely from the stereotype of the conformist diplomat, though it might be too much to claim that Yoshida's propensity for 'wanman' politics in the 1950s was something that he learnt in Britain in the 1930s. And, of course, there were others who preferred to live 'far from the madding crowd'. Thus Hirokichi and Ethel Mutsu whose family photograph is reproduced on the cover of this volume chose to leave diplomatic circles and spend the latter part of their lives doing charitable work in Kamakura, an important aspect of the Anglo-Japanese relationship.

The British link was of the greatest importance in the Meiji period. Many of the British nationals treated in this volume spent so long in their country of residence that they became citizens of the world, to some extent remote from their homeland. Those like Hannah Riddell, Ponsonby-Fane and Dr Batchelor adapted to Japan and appear to have found it hard to contemplate re-settling in their own country. Those like John Gubbins who after three decades of residence in Japan did retire to Britain found it hard to settle back without the prospect in those days of a return trip to Japan.

After the Asia-Pacific war the Anglo-Japanese relationship

changed. For some decades after 1945 Japan came under the American shadow; and it was often a benign American shadow since British people were several degrees less liberal in their views towards Japan than the Americans. But some who had special experiences were deeply influenced by the Japanese. Such was Christmas Humphreys (ch.20) who, having served part of 1946 on the legal team at the International Military Tribunal for the Far East in Tokyo, spent much of his later life writing about Buddhism. Sir Vere Redman merits a specially long essay because it is based on the reminiscences of his many friends and some autobiographical fragments, skilfully drawn together by Hugh Cortazzi. His work in Japan covered a long period, first as teacher from 1927 and then from 1946 in the Tokyo embassy (and its antecedents) until his retirement in 1961. Redman's responsibilities were in the field of cultural relations. It is therefore linked to the final essay in this collection on one of the phenomena of the post-war period: the number of contemporary Japanese novels translated into English and their impact on British publishers and readers (ch.24).

Much of the Anglo-Japanese relationship since the war has concerned commerce and Europe. Of course, these commercial connections go back to the bankers of the Meiji period; and we have included one with long-standing Japanese links, A.A. Shand (ch.5). Sadao Oba also focuses on Viscount Kano, one of the key bankers in London in the inter-war period. The central event in the economic history of the post-war period, however, was the Anglo-Japanese Commercial Treaty of November 1962 which was many years in the making. It is useful to have on record a personal account of the British and Japanese standpoints from officials who were involved in one or other aspect of the complicated negotiations (chs.22–3).

Now that the course of Anglo-Japanese relations is set fair, it seems an opportune moment to look back at the many people who tried to create understanding in the past. One marvels at the variety of personalities involved and the remarkable contributions which they made.

For help with the publication of this volume, the Japan Society would like to thank the Japanese Government's Anglo-Japanese History Project. The editor would like to express his thanks to the many contributors in Britain and Japan for their cooperation throughout this endeavour; to the office-bearers and secretariat of the Japan Society for their many acts of kindness; to the publishers who have handled a difficult manuscript with courtesy and forbearance; and to my wife who for the past six months has tried to ensure my sanity with what success I cannot say.

IAN NISH
May 1996

JAPANESE NAMES – In accordance with established conventions, Japanese names are ordinarily presented with the family name first.

Sir Rutherford Alcock, 1809–1897

SIR HUGH CORTAZZI

SIR RUTHERFORD ALCOCK was the first British Minister to Japan from 1859-1864. I first attempted a reassessment of his career in Japan in a paper which I gave to the Asiatic Society of Japan in 1994.[1] It was not possible in the space available to cover Alcock's personality and performance in Japan in depth. In this essay, therefore, I propose to cover some of the aspects omitted from, or dealt with too cursorily in, my earlier evaluation. It may be helpful, however, to readers of this volume if before doing so, I summarize the key points and conclusions made in the original study.

Rutherford Alcock, who was born in 1907, was the son of a London doctor and studied medicine from the age of 15. He developed an early interest in art, learnt Italian and French, studied for a year in Paris. At 21 he obtained his diploma in surgery. In the following year he joined an Anglo-Portuguese force supporting the Queen of Portugal. Alcock then joined the Spanish Legion. On his return to England in 1838 Alcock resumed his medical career. But he had contracted rheumatic fever at the siege of San Sebastian and, losing the use of his thumbs, had to give up his career as a surgeon.

In 1844 Alcock was chosen as a consul in China. He served in Amoy, Foochow, Shanghai and Canton. One of his young subordinates in China was Harry Parkes who later succeeded him as minister in Japan. They got on well. Both believed in taking a firm line. Alcock declared that: 'a salutary dread of the immediate consequences of violence offered to British subjects. . .seems to be the best and only protection in this country for Englishmen',[2] but he did not believe in pushing things too far. His philosophy in relations with oriental peoples was one of firmness and determination combined with patience and persistence. He also had strong ethical principles and did not approve of the unruly and often unscrupulous behaviour of the British business adventurers in China. This was to be a source of trouble in Japan. One fault which he displayed in China and which was also to cause problems in Japan was his wordiness and the lack of clarity in his lengthy despatches.

ALCOCK'S ARRIVAL IN JAPAN

Alcock was appointed British Consul General in Japan in accordance with the terms of the Treaty concluded between Great Britain and Japan by Lord Elgin in 1858. In June 1859, he arrived in Japan by a Royal Naval ship (HMS *Sampson*). He decided that, to be an effective representative, he needed a higher rank and assumed the title of 'Plenipotentiary'. The Foreign Office accepted this self-promotion and made him 'Minister Plenipotentiary'. After a few days in Nagasaki Alcock went on to Edo bay where he arrived on 26 June 1859 in time for the opening of trade on 1 July, as specified in the Treaty of 1858. Despite obstruction from the Tokugawa *Bakufu* authorities he insisted on taking up residence in Edo and established his legation at Tozenji, a temple in the suburb of Shinagawa. One of his first acts was to arrange for the exchange of ratifications of the 1858 treaty to be carried out with due pomp.

The treaty specified that the ports of Nagasaki, Kanagawa and Hakodate were to be opened for trade. The *Bakufu* (camp government) authorities were reluctant to open Kanagawa as it was on the Tokaido, and they feared trouble from anti-foreign elements among the followers of the daimyo travelling on what was at that time the most important of Japan's highways. They accordingly began to develop facilities for traders at Yokohama, a fishing village across the bay from Kanagawa. Yokohama was cut off by canals and foreigners there could be largely isolated as the Dutch had been at Dejima in Nagasaki Bay during the past two hundred years. Alcock fought hard against this deliberate attempt to pervert the terms of the treaty, but British traders found the facilities at Yokohama acceptable. One of the first British merchants to establish himself in Yokohama was William Keswick of Jardine Matheson and Company in premises which came to be known as Ei-Ichiban (i.e England Number One).

Alcock had to deal with other problems affecting the British merchants. One 'of these was the currency to be used by the traders. Under the treaty all foreign coins 'shall pass current in Japan' for one year after trade began and the Japanese authorities were to provide Japanese coin weight for weight (silver and gold). Unfortunately they had grossly underestimated the demand for Japanese coins and in consequence of their scarcity Japanese silver coins were at a premium. Another major difficulty was that the relative value of gold and silver in Japan was five times whereas in the world outside it was some fifteen times. The foreign business community, and in particular the British, put in huge demands for Japanese coins whose supply had to be rationed. This led to ever increasing demands, often on behalf of obviously fictitional people including such imaginary individuals as Snooks, Doodledo, Nonsense and Is-it-not. This infuriated Alcock who considered some of the requisitions for coins were 'a positive disgrace to anyone bearing the name of an Englishman'. Alcock's criticisms of the merchants were resented not least because of the special privileges given to foreign officials who were able to augment their salaries by up to 40% as a result of the favourable rate available for transfers of salary.

Another cause of friction was the restriction on visits from Yokohama to Edo which was outside the limits set in the treaty. The ministers had very limited accommodation in Edo and there were no hotels where merchants could stay. British subjects had to get special permits for visits to Edo as well as invitations from their diplomatic representative whenever they wanted to go there.

One case which aroused a furore among the merchants was that of Michael Moss, a British merchant who was arrested by the Japanese in November 1860. Having been out shooting, he stayed the night in a farm-house outside the limits set in the treaty. While he and his servant who was carrying a wild goose were travelling back to Yokohama on the Tokaido his servant was arrested. Moss drew his gun and demanded the release of the servant. In the subsequent affray a Japanese official had half his arm blown off. This led to Moss being bound hand and foot and carted off. At first the authorities denied any knowledge of Moss's whereabouts but eventually delivered him up to the consul who under the extraterritorial provisions of the treaty arraigned Moss in the Consular Court. Moss was found guilty by the consul and two assessors and sentenced to be deported and fined $1000. Alcock, to whom the sentence had to be referred, thought that Moss was getting off too lightly and added a sentence of three months imprisonment to be served in Hong Kong. The business community considered Alcock's decision wrong and unfair. Moss, on arrival in Hong Kong, took out a writ of habeas corpus and an action for damages against Alcock for wrongful imprisonment. He won his case and was awarded $2000 in damages. Although British officials enjoyed shooting, Alcock had some justification in believing that Moss's behaviour (if repeated) could greatly exacerbate relations with the Japanese and that an exemplary sentence was called for, but he had exceeded his authority and did not take adequate account of the feelings of the merchant community.

It is clear from other evidence that members of the British merchant community in Yokohama in those days often behaved badly and arrogantly. Their sexual behaviour was also flagrantly different from those of the Victorian moralists. Alcock disapproved of the Gankiro, the foreigners' brothel in Yokohama, where syphilis and other sexual diseases were rife.

Dr William Willis, the legation doctor, who commented on the prevalence of sexual disease among the foreign community also condemned their general behaviour. In a letter dated 15 February 1863 he wrote; 'The English. . .are more hated than any other foreigners. . .We have all the air, if not insolence, of a dominant race; the facility with which we use our hands and feet in support of argument may elicit respect but not esteem. . .We may disguise it as we like, we are a set of tyrants from the moment we set foot on Eastern soil.'[3] A.B.Mitford, later Lord Redesdale, who was a member of Alcock's staff thought that his minister's criticisms of the British merchants, though bitter, were 'not more than the facts warranted'.[4]

Despite the bad blood between Alcock and the merchants in the early years, by the time he finally left Japan in 1864 the merchants paid a handsome tribute to his endeavours on their behalf. Certainly, it is clear from Alcock's despatches that he was never in doubt about the fact that the development of British trade was a, if not the, major objective of his mission.

When Alcock arrived in Japan all official communications had to be translated twice through the Dutch language. This left infinite possibilities of misunderstanding and caused vexatious delays. Alcock realized that he must have staff capable of communicating in Japanese and he ensured that high priority was given to the training of student interpreters in the consular service. Thus began the Japan Consular Service. He also made strenuous endeavours despite his age (he was 50 when he arrived in Japan) to learn Japanese. He and members of his staff collected each morning with 'our unfortunate teacher in the midst. . .bewildered and sore distraught, under a searching crossfire of questions for equivalents to English parts of speech'.[5] He found the written language particularly difficult. The almost total absence at that time of dictionaries, grammars and primers induced Alcock to produce two books devoted to the Japanese language. These were *Elements of Japanese Grammar for the Use of Beginners* which was published in Shanghai in 1861. The second was *Familiar Dialogues in Japanese with English and French Translations for the Use of Students* which was published in London and Paris in 1863. Neither book can be commended for use by the student today! But Alcock deserved high marks for effort, even if he only deserved a lesser one for achievement.

ALCOCK'S JOURNEYS IN JAPAN

Alcock visited Nagasaki on a number of occasions. In September 1859 he went to Hakodate to install Pemberton Hodgson as the first British consul there. His main problem was to secure accommodation, the Russians having got there first. Eventually, the Japanese agreed to allocate the British consul a temple which they had been preparing for the new governor.

In September 1860, after the climbing season had ended, Alcock managed, despite strenuous opposition from the authorities, to arrange for himself and a small British party to climb Mt Fuji.[6] They were the first foreigners to make the ascent. On his way back to Edo Alcock stayed a few days at Atami. Alcock did not find Atami 'gay as a place of residence. Beyond the interests attaching to the study of village life in Japan, there is nothing whatever to amuse or give occupation'.

In May 1861, Alcock travelled with de Wit, his Dutch colleague, by land and sea to Edo.[7] He was not impressed by the miserable hamlets he saw in the Inland Sea. He noted at Osaka, in what today would be considered at the very least politically incorrect, that he had 'long given up looking at temples in Japan; for after seeing one or two, it is like looking at successive negroes – nothing but a familiarity of acquaintance, which you do not desire, can enable you to distinguish any difference between them'.

THE BAKUFU AND THE SAFETY OF FOREIGNERS AND FOREIGN MISSIONS

Alcock found dealing with the *Bakufu* authorities was at best frustrating; at worst they seemed to him to be deceitful and obstructive as well as insulting and threatening. As early as 9 August 1859 he sent a note to the Ministers of Foreign Affairs in which he complained that his officers could not walk outside their missions 'without risk of rudeness, offence and. . .violence of the most determined and wanton character. . .These outrages can only be considered as a reproach and scandal'. Alcock's protests had no effect. The first of many murders of foreigners occurred in Yokohama on 25 August of that year when a Russian officer was killed in the street. In November Alcock's servant was attacked before his eyes. In his note of 8 November to the Ministers of Foreign Affairs he gave a graphic account of the encounter with some drunken, armed samurai. Alcock became so frustrated that on 14 December he addressed a note to the authorities which contained a threat of armed retaliation. This earned a rebuke for Alcock from Lord John Russell, the Foreign Secretary: 'Time and patience may remove many of the difficulties of which you complain. . .You should endeavour rather to soothe differences than to make and insist on peremptory demands. Our intercourse is but duly begun; it should not be inaugurated by war.' Lord John's view from the safety of London inevitably differed from that of his minister enduring the threats and risks to life in Japan at that time.

On 14 January 1861 Heusken, the Dutch interpreter to Townsend Harris, the American minister, was waylaid and murdered on his way back from a visit to the Prussian legation in Edo. This led to an acrimonious quarrel between Alcock and Townsend Harris. The quarrel began after the funeral which the diplomatic corps against the advice of the *Bakufu* authorities had all attended. Alcock invited his colleagues to discuss what action they should jointly take. Alcock who took charge of the proceedings urged that, because of the failure of the authorities to provide for their security, they should all withdraw to the comparative safety of Yokohama. The other diplomats concurred but Harris demurred declaring that Heusken had exposed himself to attack by going out at night against the advice which had been given him. He failed to attend a second conference called by Alcock, telling him that, by withdrawing to Yokohama, the diplomats were playing into the hands of the

Japanese authorities who would be thus relieved of 'anxiety, responsibility and expense' and they would never be able to return to Edo. The lengthy and bitter correspondence resulting from this quarrel was duly published in London and Washington. Both ministers appear to have behaved intemperately and neither was blameless, but Alcock who had been exposed to danger in many places and occasions cannot justifiably be accused of cowardice.

In fact, the Ministers were able to return to Edo in March 1861 following discussions with *Bakufu* officials in Yokohama. However, their safety had by no means been assured. In July 1861, shortly after he returned to the legation following his journey overland from Nagasaki with de Wit, the legation was attacked in the middle of the night by *ronin* (masterless samurai). Ten of their guards were wounded and two killed. The next morning the legation 'looked as if it had been sacked after a serious conflict'.[8] Alcock was provoked by the appearance after the incident of a Japanese official who called to congratulate him on his escape and prayed him 'to accept a basket of ducks and a jar of sugar in token of amity'. Alcock rejected this peace offering and demanded 'justice and redress, not ducks or sugar'.

Alcock's task in these days was complicated not only by the fact that it still took some four months to get a reply from London but also by the inability of the foreign secretary to understand the situation on the ground. This was partly Alcock's own fault because his meaning was often clouded by his emotions and verbosity. Alcock also could not easily call for assistance from HM ships in Far Eastern waters. These were limited and communications with them were subject to frustrating delays.

HOME LEAVE 1862/3, AND RETURN

In March 1862 Alcock, having arranged for a *Bakufu* mission to Europe to travel in one of HM ships, departed on home leave. By this time he had come to the conclusion that Britain should not insist on the opening on 1 January 1863 of additional ports as specified in the treaty but should accept the Japanese proposal to defer the opening of these ports until 1 January 1868. He accepted that a refusal to agree to postponement could provoke civil war and anarchy. (For further comments on this and the discussions leading up to this recommendation see below.) Although Alcock recommended this concession, his own attitude subsequently hardened, as did that of Lord John Russell who was clearly irritated by the attempts of the Japanese envoys to extract further concessions from the British during their stay in London. By the time of his return to Japan Alcock had determined that he would insist on the fulfilment by the Japanese of the terms of the treaties and that he would, if necessary, use force for this purpose. The British Government, however, still seemed to believe in a conciliatory approach despite the Namamugi incident of September 1862 in which Richardson, a British merchant from Shanghai, had been murdered by Satsuma samurai while he was riding on the Tokaido near Yokohama. This led in due course, after the British had failed to get redress from Satsuma, to the bombardment of Kagoshima. This retaliation was criticized in parliament and may well have been one factor in the government's preference for conciliation over force.

Alcock who had just returned to Japan made it clear in a despatch of 31 March 1864 that he regarded the protocol signed in London as 'the culminating act and fitting end of the conciliatory policy'. All in authority in Japan 'should clearly understand that we intend to enforce respect' for our Treaty rights and will 'resist with arms, if need be, all attack'.

On 6 May, he declared that as the *Bakufu* had failed to take effective action against the daimyo of Choshu who had closed the straits of Shimonoseki to foreign shipping firm action would have to be taken to reopen the straits. Foreign Secretary Russell did not agree, but his instruction arrived too late to prevent the action which Alcock had engineered. Alcock was at this time much concerned about the position of the community in Yokohama as the *Bakufu* had declared their intention of closing the port of Yokohama to foreign commerce. He and his colleagues had by now begun to get a better appreciation of the relationship between the Shogun, the Daimyo and the Mikado. Their understanding had been helped by a conversation which Ernest Satow, who had made much progress as a student interpreter in the consular service, held that spring with Ito Hirobumi and Inoue Kaoru, two young samurai from Choshu who were to be among the main leaders of the new Japan.

Alcock was careful to ensure that he had the support of his diplomatic colleagues over action to reopen the Straits. Harris had gone and Alcock found Pruyn, the new American Minister, easier to deal with. The main complication was with the French because, by a convention signed in Paris by Japanese envoys and the French Government, the Japanese had undertaken to open the port of Shimonoseki to foreign trade. However, the *Bakufu* settled this difficulty by refusing to ratify the convention as they were powerless to effect the opening of the port which was controlled by the Choshu authorities.

The straits of Shimonoseki were reopened largely by a British force which avoided using the sort of indiscriminate bombardment which had aroused public opinion in Britain against the attack on Kagoshima in 1863. Alcock argued vigorously in his despatches that the strong action taken in the straits had been justified. He asserted in his despatch of 28 September 1864 that 'there was but one means of efficaciously protecting Yokohama, and that was by a bold and decisive blow levelled at Choshu, to paralyze his party, and take the heart out of them for any such enterprise'. Lord John Russell in a despatch dated 2 December 1864, declared that Alcock had made 'a successful vindication of the policy you have pursued'. However, before this Alcock had been recalled to explain his actions and had left Japan under a cloud. Having been vindicated, he was promoted to the post of minister in Peking and did not return to Japan. He did, however, continue to write about Japan in British journals and his book *Art and Art Industries in Japan* was published in 1878.

I concluded my Asiatic Society paper by quoting Grace Fox's assessment of Alcock in her book *Britain and Japan, 1858-1883* (Oxford, 1969). She wrote that Alcock 'was subjected to the calculated duplicity of the *Bakufu* and the assaults of the anti-foreign or anti-*Bakufu* terrorists, denied contacts with the elite classes, and was often thwarted in his efforts at justice, by the defiant behaviour of British subjects. Yet by 1863 his analysis of the situation and recommendations for ending Japan's obstructions and opposition to the foreign treaties set the goals for British policy until after the Restoration'.

I concluded that by the standards of his age Alcock should be counted among the more effective of our pro-consular envoys in the Victorian era. The following pages which summarize other aspects of Alcock's career will, I hope, throw some further light on his personality.

ALCOCK AS AN ADMINISTRATOR

Alcock, as Minister Plenipotentiary and Consul-general, was in charge of the total British official establishment in Japan and, because of the unavoidable delays in communication with London, had to take many decisions on his own authority which in posts closer to home would have been referred to the Foreign Office.

Policy towards Japan, the protection of British subjects and the promotion of British trade were no doubt the most important of his tasks. He also had to act in a semi-judicial capacity in view of the extra-territorial provisions of the treaty. As we saw in the Moss case, he did not always carry out this part of his responsibilities with due respect to the law. Beyond these important tasks he had to run an organization where the ordinary necessities such as stationery were unavailable locally and where there were as yet no banks and no telegraph.

The administrative problems which Alcock faced are set out in his despatch of 13 July 1860 in which he reported on 'the principal items of expenditure hitherto incurred upon my authority'. His total annual expenditure had amounted to £7,679. This seems a modest sum even by standards of the time.

His first concern was to ensure that the establishment of staff for the legation and the consulates was adequate to the tasks they faced. He requested the appointment of a Secretary of Legation to act as his deputy and take charge when he was away.[9] Because of language problems he urged an increase in the complement of Dutch interpreters to at least five. He also called for the appointment of assistants to the consuls and for a medical officer for the legation.[10] Adding up all his recommendations he proposed an additional expenditure of £4,000 per annum. He concluded that 'the service cannot be efficiently and satisfactorily performed by a smaller establishment'.

Turning to the subject of buildings and repairs, Alcock reported that these costs had amounted to £564:15s:11d. The next largest item had been special contingencies including office furniture, iron chests etc. These came to £357:18s:7d. He noted that the rents paid for consular premises had been moderate amounting to about £100 for each consulate. He had so far successfully resisted Japanese pressure to build a legation and consulates, but it was 'very inconvenient' for the Japanese 'to have all their best temples at the ports occupied by foreign Consuls'.

Alcock's administrative problems were complicated by the fact that 'at present there is absolutely no exchange; and no funds can be obtained here or at any of the ports upon bills'. This despatch suggests that Alcock was a competent and reasonably economical administrator and coped well with the serious administrative difficulties he faced.

In his despatch of 11 July 1860, Alcock recorded that trade in the first year had amounted to nearly £1,000,000 sterling 'and with large profits'. He noted the beginnings of a trade in tea and silk. He understood that some 15,000 chests of tea and no less than 3,000 bales of silk had been exported. Merchants were, he said, counting on a supply of 15 to 18 thousand bales of silk being supplied while 'hundreds of tea-chests' were being manufactured in Edo. Other potential exports included vegetable wax and oils, mother-of-pearl shells, camphor and gall-nuts. He also referred to Japan's known mineral wealth although 'little progress has been made in conquering the repugnance of the Government to see any of the produce of their mines exported'. He had to add that: 'Of imports little can be said: the Japanese are only just beginning to show a disposition to buy any of our manufactured goods. This is a trade yet to be made, and wants must first be created in the natives.'

Before trade could develop the obstructionist attitudes of the Japanese authorities had to be overcome and security assured. Rightly he gave priority to these requirements, but throughout his service as minister he was conscious of the importance of developing trade with Japan.

ALCOCK AND THE RUSSIAN THREAT

On 18 November 1860, Sir John Crampton, HM Ambassador at St Petersburg, sent Lord John Russell at the Foreign Office a despatch in which he warned of a Russian push southwards towards Japan from their territories in the Far East. He declared: 'There is abundant evidence to show that the seizure of the Island of Matsmai[11] forms part of the Russian scheme of aggrandizement in the Pacific.' He added that 'the Japanese Government might be glad to know that both Sahalin [Sakhalin] and Matsmai are coveted in Russia'.

On 2 August 1861 Alcock addressed a despatch to Lord John Russell on Russian policy in the Far East. Having outlined the progress of the Russians in the area, he declared that Russia had gained 'a commanding position as regards the territories of China and Japan, and still more in reference to the great commerce of the Pacific'. He considered that one of the writers quoted by the embassy in St Petersburg had made 'a frank declaration of a policy of continuous aggression and conquest'. In Alcock's view, developments in the area called 'for the vigilant observation of the maritime powers of Europe, and of none so urgently, in view of the magnitude of the interests at stake, as Great Britain'.

Alcock was particularly concerned by the presence of Russians along the coast of Korea and in the Tsushima islands. A Russian corvette, the *Possadnick*, commanded by a Captain Barileff, was laid up in the Sound running between two of the Tsushima islands, 'apparently refitting, and quite dismantled, with work-shops and quarters on shore'. Here Alcock's despatch becomes muddled and goes off into a sidetrack. According to information he had received the daimyo of Tsushima had written to the 'Taicoon' saying that he had been attacked by the Russians but did not need any assistance. There had followed the attack on the British legation in Edo which 'was confidently affirmed, by the popular voice, to have been the act and deed of the Prince of Tsushima, in revenge for the violence and defeat he had suffered in his territories from the Russians'. Then, allowing his emotions to run away, Alcock went on: 'That all members of a Legation, with their Chief, should be thus indiscriminately immolated to the outraged pride of the Daimio, appeared to be considered in perfect accordance with Japanese traditions and habits.' He had to admit, however, that 'no legal or undoubted proofs have been attainable'. Indeed, the story about the involvement of the daimyo of Tsushima in the attack on the legation was a complete fabrication.

Reverting to the Russian threat he declared that he would not be surprised 'if at any hour the news arrived that, as a preliminary whet to this appetite for appropriation, Tsushima was in Russian hands'. This led him on to a discussion of what action should be taken to deal with the implied threat to British interests. One possibility would be for the British admiral in the Far East, Sir John Hope, if on close inspection he concluded that the Russians had 'any immediate intention of making a pretext for seizing Tsushima', 'to give their senior naval officer notice that this could not be permitted, on the grounds that it would prejudice our Treaty rights'. Another alternative would be for the British to take possession of the islands either by a convention with the Japanese in exchange for certain treaty rights they were anxious Britain should renounce 'or by force as a reparation or indemnity for injuries suffered at their hands in violation of the Treaties, for which no redress could otherwise be obtained'.

Sir John Hope, with whom Alcock discussed his proposals, did not agree that the Tsushima islands 'could properly be considered as giving any command of the Straits, or being otherwise a desirable possession to Great Britain'. The admiral was, however, willing to take a look at the situation in the Tsushima islands and, if he concluded this was necessary, to give an appropriate warning to the Russians there. Hope, in a separate memorandum for the Admiralty, explained his views thus: 'I am disposed to consider even the temporary occupation of any portion of Japanese territory, as a measure of coercion, to be most inexpedient, in as much as it would not only strengthen, but justify, that jealousy of foreign intercourse which has given rise to by far the larger portion of the difficulties in which our Minister has been involved – an intercourse, in all equity let it be remembered, that we have forced upon Japan.'

Alcock whose imperialist sentiments clearly exceeded those of the admiral concluded his despatch with an attempt in colourful terms to justify his attitude. He declared: 'And the day of grace seems nearly to have passed; with the beak and talons of the Russian eagle sharpened; and Japan not only without any alliance, offensive and defensive, to supply her with the strengths she wants to meet such a foe, but resolutely refusing to see her danger. The Japanese rulers are too much absorbed in measures for driving the other Powers from her shores, not seeing that they form their best security, and thus blindly would rush on to their fate.' Finally he declared: 'No doubt there are many people in England who would be quite ready to cry out, and condemn as flagitious the whole scheme sketched out. But to all such I would say, if the answer rested with me, there are necessities in self-defence, with national as with individual life; and that which is now threatened by Russia is vital to the interests without which our national life must perish. If no other or milder course be open whereby to avert it, the necessity would in this, as in a thousand other cases, prove its justification.'[12]

Laurence Oliphant who was returning to Britain after having been wounded in the attack on the British legation accompanied Commander Craigie on a reconnaisance mission to Tsushima in HMS *Ringdove* and reported the results of these investigations to Hammond, the Permanent Under-secretary in the Foreign Office, in a letter from Shanghai dated 2 September 1861. Craigie's mission was followed up in August 1861 by a visit by the admiral in HMS *Encounter*. In his report to the Admiralty

Hope reported on the actions of the Russians and of the exchange of letters which he had had with Captain Barileff. In his letter of 28 August to Barileff, the admiral had pointed out the treaty between Russia and Japan did not permit Barileff to create establishments ashore or to survey the coast without Japanese permission. He asked whether the Russian would leave in October as he had previously stated and whether he had any orders to create a permanent establishment. Barileff's reply in French took a tone of injured innocence, but affirmed that he had received no orders to occupy the island. The date of his departure was uncertain.[13] Partly as a result of British pressure and strenuous protests by the Japanese the Russians withdrew from Tsushima in the autumn of 1861.

ALCOCK AS A NEGOTIATOR WITH THE JAPANESE AUTHORITIES

Alcock's verbosity and his emotional reactions to events frequently detracted from his abilities as a negotiator and reporter. However, in the negotiations leading up to the British agreement to accept postponement of the opening of the additional treaty ports in 1862, Alcock showed both a readiness to make concessions where these seemed justified and an increased understanding of Japanese difficulties which he had failed to grasp earlier on. His firmness in negotiations at the time of the Shimonoseki affair, on the other hand, showed that he could remain firm in the face of recalcitrance.

Key meetings with the Japanese foreign ministers, leading up to Alcock's recommendation of a concession on the opening of additional ports took place in Edo on 14-15 August 1861. Alcock's lengthy and rambling despatch to Foreign Secretary Russell includes his account of these crucial meetings. We also have Oliphant's clearer record in his 'Compte-Rendu' submitted to the Foreign Office. Indeed, Alcock's despatches were so diffuse that Russell felt impelled to summarise briefly the position as he had gathered it from Alcock's correspondence. He noted that 'Alcock evidently does not wish to insist on the opening of the two ports which still remain to be opened according to Treaty. The question will be, whether we ought to waive the fulfilment of those articles, and if so, what conditions we shall ask in return for such concessions'.

Alcock in his despatch of 16 August said that: 'it is, indeed, impossible not to feel, here on the spot, that we have arrived at a turning point in the history of all foreign relations with Japan'. He declared that a false step at this juncture 'might plunge the country into a civil war'. Excessive caution, on the other hand, might 'give such encouragement to the hostile agencies at work, that the position created by Treaties will be too far lost to be ever recovered by peacable means'. He thought that the Japanese anxiety to get agreement to the deferment of the opening of the ports and their embarrassment at the attack on the British legation made this an opportune moment to try to develop a confidential dialogue with the Japanese ministers. The arrival of Admiral Sir John Hope and Sir Hercules Robinson, the Governor of Hong Kong, provided an excuse to seek a substantive meeting.

The Japanese Ministers eventually agreed to a confidential meeting. The *Ometsuke* (or 'Chief Spy' as Alcock called him) with all subordinates and attendants were excluded leaving the three 'Governors' of foreign affairs and Moriyama their interpreter. Alcock kept with him only the admiral, Oliphant (Secretary of Legation) and Myburgh, his Dutch interpreter. With Moriyama on the floor between the tables and all the rest huddled close around, the discussions began 'in a tone so low that had anyone been behind the screens in the vicinity, the Ministers must have felt it would have been impossible to overhear'. The conversation involving double interpretation lasted for three hours and was adjourned to the following day. All in all, the conversation lasted some ten hours. It certainly helped Alcock to get a better understanding of the real position of the *Bakufu* in relation to the Mikado and of the problems which they faced.

Alcock felt that his persistence in remaining at the legation despite the armed attack on it 'while not without some risk' had gained him some advantages and that the position of the foreign representatives in the capital was now 'more firmly established'. He was encouraged by the willingness of the ministers of foreign affairs to explain their difficulties and considered that there were 'grounds for this improved feeling' with the Japanese. He had reached the conclusion after consulting his diplomatic colleagues that 'Of decided bad faith and unwillingness on the part of the Japanese Government to protect foreigners...there is not sufficient evidence. On the contrary I have come to the conclusion that they do really desire our protection.' But their inability to provide adequate protection compelled him to seek a British guard.

Alcock, however, a few paragraphs later reverted to form and declared that it would be long before Edo became 'either a pleasant or safe place of residence to the foreigner, exposed to the machinations of a race of political thugs, who take to assassination and massacre as a form of patriotism; for no criminals are so dangerous as those who can reconcile to their notions of virtue the pursuit of their objects'.

Alcock followed this with a lengthy review of the attitudes of his colleagues and of British business. He then turned to the proposal to delay the opening of the additional ports noting 'the grievous want. . .of more full and reliable information as to the actual Government of the country'. Behind the Tycoon and his councils 'in more or less vague and shadowy outline, though real in substance, only enveloped in a haze of mystery, are, first, the only acknowledged Sovereign of the country, the "Mikado". . .But, although to the Mikado is due the profound respect and allegiance of every Japanese yet, as he is held not to meddle with the outer world and its vulgar interests, his demands upon them must be very small. . .Nevertheless, the Ministers told me the Mikado did, through his female Court, receive from time to time news of what was going on outside.' Alcock concluded that 'The Mikado is thus not altogether a myth.'

After a rambling discussion of history and the present position in Japan he noted that the Japanese 'know something. . . of our past history. . .in the East – how all began by a petition to trade, and ended by massacres and conquest. . . shall we wonder, or be impatient and indignant, that they distrust us.' He concluded that 'We must be patient, then, and either leave them to themselves – the only boon for which they would be really grateful – or consent to bear the natural penalty of a past it is out of our power now to change, unless we are prepared to justify their fears and hatred by making our trade a pretext for all the calamities of war and the conquest of the country.' He was sure that HM Government would reject the latter alternative. In that case Britain had no real alternative but to accept the Japanese proposal. Unfortunately, Alcock muddied this recommendation by suggesting that Britain should accept the offer of the opening of the port of Tsushima during the deferred period. (This idea fell by the wayside.)

He urged the conclusion of a protocol or convention recording that the deferment had only been accepted 'on the distinct assurance that the Tycoon hoped thereby to succeed in allaying the public discontent, from which all danger sprang and that trade might go on without restriction or obstruction'. Lord Russell had great difficulties in making sense of Alcock's despatches.

Alcock, rather arrogantly, told the Japanese ministers that Britain 'was enabled to enforce her views . . .and if in the course of her future relations with Japan, she saw fit to waive any of her Treaty rights, it was not likely that any other Power would insist upon them'.

Alcock asked why he had not been able to call on any daimyo. The minister's reply was: 'In Japan it is not the custom for any blood relation to call upon each other. We are, for instance, both Daimios, but we have never visited each other. If you were to live here for ever you would never be able to call upon a Daimio.'

At the second meeting the President of the Goroju 'and consequently the first Minister in the Empire' attended but 'under no circumstances does he ever take part in the conversation, and seldom manifests the slightest appearance of interest in what is going on. Upon the present occasion, however, he seemed occasionally to listen with great interest, though he never hazarded a remark.'

The ministers, commenting on the form of government in Japan, declared that this was very different from that of European countries. 'With us there is a spiritual Emperor, who really is the Emperor of Japan. . .Of course the Tycoon honours the Mikado, from whom he takes his investiture. . .The Mikado lives shut up in a house in Miako [Miyako i.e. Kyoto], and no one sees him; he is looked upon as a God, as sacred as if he was upon an altar; he has no communication with the outer world, and he does not know the actual circumstances in which the lower classes are placed; but he now and then receives rumours of discontent arising from foreign trade. . .It is our intention to inform him of the actual state of matters, but as he is invested with so much honour it will take some time. . .Osaka and Hiogo being in the neighbourhood of Miako, the Mikado is very much against their being opened; he has some very unruly subjects (this is a secret), and if they were opened there is no saying what collision might be brought about between the Mikado and the Tycoon. . .He is waited upon by women, and they get information and give it to him, and he occasionally writes to the Tycoon, and the latter occasionally writes and asks him about matters.' (As a description of the relative position of, and relations between, the Mikado and the Tycoon these comments make interesting reading!)

On being pressed by Alcock to say what assurance the ministers could give that, if the concessions requested were made, the discontent from which the dangers came would cease, the ministers could only assert that 'in the course of time the popular discontent will be abated'. They did, however, assure Alcock that they had no intention of seeking further concessions. (This, of course, they did during the mission to Europe.)

Alcock's recommendation that the British government should agree to the postponement of the opening of the additional ports was wise in the circumstances prevailing at that time in Japan, even if his arguments in support of his recommendation were rather muddled. The ministers' assurances were, however, of no practical value as they were in no position to influence opinion in Japan. The main interest of the meetings lies in what they reveal about Alcock who clearly enjoyed the conspiratorial nature of the discussions and about the ministers whose revelations should hardly have required such 'confidentiality'.

ALCOCK'S JUDGEMENTS ABOUT JAPAN

In *The Capital of The Tycoon* Alcock commented that: 'Japan is essentially a country of paradoxes and anomalies, where all – even familiar things – put on new faces and are curiously reversed. Except that they do not walk on their head instead of their feet, there are few things in which they do not seem, by some occult law, to have been impelled in a perfectly opposite direction and a reversed order.' This comment has often been quoted, usually with approval, by writers about Japan who put pen to paper after a limited stay. It is, of course, one of the many myths about the Japanese.

In general, however, Alcock was a careful observer of Japanese life and nature and, except in relation to the *bakufu* authorities with whom he had to deal, he was rarely anti-Japanese. His prejudices which were those of a Victorian middle-class moralist inevitably coloured many of his comments on Japan. He particularly regretted the lack of the Christian ethic.

Alcock could rarely resist the temptation of railing against the *Bakufu*. In his despatch of 11 July 1860 he encapsulated one of his favourite themes, namely the systematic policy of isolation and restriction on all foreigners which together with 'insecurity of life, and denial of justice when either life or property is sacrificed, are the greatest difficulties now to be encountered in Japan'. He noted that relations with Japan were at all times 'at the mercy of the Government of the day, and may be interrupted by a turn of the Tycoon's fan'. Alcock's feelings on this score were understandable in view of the many frustrations he suffered.

As we have seen, Alcock had no liking for Japanese temples and thought nothing of Japanese architecture, but he was interested in Japanese art objects and tried e.g. through the exhibits which he collected for the International Exhibition in London in 1862 to promote the export of Japanese works of art. He studied Japanese art with some care, if not always with aesthetic discrimination. His book *Art and Art Industries in Japan* is a competent survey of certain aspects of Japanese art which were available to him. He wrote in this: 'Of high Art, such as has been cultivated in Europe since the dark ages, the Japanese know nothing. But the range of true artistic work in its application to industrial purposes in Japan is very wide, and more varied than anywhere in Europe. There are a peculiar grace and delicacy, both of design and execution, in all their work, even in utensils for the common purposes of daily life. . .' In Alcock's view, 'all branches of Japanese Art, apart from their popular picture-books, are decorative in their main purpose' but he wanted to avoid 'any hasty inference that decorative Art should be regarded as something inferior or ignoble'. His final conclusion which is a fair one was that the lesson to be derived from the study of Japanese Art was one of universal application – 'that only those who love their work, and find satisfaction in its excellence, can feel true pleasure in anything they undertake'.

CONCLUSION

These further comments on Alcock's work in relation to Japan do not call for any fundamental change in the assessment which I reached at the end of my study for the Asiatic Society of Japan. Judged by the standards of his time, he was generally successful as a pro-consular envoy. By the standards of today he must be adjudged an imperialist with a limited outlook. As an administrator he was competent but he would never have prospered in the modern diplomatic service unless he had controlled his verbosity and achieved a greater measure of clarity in his recommendations. He would also have had to curb his emotional reactions to events and people. Still as the first British minister to Japan his achievements were considerable and he is surely a worthy object of study.

Inoue Masaru – 'Father' of the Japanese Railways[1]

YUMIYO YAMAMOTO

IN 1863, five bright, ambitious young noblemen were sent by the Choshu clan to England to study. All of them – Ito Hirobumi, Inoue Kaoru, Yamao Yozo, Endo Kinsuke and Inoue Masaru – would play a vital role in the growth of Japan during the Meiji period. Inoue Masaru, in particular, applied the knowledge of railway technology, which he had acquired in England, to building railways in Japan from scratch and to supervizing their development until his death in 1910.

Born in the provincial town of Hagi on 1 August 1843, Inoue Masaru, the third son, was greatly influenced by his father, Inoue Katsuyuki, *Daikan* and *Ometsukeyaku* of the clan, a most progressive man despite his high feudal position. Adopted into the Nomura household at the age of six, he took the name of Yakichi. Masaru was kept in close contact with his father who would often visit his foster home and discuss the West animatedly as he drank. At 16, Yakichi was selected to study at the Academy in Nagasaki, an educational base founded by the shogunate where promising boys from the clans were taught by Dutchmen especially Military Science, Physics and Chemistry. Yakichi showed a flair for languages and asked to be sent to Edo [Tokyo].

After a period at the Yakuro Saito juku, he entered the highly-reputed Banshoshirabedokoro, an educational institute set up by the shogunate primarily to educate interpreters and translators by familiarizing them with the West through the study of 'barbaric books'. Having found that English was a language more spoken than Dutch, Yakichi went to Hakodate to enrol at the

Shojutsushirabesho, an institute renowned for the quality of its English teaching. He took English lessons at the British consulate and benefited from the accessibility of foreign books and Western technology from foreign ships arriving at the port.

It was while he was doing a tour of duty in Edo that Yakichi heard of the clan's daring plot to send some youths abroad to study in order to profit from the modern techniques of the West. Outwardly they were to be expelled in view of the ban, but actually they were to be given some money and five-years' leave. The party was ultimately made up of five – Ito Shinsuke (the later Ito Hirobumi), Shido Monta (the later Inoue Kaoru), Yamao Yozo, Endo Kinsuke and Nomura Yakichi (the later Inoue Masaru). Thanks to Yakichi's English abilities and the cooperation of Jardine, Matheson & Co., passage to Shanghai was secured. Their top-knots cut, they hid under cover of darkness in the coal-hatch of the *Chelswick* which sailed on 27 June 1863. Split into two groups for the next leg of the journey, after a dreadful 130 days aboard the *White Adder*, Yakichi, Yamao and Endo were re-united with Ito and Monta on the arrival of the *Pegasus* in London on 4 November.[2] Great as the shock had been in Shanghai, it was nothing compared to London, but this only made them more eager to study the West. The five were then taken to Matheson & Co. on arrival. Hugh Matheson induced Dr Alexander William Williamson, F.R.S., professor of chemistry at University College, London, to receive them. Williamson had made an 18-month tour of the East in his younger days and this had stimulated his interest and heightened his sense of social purpose.

He therefore arranged that, after learning English, the Five should be placed in classes that would lay the groundwork for a really good education.[3] Since the Five had come over to England to make a systematic study of European science and civilization, it cannot be doubted that University College, set in the heart of London, was the obvious choice. Its Chair of Civil Engineering, the very first of its kind in the country, had been set up in 1841: the 'Godless Institute', moreover, was still the only university institution in England open to all races regardless of religion, class or political beliefs.

Ito, Endo and Yakichi boarded with Professor Williamson, but, since he was only able to take in three, Monta and Yamao stayed with a Mr Cooper in Gower Street. Fortunate indeed were the Five to be taken under the kind and caring wing of

Professor Williamson. Persevering in his studies despite a severe handicap,[5] he possessed 'great strength and decision of character' and was 'admirably well qualified to exercise a beneficial influence on the band of earnest young inquirers'.[6] Having studied mostly in France and Germany, he had a broad outlook and was freer of narrow prejudices, and no doubt his personal experiences on the Continent had made him more sensitive to the needs of these youths in a foreign land. He and his wife took the Five to their hearts as well as their home, Yakichi becoming so much part of the family that he even got 'engaged' to their seven-year-old daughter.[7] Mrs Williamson not only helped them with their English, but also educated them in the manners of proper English gentlemen.

All save Monta enrolled in Professor Williamson's classes in Analytical Chemistry as of July 1864, recorded as 'Yamarou', 'Shunski Ito', 'Endo' and 'Nomuran'.[8] Although, prior to his smuggling out of Japan, Yakichi had officially reverted back to Inoue so as not to inconvenience his foster home, he went, in the West, by the name of Nomura Yakichi. The most fluent in English, Yakichi was the first of the Five to adjust to life in London. A great lover of sake, he soon acquired a taste for Western spirits, his vicarious drinking and heated debates earning him the nickname of 'Nomuran' or 'Wild Drinker', a name which stuck, even appearing on the Geology Certificate he received in 1867. But no doubt the misspelt entries were due simply to the College scribes being unable to spell such unfamiliar names, and their inability to rectify the errors. It is somewhat dubious how seriously the Five followed the course:[9] registration no doubt had other uses by giving access to other lectures and University facilities. Besides giving personal tuition on science, maths and other subjects, Professor Williamson took them on various field tours, and introduced them to other students, one Carpenter in particular[10] being most helpful and taking them to places of interest such as the British Museum and the Houses of Parliament.

Having studied military arts in Japan, Masaru had been inclined to continue such studies in England, but, on seeing the wonderfully developed transportation systems of London compared to the non-existent state of the infrastructure in Japan, he decided otherwise. Japan was still at an age where the only means of transport was by foot, horseback or by 'kago' (a palanquin borne by two stout men). Of this last method one provincial lord stated that it would be punishment enough for any criminal to be sent to Edo in such a way.

Monta and Ito returned to Japan after a mere six months, on the news of the Choshu disputes with the foreign powers. Endo also returned in 1866 for health reasons; initially put into Customs, he later did great work in the Osaka Mint. Yakichi and Yamao remained, and made considerable progress, being sent also to 'Glasgow, Newcastle and other places to study mining, ship building and other large industries'. Yakichi even apparently having joined 'a regiment of Rifle Volunteers'.[11] Yamao moved to Glasgow in 1866, to study in the Napier shipyards and at the Andersonian (forerunner of Strathclyde University), but Masaru remained at University College with the Williamsons, registering for, in addition to Chemistry, Mathematical Physics, Mathematics, Geology and Mineralogy, English and French, and obtaining a certificate of honour in Geology for the 1866-7 session.[12] Although paying college fees from 1864, he remained an unmatriculated student throughout his stay: it was not however unusual even for British students at the time to enrol for courses without going on for a degree.

Yamao and Yakichi returned in late 1868 looking the very picture of young English gentlemen, deeply aware and grateful for the kindness and care shown to them, and eager to put to good use their acquired knowledge for the progress and modernization of Japan. Faced with the task of setting up a new system and thirsting for knowledge of the West, the Choshu clan hailed their return with joy. Greatest of all, however, was the delight of Yakichi's father, who had suffered a dreadful time, even within the clan, for having 'such a treacherous son'. Reinstating Yakichi under his eldest son, Katsuichi, he awarded him the new name of 'Masaru', taking the first character of his own name, meaning 'Victorious'.

The new-born Inoue Masaru was initially set to work on the clan's mines, but it seemed a waste to bury such talent in a distant province, and he was ordered to Edo to work for the new Meiji government. Appointed Commissioner of the Mint and Head of Mining, Masaru was later ordered to dedicate himself solely to Mining Affairs, and sent to supervize the Aikawa Mines in Sado.

★   ★   ★

The British and French, in particular, had been trying in vain for permits to build a railway in Japan, but it was the Americans who unexpectedly turned up with a construction permit they had obtained from the Bakufu powers. Dated after the fall of the Tokugawa Shogunate, the contract was clearly null and void but, with the American Consulate involved, the matter required careful handling. Boarding with Ito Hirobumi at the time, Inoue Masaru remarked that, while construction funds might be obtained from abroad, for Japan to allow foreigners to operate the railway would, in effect, amount to colonization. At the end of the meeting between the Japanese authorities and the American Minister, de Long remarked that, although he was disappointed that no agreement had been reached, it had been worthwhile to learn that there was a Japanese who could speak such fluent English as Masaru, who had acted as interpreter. Not returning his smile, Masaru replied shortly that it was simply the result of five years in London, and that surely Japanese, too, could be mastered by living in Japan. Never one to fawn, 'Nomuran' had evidently done more than simply drink away his time in England.

Influenced in part by such actions by the foreign powers though more so by the repeated recommendations by the British Minister, Sir Harry Parkes, Ōkuma Shigenobu and Ito became aware of the importance of a transportation system linking the capital to the provinces, which would not only allow for freer movement of people and goods, but also enable the authority of the new Meiji government to spread throughout the country. Sir Harry put forth the suggestion that, although British engineers and financial assistance would be utilized, full autonomy would be retained by the Japanese. An informal meeting was held in Sanjo Sanetomi's residence on 6 December 1869 to consider this proposal, at which Masaru was again called in to interpret. Given the unstable domestic situation, this had to be conducted in great secrecy, even within the government, in order to avoid antagonizing those who would kill it if they thought that assistance was being sought from the 'red-headed barbarians'.

Assuring them of his cooperation, Sir Harry further recommended the agency of Horatio Nelson Lay, CB, ex-inspector general of the Customs Service in China, whom he knew from his own days there. A meeting was held with Lay, at which agreement was reached that the Japanese government would borrow one million pounds from Lay at 12%, secured with the guarantee of future revenue from tariff and fares.

Perhaps blinded by the introduction through Parkes, neither Ito, Ōkuma nor Masaru (who again acted as interpreter) was able to see through Lay or his plans. It emerged that Lay had acted contrary to their interests and publicly announced the sale of Japanese governmental bonds.[13] His services were terminated in December 1870.

With materials ordered and in the process of shipment, engineers hired and some even already at work in Japan, it was decided that, despite Lay's discharge, the plans should be continued to be handled by William W. Cargill, an inspector of the Oriental Bank, along with the public bonds issue. So capable did he prove as Director of the Railway that, on expiry of his time with the Bank in Japan, the Japanese government pleaded for his extension on the grounds of his being 'indispensable'. This being in vain, he was eventually hired directly (for a colossal sum) on a five-year contract, until 1877.

The first railway in Japan was to run between Shinbashi and Yokohama.[14] Far from the centre, these two ends were chosen for their proximity to the foreign settlements, allowing a close eye to be kept on foreigners and Japanese alike, and at the insistence of those dependent on the old systems for their living such as *kago*-bearers, pack-horse drivers and inn-keepers, strongly opposed to a new system likely to deprive them of their livelihood. Survey work from the Yokohama side which was commenced in April 1870 was a constant battle with mud, bureaucracy, anti-railway sentiment and cross-cultural differences.

Prior to assuming his duties, Cargill requested the appointment of a Commissioner of Railways, suggesting 'a Japanese gentleman of sufficient rank and importance to insure implicit obedience', having 'the perfect confidence of the Japanese government' so as to be able to give 'prompt decisions on matters not admitting delay', possessing good judgement and able to deal with persons of every rank and, 'if possible, able to speak English'.[15] Ōkuma and Ito immediately thought of Masaru, but since he was engrossed in the mines at the time and about to see one of his projects take off, they decided to bide their time.

The Yokohama line partially completed, a trial run was held in August 1872 for high-ranking officials, after which even those who had harboured grievous doubts of such 'Western sourcery' became converted enthusiasts and believers. When a major re-shuffling of the Public Works Ministry took place, a Railway

Bureau was set up, and the need for an appointment became desperate. Masaru was finally persuaded to take up the post of Chief Commissioner of the Railway. He was then 29.

On appointment, Masaru worked tirelessly, looking the sites over and talking to the workers, even going to Yokohama to inspect the shipments of materials as they arrived from England or India. One official, voicing his delight over the abundance of goods, was silenced by a thundery 'You fool! Half of these could easily be procured in Japan, not at such expense from overseas!' A mild man by nature, Inoue could be most voluble when provoked, thus earning the nickname 'Mr Thunder'.

Endlessly frustrated by Japanese ignorance and heavy bureaucracy, Masaru tendered his resignation on more than one occasion in protest at the lack of Japanese official coordination. Possessing amazing strength and perseverance, he was also a most stubborn and difficult man; quick to praise his subordinates, he was never one to let his superiors have an easy time of it. For them, it was a constant 'Get rid of him and find a replacement' – such were the people by whom revolutions were made.

After much ado, the Yokohama-Shinbashi line was at last completed and, although the State Opening had to be postponed until October 1872, due to bad weather, spirits were not a whit dampened. The ceremony was hailed as 'the greatest celebration since the time of the Emperor Jinmu'.[16] Despite a rather unpromising dawn, crowds began to gather as early as seven o'clock, the streets bedecked with flags and flowers, while top-hats and tails mingled with court robes and kimonos. The train chuffed out of Yokohama at eight, reaching Shinbashi a little before nine.[17] The Imperial procession had in the meantime left the Palace, moving amidst reverent silence towards the bravely decorated station. At 9:45 the gates were thrown open to receive the State coach, to be met by the Minister of Public Works Yamao Yozo and Chief Commissioner of the Railways, Inoue Masaru. The Emperor addressing a few words of acknowledgment to the representatives of foreign powers and ministers also gathered there, Masaru then humbly presented a plan of the railways, drawn in his spare time.

What excitement there was as the train chuffed out of the station, leaving behind rows of footwear! One man, pitying the 'perspiring' engine, concernedly threw a pail of water, only to be severely reprimanded for his pains; another would race his horse, trying to outrun the 'thing moved by Christian magic'; others sank to the ground in sheer terror at being devoured as the 'monster' approached; one young man burst into tears regretting his father having died four days earlier with a curse on his lips instead of rejoicing at the dawn of civilization.

All the way to Yokohama, the line was streamed with flags and people, men-of-war in Kanagawa harbour saluted, and bands played their music. The train reaching its destination in little under an hour, the Emperor was there met by the Director of the Railway, Cargill, Chief Assistant Commissioner Takeda Harukazu, Robertson of the Oriental Bank, and the other Japanese and foreign staff proudly lined up on the platform. It was a novel occasion in that the Emperor himself acknowledged the services of those foreigners whose knowledge and experience had made the railway possible, and of the important part played by the hitherto despised merchant classes in the economy of the country.

The various speeches over, the train returned to Tokyo, the Emperor there expressing his great pleasure that it was 'so great a source of convenience' and meriting 'the perseverance and energy' as 'worthy of high praise'. The Emperor returning to his castle, the foreign ministers were entertained at Hamagoten before returning to Yokohama around 5 pm, but the festivities of the populace went on till well into the night, the streets lit with thousands of red and white paper lanterns.[18]

At the celebration party for all concerned with the railway, there was, however, one sad noticeable absence. Worn out by toil and stress, Masaru had tottered home to nurse a raging fever once the formalities were over. Sorely missed, Cargill paid tribute in his speech to his untiring dedication and work, but above mere words, Masaru was supremely happy with the accomplishment. The ending words of the Emperor: 'It is my intention to develop the railway still further, and, I hope, beginning with this line, to spread it throughout the country', were ringing in his ears, giving him fresh energy and the will to commence work anew – next day.

The 'perfect marriage' between Cargill and Masaru, based on mutual trust and respect also played an important part in surmounting difficulties. Added to his clan background, Masaru was invaluable because of his technical efficiency and management skills in handling Japanese and foreigners alike and, under his enthusiastic leadership and the guidance of foreign technicians, rapid progress was made, enabling the Japanese railway to ultimately pass from the phase of total dependence on foreigners and turn out their own engineers and workshops.

The Tokyo-Yokohama ceremony over, Masaru went to inspect the Osaka-Kobe line, which, although work had commenced, showed but little progress. It emerged that this was mainly due to the lack of an able Japanese leader, inadequate telecommunications also hampering receipt of orders and instructions from Tokyo. Masaru, therefore, suggested the temporary removal of the Railway Bureau to the Kansai area so that he personally might supervise the work and help overcome problems. This, however, met the unexpected opposition of Yamao, the Minister of Public Works. Frustrated with the lack of understanding Masaru resigned on 22 July 1873.

Having had clashes before on other issues, the relationship between Yamao and Inoue completely deteriorated after this event. Both were stubborn, independent men; and their views may also have been influenced in part by the careers they had chosen. It is interesting to note that of the Five, only Endo and Masaru trod the path of 'pure' technicians, the other three going the way of administrative bureaucrats. The avoidance of colonization immediately before the opening up of Japan owed much to the work of Japanese technicians and specialized civil servants like them in a society where ranking was by class. Personal issues aside, their different paths must have only furthered the divide between the two.

On his return to Japan in September from Europe, where he had been accompanying Iwakura, a shocked Ito set to work trying to heal the breach, and Masaru was finally persuaded to resume his post in January 1874, on condition that he might have a free rein and, by working round the clock, the Kobe-Osaka line was completed in May. The Railway Bureau was abolished in 1877, a Railway Commission was set up within the Public Works Ministry in its place to greet Masaru as Commissioner. Financial difficulties hampered the Osaka-Kyoto line but this too was officially opened with great pomp and ceremony on 5 February 1877, completing a 75km (47-mile) track linking Kobe, Osaka and Kyoto. Continually hindered by communication and administrative problems, Masaru felt the need to break out from dependency on foreigners and to educate skilled Japanese engineers. In May 1878, he set up an educational institute for civil engineering at Osaka station, with such experienced technicians as Thomas R. Shervington, Edmund G. Holtham and Iida Toshinori as principal instructors, and with himself also lecturing when time permitted. Masaru took the daring step of assigning his newly-fledged students to various sections of the Kyoto-Otsu line, plans for which were drawn up by British engineers, but all actual construction work was to be conducted by the Japanese at his insistence. Begun in August 1878, foreigners and Japanese alike were naturally sceptical, but to the credit of both teachers and pupils, despite serious tunnelling problems, the 10-mile line was completed in June 1880. Along with the appointment of the first Japanese engine-driver, this marked a real first step in the independence of the Japanese railways, filling people with a new sense of confidence.

The education of the Japanese technicians apart, the sheer expense of having 'oyatoi' ('foreign employees') was undoubtedly one strong reason for urging speedy independence. 83 'oyatoi' were employed on the railway on its first operation in 1872, reaching a peak of 115 in 1874. This was in itself a huge financial drain, but the 'oyatoi' power, especially when backed by their home governments, was at times so strong as to intervene in internal affairs. Excessive 'Europeanization' led to the emergence of a backlash nationalist reaction. After the success of the Otsu line, Japanese officials remarked that the Japanese were better able to understand their own terrain and the assistance of foreign technicians became less and less acknowledged, perhaps influenced by a general desire to avoid recruiting foreign employees. With the emergence of competent Japanese technicians, this figure dropped to a mere 14 by 1888.

All this time, Japan was constantly wracked with internal and external strife, and it was only by dint of much bullying and cajoling that Inoue was at all able to obtain resources from a government concerned with matters of war and projects with more immediate returns than the railway. Desperate that his carefully trained body of engineers should not go to pieces for want of work, he endeavoured to enable them to continue construction, in however piecemeal a form.

Around the 1880s came the emergence of private capital and the conviction of the strategic importance of the railway. The Ueno-Takasaki line which was financed by the Nippon Railway Company, an association formed by former peers, was begun in 1882 and completed in less than three years, becoming a commercial success. This caught the attention of various capitalists and local politicians, causing a private railway building craze. Inoue held the staunch belief that the railways should be public property, run and owned by the government, and was highly critical of the sudden growth in private lines, pointing out the speculative interest and political incentives behind the emergence of many unnecessary or even useless lines. So strongly did he feel that in 1891 Masaru presented a 'Proposal for Railroad Administration' to the government, in which he urged the predominance of government lines and the buying-up of private lines; but it was not until the nationalization law in 1906 that his recommendation was finally accepted.

In 1887, Inoue Masaru was made a viscount. In 1889, less than twenty years after the very first railway, public and private included, the construction of the 1000th mile was reached, celebrations for which were held in Nagoya. Dedicating himself so completely to the railway, Masaru had no private life to speak of; even his own house became a sort of railway club. Convinced of his vocation in the railway, he would often set off in straw sandals and a tunic of his own creation, ready to set to work immediately if any emergency work was at hand. On site, he would sit and dine amongst his subordinates, and hold animated discussions which only endeared him further; becoming the First Chief Commissioner to the Railway Agency in 1890, he was also elected to the House of Peers that year, to be re-elected two years running.

During the final stage of the Tokyo-Amori line in 1891, Masaru had occasion to visit Iwate. Expressing his regret over the many carefully-tended pastures and paddy fields that the railway must have destroyed and the hardships the farmers must have suffered, he discussed on his return to Tokyo the possibility of providing a large plot of farming land with Ono Yoshinobu, Vice President of the Nippon Railway Company, who in turn talked to Iwasaki Yataro. This led to the establishment of Koiwai Farm, taking the first characters of the founders' names.

Great was Masaru's dedication and love of the railway, but great also was his stubbornness, especially when it came to his belief in the public ownership of the railroads of Japan. His views getting in the way, speculators and politicians with a stake in the railroad pie began to issue propaganda so as to make out that this was a ruse to increase Masaru's own power and wealth, creating also ready material to be used against the government itself. Perhaps simply tired of all the pressures and petty squabbles, and not wishing to cause further trouble to his friends in government, especially Ito, Masaru resigned on 16 March 1893, at the age of 51.

Horrified, Ito tried to dissuade him, and then to persuade him to accept a position as Lord Privy Seal, but in vain, Masaru saying it was not for the likes of a humble technician like him. In appreciation of his work, the Meiji Emperor presented Masaru with a beautiful set of saddle and spurs, and a big farewell party was thrown, at which his subordinates gave him a set of silk screens, in return for which he gave them a cherished photograph of himself as an ambitious youth holding a shovel, taken in England so many years earlier. His love of the railway continued strong, and he was known to scold ticket officers and passengers alike for misbehaviour on trains and, if he felt bumps on the ride, he would throw some little pebbles he kept in his pocket out of the carriage window as markers, and demand at the next station that inspection take place.

After retirement, he first became adviser to one or two private rail companies, attempting to set an example of how private lines could work for the public good, but they were only interested in the profit they could gain from having him. Quickly disillusioned, he soon left.

Because Japan was suffering from a shortage of railway carriages, Masaru set up such a manufacturing company in 1896, which, with the outbreak of the Russo-Japanese War, became a great success, encouraging other private companies to set up also, and thereby helping accelerate the development and independence of Japan's railway enterprise, which celebrated its 5000th mile in 1903. Ever since the Sino-Japanese War in 1894, Masaru had been harbouring plans for a pan-Asian railway system, advocating his views whenever he visited the Asian continent and sending out Japanese technicians of his own so that they might apply some of their technology and contribute to development there. As time passed, his ambitions grew, and he began to dream of a railway that would stretch over Asia and into Europe. To this end, he yearned for an opportunity to be able to study the developments of the railways of Europe once more, but chance did not readily come his way.

This came at last, however, in 1910, on the occasion of the Japan-British Exhibition in London. The rail nationalization, so often advocated by Masaru, had finally been accepted and realized in 1906. This in turn led to the enlargement of the railway network, leading to the forming of a new Railway

Agency in 1908. Its first President, Goto Shinpei, requested that a study of European railways be made by Inoue as adviser. Because he was 68 by this time and suffering from kidney disease, his family, friends and relatives did their utmost to prevent his undertaking such a suicidal trip, but there was no stopping the overjoyed Masaru. Taking but one young attendant and one small suitcase (which also contained a white funeral robe), stubborn old Masaru set off on 8 May 1910. The object of the trip being the study of the European railways, he was eager to try out the newly-opened Siberian railway, insisting on travelling overland from Asia into Europe, as had become his dream.

Connections necessitating a day's stop-over in Dairen, Masaru wrote a detailed letter to his family back in Tokyo, which was in effect a will. He requested that, should he not return alive, his ashes be scattered over the tracks, one bone to be buried in Tokaiji temple, near the busy rail junction of Shinagawa.

The half-month journey overland to London would have tired even the fittest of men. But, hardly sparing the time to leave his belongings at the hotel, Masaru hurried to the Williamsons, eager to thank the good professor who had taken the penniless 'Nomuran' into his heart and home, and had helped his dreams of study come true. The house was exactly as he remembered it, Mrs Williamson greeting him with great delight. Sadly, the professor had already passed away, Endo was no more and Ito had been assassinated in Harbin station some seven months earlier. The two, however, talked only of the happy bygone days. Masaru spent the next few days trying to look up those who had been so good to him in London long ago, with little success; the kindly Hugh Matheson had also passed away and Carpenter had vanished, as had so many of the others.

Concerned at how pale and sickly he looked, Mrs Williamson urged that he see a doctor, appearing at his hotel with one in tow. To appease her, Masaru had a check up, to be told that his liver was in a serious state and that he should spend a few days in hospital. He spent a few days quietly in his hotel, but insisting he had work to do, the stubborn Masaru was off on a months' tour of Europe – France, Germany, Italy, Spain and Portugal. Returning to London in the heat of late July with far greater results than he had expected, he found also that the trip had been a great strain. On leaving Japan, he had declared that he would set a good example to 'all those modern spendthrift government students wasting good money on extravagance' (surely easier since he was now unable to drink!). It is suggested that his illness was worsened by his insistence on tramping the hard streets instead of taking a cab. Aided by some resident Japanese and Mrs Williamson, he was taken into Henrietta Hospital, fondly hoping that 10 days' good rest would set him back on his feet; sadly, he passed away within that period, to be cremated at Golders Green on 3 August.

His faithful young attendant carrying his ashes back over the seas, Masaru was buried in great pomp and ceremony in Tokaiji Temple on 2 September 1910, to keep an eye on his beloved railway, according to his wishes. Before retirement, wild rumours had flown that he had accumulated great wealth through the railway and that he had a fat vault hidden away in London, but his death revealed that he had only his pension and house to his name.

Inoue Masaru's bronze statue stands in front of Tokyo station, humbly hidden amongst some trees. For four decades he had applied with the greatest dedication and single-mindedness the railway technology which he had first observed in London.

Laurence Oliphant and Japan, 1858–88

CARMEN BLACKER

LAURENCE OLIPHANT, 'traveller, diplomat and mystic' was accounted one of the strangest and most variously gifted characters of his period. He was an enthralling and witty talker; he was well connected and widely read; he was a talented writer and a daring traveller. On Christmas Day 1854, he recalled, he was in Quebec. On the same day 1855 it was Trebizond. In 1856 it was New Orleans and in 1857 the Canton river. Wherever drama or crisis was brewing, indeed, Oliphant was unerringly on the spot to record the scene. He had a seat in the House of Commons. He was welcome in every fashionable drawing-room. He hobnobbed with princes, Red Indians, mandarins and Garibaldi. He might have succeeded Gladstone, or even Sir Harry Parkes.[1]

His career was ruined when he fell under the spell of a fraudulent American guru. Thomas Lake Harris, though puny by comparison with modern religious charlatans, was nonetheless shocking to the uninvolved observer of a century ago. The evangelist Hannah Whittall Smith, mother of Logan Pearsall Smith and author of the daring book *Religious Fanaticism*, described him from personal knowledge as a 'greedy and dangerous sensualist, arrogant, harsh and revengeful'. The closer one came to understanding his doctrines, the more repulsive they became.[2] Margaret Oliphant, that prolific Victorian writer who numbered among her 125 books the first biography of her cousin Laurence, was equally uncompromising: Harris was a spiritual tyrant, who exercised an extraordinary despotism over his disciples while himself living in debauched luxury.[3]

This alas was the man who came to exert so potent a

magnetism over Oliphant as to cause him to abandon his career, his freedom and his friends, to submit himself for more than fifteen years to a discipline both humiliating and spiritually nugatory. To the end of his life, indeed, he never entirely freed himself from Harris's malign influence.

Oliphant's encounters with Japan fortunately occurred before his infatuation with Harris. He visited the country twice, each time leaving a fascinating account of his adventures. As Private Secretary to Lord Elgin on his mission to draw up a Treaty with the Bakufu, he went to Edo as early as 1858. The record of his visit, *Narrative of Lord Elgin's Mission to China and Japan*,[4] remains one of the most observant and enthralling accounts of Japan at a time when barely a half dozen foreigners outside Nagasaki were allowed to reside on Japanese soil.

His second visit, as First Secretary to the British legation in 1861, was tragically curtailed. Hardly had he arrived when the legation was attacked by fanatical *rōnin* of the Mito clan. Oliphant was so badly wounded by one of the assassins that he had to be sent home on the next boat.

He never returned to Japan. But his last 'encounter' was nonetheless of consequence, for he introduced six of the Satsuma *ryūgakusei*, that talented group of young students which included the future Education Minister Mori Arinori, to the 'utopian community' run by the sinister Harris in Brocton N.Y. All but one left the Brotherhood while their impressions of the guru remained positive.

Laurence Oliphant was born in Cape Town in 1829, the only child of Sir Anthony Oliphant, the Attorney-general. He later lived with his parents in Ceylon. He travelled to Italy during the revolution of 1848, and to Kathmandu and Russia on a daring journey from St Petersburg to Sebastopol. He was invited to Washington as Private Secretary to Lord Elgin on a treaty mission, and later to Quebec, where as Superintendent of Indian Affairs he lived in the wigwams of the local chiefs. After a spell in the Crimea with Lord Stratford de Redcliffe, he was in 1856 invited once more to accompany Lord Elgin, this time on a special mission to China and Japan. The mission to China was occasioned by the Arrow Affair of 1856 and the political rupture with Commissioner Yeh. It resulted in the Treaty of Tientsin of 1858.

The visit to Japan was accomplished during the interlude while waiting for the Chinese Treaty to be ratified.[5] It was necessarily a short one, lasting less than a month. But it was long enough to convince Oliphant that St Francis Xavier had been entirely right; the Japanese surpassed in virtue and probity all other nations hitherto discovered. Indeed, the account in the remarkable two-volume *Narrative* (1859) well exemplifies the tendency noticed by Yokoyama Toshio in the writings of early Western observers: to see Japan as a pocket of unfallen, uncorrupted man, a survival of the sinless conditions of the Garden of Eden. His impressions of Japan throughout his visit remained paradisal.

The purpose of Lord Elgin's Mission was, however, to secure from the Bakufu a Treaty of Commerce and Friendship for Britain on the model of that just concluded by Townsend Harris for the United States. Lord Elgin had also brought a yacht as a present from Queen Victoria to the Shogun. After a few days in Nagasaki, therefore, during which Oliphant was enchanted by the amiable contentment, the semi-nude languor, of everyone he saw, and by the absence of the beggars and foul smells so omnipresent in China, the mission, with the yacht in attendance, set off for Edo.

They stopped en route at Shimoda, where the American Consul Townsend Harris and his secretary, Heusken, had just returned triumphant from their successful treaty coup in Edo. Harris kindly lent Elgin both a palanquin and Heusken, whose knowledge of both Dutch and Japanese proved invaluable to the mission during the succeeding weeks. Thus equipped, Lord Elgin took the unprecedented step of steaming past Kanagawa and dropping anchor in Edo Bay off Shinagawa. There he stoutly refused to budge until a suitable treaty was concluded. On 17 August the party was eventually allowed to land in Edo, and to ride in procession through wildly excited crowds to the Buddhist temple thoughtfully equipped for their accommodation.

The mission was lucky to have among its members a talented artist, F.C. Bedwell, who managed to make 'truthful' sketches, later worked into fully tinted lithographs, both of the striking features of the city of Edo, and of the high moments of the party's political negotiations. The moment when Full Powers were exchanged between Lord Elgin and the Japanese Commissioners, the important evening interview, candlelit, between Lord Elgin and the Prime Ministers of Japan, embellish Oliphant's *Narrative* as vividly as might photographs.

The mission was lucky to see Japan at a moment when the

feudal regime of the Bakufu was still in power, and before any foreign influence had affected the 'purity' of the culture which had remained closed to the outside world for more than two centuries.

They were lucky, too, to see Edo before anti-foreign feelings among the *bushi* class made life perilous for foreigners. The crowds which lined the streets wherever they went were friendly. The five 'Commissioners' detailed to negotiate the Treaty were 'capital fellows', extremely well disposed, full of jokes, and liable to call just at lunchtime when their remarkable predilection for ham and champagne notably smoothed the negotiations.

Between working sessions with the commissioners, they were encouraged to make expeditions, on horseback, to well known beauty spots surrounding the city. On the first such jaunt, they rode for three hours through the streets of Edo, lined with peach trees, past the spacious palaces or yashiki of the daimyo. The palace and estate of the powerful Prince Kaganokami, Oliphant noted, was so immense that it could accommodate 10,000 men.

Another jaunt took them over the great 'Nipon Bas' bridge to the celebrated 'Quanon Temple', where in the surrounding fair they were enchanted by the toyshops and aviaries, and where Lord Elgin bought two pigeons. Their purchases, indeed, seem to have been exuberant. There was a 'rage' among the party for lacquer and eggshell china, and an even more extravagant 'mania' for dogs. These little creatures, which Oliphant describes as resembling King Charles spaniels,[6] with bulging eyes and underhung jaws, were presumably *chin*, the breed later given the name of 'Japanese spaniels'. B.H. Chamberlain includes an article on them in his *Things Japanese*, which stresses their goggle eyes, their habit of sneezing, and their sickly constitution which requires them to be fed on a light diet of rice and grated dry bonito. Every member of the party except Oliphant bought three or four of these little dogs, many of whom subsequently died in the 'paper kennels' in which they were confined. Whether any survived the journey home, which included a lengthy stop en route in China, is not mentioned.

On their last day, 26 August, the treaty of Edo was triumphantly signed by Lord Elgin and the five commissioners. The Tycoon himself was not present. It secured for British subjects much the same 'unequal' privileges that Townsend Harris's 1854 treaty had done for Americans. Its twenty-four articles declared the ports of Hakodate, Kanagawa, Nagasaki and Hyōgo open to British residence and trade, the first three to be opened on 1 July 1859; it allowed British subjects free exercise of their religion and the right to be tried for crimes against Japanese on extraterritorial land by their own consul.

Lord Elgin, on behalf of Queen Victoria, handed over the yacht to the Tycoon, and the Japanese flag was promptly raised thereon. The deck of the *Furious*, in return, was piled with presents from the Tycoon which included a set of silver storks and thirty 'dressing gowns of state'.

The gigantic purchases of the party were duly paid for and packed. A last grand banquet was provided by the Tycoon, who again sent his apologies for failing to receive the party. (He was in fact dead at the time, though none of the party was aware of this.) The banquet concluded, the mission took its departure with sincere demonstrations of affection on both sides, and satisfaction on Lord Elgin's at the success of the treaty.

Oliphant's massive two-volume *Narrative of the Mission to China and Japan* is something of a tour de force. He did not reach England until the spring of 1859, having 'with inexpressible delight' seen the last of China on 4 March. Yet the work was published, with all Bedwell's tinted lithographs, within the same year. Nor was it a mere diary account of what he had seen. His own personal adventures in Edo are skilfully blended with a remarkably vivid and competent background description of the language, manners and skills of Japan, its feudal government and institutions. Oliphant in the short time available had managed to read and digest virtually all the available literature about the country and its history. He quotes happily and relevantly from Siebold, Thunberg, Titsingh, Xavier, Golownin, Klaproth, 'old Kaempfer', 'old Father Froes' and even Père Charlevoix. He is also an accurate and retentive observer, including in his narrative minute descriptions of horse harness and straw shoes, lavish dinners of unfamiliar dishes, and the ghastly white faces and blackened teeth of married women in Nagasaki.

So enchanted had Oliphant been by his brief visit to Japan that he lost no time on returning to England in pulling every string to return there. With his numerous connections, and a special recommendation from Lord John Russell, he was not long in obtaining an official diplomatic post. He was appointed First Secretary in the legation, by then established in Edo. He arrived at the end of June 1861 full of hope and enthusiasm. His 'tour' was alas to be brief and disastrous.[7]

He was dismayed in the first place to find the mood towards foreigners had changed dramatically since 1858. Gone were the amiable smiling faces which had lined the roads three years before. Gone, too, were the carefree shopping sprees to temple fairs, and the leisurely jaunts to beauty spots. Now all was suspicion, hostility and rumours of death from the assassin's sword. No member of the legation could venture outside the temple in which they were quartered without a compulsory escort of at least twenty 'yaconins'. Scowling multitudes in the streets, apparently thirsting for their blood, made them grateful for the extra guard of 150 men allotted to the legation by the Bakufu.

Worse was soon to follow. On the night of 5 July the legation was attacked by masked assassins. Oliphant, armed only with a hunting crop, found himself engaged in desperate combat with an assailant with a sword. He was saved by a horizontal beam, the deep sword cuts in which could be seen years later. The assassin was shot by Mr Morrison, but not before he had wounded Oliphant severely in the neck and left arm. Sir Rutherford Alcock awoke to see 'Mr Oliphant covered with blood which was streaming from a great gash in his arm and wound in his neck'. He instantly put his medical knowledge to good use by binding up the wound, while the temple was resounding with a frightful din of clashing swords, sharp yells and breaking glass. The assassins, lost in the labyrinthine corridors, slashed wildly with their swords, transfixing mattresses in the hope of impaling a sleeper, severing Bibles clean through and wounding Morrison.

At last, none too soon, the guard of 150 yaconins appeared with more breaking glass and routed the assailants. The legation was saved. Charles Wirgman, the artist of the *Illustrated London News*, who had sensibly taken refuge under the house, emerged coated with mud, and with 'the true spirit of his calling set about portraying the most striking features of the episode for the benefit of the British Public'.[8]

When Oliphant eventually tottered back to bed, he trod on something like an oyster. He perceived it to be a human eye. Another corpse lay nearby with the entire front of the head sliced off, leaving visible only the back of the brain. 'I have seen many a battlefield,' Sir Rutherford recalled, 'but of sabre wounds I never saw any so horrible.' He gave thanks for their deliverance from such a mangled and hideous fate.

The next day a survivor of the gang revealed that the assailants had been 'Lonins' from the domain of the Mito daimyo, a noted hater of foreigners on Japanese soil, who had planned the attack in the hope that it might frighten them all away.

Oliphant adds an extraordinary coda to his account of the incident. Several years later, having been of service to a group of Japanese in London, he mentioned to one of the party that he had been in the legation on the night of the attack. 'How glad I am that you escaped safely,' the man replied. 'For I, to whom you have shown such kindness, planned the whole affair!'

Oliphant was soon moved to the captain's cabin on the *Ringdove*, where he suffered far greater torments at the hands of the ship's surgeon than he had from the assassin's sword. Both arms were firmly bandaged to his sides; boils burst out all over his body; ophthalmia infected both eyes so that he had to lie blindfold in total darkness. The thermometer stood at 95°. He was 'red as a lobster with prickly heat which produced incessant irritation', while the cabin buzzed with mosquitoes like a beehive.

Hardly had the ophthalmia cleared than Sir Rutherford Alcock informed him that he was to be sent home forthwith, with a personal letter from the Tycoon to Queen Victoria apologising for the outrage.

He thus left Japan after a stay of barely two months, only a week of which had elapsed before he was too severely wounded to carry out his duties.

En route to England, however, barely convalescent though he was, one more diplomatic task was required of him. He was to proceed to the island of Tsushima to investigate reports that the Russians had, contrary to treaty, made a secret settlement on the island. Vladivostok being frozen in winter, Tsushima with its quiet lagoons would make an ideal alternative as a maritime station.[9]

Tsushima in 1861 was the territory of the daimyo Sō Yoshihira. Oliphant on arrival at the port of 'Fatchio' was told that he could not be received and must leave the island forthwith. He landed, nonetheless, installed himself in a 'pretty little summer house' on the seashore, and declared himself ready to stay there indefinitely until he could have the necessary audience with the daimyo.

A 'norimon' soon appeared on the beach, carrying a senior official of the domain. The daimyo being ill, he was informed, a meeting with the chief minister had been arranged at midnight that night. To this rendez-vous he was escorted through the dark and shuttered town by twenty of the daimyo's retainers, carrying lanterns. After half an hour's walk they reached a building where he was conducted to a room lit by four enormous candles.

After preliminary courtesies, Oliphant broached the reason for his visit. Had any Russians recently visited Tsushima? Oh no, was the reply, no Russians have ever been here. But after two hours, during which Oliphant put into practice his own special technique of persuasion and reassurance, he extracted the information that the Russians had indeed been on the island for six months. They refused to be dislodged, and the daimyo was extremely worried by the situation. The Russians had furthermore extorted, under dire threats, promises of secrecy as to their presence. The Minister, though delighted at the prospect of being rid of the unwelcome strangers, refused to divulge the spot where they had settled. Dawn was breaking when this strange interview came to an end.

The *Ringdove* accordingly was set to coast round the island in search of the Russian hiding-place. Eventually, they reached an extraordinary hidden lagoon, apparently uninhabited. Oliphant set off in a boat to explore the mysterious haven. Suddenly, winding through a labyrinth of deep creeks, he came upon a Russian frigate, the *Possadnik*, moored to the branches of two giant trees. The Russian captain, who had lived in this hidden place and complete solitude for six months, was astonished by his appearance. But he professed himself delighted to receive the English callers, invited them aboard for refreshment, and assured them that his sole purpose in being there was a hydrographic survey. It later transpired that he had founded a comfortable settlement, with a hospital, dairy, Russian steam bath and vegetable garden.

Oliphant gently reminded him that his presence was contrary to treaty, and at a subsequent most amicable dinner on the *Ringdove* the captain promised to apply for orders to evacuate the *Possadnik*. Nothing would give him greater pleasure, he declared, as he was heartily sick of his exile.

In such circumstances, Oliphant remarked, were the Russians frustrated in their attempt to hoist their flag on the island of Tsushima; and such was Oliphant's personal contribution, convalescent though he was, to what was subsequently known as the Tsushima Incident.

These two affairs, the 'Attack on the British Legation' and 'A Visit to Tsushima', are vividly described in Oliphant's *Episodes in a Life of Adventure*, 1887. They stand alongside accounts of the overland route to Ceylon in 1841, an address to a tribe of Red Indians in a chapel near Quebec, Calcutta during the Mutiny, and encounters with Garibaldi and with pillaging Cossacks.

Oliphant could have returned to Japan to resume his duties at the legation. That he decided against doing so may have been one of the greatest mistakes of his life. He resumed, instead, his other customary avocations. He wrote a society novel called *Piccadilly*, he travelled to Poland to witness an insurrection and was taken for a spy. He frequented fashionable drawing-rooms in London, where Lord Redesdale saw him as 'a mystic in lavender kid gloves, full of spiritualism and strange creeds'.[10]

But he also exerted himself to be of service to any Japanese whom he might encounter in the London of the 1860s. By no means disenchanted with Japan, though he never fully recovered from the effects of his wound, he took particular pains to welcome and help the group of young men from Satsuma who in 1865 arrived in London to study Western science and law.[11]

Japanese visitors at this time were necessarily few, since any attempt to leave Japan without official permission was still a crime punishable by death. But various domains, notably Chōshū and Satsuma, had succeeded in sending groups of promising young samurai to London with a view to acquiring knowledge useful to their daimyo in the coming new age. The Chōshū group arrived in 1864. The Satsuma group, having eluded the Bakufu spies by changing their names and hiding in a fishing village before embarking on a boat of the Glover Company, arrived in 1865. They were a remarkable group in so far as nearly all were later to make a notable mark on Meiji history as diplomats, government ministers, educators or captains of industry. Mori Arinori, for one, was later to become minister in London and Washington, Minister of Education and author of the state school system in Japan.[12]

To this interesting group Oliphant became guide and mentor. He introduced them to the relevant authorities in London University, where they were assigned their various studies. He took Terashima Munenari, a senior member of the group, to the Foreign Office to explain their presence in London and the relationship of Satsuma to the Shogun. The Satsuma students were fortunate, wrote Ivan Hall in his biography of Mori, to have as their preceptor a man so sophisticated, well connected and so sympathetic to Japan.

Oliphant's last service to the group was a more equivocal one. He persuaded six of them to accompany him to America to join the Brotherhood of the Good Life in Brocton, N.Y. Here it was that Thomas Lake Harris presided over a community, described as 'utopian', of some forty disciples.

Oliphant's infatuation with Harris seems to have begun during the early 1860s, when the guru paid a couple of visits to England. He quickly became convinced that Harris held the keys to the good life, the rejection of a corrupt world and the gates of a new regenerate one. He awaited only a formal summons from Harris to renounce his prospects, career and friends, and to embrace the disciplines of the Brotherhood in America.

Compared with the cults all too rampant today, Harris's Brotherhood was relatively innocuous. Harris is not to be compared with Jim Jones, David Koresh or Asahara Shōkō. His followers did not commit indiscriminate murder or mass suicide. He is nonetheless true to an increasingly familiar type on several counts. His disciples were required to believe him infallible and divinely inspired, even to be a Second Christ. They were further required to make over their entire estate, in both land and investments, to Harris's use. And finally, though they were required to live in complete chastity, as well as poverty and obedience, it became increasingly clear that Harris himself was living a life of arbitrary luxury and debauchery. The female adorers who ministered to his lightest whim were in fact his harem.

Harris's teachings and the peculiar magnetism they held for intelligent people are not easy to summarize. He preached an imminent doom for a corrupt world and church. He himself, however, was empowered to save from this cataclysm those favoured souls who joined his band and did his bidding. To survive, it seems, they first had to practise a special breathing technique known as 'arch-natural breath'. This would in time transform their physical bodies to another substance deathless and immortal. Next, they must find their Counterpart, a spiritual mate, man for woman, woman for man, without whose partnership they were only half their true selves. Only Harris was able to identify the correct counterparts of his disciples, who might exist in the spirit world, or might manifest in a physical person. Existing husbands and wives were never their own counterparts. Harris's own Counterpart was known as the Lily Queen, whom he came to identify successively in the bodies of his female adorers.

Laurence's cousin, Margaret Oliphant, confesses to a sense of 'moral vertigo' when she discovered for what creed he had abandoned his brilliant prospects. But such was the doctrine which prevailed at Brocton Brotherhood in 1867 when at last Oliphant received a formal summons to join, and took with him six of the Satsuma students.

New arrivals at Brocton were subject to a hard probationary discipline for at least three months. Family ties were strictly abjured. Parents were separated from children, husbands from wives, friends from friends. Oliphant himself was required to sleep in a barn, to get up at 4 o'clock in the freezing cold, and to spend the day until late at night carting manure. He was given a silly nickname, and forbidden to speak to anyone. His meals were brought to him in silence and solitude.

He continued to believe, however, as is abundantly clear from his correspondence with the evangelist William Cowper, later Lord Mount Temple, that Harris was a divinely inspired link with the Lord. He also reported that the Japanese were as happy as larks. 'Dear souls', he wrote, 'they say they never knew what happiness was before.' Natures such as theirs, so simple and noble, sensitive and open, what a privilege it was to feel that he was bringing them to a knowledge of the Lord.

And, oddly enough for young men educated in the strict Confucian and martial traditions of *han* schools such as the Gōjū and the Zōshikan, the six Japanese were apparently as happy as larks.[14] They spent their days chopping wood, washing dishes and making beds, but these menial tasks gave them nothing but satisfaction. They were especially good at the 'arch-natural breathing', with a noticeably demonstrative style. They were apparently delighted with the simple life, so reminiscent of the training of a Zen monk, and with the knowledge that they were hastening the coming of a new age such as had been expected at home.

By the spring of 1868, however, five of the six had left the Brotherhood. Their reason for leaving Brocton after only nine months was not, apparently, disillusionment with 'Father Faithful', or the discovery that his precepts for his disciples did not coincide with his own personal practice. Trivial quarrels among themselves made them restless and the news of the Meiji Restoration, in which Satsuma played so important a role, made them wish to do their patriotic duty at home.

They left, remarkably, without any mental or spiritual scars. They had by no means been brainwashed. Indeed Mori's biographer, Ivan Hall, believes that Mori, for one, derived nothing but benefit from his stay at Brocton. None of the group saw Harris as a spiritual hypocrite. On the contrary, he was the 'new Confucius', just as Oliphant had described him, who confirmed their perception of the moral dimension in Western thought. Even further, the lessons they had learnt in Western moral thinking went to strengthen their later resolve when the time came to propagate the ideals of the new Meiji regime.[15]

The only member of the group to remain in the Brotherhood was the youngest, Nagasawa Kanae. A child of twelve when he left Japan in 1865, he was sent on arrival in London to a school in Aberdeen and to board in the home of the Glover family. It is good to learn that for him, too, the experience of the Brocton Brotherhood proved wholly beneficial. Far from being brainwashed or mentally crippled by the influence of Harris, he rose to a prosperity, wealth and importance that he might never have achieved even in Meiji Japan. He became the indispensable secretary and assistant to 'Father Faithful' and eventually manager of two thousand acres of vineyard in the Brotherhood's new premises in Santa Rosa, California. Even more remarkably, on Harris's death he was designated sole heir and legatee. He thus became the owner of a large estate, ran a prosperous wine-making business, and died as late as 1934 rich, respected and in no way affected by past scandals.[16]

With the departure of the Satsuma students, Oliphant's connections with Japan were at an end. Several more Japanese arrived at Brocton during the next few years, but Oliphant makes no special mention of them in his correspondence. He himself was to remain under Harris's spell for another dozen years. It was only in 1881 that the scales fell from his eyes and he saw Harris as a spiritual charlatan and despot. His wife, Alice le Strange, whom he had married without Harris's permission in 1872, was asked to certify him as insane. The scales fell from her eyes too.

The remaining years until his death in 1888 were spent principally in Haifa where, apparently still obsessed by Harris's doctrine of Counterparts, he evolved a new version of the dogma which he called Sympneumata. His efforts to found a new community based on the practice were doomed to a mildly scandalous end. It was testified by several potential female members that 'Mr Oliphant's idea was that sexual passion was the only real spiritual life, and that in order to be spiritually alive, you must continually keep that passion excited.' He could only write, it was further alleged, when his passions were aroused. The naive confusion of sexual excitement and spiritual afflatus was to prove his final undoing, and Mrs Hannah Whittall Smith was surprised that to the end he managed to avoid a humiliating scandal. But he was always so brilliant, she added, so charming, so persuasive about his wonderful experiences, that he always seemed the very last person to be guilty of such an odd secret inner life.[17]

Had he but returned to Japan in 1862, he might have risen, with his varied talents of diplomat, writer and linguist, to follow notably in the footsteps of Sir Harry Parkes or perhaps Ernest Satow. He might have left us another volume like *Diplomat in Japan*. He might have explored the byways of Japanese religion with a curiosity shared by few of his Western contemporaries. In fact he has left us a brilliant evocation of Edo in 1858, an eye-witness account of the attack on the legation by 'Mito-lonins', and another lesson in the fearful and frequent subjection of intelligent reason to the exigencies of bogus magnetism and personal myth.

Edmund Morel, a British Engineer in Japan

YOSHIHIKO MORITA

IN *GAIJIN-BOCHI*, the foreigners' cemetery in Yokohama, lies the tomb of a British engineer, Edmund Morel. Although he died only one-and-a-half years after his arrival in Japan, immediately after the Meiji Restoration of 1868, Morel nevertheless made a number of distinguished contributions to the modernization of Japan. Beside him in his grave lies his wife, said to be Japanese.

In 1962, the then governor of Japan National Railways, Sogo Shinji, dedicated Morel's tombstone, on which the following epitaph is inscribed:

> Edmund Morel was born in 1841. He studied and mastered civil engineering, both in London and Paris, and came to Japan in March 1870 as the Chief Engineer for the construction of the first Japanese railway. He acted as superintendent for the construction of the railways between Shimbashi and Yokohama, and between Kobe and Osaka. His contribution to the foundation of the Japanese railway system was remarkable, and he was never afraid of offering his frank opinions to the government. His views were always appropriate and in touch with the times, guiding progress and innovation in Japanese civil engineering.
>
> Sadly Morel died on 23 September 1871, in the midst of construction work, from the worsening of pulmonary consumption, brought on by overwork. His wife died just 12 hours later.

Alongside the Japanese inscription on the tombstone is an

English one from which we can additionally glean that Morel was a member of the British Institution of Civil Engineers.

The tombstone's allusion to Morel offering his 'frank opinions' to the government, which were 'appropriate and in touch with the times', refers to his proposals to the then Minister of Civil Affairs and Finance, Okuma Shigenobu,[1] and his vice-minister Ito Hirobumi.[2] Morel suggested the establishment of independent authorities to take charge of major public works, and educational institutions to train engineers.

Morel's proposals were realized with the formation of the Ministry of Public Works (Kobusho) in 1870, and the Imperial College of Engineering (Kogakuryo) in March 1872. Kobusho and Kogakuryo formed a major axis of pragmatic thinking during the modernization of Japan in the Meiji era, and so had an enormous impact in determining the country's economic direction. A British engineer who left such a giant mark in such a short period should hold some interest for us all, even today.

By contrast, Morel's life was less significant for Britain. It can be said that this British engineer was a person of little distinction in Britain. His name is only briefly mentioned – a few lines to a couple of pages – in books about foreign employees in government service in Japan during the Meiji period of modernization.

The Times newspaper of London has long been famous for its obituary articles on persons of note. A thorough search I made of the period concerned produced no such memorial of Morel's death, probably due to the fact that his main activities were overseas, in countries such as Australia, New Zealand and Japan. There was a brief mention of him on 5 April 1870 in relation to a railway construction project:

> Arrangements have been fully completed for the first introduction of railways into Japan. The work will belong to the Japanese Government, but it is to be carried out under the advice of English engineers appointed by Mr Horatio Nelson Lay, by whom all negotiations have been conducted, and who has already selected Mr Edward [*sic*] Morel as principal engineer, who has been summoned from Australia, where he was engaged in works for Mr Edwin Clarke.

Horatio Nelson Lay, who enters the scene at this point, went to Japan in 1869 to conclude a loan agreement for one million pounds – secured against future customs duties and railway revenues – to finance railway construction, negotiating with Okuma and Ito on the Japanese side, about whom we will hear more later. With some misunderstandings about the loan contracts on the Japanese side, Lay raised the necessary funds through issuing a Japanese Government Bond on the London market, against the real intentions of the Japanese government. Lay's appointment was subsequently terminated in an out-of-court settlement.

Although Morel appeared to be actually selected on the recommendation of the British Minister in Japan, Sir Harry Parkes, Lay's contract with the Japanese government, which was later cancelled, authorized him to employ engineers and fix their remuneration. Formally, therefore, Lay made the employment contract with Morel.

The relationship between Lay and Morel is an interesting story in itself. When conflict emerged between Lay and the Japanese government over the loan agreement, Morel was already in Japan and somewhat apprehensive on Lay's behalf. He wrote to Lay urging him to come to Japan as soon as possible and explain the circumstances to the government. Unfortunately, it was not easy to communicate clearly in those days across the distance between Japan and London. The relationship between the two men gradually turned chilly, to such an extent that Lay wrote to Okuma and Ito on 7 December 1870, one day after the loan agreement had been cancelled, saying:

> Morel was appointed on the recommendation of Minister Parkes, even though his technological skills may prove not adequate to the task. I disclaim any responsibility for problems in construction due to his performance.

Further, the *Japan Weekly Mail* – a weekly newspaper published in Yokohama for foreign residents – carried an article on 4 March 1871 on Lay's one-sided disclosure of his private correspondence with Morel.

Morel was much grieved by the worsening relationship. According to the obituary in the same newspaper on 11 November 1871, Morel had intended to write an explanatory article on the relationship just before his death, but was persuaded by those close to him that he was not at fault and there was no case to answer. His contribution was fully recognized by the Japanese government, so an article responding to the attacks was never written.

BIRTH AND HEALTH

Morel's tombstone in *Gaijin-bochi* says he was born in 1841 and died on 23 September 1871. When I tried to trace his records in Britain, using the clue on his tombstone that described him as a member of the Institution of Civil Engineers, I found an obituary of him in the Institution's *Proceedings* for 1872-3.

That obituary seems to have been the source for various documents about Morel written in Japan. It records his date of birth as 17 November 1841, and the tombstone has his date of death as 23 September 1871, which is 5 November 1871 in Western-style dates. This is confirmed by the death certificate issued by the British Register Office. Morel therefore appears to have died just a few days before his thirtieth birthday. The birth date of 17 November 1841 is rather questionable, and his age was probably 30 years when he died.

Morel's entrance registration at King's College School in March 1857 shows his age as 16 and his date of birth as 17 November, implying that his real date of birth was 17 November 1840. If his date of death is as reported, that would make his age just short of 31 years when he died on 5 November 1871.

A search of the British Register Office confirms the earlier birth date, with the certificate recording that Morel was born on 17 November 1840 at 1 Eagle Place, London. His father was Thomas Morel, a wholesaler and importer of wine and other products from Italy, and his mother was called Emily. The birth was registered in the St James' district of central London, near to Buckingham Palace.

So there appears to have been some confusion about the date of birth; and the tombstone – which says 1841 – is probably wrong. I am inclined to think that Morel was actually born in 1840 and was therefore 30 years old when he died.[3]

According to Morel's entrance registration form at King's College School, he lived in those days at 20 Ladbroke Villas, in the Notting Hill district of London, west of Hyde Park. The records of the local borough indicate that the name of the street was changed to the current name of Ladbroke Road on 21 December 1866. I went to visit this place and found a nearby pub which was established in 1843. Morel and his father might have passed some time drinking beer here. Another old pub nearby is called *The Windsor Castle*, and is one of the oldest pubs in London, built in 1828. It stands at the top of a gently-sloping hill. It took its name from the fact that, in those days, if you looked westwards, you would have an unbroken view as far as Windsor Castle itself, while to the east the whole of London would be laid out before you.

Edmund Morel had a delicate constitution in his youth. He attended the King's College School, but only for one term during the summer of 1857. According to the school's archivist, Morel's results were recorded as 'good', but it was also noted that '[the student was] impeded by absence from illness. He was absent from school no fewer than 17 times in that one term'. The Institution of Civil Engineers notes that his death was due to 'pulmonary disease'. In those days London was completely polluted by smoke and soot. Natsume Soseki (1867-1916), the famous novelist who stayed in London, wrote in his diary during January 1901: 'For a test, just spit out. You will be shocked to see pure black phlegm.' It is likely that Morel, who had suffered from respiratory problems since birth, said farewell to London for health reasons in 1862. He went to New Zealand and Australia, working as a civil engineer in railway construction and other fields between 1862 and 1865 and was able to breathe cleaner air.[4]

Following this line of reasoning, it is likely that, when a man of such delicate constitution came to Japan in 1870 to work on construction sites, he must have found the going difficult. Japan was notorious for the severe conditions which were imposed on foreigners in government service. This can be guessed from the record that, of the 19 British workers employed in the early stages of railway construction, four of them – including Morel – perished, while three others had to return to Britain because of ill-health.

It is recorded that Morel joined a group of officials – including the British Minister to Japan, Sir Harry Parkes and Okuma Shigenobu, an important politician – who travelled by sea from Yokohama to the opening of the Mint Bureau in Osaka in early 1871. During this period, his tuberculosis might not have been so serious, but it appears later to have rapidly worsened. The government hired a foreign doctor, Assistant Surgeon Purcell, to treat its foreign employees in May 1871, but even Dr Purcell could not treat Morel's congenital illness. Although given permission to go to India for a change of air on 19 September 1871, he died in Yokohama four days later on 23 September (5 November 1871 in the Western calendar).

The obituary in the *Japan Weekly Mail*, published on 11

November 1871, noted that Morel chose to work in Japan despite an offer of another project in Australia. I wonder what drove a man already ailing with lung problems to go to Japan.

CONTROVERSY OVER RAILWAY CONSTRUCTION

Soon after his arrival in Japan on 9 April 1870 (or Meiji 3, March 9 Japanese style), Edmund Morel began work on a survey of land for the Shiodome area, as the first stage of the Yokohama-Shimbashi railway, on 25 April (Meiji 3, March 25). The task of railway construction was extremely arduous in those days.

First of all, there was considerable personal risk for the foreign engineers. The opening-up of Japan, and the consequent influx of foreign workers, had provoked Japanese xenophobia, and waves of anti-foreigner sentiment swept the country. In April 1871, for example, the government found it necessary to order the prefectures involved to provide bodyguards for foreign engineers passing through their territory. In answer to an enquiry from the Odawara domain (in south-western Kanagawa) as to how many bodyguards were necessary, the official response was that each foreigner should be accompanied by four guards.

Railway construction also raised diplomatic issues. Britain and America, in particular, played a heated game in the competition for construction contracts in this newly-opened market. In the end, the Meiji government decided to place the order with the British, favouring the approach submitted by Minister Parkes, which respected Japanese independence and aimed to foster harmonious cooperation. This provoked an immediate angry response from the American government.[6]

Railway construction was a source of controversy on the domestic front too. The camp supporting the venture involved Saga domain (now Saga Prefecture), led by Okuma Shigenobu, and Choshu domain (now Yamaguchi Prefecture) led by Kido Koin[7] and Ito Hirobumi. In later years (May 1902) Okuma was quoted as saying, at the regular meeting of the Imperial Railway Association:

> In those days, neither Ito nor I had strong political authority, but we tried to work towards abolishing feudalism. In order to unify the general public behind abandoning feudal practice, we thought it important to make transport more convenient. Also, to destroy feudal ideology holding on to its own sphere of influence, there must be some enterprise that surprises and excites public

feeling. Thus we came to the idea of establishing a railway system.

Kido Koin, the representative of the Choshu domain supported Okuma and Ito, but Saigo Takamori,[8] the leader of the Satsuma domain (now Kagoshima Prefecture), opposed their ideas, saying:

> Although we should open Japan to the world as soon as possible, we must be careful not to fail by overstretching our body, by envying the prosperity of foreign countries and following them without considering our financial capacity. The extravagant enterprises of installing steam-operated machines and constructing railways should be stopped completely, and efforts made to improve our military capability, going back to the basics.

Another influential critic was Okubo Toshimichi,[9] one of the most able men to guide Japan during the Meiji Restoration, who preferred to take a neutral position:

> We should not rush into an empty embrace of the new-fangled. We should distinguish urgent matters and leave the rest, choose our priorities and not make unnecessary haste.

Records show that Morel was granted interviews with Okuma, Ito and Okubo from time to time. It can be imagined what additional pressures were piled on the man responsible for constructing the railway by such conflicts within the Meiji government. In fact, he wrote in a letter to Lay in May 1870: 'Among the leaders of the Japanese government, only Okuma and Ito are our supporters.'

★ ★ ★

When considering the background to the Japanese railway system, one must recall the five students who arranged to be smuggled out of Choshu domain in 1863 in order to go to Britain to study. Three of the five left a considerable mark on the railways, and were among the guest passengers at the official opening in October 1872. They were Inoue Masaru, then head of the railway system; Yamao Yozo, vice-minister of Public Works; and Inoue Kaoru, the Minister of Finance. Ito Hirobumi was also among the five who illegally went to Britain, but was not able to attend the opening because of his involvement in a government mission to Europe, led by Iwakura Tomomi between 1871 and 1873.

The five students, including the fifth, Endo Kinsuke, arrived in London in November 1863 and began to attend the classes of the famous science professor, Williamson, at University College. Although I could not find Inoue Kaoru's entrance registration in the college archives, it is known that he, Ito, and Endo stayed at Professor Williamson's home. When I visited the location, it proved to be in the Chalk Farm area, next to what was then one of the largest railway marshalling yards in London. The nearest station was Camden. I can imagine these Japanese students commuting from Camden to Euston, the nearest station to University College, that line having been opened in 1837.

When at the height of the Meiji Restoration, the government was looking for 'an enterprise that will excite public feelings to abolish feudal domains and the feudal rivalry of local lords', in Okuma's words, Ito must have remembered commuting by railway train in London, and the sight of Chalk Farm marshalling yard. It is possible that Okuma had already studied steam power by inspecting a steam-engine model produced in Saga domain. This effort had been stimulated by a model brought to Japan by a Russian naval party, led by Admiral Putiatin, in 1853.

MOREL'S CONTRIBUTION TO RAILWAYS

Let us now turn to Morel's reputation as an engineer, starting with the Japanese account.

In Japan Morel was much appreciated. Less than one week before his death, on 19 September 1871, the Meiji Emperor, through the Vice-Minister of Public Works, presented him with a testimonial of gratitude and a prize of 5,000 ryo[10] (about £1,000, a huge sum at that time). It reads:

> . . . you have laboured diligently and without ceasing, from morning till night, at engineering under the Board of Works: in consequence of which the railways between Tokio and Yokohama, and Kobe and Osaka have nearly arrived at completion, the science of engineering has also, at the same time, been introduced, from which our people will receive great benefits to the end of time. This result has been brought about solely by your indefatigable energy and your talents, and your services have not been small.

When inclement weather prevented field work, Morel would

invite Japanese colleagues to his home and lecture them on engineering.

Another interesting anecdote concerns the proposal by a consulting engineer in Britain to supply steel sleepers for the railway, as he was doubtful that wooden sleepers would last long enough. Morel insisted that they should use wood. He pointed out that Japan had abundant timber resources, that techniques for the preservation of wood against decay were very advanced, and that wood sleepers would be much cheaper. The Meiji government took his advice and over-ruled the consultant. This incident indicates Morel's attunement to the sensitivities and limitations faced by the government in carrying out construction projects. Undoubtedly this contributed to his high reputation in Japan.

On the other hand, there are accounts which raise technical questions about the Shimbashi-Yokohama railway. Holtham, a railway engineer who came to Japan one year after the opening, inspected the system and reported: 'I found many technical mistakes that will necessitate reconstruction.' In response, the railway's chief engineer of the time, Boyle, commented that the sudden death of Morel had prevented the efficient transfer of duties and so led to some unfortunate developments. Another British engineer was Richard Henry Brunton, who had arrived in Japan in 1869 to take charge of lighthouse construction. He was also experienced in railway work in Britain and offered harsh criticism:

> The making of this line was, perhaps, not unnaturally, attended by a series of the most unfortunate mischances and mistakes.

Technical evaluation must naturally be left to specialists. Brunton's criticism could have been coloured by spite, as he was an experienced railway engineer passed over by the government in selecting Morel to head the railway construction. We must also consider Morel's extremely short period of involvement with actual construction of the railway before criticizing. Anyway, it seems clear that from a technical perspective Japan's first railway faced a number of problems.

In 1902 Ito Hirobumi referred to Morel in his address to the regular meeting of the Imperial Railway Association. He noted that:

> Morel had been engaged in construction projects in

Australia. Although not very experienced in railway construction, he was loyal and seemed a not inappropriate person to build Japan's first, short railway.'

It was his extreme myopia which prevented Morel from acquiring an official engineer's certificate in Britain. His career in Australia and New Zealand before going to Japan was not specifically in railway construction, but in port, road and railway civil engineering in general. Ito's remarks amount to a very precise estimation of Morel's level of skill.

Since the first track was laid from Yokohama to Shimbashi with the relatively narrow track gauge of 3 feet 6 inches, there remains the unsolved question of why this gauge was chosen. There are two theories about the origin of this particular gauge. One is that the proposal came from the consulting engineer White, who was in charge of material procurement from Britain, as mentioned in a letter from Lay to Morel in September 1870. Another opinion is that it was Morel's idea.

In Britain at that time there was still some confusion over the best railway track gauge. After passing through the co-existence of 4ft 8½in, 7ft 0¼in and 5 ft gauges, finally in 1846 the standard was set at 4 ft 8½in. It therefore seems unlikely that the Japanese narrow gauge of 3ft 6ins could have originated from Britain. It is more probable that it came from New Zealand, which has some similar geographic features to Japan, such as mountainous and volcanic terrain. Budget restrictions would have encouraged the adoption of a narrower gauge, and Morel had working experience on the railways in New Zealand. Before coming to Japan, Morel had written to Lay on 18 January 1870 referring to the applications of narrow-gauge track at 3ft 6in. Okuma Shigenobu related the circumstances in his address to the Imperial Railway society in 1920, when he was appointed its Chairman:

> An English engineer called Morel, who had worked on railway construction in Australia, was hired. I asked him, 'What kind of railway are you going to build?' and his response was a question: 'What about the gauge?' My response was also a question: 'What is a gauge?' Gradually I became more familiar with these concepts through Morel's explanation, and then said: 'Japan is a poor country, so it should perhaps have a narrow gauge. Are there any suitable examples anywhere else in the world?' His reply was: 'A narrow-gauge railway was built in Australia last year and has

a good reputation.' I expressed my opinion that he had better build a railway after the Australian example. And so the decision was made.

Even today, New Zealand uses the narrow 3ft 6in gauge and Australia seems to have made separate gauge decisions state by state.

In later years, the Meiji government reviewed the gauge issue in 1873 but the idea that it should be changed was dismissed on the grounds that it was too early to consider such a move. The gauge issue was reviewed again in 1896 but the proposal to change was again rejected, this time because the investment required was too great. That has remained the position to the present day, except for the *Shinkansen* (Bullet Train) which uses standard gauge.

MOREL'S ADMINISTRATIVE RECOMMENDATIONS

Another aspect of Morel's contribution to the modernization of Meiji Japan was his proposal for the establishment of a Ministry of Public Works (Kobusho) and an educational institution for the training of engineers (Kogakuryo).

Until that time, major public works had been administered by the Ministry of Civil Affairs and Finance (Minbu-Okurasho). Morel provided advice and guidance as requested by Ito Hirobumi, suggesting that public works would best be handled by a sole specialist ministry comprising three main units, responsible for construction, accounting and teaching respectively. He pointed to organizations along these lines in various other countries.

Morel emphasized the need to train engineers by arguing that Japan must plan to become self-sufficient in these skills for the future, not dependent for ever on importing them from the West. An institute that could select and train suitable young people to become engineers would eventually contribute local skills to many different fields of engineering and manufacturing. He urged that an engineering school should be set up in Tokyo or Osaka.

These recommendations were made on 28 May 1870, just one-and-half months after his arrival in Japan. Morel clearly played an important role from the outset as adviser to the leaders of the progressive camp that guided Japan in its formative years as a modern nation-state, primarily Okuma and Ito, and their officials.

Okuma and Ito submitted Morel's proposal intact, now endorsed by Minbu-Okurasho, to the Dajokan – the Grand Council of State that was the central decision-making body of the Meiji period. As a direct result, on 20 October 1870 a new Kobusho (Ministry of Public Works) was decreed. Its brief was to supervise all major works such as construction of railways, mines, steelmaking, shipbuilding, lighthouses, telecommunications, machine manufacturing, scientific plants, etc., as government enterprises. In April 1871 the new Kobusho submitted a report to Dajokan suggesting the establishment of Kogakuryo, an engineering college. This was accepted and the college set up in March 1872. Ito Hirobumi referred much later, in 1902, to Morel's recommendations, saying:

> Morel told us such things from the beginning, and it was realized, as with Kobusho.

Much credit for setting in motion the enormous reforms implied in the establishment of a new ministry and college must go to Morel. In this sense, his influence over modernization and technological innovation in Japan lasted for a long time. But we should not ignore the political dynamics of power struggles within the Meiji government that made the task easier.

Morel's arrival in Japan and the start of railway construction in March 1870 coincided with a period of struggle between two rival factions in the government. The progressive modernization camp of Kido Koin, including Okuma and Ito, was based on the Minbu-Okurasho ministry. Their rival was the Sangi group, or Councillors in the Meiji government, led by Okubo Toshimichi. This group also included Soejima Taneomi and Hirosawa Saneomi.

The accepted view is that the power struggle had its origins in July 1869 when Minbusho (Ministry of Civil Affairs) and Okurasho (Ministry of Finance) were merged, creating a greater concentration of power. The Sangi group tried to counter the concentration by strengthening the control exercised by the Dajokan, and by trying to split the combined ministry again. Kido took steps to appoint his faction-member Okuma to a sangi (councillor) position, the better to support the consolidated ministry from the centre. As a compromise between the two factions, Minbusho and Okurasho were divided again in July 1870, and Okuma was appointed to a sangi position in September of the same year.

If we carefully review the series of actions taken – Kobusho established in October 1870, Okuma appointed sangi and also as commissioner of the new ministry – from a political perspective, Kobusho was clearly going to have a major role to play in the encouragement of industrialization and increases in productive capacity. Morel's proposals had truly borne fruit.

DEATH IN JAPAN

The inscription on Morel's tombstone records that he:

> . . .died on 23 September 1871, in the midst of construction work, from the worsening of pulmonary consumption, brought on by overwork. His wife died just 12 hours later.

Next to the joint tomb in the *Gaijin-bochi* foreigners' cemetery in Yokohama was a white *ume* (Japanese apricot) tree. According to Japanese sources, when blossoms appeared for the first time there were red and white flowers together on one branch. The *ume* was called 'Eternal love' and became an attraction for the public in Yokohama.

Morel, as we have seen, was born with a weak constitution and it seems to have worsened over time. The diary of Kido Koin records that he met Morel at Kawasaki Station on 16 October 1871 but Morel's condition seems then to have rapidly declined. On 28 October Morel filed an application to go to India for two months for a change of air, and this was approved on 1 November. According to the *Hyogo Times* – the newspaper for foreign residents in Kobe – on 11 November, the condition of Morel's illness was serious enough to prevent his receiving visitors by the end of October. About the time he had received permission to go away for recuperation, he fell into a critical condition, requiring constant medical supervision. On the same day, Inoue Kaoru – who had received news of Morel from a British colleague – passed on the information of Morel's declining health to Okuma Shigenobu, through Goto Sho-jiro[11] and Inoue Masaru. At 1.30pm on 5 November Morel passed away.

While the circumstances of Morel's demise are clear, that of his wife raises a number of mysterious issues. Of a number of Japanese sources which mention Morel, several record his wife as Japanese, and include specifics: that her name was Kino, and that she had been a housemaid to the wife of Okuma Shigenobu. Apparently the marriage had been arranged by Mrs Okuma. But it was only in 1873, two years after Morel's death, that mixed marriages between Japanese and foreigners were legalized by State Order 103 of the Grand Council. If his wife was Japanese, then the marriage could not have been legally approved.

Sources on Morel present conflicting views, some saying that Mrs Morel killed herself after his death, others that she caught his disease through long nursing of him. There is a note written to Inoue Masaru by a British engineer on 6 November:

> Morel's wife had been suffering with asthma for two days and also passed away at 1.30am this morning.

Another item is the telegram sent to the Railway Agency saying:

> Yesterday at 1.30pm Mr Morel passed away. Since then his wife had several fits and finally also passed away at 1.30am.

These sources indicate a natural death, but, with only 12 hours between the deaths, it was perhaps inevitable that someone should invent a suicide theory to explain the unusual event – and add an element of romanticism.

An important clue on Mrs Morel and her death can be found in the diary of Kido Koin. When he was informed of Morel's demise on 7 November he records:

> After the British engineer Morel died, his wife is said to have died too, after becoming mentally deranged. When I went to Kawasaki and Yokohama by train on 6 September [Japanese calendar], twenty-odd days ago, I was sent off by Mr and Mrs Morel.

Going further back, we find the *Japan Weekly Mail* of April 1871 and the *Hyogo Times* both carrying articles about the opening of the Mint Bureau in Osaka. Both newspapers report that Mrs Morel attended a luncheon reception with her husband, and that she was seated at the second table between a Mrs Konthals and Captain Blake of the US vessel *Alaska*. This would be the table next to that of the host, Sanjo Sanetomi. There is some incongruity here. It seems unlikely that she would have been permitted to send off Kido Koin, one of the highest ranking politicians, or invited to an official event such as this and treated with such honour, if she was Morel's Japanese wife who was by definition not legally approved.

With this in mind, I proceeded to further investigations and luckily found a funeral record for the Morels in the Yokohama Historical Archive.[13] Concerning Mrs Morel it says:

> Harriett Morel, died 25 years of age on 6 November 1871 (Western style).

Based on this information, I contacted the Registrar of Births, Marriages & Deaths in London. Here it was possible to trace the record of the deaths of Mr Morel on 5 November and Mrs Morel on 6 November, both registered on 8 November 1871 with the British Consul in Yokohama.

There is no clear indication of the cause of Mrs Morel's death, especially no indication of suicide. While suicide would be believable in the circumstances if she were Japanese, this seems an open question if she were British. Although I can neither agree nor question Kido's 'mentally deranged' comment, primary information indicates a natural death. This clearly requires further investigation, but, at this stage, I am inclined to take the view that she died from infection and fatigue after long nursing of her husband. The feeling of lost support after his death could have led to her own 12 hours later.

Despite the *Gaijin-bochi* foreigners cemetery in Yokohama having a display on 'Harriett Kino', I now believe Mrs Morel to have been British. But, with such a strong theory to the contrary, and the anecdote of the 'Eternal love' *ume*, it is difficult to reject the existence of the Japanese lady close to Morel completely. I am hopeful of finding new revelations, new drama, in this area.

★   ★   ★

What a story we have here! Morel was able to survive only a brief one-and-half years in Japan, dying halfway through major railway construction projects. There was conflict between Britain and America over the projects, and conflict between Morel's patron Lay and the Meiji government. Morel enjoyed apparently intimate relationships with influential leaders such as Ito and Okuma, caught up as they were in the whirlpool of political strife in the Meiji government. And finally there is a Japanese shadow of a lady close to Morel, and a wife who died just 12 hours after her husband, apparently sacrificing her own health through nursing him.

The question arises as to what kind of existence Edmund

Morel had in the context of Anglo-Japanese relations immediately after the Meiji Restoration. Brunton, as mentioned earlier, came to Japan as a lighthouse engineer. In his book about how a foreign employee in government service should behave he notes that:

> ...there are two basic approaches. One is to be a man of initiative, using progressive western ways. The other is just to respond with proposals whenever asked, respecting the Japanese ways.

It is easy to imagine Morel as well balanced between the two types. His constitutional weakness may have made it easy for him to control his self-assertion, concentrating on pragmatism and insight into his surroundings.

Morel appears to be neither known nor respected by the British. He was unable to attend school due to weak health, and his short-sightedness prevented him from acquiring official certification as an engineer. Then there are the technical criticisms of his railway from Yokohama to Shimbashi. Nevertheless, it cannot be denied that he played a significant role and rendered major service as an adviser to influential bureaucrats such as Ito and Okuma, who went on to guide Japan during her formative years as a nation-state. In some way he acted as a bridge during these early years of the Meiji era between the advanced technology of Britain and a Japan eager to learn. We have seen how symbolic railway construction was at this time.

It is probable that the ideas of establishing a Kobusho and Kogakuryo were already in the minds of Ito and Okuma, however vaguely. We cannot ignore the political power-struggle in the Meiji government that was pushing matters that way too. Nevertheless, we should not underestimate Morel's role in providing direction to the government. As a result, Japan went the way of organized industrialization, and adopted modernizing approaches in many areas. It was Morel who crystallized the vague ideas of the leaders into practical action. His obituary in the *Japan Weekly Mail* of 11 November 1871, said:

> The making of a railway was not with him a mere question of laying out so much road along which trains should travel at a certain speed, or so much more merchandise should be conveyed. It was a means by which the human race was advanced in civilization, by which governments could consolidate their authority, and by which the comfort, happiness and enlightenment of mankind were advanced.

Morel can also be regarded as an educator to the Meiji Government, as well as an engineer. Perhaps it should be summed up this way. Because Morel cast himself in the role of 'engineer', his contribution was easily accepted by the Japanese government, which had its own policy of self-sufficiency and reduction of dependence on foreign help. It also made it easy for him to provide frank and practical advice to the progressive leaders of the Meiji government, in turn giving rise to the great respect they accorded him and the towering reputation he left behind in Japan.

Alexander Allan Shand, 1844-1930
– a Banker the Japanese Could Trust

OLIVE CHECKLAND & NORIO TAMAKI

ALEXANDER ALLAN SHAND was one of a rare breed, a Western banker who, during the Meiji period, earned the trust of the Japanese. His 'Japanese' career was in two parts. In the 1870s in Tokyo, he was invited to teach the first generation of young Japanese bankers the elements of modern Western banking, book-keeping, auditing and accounting. In the 1900s, in London, he was an important agent who smoothed the way for the Japanese government to borrow large sums on the London money market.

A closer look at Shand's career clearly demonstrates the remarkable progress which Japan had made in the management of its financial affairs over the hectic Meiji years. During the early 1870s, when Shand was first involved, there was little or no order in Japanese banking. The country was awash with debased paper money, including *hansatsu*, the paper money of the disbanded clans. The idea of a nationwide banking system had yet to emerge and the confusion endemic in the country fuelled inflationary pressures. By 1900, due largely to the control exerted by Matsukata Masayoshi,[1] the strong man of Japanese banking, Japan was on the Gold Standard (1897) and from 1902 was linked through the Anglo-Japanese Alliance with Great Britain.

Alexander Allan Shand was a Scotsman, born in Turriff, Aberdeenshire, on 11 February 1844[2] the son of James Shand, surgeon, and Margaret Allan. He is thought to have been trained in a Scottish bank in Aberdeen; he may have moved to serve in a bank in London before becoming, by 1863, an officer in the Chartered Mercantile Bank of India, London and China in Hong Kong.

Early in 1864 A.A. Shand, at the age of 20, was appointed acting manager of the newly opened office of the Chartered Mercantile Bank in Yokohama (at Lot 78, which was situated south of the great pier, some half mile inland) with W.D. Henderson as acting accountant and J. Watson as his assistant.[3]

It was an extraordinary time to be in Japan. Yokohama, a mere sixteen miles from Edo, later renamed Tokyo, the power base of the Shogunate, had (together with Nagasaki and Hakodate) been opened to foreign merchants as a treaty port on 1 July 1859. Traders, mostly British, had rushed ashore, eager to gain trading advantage. Inevitably, but more reluctantly, Western bankers, including, first, the Central Bank of India and secondly, the Chartered Mercantile Bank, opened sub-offices, to follow the merchants.[4]

It was a turbulent period, presaging the fall of the old Bakufu regime. The bombardment by Western guns of Kagoshima, the capital of the Satsuma han, in August 1863, and that of the batteries of Choshu at the Straits of Shimonoseki in September 1864, shattered the myth, for some intelligent Choshu and Satsuma samurai, that the Japanese had the option of keeping the foreigners out. In March 1866 some Choshu samurai led by Kido Takayoshi (1833-1877) and some Satsuma samurai, led by Saigo Takamori (1828-1877) sank their differences and concluded the Sat-Cho Alliance. This was the preliminary to the military campaigns of 1867-68 which routed the Shogunate and elevated the young Meiji Emperor to a crucial role as the head of a forward-looking reforming government.

From 1864, during these unsettled years, Shand remained in Yokohama doing business and familiarizing himself with Japanese society. It is interesting to note that sometime after November 1866 Shand employed Takahashi Korekiyo,[5] later finance minister and prime minister, as messenger-boy at the bank. This was Takahashi's first sight of the business of banking. Although there is no evidence that Takahashi was involved again with banking until 1892 (when he became a junior officer in the fabric maintenance office of the Bank of Japan)[6] it is possible that he may have become aware of the relevance of banking to a successful country at this time.

The most urgent task for the new Meiji administration was the building up of a financial structure, on which the new polity could establish itself firmly. In February 1868, the fledgling government set up the accountancy bureau, which was, in April, enlarged as the accountancy office. In June a tax department was added which started issuing in July, *dajokansatsu*, or government notes. A year later, in July 1869, the accountancy office was reorganized as the Ministry of Finance. By July 1870, the finance ministry had six departments, these were cash, supply, building, mint, tax and overall supervision. Under this system, the new coinage decree was promulgated in May 1871 and the newly-built mint in Osaka started to strike new coins with British-made machinery (which had been bought from the defunct Mint in Hong Kong) and British staff. The time had come for the young Meiji oligarchs to consider a banking system on the Western model with the aim of circulating paper currency alongside metal coins.[7]

Early in 1869, the government set up eight exchange companies through which it intended to circulate government money. These companies were given the right of note issue and expected to finance local industries by using both types of notes.[8] The companies were initially reliant on ex-*kokusankaisho*, or domain exchange houses, but this proved unworkable as subsequently, in 1871, the domain system was replaced by a national system of prefectures. Because of the imminent departure of a large overseas mission led by Iwakura Tomomi, Okubo Toshimichi and Kido Takayoshi (which was to leave Japan in late 1871 to renegotiate the Ansei treaties with the Western powers and investigate things Western), the matter became urgent. A hurried compromise was reached towards the end of October 1871, when the financial authorities resolved to base their system on the American National Bank model. It was against this background that A.A. Shand was chosen by the Meiji oligarchs to guide them in building an early banking system and in training the first generation of modern Japanese bankers.

KIDO TAKAYOSHI AND SHAND

It seems likely that Shand came to the attention of the senior Japanese oligarchs through his friendship with Kido Takayoshi, one of the most astute and perceptive of the new Japanese leaders. They first met in September 1869 in Hakone, a summer resort west of Tokyo, where Kido was taking a brief leave on account of ill-health. Okuma Shigenobu should also have been of the party but he was detained on official business in Tokyo.[9] Later, back in Yokohama, they continued to meet occasionally. Kido wrote:

> . . . This evening I had a few drinks with my friends. By chance two British army officers, Strong and Hood, as well as Shand of No. 78 (Yokohama) came to the room of Wilkin of No. 3 on the coast; and I asked them to sing us some songs of their own country, so the three men burst into song in unison. They also talked about several things relating to their home country. It was quite a diversion.[10]

When they next met, it was Kido who paid a visit writing, '. . . after 2 I went to visit Shand at the foreign money exchange at 78'.[11]

It is highly likely that Kido discussed banking questions with Shand, say, on the Yokohama Exchange Company which had been launched several months before. This Company was in serious trouble as their paper bank notes had failed to circulate in the community. It seems likely that Shand explained to Kido why, without public confidence, the notes of the Yokohama Exchange Company would never circulate. Talking to Kido reminded Shand of the difficulties which all Japanese then faced in understanding the complexities of a modern banking system:

> . . . I had an appointment with the Englishman Shand; so I went to his house with Schmidt and Shojiro. He had seven other foreigners as guests, among them the Army officer who accompanied Shand to Miyanoshita in Hakone last year. I returned to my inn after 10.[12]

The last arranged meeting between them was shortly before Kido's departure on the Iwakura Mission to America and Europe:

> Fair. I went to the Palace at 10. This evening Prince Sanjo and three of the Imperial councillors were summoned into the Imperial Palace, and served saké. I returned home after 5. This evening I had an appointment with the Englishman Shand who came over to talk. Yamao Yozo and Nomura Yasushi joined us for the discussions. Shand was acquainted with Morel.[13]

In 1871 there were four councillors on the *dajokan*: Saigo Takamori (1828-1877), Okuma Shigenobu (1838-1922), Itagaki Taisuke (1837-1919) and Kido himself. Among the four, Okuma was a recognised financial expert in the government, being responsible for drafting the National Bank Decree to be promulgated in the following year. Yamao Yozo (1837-1917), one of the Choshu Five, who was familiar with life in Britain having spent two years in Glasgow, between 1866 and 1868, and who spoke serviceable English, was then a high official in the Ministry of Works. Nomura Yasushi (1842-1909), another ex-Choshu samurai, was a high official in the Foreign Ministry due to join the Iwakura Mission. Edmund Morel (1841-1871), the British railway engineer responsible for constructing the first railway in Japan had died on 5 November 1871, shortly before their meeting. Morel's death, and his wife's subsequent suicide, were indeed still a tragically vivid memory for them all. But it could not be a focus of 'the discussions'.

It is conjecture but it seems likely that Kido quizzed Shand on banking matters from the beginning. The presence of Yamao who was especially useful as an interpreter, at the meeting of 11 November may also be significant. At the same time a struggle was going on between Ito Hirobumi (1841-1909) and Yoshida Kiyonari (1845-1891) over the direction of any new banking initiative in Japan.[14] Ito, representing Choshu, succeeded in discrediting Yoshida's (Satsuma) ideas, although in retrospect these might have been more successful.

The meeting of 11 November could have been held to persuade Shand to join the Finance Ministry to support the banking scheme launched by the Choshu initiative. It was also highly probable that at some stage during 1871 Shand met Okuma. The Iwakura Mission, bearing Kido and Ito away from Japanese shores for some two years, left Yokohama on 23 December 1871. It was in fact Okuma with whom Shand would work, and they became close allies. Shand, with a natural tact, always deferring to the Minister Okuma as 'His Excellency'.

SHAND IN THE MINISTRY OF FINANCE, 1872-1877

In August 1872, four months before the proclamation of the National Bank Decree, Alexander Shand was, provisionally, employed by the Ministry of Finance as an adviser to the department of issue. Joseph Heco, or Hamada Hikozo (1837-1897), Japanese seaman turned American, merchant and interpreter, who was known to Kido long before the Meiji Restoration, writes:

At the request of the Minister, I attached myself to the Bureau of Currency under Mr Yoshikawa. It was occupied with the task of establishing National Banks on the American model, to help forward the capitalization and commutation of the Samurai's incomes. An English expert in banking matters, of high standing, Mr S., had been engaged in connection therewith to compile regulations and to establish a system of Bank book-keeping.[15]

As Heco noted, Shand started writing a book on bank book-keeping in August 1872, before the formal contract had been signed. He finished writing by the summer of 1873, and his draft was immediately translated by Joseph Heco and his team in the ministry of finance. The book, *Ginkobokiseiho*, or Detailed Accounts of Bank Bookkeeping was published in December 1873.[16] This five-volume work provided the first information on Western banking accountancy technique to be introduced into Japan. In the meantime, on 1 October 1872 the formal contract between Shand and the Ministry of Finance was concluded, with a salary of 450 yen per month, soon later increased to 500 yen. Such a high salary, which was equivalent to that of a government minister, was remarkable, but it should be remembered that Shand had given up the security of his post in a Western bank.

Following the death of an infant son in Hakone in the summer of 1873, Shand was granted home sick leave. On the P&O steamer *Hindustan*, near Aden, on 9 November 1873 he wrote a Memorandum which was sent to Okuma and which gives some idea of the recommendations which Shand was giving to the Japanese.

SHAND'S MEMORANDUM
(P&O STEAMER, *HINDUSTAN*, NEAR ADEN, 9 NOVEMBER 1872)

1. It is desirable that a new and improved system of accounts should be introduced into the department of the government with the view of preventing fraud, diminishing expense and encouraging rapidity and accuracy.

2. It is desirable that there should be in the Banking department of the Shiheiryo (Mint) certain officers who have not only studied the general principles of banking, but who have also had opportunities of studying the mode in which banking is conducted in foreign countries.

3. For the attainment of these objects it was proposed to Chief Commissioner of the Treasury by Mr Shand, Secretary to the Comptroller of the Currency, that he, in conjunction with such officials as the Government might select, should proceed to Europe to obtain the necessary information for the introduction of a new system.

4. This proposition was submitted by Mr Okuma to the Privy Council and was rejected by them on the grounds following viz:-

A. That as Mr Shand was about to proceed to England on sick leave it would not be expedient to entrust him with duty.
B. That if he should be retained as a paid servant while suffering from sickness it would create a dangerous precedent in respect of the relations of the government with its foreign employees.
C. That the government was not prepared to spend such a sum of money as would be required to accomplish the end sought for. As there now appears to be every hope that Mr Shand's health will be soon completely restored he ventures to put forward the following modifications of his former proposition in the hope that it may meet with the approval of Mr Okuma and of the Privy Council.

5. That the government shall send to the Japanese ambassador either in London or Paris a discretionary power to entrust to Mr Shand the carrying out of the objects mentioned in paragraphs 1 and 2.

6. That before doing so the Japanese ambassador shall satisfy himself that Mr Shand is in a fit state of health to perform the duties required of him.

7. That the Japanese Ambassador shall select from among the students under his control as many as it may be desirable to employ, to act in conjunction with Mr Shand and to receive instruction from him in matters relating to banking and accounts.

8. As to Mr Shand's remuneration he would propose that the Japanese ambassador be entrusted to arrange with him, or if the government prefer it they can pay to Mr Shand any sum they may consider fair after his return to duty in Japan.
It will at once be seen that if this proposition should be carried into effect, the expense will be comparatively trifling and the advantage to the government in having officials who understand

accounts and banking matters will be considerable even if the government should not immediately re-organize their system of accounts. But if they should decide upon doing so, the importance of having such officers can hardly be over-estimated. Any difficulty that there may be about Mr Shand's sickness will be obviated by the Japanese ambassador seeing him personally from time to time and satisfying himself that the work is progressing.[17]

Officially, this Memorandum was not accepted by the Ministry of Finance.

And yet, a small group of young Japanese bankers were in London over the period when Shand was also there on sick leave. Was this pure coincidence? These future bankers included Koizumi Nobukichi (1853-1894) who became in 1880 first Vice-President of the Yokohama Specie Bank, Nakamigawa Hikojiro (1854-1901) a nephew of Fukuzawa Yukichi, who later became the chief executive of the Mitsui Bank, Sonoda Kokichi (1848-1923) who became president of the Yokohama Specie Bank in 1890 and Soma Tanenaga (1850-1924) who became president of the Yokohama Specie Bank.[18]

One can only suggest that Shand was able, informally perhaps, to introduce these young men to banking circles during his period of sick leave in London.

In November 1874, back in Japan, Shand was commissioned to organize courses on public finance in a banking science section, newly set up in April that year in the department of issue. The courses were divided into two; one introductory and the other standard. In the preliminary course, there were lectures on economics, bank regulations, bookkeeping and arithmetic. In the regular course there were lectures on banking, translation, bookkeeping, arithmetic, bank history, bank regulations and commerce. Shand himself was responsible for lectures on J.S. Mill's *Principles of Political Economy* and his own Detailed Accounts of Bank Bookkeeping. These courses, which were the principal training this first generation of Japanese bankers received, operated for five years until 1879. In total, 341 students qualified and continued to serve the banking and financial world in Meiji Japan, of whom 118 were in the Ministry of Finance itself while 42 served in local government and 181 became bank managers or officials.[19] One must wonder at Hazel Jones' remark that Takahashi was 'one of Shand's most able pupils' at these classes.[20]

In October 1874, Shand was asked to undertake the first bank inspection in Japan's history. The failure of the house of Ono, one of the largest shareholders of the First National Bank of Tokyo, in the autumn of 1874, had aroused grave doubts about how the Bank had been conducting its business. The first inspection, executed by Shand by March 1875, gave priority to searching out bad debts, in the accounts of both the First National Bank and the Second National Bank of Yokohama. Besides these investigations Shand pointed out two other basic shortcomings in modern Japanese banking; a necessary reform in the method of note issue and awkwardness in allowing more liberal overdrawing facilities. Shand took special measures to advise Shibusawa Eiichi (1841-1931), the auditor of the First Bank, personally on these matters. Shand's inspection was a rare example of an independent audit in the history of Japanese banking.[21] It is important to note that, although this type of inspection was built into the National Bank Decree, it was never used and became a dead letter. The Japanese never did incorporate the British system of independent and unexpected bank inspection as Shand would have wished.

In the last two years of his duties in the Finance Ministry, Shand was ever more active and involved in enlightening the financial authorities and assisting the ex-*ryogae* merchants to transform themselves into modern private bankers. The Finance Ministry, without any resources in the form of modern banking textbooks, accepted Shand's advice and published a translation of Arthur Crum's *A Practical Treatise on Banking, Currency and the Exchanges*. Shand himself drew up a manual for national banking in Japan, which appeared in serial form in the ten issues of a magazine published by the Finance Ministry and entitled *Ginkozasshi* (or *Bank Magazine*), between 1877 and 1878. Before he finally left Japan in 1877 for London, Shand himself wrote a short book, *On Banking*, which was translated as *Ginkotaii* and published in May 1877. The book was a concise introduction to banking which was of course based on British practices.[22]

Shand thus contributed substantially to the development of Japanese banking ideas and practices. In the summer of 1876, the national bank system, which was already in the doldrums with only four banks established, was about to undergo a major reform. The government tried to assist would-be bank proprietors to set up their banks more easily and also tried to find a way forward politically. As banking adviser to the Japanese government Shand prepared a scathing indictment of the financial authorities. He listed his objections under 59 heads. His lengthy paper was harsh, he used examples from the West, citing a variety of banking authorities, particularly about the urgent necessity of keeping bank note issuing business separate from banking business. Uncomprehending, the Japanese authorities dismissed his advice.[23]

The refusal of the Japanese monetary authorities to listen to Shand's advice was to cost much in the ensuing years as run-away inflation brought severe suffering and hardship.

SHAND, THE BANKING ADVISER, IN LONDON

The second half of Shand's career as a Japanese banking adviser began sometime after April 1898 when Takahashi Korekiyo made contact in London with Shand and through him with Parr's Bank and its officials. Takahashi, as deputy governor of the Yokohama Specie Bank, had been requested by Inoue Kaoru, then Minister of Finance, to make enquiries about the possibilities of raising a foreign loan. Takahashi journeyed to London and sought out A.A. Shand.

When Takahashi and Shand met again in April 1898 some thirty years after their earlier association the roles had been reversed. Whereas in the 1860s the young aspiring Takahashi in Yokohama had served as messenger boy to Acting Manager Shand at the office of the Chartered Mercantile Bank; in the late 1890s, Takahashi, now the deputy governor of the Specie Bank met Shand, a sub manager of Parr's Bank.

It is not known how difficult it had been for Shand, at the age of 33, to find a new banking job in London, suffice it to say that on his return from Japan in the late 1870s, he joined the Alliance Bank and remained with them until they amalgamated with Parr's Bank in 1892.

The union of Alliance and Parr's seems to have increased Shand's responsibilities. After 1892 he was one of the signatories entitled to sign cheques on the Bank's behalf, in its dealings with the Bank of England.[24] At the same time he became manager of the Lombard Street branch of Parr's Bank at a salary of £1,000. On 9 October 1902, A.A. Shand was transferred to the Bartholomew Lane office as head office manager at salary of £1,500 per annum.

After his return to London Shand continued to undertake small but significant services for the Japanese. In 1881 Shand had helped S. Hihara[25] (of the Yokohama Specie Bank) to open a private account at the Alliance Bank, Bartholomew Lane branch, and in 1885 he had arranged for the Yokohama Specie Bank to open an account in the same way. Parr's Bank (after 1892) took over the Yokohama Specie Bank's account allowing unsecured advances to be made.[26] Shand also may have encouraged the first teaching of Japanese at the School of Oriental and African Studies in London between 1903 and 1907.

Shand's availability in London, to Takahashi and other Japanese, was of importance for he was to prove a valuable ally throughout the succeeding years when Japan was seeking to borrow on London, especially over the Russo-Japanese War period of 1904-5.

From Takahashi's own enquiries in London he reported to Inoue Kaoru, the Finance Minister, as follows:

> . . . a foreign loan might be arranged at 4 or 4.5 per cent for less than £5 million at 90 per cent, the loan issue should be divided into a three-year consecutive operation.

Takahashi also recommended that while the Japanese Minister in London should supervise any loan arrangements, a loan commissioner should be appointed from the staff at the London legation to develop good relations with the City.[27] In fact, in the long and difficult years before 1914, when the Japanese were arranging loans in London, it was the London manager of the Yokohama Specie Bank who *de facto* became the agent for the Japanese government and so involved with the borrowing.

From Shand, Takahashi learned something of the complexities of launching a loan on London and the necessity of forming a syndicate. In June 1899 the 'Prospectus of the Imperial Japanese Government 4 per cent Loan for £10 million, secured by Customs duties and redeemable in 55 years' was issued.[28] The attempts to raise this loan were not successful. The Japanese government had eventually, through the Yokohama Specie Bank's London branch office, to accept that it could only raise £4.5 million. It was an inauspicious time as the Boer War had broken out and the British were pre-occupied with setbacks and casualties in South Africa. Fifty-five years was also a very long period, unacceptable to London bankers. Of this Japanese loan only 10 per cent was subscribed on the open market. This meagre 10 per cent was in fact a warning that despite the fact that Japan was on the Gold Standard, lending money to this 'new' country was still regarded with suspicion as far as the conservative bankers of London were concerned.

The Russo-Japanese War broke out in February 1904 sending Japan, as borrower, back to the London money market. 'Shand was again the vital Japanese contact'.[29] But by this time Shand had found an ally in Jacob Schiff,[30] of Kuhn Loeb & Co. in New York. Through the intervention of Schiff, the National City Bank and the National Bank of Commerce in New York, agreed to join the syndicate. As a result, a £10 million loan at 6 per cent and redeemable in seven years, was successfully launched. Between 1899 and 1907 £140 million were raised to the Japanese government as loans on the London money market.

Shand remained the key figure, in the sense that he was the only Westerner consulted at every stage throughout these years. The point might be made that, despite Shand's importance as Head Office manager of Parr's Bank, he was not a nationally known banking figure whose confidence in Japan could have influenced the London money market in Japan's favour. Shand's younger brother, Hans George Leslie (born Turriff 20 January 1853) was private secretary to Mr Gladstone during the fourth Gladstone administration (1892-94) and remained associated with the Gladstone family after W.E. Gladstone's death in 1898.[31] It is not known whether A.A. Shand was ever introduced into political circles by his younger brother.

But there were other powerful Western bankers who took a pro-Japanese stance. As early as 1892 the German/American Jacob Schiff, based in New York, as well as Ernest Cassel, based in London, were in consultation with Yoshida Kiyonari who was trying to arrange Japanese government loans.

The engagement of Jewish financiers in Japan's campaign to raise loans on London did in fact transform their prospects. Sir Ernest Cassel (1852-1921), an intimate of King Edward VII, who was acclaimed for his lavish philanthropic gifts, moved in influential circles, far removed from those of A.A. Shand. Jacob Schiff was a friend and associate of Cassel's. Schiff's fervent anti-Russian stance, perhaps engendered by Russian pogroms of the Jews, encouraged his determination to ensure that Japanese government loans were successful. But Schiff did more; by finding supporters of the Japanese loans in the United States, he emphasized the availability of money markets other than London and so did perhaps weaken the position of London as the world's top money market.

Shand's position as the foremost banking contact of the Japanese in London was recognized not only by his own bank but also by the Japanese. In August 1899 Mr. Shand's contribution received the first, of several, substantial gifts. As was reported:

'It having been determined at last Board meeting, subject to the approval of the Chairman, to present Mr. Shand with £1,000 as an acknowledgement of his services in the matter of the recent Japanese loan and generally in maintaining for the Bank the Japanese connection. It was reported that Mr.Shand had, with the consent of the Rota Committee accepted a present of £1,000 from the Yokohama Specie Bank for his good offices to them over a series of years and especially in connection with the recent Japanese loan and it was resolved to confirm the resolution of the previous meeting to give Mr. Shand a present of £1,000.'[32]

It seems abundantly clear that Parr's Bank found the Japanese loans business exceedingly profitable. From the Japanese point of view Parr's Bank offered 'the cheapest and safest issue terms'.[33] Repeatedly (29 December 1904, 7 December 1905, 14 March 1907) the Minute Books report bonuses of £1,000 to Mr Shand 'for his good offices in the matter of the Japanese loans'.[34]

Shand retired from his Head Office managership at the end of 1908. On 31 January 1909 he was 'unanimously elected a director of the Bank to fill the vacancy caused by the death of Sir Ewan Cameron'.[35] He remained a director until 1918 and so retired finally at the age of 74. The Emperor Meiji conferred on Shand the Fourth Order of the Rising Sun (1902), the Third Order of the Sacred Treasure (1904), the Third Order of the Rising Sun (1906) and the Second Order of the Sacred Treasure (1908).

A. Allan Shand, as he signed his name in his letters, was a good friend and supporter of the Japanese in Tokyo in the 1870s and in London in the 1900s. His pioneering work in teaching over 300 Japanese, the first generation of modern bankers, was a significant achievement. Some of Shand's advice in the 1870s – notably his insistence on the absolute necessity for Japan to keep banking business strictly separated from note issuing business – was rejected. But this was because the Japanese could not understand the validity of the advice they were being given.

Shand's role in London as adviser and confidant to the Japanese during the hectic decade when Japan was seeking loans, for which there was no great enthusiasm, on the London money market, was equally important. Because he knew the Japanese with whom he was working he was able to give his wholehearted support. It is not wholly fanciful to conclude that Shand's steadiness and competence in banking matters, together with London's supremacy as a money centre, persuaded Japanese bankers that they should, in banking matters, at that time, make the British their role models.

Alexander Allan Shand drew up his Will at his home at 2 Beulah Hill, Upper Norwood, South London, on 14 March 1914. The Will was probated on 19 June 1930[36] following Shand's death, on 12 April 1930, at his then residence Ardmore, Ardmore Road, Parkstone, Dorset. He left an estate of gross value of £7,582, and net value of £5,369. It was a substantial sum[37] for a surgeon's son from Turriff, Aberdeenshire, to leave, reflecting his achievement in becoming a director of an important London bank. But this was not all. Because of his knowledge of banking, his honesty and his integrity[38] he had become the best known foreign banker ever to have served the Japanese Government in Meiji times.

6

Royal Visits to Japan in the Meiji Period, 1868-1912

SIR HUGH CORTAZZI

ROYAL VISITS to Japan in the latter part of the nineteenth century and the early part of the twentieth century were comparatively rare, if only because travel by sea to Japan took many weeks. While a few had some political implications, most of the visits do not seem to have been part of any concerted plan to develop relations with Japan. Nor, unlike the much more frequent royal visits to Japan since the early nineteen sixties, which have been much facilitated by air travel, were they designed to support and promote commercial objectives.

Some visits, such as the first British royal visit to Japan by Prince Alfred, Duke of Edinburgh (1844-1900), second son of Queen Victoria, in 1869 and those in 1881 of Prince Albert (1864-92), elder son of Edward, then Prince of Wales, later King Edward VII and of Prince George (1865-1936), second son of the Prince of Wales and later King George V, were to some extent at least fortuitous in that they were all serving with the Royal Navy and were cruising in Far Eastern waters. Prince Arthur, Duke of Connaught (1850-1942), who visited Japan in 1890 with the duchess, seems to have come largely as a tourist or (as such visitors were termed in those days) 'a globe trotter', while the visit of his son, Prince Arthur of Connaught, in 1906 was a visit with an overtly political purpose. His task was to convey the Order of the Garter from King Edward VII to the Emperor. Prince Arthur's subsequent visit in 1912 to attend the Emperor Meiji's funeral on behalf of King George V, although not strictly in the Meiji period, must also be considered to have had a political purpose.

This essay is an attempt to describe the highlights of these visits and the results, if any.

★ ★ ★

1869, ALFRED, DUKE OF EDINBURGH

The best account of the visit to Japan of Prince Alfred, Duke of Edinburgh, Captain Royal Navy, in 1869 is that given by A.B.Mitford, later the first Lord Redesdale.[1] Mitford, then secretary of the British legation, began his account with these words: 'There was a great stir in Japan in the summer of 1869 when it was known that the Duke of Edinburgh was coming in the [HMS] *Galatea*. The Japanese Government were wildly excited for this was the first time that a Royal Prince had paid a visit to the Mikado, and they were determined to give his Royal Highness a reception at Edo [Tokyo] worthy of his rank and of the monarch who was to entertain him.' The Hama Goten (detached palace) was to be his residence in Tokyo and generous preparations were made. Furniture and other European style equipment were procured from Hong Kong for use in the 'rather ugly, ramshackle wooden house with green shutters' which 'was run up in a hurry' for the duke. The furniture from Hong Kong 'with a strong flavour of Tottenham Court Road, jarred piteously with the imaginative poetry of the Japanese artists' who decorated the interior 'with a riot of colour and gold'.

As Sir Harry Parkes noted in his despatch of 23 August 1869, however, the decision to accord appropriate honours to the duke had been the subject of much debate in the Japanese government and court. Iwakura Tomomi observed to Sir Harry 'that the reception of the Duke had caused the Government much anxious consideration; for when the subject was first mooted, opinion was by no means uniform as to the course to be pursued. An intelligent majority of the advisers of the Mikado had, however, seen that the occasion was one which should be profited by to mark their friendly feeling towards foreign Powers, and their readiness to promote more intimate relations with them, although at a sacrifice of old ideas and usages. In order, therefore, to receive the Prince in a manner that would be acceptable to England, the Mikado would have to adopt a new etiquette; but it afforded them gratification to feel that these compliments would be paid in the first instance to an English Prince, and would form, therefore, some acknowledgement of the various proofs they had received of the good-will of England and Her Majesty's Government.' (It is interesting that the stress throughout is on England, not Britain or the United Kingdom!)

Mitford was given the task of advising the Japanese in their preparations and of interpreting for the duke. For this purpose he had to learn court Japanese. In a letter home Mitford expressed the fear that he would get the blame for anything which went wrong and would receive none of the credit. Here he did an injustice to Parkes who commended his services to the foreign secretary in London.

The preparations by the Japanese authorities included prayers to 'the God of Roads' for the duke's safe journey and the performance of other Shinto ceremonies. 'The Duke arrived and departed in unbroken health and spirits; all evil influences, all malignant *oni* and *bakemono* (devils and ghosts) had been successfully exorcised', Mitford recorded.

The duke arrived at Yokohama on 31 August 1869 and 'hoisted his standard on board HMS *Galatea*. British, French and Japanese guards of honour were in attendance'.[2] The duke first proceeded to the British legation, then still in Yokohama, where he held a levee attended by the whole diplomatic corps and 12 British residents presented an address signed by some 250 British residents. The Duke was driven up to Edo in one of the Emperor's carriages. Mitford wrote: 'All along the road he was received with the same honours that would be paid to the Mikado himself. The shutters of the upstairs rooms in the houses by the wayside were hermetically sealed with bits of paper stuck across them so that no Peeping Tom should look down upon the august person. . .As the Duke's carriage went by, the people who thronged the road and streets fell prostrate, touching the earth with their foreheads.' On arrival at Edo the Duke was immediately visited by Ninnaji no Miya, a 'Prince of the Blood', who greeted the duke in the name of the Mikado.

Various entertainments were put on specially for the duke. These included a demonstration of Sumo wrestling; Mitford described the wrestlers as 'monstrous mountains of adipose tissue'. 'There were dancers, musicians, conjurors; Cho-cho San came specially for the butterfly trick.' There was also a special performance of Noh at the mansion of the Prince of Kishu (the Tokugawa branch from Owari) 'which had the reputation of being, after the Castle, the most luxurious palace in Edo'. Mitford commented: 'The ancient poetry of these pieces is full of the most delicate fancies obscured by archaic puns and plays upon words; so it was with no little difficulty that, with the assistance of a man of letters, I prepared the arrangement of the plays.'

The highlight of the visit was the duke's meeting with the Emperor in the palace which Mitford called the castle on the day after the duke's arrival in Edo. Accompanied by Sir Harry Parkes, Admiral Sir Henry Keppel and the officers in attendance, he was shown into the audience chamber 'where the Mikado stood on a raised dais with two of his personal attendants and the Prime Minister behind him'. The duke and Mitford took their places opposite the dais. Mitford found his task of interpreting 'rather nervous work. . . for it is so easy to bungle into some absurd mistake where foreign etiquette and a very stately phraseology have to be observed; however, it all went off well, there were the usual commonplaces exchanged, and then his Majesty invited his Royal Highness to meet him more privately in the garden. . .After a short delay. . .the Duke was shown into the delicious little Maple Tea-house in the castle gardens where tea and all manner of delicacies were served. Then came a summons to the Waterfall Pavilion, where the Emperor was waiting; only Sir Harry, the Admiral, and myself went in with the Duke. This particular Court ceremony was certainly something out of the common. It can never occur again. East and West were sharply defined. There were no cocked hats or gold-laced coats among the Japanese of those days. The Emperor and all his court were living pictures out of the dark centuries'. The duke presented the Mikado with a diamond-mounted snuff-box.[3]

Parkes in a despatch from Edo dated 4 September, commenting on the reception accorded to the Duke on his arrival, said: 'Any one acquainted with the past state of affairs in this country could scarcely fail to observe the remarkable improvement in our intercourse which these circumstances denote. Three or four years ago the foreigner entering Edo watched, with well grounded distrust, the movements and forbidding aspect of every armed Japanese; but on this occasion the feeling animating all classes appeared perfectly friendly and unrestrained. They acted as if they felt that they were receiving foreign friends instead of traditional opponents.'

In a further despatch, dated 30 September, Parkes reported: 'His Royal Highness expressed himself as entirely satisfied with the cordial feeling which was shown towards him. He was received by the Mikado on a footing of entire equality, and His Majesty profited by the occasion to make favourable allusions to the friendly relations existing between Japan and Great Britain.

'It is satisfactory to think that the good results which may be anticipated from this reception are not likely to be confined to the personal compliments which were paid to His Royal Highness. The event probably derives no small degree of importance from the additional and conspicuous proof which it affords of perseverance on the part of the new Government in the abandonment of a long-cherished system of isolation, and of their willingness to conduct their foreign intercourse according to the rules which obtain among Western Powers. His Majesty has been brought on this occasion into direct and personal communication with a member of one of the leading Royal families of Europe, and the knowledge of this fact and of the character of the reception of His Royal Highness can scarcely fail to exercise a favourable effect on the position of foreigners generally in this country, or to weaken those prejudices which are the result of centuries of rigid exclusion.'

Parkes had stolen a march on his diplomatic colleagues as a result of the visit and we may be sure that he was determined to extract as much benefit for Britain as he could from the visit. The duke returned to Yokohama by sea after his visit had been extended to a week. HMS *Galatea*, *Ocean* and *Pearl* had come up from Yokohama to Edo. An imperial prince, described by Parkes as Hiyobukiyo no Miya, attended the prince as far as Yokohama and returned there later to attend an official dinner and ball which Parkes gave for the duke. The duke left Yokohama on 16 September for Osaka and Nagasaki, this time accompanied by HMS *Ocean*, *Adventure* and *Salamis* under the command of Admiral Sir Henry Keppel. In Osaka the duke visited the mint, which had been procured from Hong Kong, and the castle. At Nagasaki Consul Flowers reported to Parkes, in a despatch dated 27 September, that the duke 'met with a most hearty reception from all members of the community'. There was 'a grand illumination' in which 'the whole front of the Bund was lit up'. 'Everyone appeared to vie with each other in rendering homage to the Prince ; there was no distinction of nationality.'

The visit contributed to cementing British relations with the Meiji government. It provided a useful opportunity to develop high level contacts and enabled the Meiji authorities to break away from the shadow of the old policies of isolation and seclusion. This was confirmed by the visit of Prince Henry of Prussia ten years later as a naval cadet on the Prussian corvette *Prinz Adalbert*. He was making his first world cruise and happened to be in Tokyo on 30 May 1879 which was the day on which Sir Harry Parkes was giving his Queen's Birthday Ball. As Prince Henry, the Queen's grandson, 'son of our Crown Princess' as Parkes described him,[4] 'had accepted my invitation, I felt that my arrangements should be rather more extensive than usual, as so many guests wished to be present. I have 250 acceptances'.

1881, PRINCE ALBERT VICTOR AND PRINCE GEORGE OF WALES[5]

HMS *Bacchante* with the two princes on board 'steamed up Yedo bay in the grey of early dawn' on 21 October 1881. It moored off Yokohama. On 22 October, Parkes being away on home leave, Kennedy, the chargé d'affaires, came on board to call. Two days later the two princes went ashore 'for five days leave'. They were greeted by Prince Higashi-Fushimi and other Japanese officials who had 'been educated in England,' and whom they 'used to meet at the Chiswick garden parties'. 'At the request of the Mikado' he was to stay with the princes while they were in Japan.

They went by train to Tokyo and then by carriages to the Hama Goten (detached palace) where they were to stay. The princes were accompanied by Prince Louis of Battenberg, Lieutenant the Hon A.G. Curzon-Howe, Dr Turnbull and 'two gun-room messmates' . Other officers from the squadron stayed at the legation. Their first visit was to Asakusa where they went by jinrikisha. At dinner that evening at the Hama Goten they were joined by Japanese dignitaries, including Sanjo Sanetomo and Iwakura Tomomi. The Mikado sent his own 'private band' to play to them during dinner. 'The sounds that proceeded from the inner-room where these musicians were placed were so faint and plaintive that some of the party ignorantly mistook them for preparations of a band tuning up, and as it went on for some time inquired when they were going to begin to play. This music in fact. . .appears altogether out of tune and full of discords. . .But after listening to it attentively for some time, although we cannot say we like it, yet we can understand how some people do: just as others admire Mr Whistler's pictures. . .' They found more to their taste the fire-works, juggling and conjuring which followed dinner.

On the following morning after breakfast Japanese tumblers and acrobats performed in the garden. They then visited Zojoji at Shiba which prior to its destruction in war-time raids was one of the chief sights of Tokyo. After lunch they put on their uniforms and went to call on the Mikado. At the palace they were joined by the chargé d'affaires and legation staff. The Mikado received them 'in full uniform, dark blue tunic with heavy gold braid on the sleeves and front. Although he is not thirty years old. . .he has a much aged look about the face. He is self-possessed and evidently strenuously anxious, though not nervous, to play his part well'. The Empress was also present. She was in Japanese costume. 'She is very small and would be very pretty if she was not painted up so according to Japanese fashion.' 'All the chamberlains were in European court dress which had been made at Poole's. . .One of the stout chamberlains who is thus now attired, often at other times wrestles with the Mikado.' The Mikado conversed briefly with the two princes during which 'Eddy', i.e. Prince Albert Victor, said that the Queen had ordered her portrait to be painted in oils and 'forwarded in token of friendship.' This portrait was duly delivered by Parkes to the Emperor and Empress, after his return from home leave on 18 March 1882. The Emperor thanked the minister for the portrait 'in pronouncing an imperial edict'. The portrait of the Queen, which has been preserved in one of the imperial warehouses, shows the Queen seated on a throne in robes and crown. It seems to have been a copy of a portrait painted before the death of the Prince Consort.[6]

The Emperor expressed his thanks through the princes for the hospitable reception accorded to Prince Arisugawa Taruhito who was studying at the Royal Naval College at Greenwich and who had been received by the Queen at Osborne.

'The Empress in cheerful and genial manner then tried to begin a conversation. Eddy asked her to accept two wallabies which we had brought in the *Bacchante* from Australia. These were great pets with all aboard, as they went hopping and frisking and booming about at meal hours all over the decks, as wild as hawks. . .' The Empress seemed much pleased and the wallabies were sent off next day to the palace.

The princes remained about half an hour. They then returned to the Hama Goten to see some performing birds. Some of the party then caught several old carp 'with hook and line baited with worm'. 'The elder members of the party wandered about the gardens, and found in the summer houses lacquer boxes lying on the tables filled with large cigars, the ends of which were all tipped with gilt. The cigars were very good, but the gilt came off on the lips.'

On the next day the princes watched the Mikado reviewing 'his troops'. The princes and other naval officers were provided with horses to ride. One of the medical officers unable to control his mount caused a certain amount of chaos. The princes recorded that there were some 10,000 men in the troops, but only one regiment of cavalry 'owing to the scarcity of horses in Japan. There is not a blade of grass growing in the whole empire'! Back at their palace the young princes were provided with more entertainments. The afternoon was spent 'in the town' travelling by jinrikisha. They visited the British legation and called on the wife of the chargé d'affaires. They then did some shopping, accompanied by Ernest Satow of the legation. In the evening they went to dine with the Mikado. There they noted that 'the service of gold plate was made by Garrard. . .Its only ornaments are the imperial dragon and the chrysanthemum. . .The desert service of Minton china was an exact facsimile of the blue one with roses in placques at Marlborough House'. The two princes sat one on either side of the Mikado. After dinner they 'heard a good deal from Baron Eisendecher, the German minister, about Prince Henry of Prussia's recent visit to Japan.' After dinner they went on to the British legation for an evening party attended by a good many English residents, where there was yet another conjuror.

The following day the princes were up at 6.30 a.m. riding with Prince Louis of Battenberg, the German minister and Prince Kitashirakawa. They 'went all round the Uyeno woods and parks on the north of the city'. On their return they changed into uniform to receive the Mikado who came to call on them. The Mikado had sent in advance a present of 'four beautiful bronze vases, each three feet high, and worked with silver and gold figures of dragons and flowers on the surface, and four cases containing rolls of silk brocade'. After the Mikado had left they were taken to the naval college, the *Kaigun Heigakko*. They could not stay long as they were due to lunch with Prince Higashi-Fushimi where they saw Japanese-style polo. This was followed by a visit to the tomb of the 47 *ronin* at Sengakuji temple. After dinner there was a ball at the Imperial College of Engineering.

They thought that the best that could happen to the ballroom 'built in horrid European fashion' would be that it was 'shaken down by the next earthquake when no one is in it'.

On the next day they had another early start as they went duck netting with Prince Kuroda. They returned to breakfast at 9.30 'and then the tattooer finished our arms. He does a large dragon in blue and red writhing all down the arm in about three hours'. So King George V carried a Japanese tattoo!

There were more sightseeing, dinners and other entertainments as well as the inevitable group photographs. They felt that 'they had had a very pleasant stay' in Tokyo. In Yokohama there was a cricket match at the Yokohama Club where the officers were beaten by ninety-five runs to seventy-three. They managed a visit to Kamakura and Enoshima. On the last day of October the Mikado visited them on HMS *Bacchante* in Yokohama harbour and was entertained to lunch on board. 'This was the second day of the Yokohama regatta and George had to slip away before lunch was over to get into his flannel suit to steer the officers' boat in a race.'

Ernest Satow accompanied them on their voyage to Kobe. Here Satow, having made inquiries of W.G. Aston, then Consul in Kobe, 'about the sanitary condition of the place' and this having been found 'extremely satisfactory', the admiral gave the princes seven days leave of absence to visit Kyoto and Nara. They could not have had a better guide than Satow who took them to all the main sights. Among souvenirs which they bought in Kyoto were 'drawing books' by Hokusai (presumably Hokusai's *Manga*). At a dinner in Nara 'one of the dishes was a large round pie, the crust of which being cut out flew a number of birds all over the room'. They returned via Horyuji to Osaka where they inevitably visited the mint and the castle before returning by train to Kobe. From there the squadron went through the Inland Sea and away to China.

The princes clearly had a busy and enjoyable visit. (It probably included some extra-curricular activities for young men!). If the account given really reflected what they had jotted down they also learnt a lot about Japan and, where they got this information from Satow, they were not misled. The Japanese from the Emperor down did all they could to honour the princes.

King George V remembered his visit with pleasure and told the Crown Prince, the future Showa Emperor, when he visited Britain in 1921 what a wonderful time they had had. The visit no doubt helped to develop a relationship between the British royal family and the Japanese imperial family.[7]

1890, THE DUKE AND DUCHESS OF CONNAUGHT

Prince Arthur, Duke of Connaught (1850-1942), third son of Queen Victoria, married in 1879 Princess Louise, daughter of Prince Frederich Charles Nicholas of Prussia. He was an army officer who served in Egypt and India. In 1889 he reached the rank of Lieutenant General.

The Duke and Duchess on a world tour arrived in Tokyo from Shanghai in 1890 in time for the cherry blossoms. In Tokyo Mary Fraser, wife of the British minister, recorded[8] that she had vacated No 1 House in the legation, the residence of the head of mission, and ceded it to the Connaughts who found it 'a convenient starting point for their excursions'. She added: 'They brought a good many people with them.'

The Connaughts arrived in Yokohama on board the SS *Ancona* on 14 March 1890 having called first at Nagasaki, Kobe and Osaka. At Yokohama they were received with due pomp and ceremony. At the station the British residents presented an address of welcome.

Mary Fraser noted that 'as the royal visitors had been rather overwhelmed with the entertainments given them in Shanghai and Hong Kong, the English people here wisely refrained from taking up their time in that way, and they were left free to devote it all to sight-seeing, as of course they wished to do'. She added that the Duchess was an ardent sight-seeer 'and seems to have only one dread; namely that she should miss some interesting experience which the ordinary traveller would ferret out for himself'. They had let it be known in advance that they wished to travel about unofficially with as much freedom as possible. As this was the era of the *soshi*,[9] the British minister who wished to avoid an incident supported this arrangement. Mary Fraser commented that the Emperor would have liked them to be his guests, but 'in view of their own desire to move about freely, and because of one rather embarrassing misunderstanding in the past, it was thought better that they should not accept the gracious invitation in its entirety'.

The 'misunderstanding' arose because at the Queen's jubilee in 1887 Prince Komatsu went to England to take the Grand Star of the Chrysanthemum to the Prince of Wales 'who unfortunately never returned the visit'.

The duke and duchess 'made the most of their liberty, and from the moment of their arrival in Tokyo refused to have anything to do with the Court carriages which were sent every morning to carry them about'. They insisted in going out in jinrikisha, 'a long procession through the dust, to see the curio shops'. Mary Fraser commented: 'Public jinrikishas correspond to omnibuses in London, and official people do not use them.' One of the three courtiers appointed to accompany the duke and duchess pleaded sudden indisposition and disappeared in the direction of the palace when the jinrikishas were ordered; the others meekly took their places in the procession with an expression of resigned despair.

From Tokyo they visited Kamakura, Nikko, Hakone, Miyanoshita and Atami. Mary Fraser noted, cattily, that the duchess 'rather surprised the foreign community by the extreme plainness of her dress, generally a light flannel coat and skirt (made by her sewing-maid) and a serviceable sailor hat. She is daintily neat and trim, and when she clicks her little heels together and bows straight from the waist reminds one irresistibly of a smart German officer'. The royal visitors avoided official duties although the duchess agreed to lay one foundation stone for a cottage hospital connected with an Anglican mission school. This ceremony 'took place in a pause between a flight back from Nikko and one off to Kyoto'. While at Nikko they met the artist and traveller Henry Savage Landor.[10] On 6 May the duke visited Landor at his house in Tokyo. The visitors had to take off their shoes before going in. Landor commented: 'I cannot say that, standing in their socks, they looked either pleased or happy. Less still when they had to sit on the floor, which they did, like Sir Edwin Arnold, in a sort of Anglo-Turkish style, giving plentiful evidence of agonizing cramp in their lower limbs.'

At Kamakura the duchess was bored in the evening and asked if a band could be provided. The Japanese obliged by summoning one from Yokosuka.

The Connaughts stayed at Yaami's Hotel in Kyoto,[11] used by most 'globe-trotters' in those days. They were joined by the Master of Napier, first secretary at the British legation. Douglas Sladen who was staying at the hotel noted that they had forty-two trunks and that the duchess spent much of her time in buying curios and embroideries.[12] 'The Duke, after he has shaved himself in full view (although he doesn't know it) of half the hotel, enjoys lounging about in one or other of the sunny verandahs, which, of course, are instantly vacated for the royal party whenever they step out into them by all the English people, in spite of his good natured expostulations. . .' Later Sladen commented that 'The Royal party have the very simplest habits. claret and seltzer for the ladies, and whisky and seltzer for the gentlemen, in very modest libations. . .' The servants made no particular fuss over them. Nor did the authorities!

The duke and duchess allowed Sladen to accompany them on their trip down the Hozu river rapids. They had a picnic after which the duke helped to wipe the knives and forks and pack up the drinking cups.

After their visit to Kyoto the duke and duchess were invited to dine with the Emperor and Empress on 7 May 1890 at the palace. The Emperor and Empress sat together with the duke and duchess on either side. The dinner lasted an hour while a band played under a German band master. The Emperor and Empress withdrew after coffee. 'Sir John McNeill,[13] who was at the dinner, wrote to the Queen that the scene of the Emperor and Empress of Japan conversing freely with the Duke and Duchess of Connaught was not one which could easily be forgotten.' With only one interpreter, such a brief meeting and a band playing, the conversation must have been very limited.

Various other entertainments were given for them by 'the Princes and the Ministers'. 'In an interval of sight-seeing on their second day in Tokyo' they met the minister of foreign affairs, Viscount Aoki, and his wife at lunch.

Before they departed Prince Komatsu, representing the Emperor, called unexpectedly at the legation at a quarter to nine in the morning before the duke and duchess were up and ready to receive him. He brought the Grand Star of the Chrysanthemum for the duke and the Grand Star of the Precious Crown for the duchess.

Mary Fraser's account suggests that the royal visitors were not the most considerate of VIPs although the duke's affability was the subject of favourable comment especially by Douglas Sladen; and Mary Fraser concluded that they 'had left a most charming impression, if one can judge by the outbursts of enthusiasm in the local newspapers'.

The visit hardly seems to have done much for Anglo-Japanese relations. The royal visitors' refusal to accept the offer of imperial carriages clearly did not go down well with the Japanese court whose displeasure was indicated by the delay in arranging dinner with the Emperor and Empress and their speedy withdrawal after dinner. The perhaps unintended snub to Prince Komatsu had not been forgotten. The Duke was no doubt affable in a royal way, but there was clearly a significant amount of arrogance among British royalty in the Victorian era which cannot have been helpful to Britain's foreign relations.

In 1891, the Czarevitch, Prince Nicholas, who became the last Russian Czar in 1895, was sent to Japan on an educational visit. It nearly ended in disaster as he barely escaped assassination while riding in a rickshaw (jinrikisha) between Otsu and Kyoto. If he had died, it would have been a tragic reminder that royal visits can be disastrous to relations between countries. Even the failed assassination attempt harmed Russo-Japanese relations.

1906, PRINCE ARTHUR OF CONNAUGHT AND THE GARTER MISSION[15]

The purpose of the 1906 visit to Japan of Prince Arthur of Connaught, son of the duke and duchess of Connaught, was to deliver the Order of the Garter to the Japanese Emperor from King Edward VII. The Garter Mission, as it was called, marked the high point in Anglo-Japanese relations. The first Anglo-Japanese alliance had been concluded in 1902 and revised and renewed in 1905. British sentiment had favoured Japan in the Russo-Japanese war of 1904/5 and Japanese prowess in the war had been much admired in Britain.

The mission which left Marseilles on 12 January 1906, arrived at Yokohama on HMS *Diadem* on 19 February. On their arrival from Yokohama at Shimbashi station later that day they were met by the Emperor in person (this was an unprecedented honour as the royal visitor was not a head of state), the Crown Prince and Prince Arisugawa.

The highlight of the visit was, of course, the presentation of the Garter to the Emperor on 20 February at the Imperial Palace. Lampson described the ceremony briefly in these words: 'To the strains of "God save the King" we formed a procession to the throne-room. Each member was announced in turn by Sir Claude MacDonald, [the British ambassador, the legation having been raised to the status of an embassy] and, after taking up his allotted position, the Investiture began. His Royal Highness handed to the Emperor the autograph letter and the warrant, and then read the Address, to which His Imperial Majesty replied through an interpreter. The Garter, Riband, and George Star,

Mantle, and Hat were then brought up one by one and handed by me to His Royal Highness, and by him put upon the Emperor. After which we withdrew backwards one by one and the thing was over.'

The Emperor 'at once pursued' them to the palace [at Akasaka] where they were staying. There he gave Prince Arthur the Grand Cordon of the Chrysanthemum and other decorations to members of the party. Lord Redesdale received the Grand Cordon of the Rising Sun, as did Admiral of the Fleet Sir Edward Seymour, and General Sir Thomas Kelly-Kenny, senior members of the prince's suite. That evening the Emperor gave a large official dinner. Prince Arthur drove to the palace in a carriage accompanied by Admiral Togo who was awarded the British Order of Merit (also conferred on Field Marshals Yamagata and Oyama). Prince Arthur proposed the toast to the Emperor who in reply proposed the toast to the King.

The mission had a busy programme, including visits to Yokosuka naval base, lunches and dinners as well as duck-netting, a charity concert at Ueno, *kabuki* where they saw a play about William Adams, and shopping at Mitsukoshi. The official programme ended on 26 February with a visit by the Emperor to the prince to bid farewell.

The unofficial part of the visit included a tour which took them to Shizuoka, Kyoto, Shimonoseki, Sasebo and Kagoshima. They then went back to Honshu to visit the naval college at Etajima and on to Kure, Hiroshima and Kobe where they said farewell to HMS *Diadem*. They were now free for sightseeing in Kyoto, Nara and Nagoya, returning to Tokyo on 13 March to dine with Prince Saionji, then Japanese prime minister. They finally left from Yokohama on 16 March by the Canadian Pacific *Empress of Japan*. It had been a sentimental journey for Lord Redesdale and the party had been given a marvellous time and a very warm welcome. It could never be quite the same again.

Prince Arthur of Connaught was to return to Japan to attend the Emperor's Meiji's funeral and in May 1918 as leader of a wartime mission to confer on Emperor Taishō the baton of field-marshal in the British army – thereby acknowledging Japan's 'allied' contribution in the World War (and hoping it would continue). At the time, there was little reason to imagine the war would be over in six months. Prince Higashi-Fushimi reciprocated the gesture by making a 'visit of inspection' later in the year.

CONCLUSION

'Royal' visits to Japan in the Meiji period do not seem to have had any economic or commercial content. Most were more of symbolic than political import, but in the absence of monarchical despots it is inevitable that 'royal' activities are primarily symbolic. Symbols can, however, have political implications. The most significant in this respect were those of the Duke of Edinburgh in 1869 and Prince Arthur of Connaught with the Garter Mission in 1906. The visit of the Czarevitch in 1891 which was not discussed here had the greatest negative impact.

The striking changes in Japan during the period are apparent from the different conditions which the visitors encountered. The court quickly adapted its ceremonial to Western ways but then saw no reason for further adaptation.

The Emperor Meiji never learnt any English and does not seem to have been able to relax in conversation with foreigners. Nor does he seem to have shown much personality in his dealings with his visitors. However, he played his part conscientiously and the accounts suggest that the Japanese were consistently courteous and generous to their 'royal' visitors. In some cases at least they seem to have behaved better than the visitors.

As history the visits were of little significance and most of the doings of the visitors are of only very limited interest, but some of the comments by the visitors (or their amanuenses) have a pleasing touch of irony.

Britain's Japan Consular Service, 1859-1941*

J.E. HOARE

AT THE TIME of the 'opening' of Japan in the 1850s, Britain had three British consular services. A general service operated in most of the world, primarily for the protection of trade. It was the oldest and least organized service. Theoretically reformed in 1825, it was not held in esteem.[1] Better regarded was the Levant Service, covering parts of the Near and Middle East. Its origins, too, lay in trade but its officers also had political and judicial functions. Formally organized as a separate service only in 1877, its origins went further back, to the foundation of the Levant Company. The company was wound up in 1825 and its consular establishments passed to the crown. Its staff were systematically recruited, properly paid and exercised jurisdiction over their countrymen.[2]

By 1858, the China Consular Service resembled the Levant Service rather than the general service. Until the abolition of the East India Company's monopoly over China trade in 1834, Britain had left the protection of its citizens to the company. There followed a disorganized period until the 1842 Treaty of Nanking opened five ports for trade and residence, with a consulate at each. At first these posts were filled by anybody available, and no knowledge of Chinese was expected. Gradually, a professional Chinese-speaking service emerged. It was well-paid, and its members, unlike diplomats, were not expected to have a private income.[3] This was the model for the Japan Service.

THE EARLY YEARS

By 1858, the China Service had developed a structure which lasted until the 1940s. Candidates were recruited specifically for a career in China. Knowledge of Chinese was required for the conduct of business and in 1849, Palmerston laid down that this was essential for promotion.[4] After an initial group of recruits drawn from military and merchant backgrounds, the net was widened to include university graduates and others with a good education. By the late 1850s, the principle was accepted that outsiders would not fill senior positions; those who qualified as interpreters would fill such slots as they became available. As in the Levant Service, rules against trading were strictly enforced. There would be proper salaries and allowances during an officer's employment and a pension at the end.[5]

In 1854, in preparation for the opening of Japan, Clarendon, then foreign secretary, wrote to several university colleges seeking nominations. Those selected went to Hong Kong as 'supernumerary interpreters'. It is not clear if any of them took up appointments in Japan. Certainly none was ready in 1859.[6] Instead, the foreign secretary assigned A.J. Gower, private secretary to the Superintendent of Trade, Sir John Bowring, to Japan '. . . as I understand that during his employment . . . he has directed his attention to Japanese'.[7]

As in China, consular officers were to report to the senior diplomatic representative in the country. This was Rutherford Alcock, former consul at Canton. Sent out as consul general, he soon became envoy extraordinary and minister plenipotentiary, with detailed instructions on the management of the new service, and was enjoined to strict economy in selecting consular premises.[8] Salaries for the new service were relatively generous, though less than in China. The consul general would receive £1,800 (raised to £2000 in February 1860); consuls £800; vice consuls £750; interpreters £500; assistant interpreters £405 in Edo and £324 elsewhere; and student interpreters £200. Later, consuls received £1000. The posts were at Edo, a vice consul, an assistant, a Dutch interpreter and two students; Nagasaki, a consul and a Dutch interpreter; Hakodate, a consul and a Dutch interpreter; and Kanagawa (soon to be replaced by Yokohama), a consul and such staff as could be spared from Edo. Consular officers received free quarters, medical attention and, in the case of the single men, free messing.[9]

The earliest appointments were mixed. Some came from the

China Service, others caught the attention of the foreign secretary. None was particularly well-qualified to live in the tense atmosphere of Japan. Within a few months, Alcock reprimanded G S Morrison, transferred from China to Nagasaki, for his behaviour to the Japanese authorities. Morrison was to retire early in 1864, angry at being passed over for promotion and convinced there was a plot to kill him at Nagasaki.[10] C. Pemberton Hodgson, consul first at Nagasaki and then at Hakodate, was also aggressive towards the Japanese, his servants and the British community, failed to keep accounts and drank heavily. He admitted that he was sometimes drunk, but said he was not always so, and claimed mitigating circumstances for his other faults. It was to no avail and he was dismissed.[11] Captain Vyse, consul at Kanagawa/Yokohama, was forced to resign in 1866, following the robbery of Ainu bones for 'scientific' purposes.[12]

There were also difficulties with interpreters and language training. Because the Dutch maintained a trading post at Nagasaki from the mid-seventeenth century, Dutch was the only Western language widely known in Japan. Britain, therefore, at first employed Dutch speakers in Japan. There was perhaps some optimism about the extent of knowledge of Dutch in Japan, but the use of Dutch was only a short-term measure until staff were trained in Japanese. Four Dutch interpreters were selected in London: A. Annesley, C.F. Myburgh, F.M. Cowan and Richard Eusden. Martin Dohmen, a supercargo on a Dutch ship, later joined them. Another Briton, J.J. Enslie, was appointed in 1861.

Cowan died in the autumn of 1860, Myburgh in 1869. The others stayed, even though it was obvious that officers who understood Japanese would be required. As early as 1861, Alex von Siebold, was employed as a supernumerary interpreter because he knew Japanese. Ernest Satow, joining the legation in 1862, found that Eusden, 'The Japan Secretary', knew not a word of Japanese, yet was supposed to provide language supervision for the students. This lasted until 1867, when a consular post was found for Eusden, and Satow himself took over as Japan Secretary. The others served on. Enslie acquired sufficient Japanese to pass an oral examination in 1878. Annesley, denied promotion, eventually left, becoming consul at Reunion and then at Portland, Maine, before retiring in 1885. References to Dutch interpreters disappeared in 1872.[13]

Extraterritoriality, provided for in the 1858 treaty, also brought problems. British subjects were to be tried under British law by British officials, an obligation Britain took seriously. At first Britain operated a system of consular jurisdiction. Consular officers had the power to try cases, with assessors drawn from the local community in more serious matters. Appeals were to the minister. But often neither consul nor minister had legal training, and the result was botched cases. One remedy was to encourage consular officers to undergo legal training, but that took time. To improve matters, an Order in Council in 1865 replaced the British minister as the supervising and appellate authority by a chief justice in Shanghai, with a judge at Yokohama. The British courts were now circuit courts under the control of the supreme court in Shanghai. Consular officers still lacked legal training, but they had a legally trained officer to whom they could apply for help, while appeals would be heard by a trained judge in Shanghai. The Order in Council also gave the British minister law-making powers to meet situations not otherwise covered in British law.[14]

LANGUAGE TRAINING

Whatever A.J. Gower's language abilities, they were no match for the reality of Japanese in practice. He was widely regarded as a good sort, but was no good at either running the legation or learning Japanese. He retired in 1874 with everybody's good wishes.[15]

Language training was deemed vital to the Japan Service, but it was not systematically organized. Satow, recruited in 1861, was sent to China initially, since Alcock believed that knowledge of Chinese would help him to acquire Japanese. Urgent need cut short the experiment, and Satow, R.A. Jamieson and Russell Robertson set out for Japan in August 1862. Jamieson left at Shanghai to become a newspaperman. The other two went on to begin language training.[16] On arrival, they found that there were no arrangements for teaching them, Western books on Japanese were few, out of date and not easily obtained in Yokohama. There were no teachers, and no funds to pay for them. They had to devise their own methods of learning. At first they worked on their own, but were eventually allowed to employ an American missionary for two hours a week at public expense . A Japanese teacher was also provided at public expense. They paid for a second one themselves. The Japanese were in no sense qualified teachers, which created its own difficulties. There was also the problem of time for study. Satow had it in writing that his task was to learn Japanese, but his seniors in Japan shared the general view that the best training for those embarking on a diplomatic or consular career was to learn about current issues by copying. It took much effort to persuade them otherwise.[17]

They learnt spoken and written Japanese by puzzling out the language with books and a Japanese teacher, and Satow remained wedded to this method for the rest of his life.[18] By June 1863, he could provide an adequate translation of a Japanese document. (Robertson had gone home on health grounds, but resumed his studies later.) In 1865, on the recommendation of the new minister, Sir Harry Parkes, he was appointed as 'Interpreter for the Japanese Language,' with a salary of £400 per annum, double that of a student, but less than the senior Dutch interpreter. Eusden finally moved in 1868. Satow became the Japan Secretary, with a salary of £700, ranking with, but after, the diplomatic second secretaries. By then, he had a circle of Japanese friends and acquaintances who were to be useful in the years to come.[19]

The need to study Japanese was clear. Few Japanese had any knowledge of English, at least in the 1860s and 1870s, and the consular officers had to conduct business in the local language. Passing the interpreters' examination, and thus moving on to an assistant's post, however, was itself no easy task. It was never achieved in the two years allowed. Even though copying gave way to typewriters and carbon, to the end of the Japan Service, there were always other requirements which took the student interpreters away from their main task.[20] Yet, having passed the examination, officers were not required to requalify, and there was some concern that they would sit on their laurels or 'devote their leisure to dissipation and extravagance'.[21]

OTHER TRAINING

There was little attempt at other training. Officers learnt on the job. Copying was still seen as the best way to understand current issues. Concern was expressed in London in 1885 when it was found that the constables were doing it, rather than assistants. The minister, Francis Plunkett, argued that it gave the constables something to do, and allowed assistants the time to keep up their Japanese.[22]

The exception to the general lack of training was that officers were encouraged to read for the bar. If the minister agreed, then an officer with five years' service was allowed an extra year's leave on full pay to qualify as a barrister. Several did so, including both Satow and Russell Robertson. But the acquisition of barrister status did not automatically result in promotion, and there was resentment and at least one resignation at this failure to reward hard work.[23]

THE ESTABLISHED SERVICE

Early recruitment was haphazard, but from 1862 onwards, more systematic arrangements were in operation. At first, Clarendon's practice of writing to selected schools and universities for nominations continued. Requirements for China and Japan, and later Siam, were similar, and candidates were recruited together until 1902. There were even occasional exchanges after the initial appointment.[24] From 1860 onwards, candidates were also certified as qualified by the Civil Service Commissioners.

From the late 1860s, nominations were no longer sought for recruitment. Instead, those who had enquired since the last examination were invited to apply. In 1872, the specialist consular services were opened to all by advertisement. This was eventually considered too egalitarian, and after 1907, it was again necessary to secure the secretary of state's nomination before taking the examination. Applicants had to be natural-born British subjects, of good health and education, between 18 and 24 – or 29 if they were already in the Foreign Office – and unmarried. They sat obligatory examinations in English composition, arithmetic, French, Latin and law, and could offer optional Italian, German and geography.[25]

This produced a standard of consular officers higher in ability and social status than in the general service. A.B. Mitford said in 1870 that student interpreters in China and Japan were of a higher class than 'dragomen' in the Levant: '. . . young gentlemen who come out principally from the Irish universities'. Asked if they were of the same class as diplomatic attaches, Mitford replied that they were not. The First Civil Service Commissioner put it more gently in 1914. Recruits for the Far Eastern Services were like diplomats 'but not so highly qualified'.[26] In fact, the social origins of entrants to the Japan Service were firmly middle to upper class. Mitford's 'Irish universities' and Irish schools were well represented. Many were sons of the clergy. Those from Ireland included J.J. Quin, consul at Nagasaki; J.H. Longford, who was another consul at Nagasaki and later became professor of Japanese at King's College, London; J.C. Hall, consul general at Yokohama; W.G. Aston, who like Satow acquired a considerable reputation as a scholar and became the first consul general in Seoul; and H.S. Wilkinson, a noted lawyer. Those from Scotland included L.W. Kuchler, appointed a student interpreter in 1878.[27] Satow, educated at University College London, was the son of a merchant. Russell Robertson, consul at Yokohama, was the son of Sir Daniel Brooke Robertson, the first consul at Canton, and a friend of Parkes. Parkes's nephews, H.P. and T.R. McClatchie, who joined respectively the China and the Japan Services, were the sons of a missionary. J.H. Gubbins, another scholar and the chief British negotiator of the 1894 revised treaty with Japan, was a nephew of the Duchess of St Albans. His father had been in the Indian Civil Service. E.M. Hobart Hampden, a student at Brasenose College, Oxford, who joined in 1888, was also from an ICS background.[28]

THE WORK

After two years, students became assistants. There were three assistant grades, at £300, £350 and £400 respectively. In addition, an allowance of £100 was paid to up to six officers who had passed the interpreter's examination. Parkes drew up a training scheme in 1870 under which third class assistants spent one year at the court at Kanagawa (Yokohama), for legal training, and one year at a consulate for practical experience.[29] In practice, assistants were often called upon to do more advanced work before completing formal training. Henry Bonar found himself acting consul in 1882, with no legal training and no previous consular experience.[30]

Office hours could be long, five or six hours a day minimum, and an assistant's lot was not exciting. Apart from the ubiquitous copying, there was much translation. Parkes discouraged the Japanese from writing in English, and it was not until his departure that such communications were generally accepted. Plunkett, Parkes' successor, noted in 1885 that a first assistant kept accounts, prepared despatches and letters to the Japanese authorities, kept the land and other registers and undertook notorial acts. In addition, if the consul was absent, he acted as judge. The junior assistants looked after the Japanese-language archives, translated from Japanese, registered claims, and copied most of the outward letters and despatches.[31] Each assistant level took two to three years. An officer then become a vice-consul, or, if good at the language, assistant Japanese Secretary. Another three or four years would take him to consul. It was normally at least ten years before a man became consul. Some took longer, but periods as acting consul softened the blow of delayed promotion.[32]

There were two main strands of work. The best linguists went to the Japanese Secretariat in the legation. There, two or three officers were in charge of the Japanese language work of the legation, and supervized the next generation of language students. Satow was the doyen of Japanese Secretaries, but successors included W.G. Aston and J.H. Gubbins, both also prominent scholars. For other officers, their normal career was as consular or judicial officers at the open ports or cities. After the opening of Hyogo (Kobe), Niigata, Osaka and Tokyo in 1868-9, no more Japanese ports or cities were opened to foreign trade or residence until after 1899. There were at first consulates at all the open ports and cities. British interests were small at Osaka and Tokyo, which were left to vice-consuls. They were non-existent at Niigata and after 1871 the British consulate functioned only occasionally. Hakodate, the most northerly of the treaty ports, was reduced to a vice-consulate in 1882.[33]

Work at the consular posts was straightforward. Notorial duties became heavier as the communities grew. But they were outweighed by the demands of the Merchant Shipping Acts. The signing on and off of crews played a big part in most consuls' lives. By 1879, there were some 15,000 seamen passing through Yokohama each year, and there were some 3000 residing ashore at any one time. The majority of these were British or on British ships. Yokohama was also a minor centre for shipbuilding, and therefore for registration.[34] Even Hakodate enjoyed a new lease of life in the 1890s, with the development of the pelagic seal trade. Henry Bonar noted in 1896 that 'The sealers have kept me busy morning noon and night.'[35]

Commercial work was also important, especially the provision of commercial information and the protection of merchants' rights. Consuls were not, however, expected to push specific British trade interests, nor to be advocates for a particular company or product. As late as 1914, the London Chamber of Commerce complained that it was still necessary to persuade consuls to abandon prejudices against supporting trade.[36] The provision of information was also not without difficulties. The main method was an annual consular report, which was then published in a regular series. According to the treaty port press, most British merchants found the Japan reports lacking. In 1880, the Japan Gazette said that the Hakodate report was late and that, instead of an incisive analysis of trade, '. . .we are treated to lengthy dissertations upon the disastrous fires . . .[at] Hakodate, written in terms which would have been appropriate [from]. . . a cheerful old lady addressing friends at home. . .'[37] The *Japan Mail* defended the reports, arguing that they were prepared by people with considerable knowledge. But even it felt that they were too stereotyped to be of real use.[38] In due course, a new attitude began to develop towards trade promotion and consuls became more willing to identify market opportunities.

Most important was the legal work. The courts handled large numbers of cases; even at the end of the 1860s, Yokohama handled two to three hundred legal cases a year, and even a small post might have twenty or so. Theoretically, all were handled by men with legal training. Britain, alone of all the countries operating extraterritoriality, tried to make reality match the ideal. Joseph Longford, a former consul, claimed that 'no crime committed by a British subject in Japan ever failed to be visited with its proper legal penalty. . . nor did any civil claim against a British subject ever fail to be equitably adjudicated', and Satow said much the same in private.[39] But the 'exigencies of the service' meant that consular officers had to act in legal proceedings without training or experience. Satow, knowing neither how to register a birth nor to conduct a case, was a consular officer, and found himself filling an unexpected gap at Tokyo.[40] The Chief Justice at Shanghai put it to Clarendon that it was as if 'your lordship insisted upon appointing me chief surgeon to a London hospital'.[41]

Not surprisingly, there were criticisms over poor judgements which continued to the very end of extraterritoriality.[42] Yet the system worked and there were few serious mistakes. Even at the end, the British arrangements were working well. Japanese objections to extraterritoriality hinged on the basic unfairness of the system, rather than to individual miscarriages of justice.[43]

CONDITIONS OF SERVICE

Salaries remained at the 1859 levels, supplemented by allowances. Some allowances stopped when an officer went on leave. Housing was supplied, or an allowance in lieu, but not furniture until the twentieth century, and staff suffered losses each time they moved. Housing was a mixed blessing. The Yokohama consulate surpassed the Shanghai club for the title of the ugliest building in the east, while the Nagasaki consul's house was uninhabitable in 1885. Although the wells were tainted, the Treasury refused to pay for the piped water for Yokohama consulate. Houses were hot in summer, cold in winter.[44]

To casual visitors, Japan seemed cheap. But living in European style was not, and the salaries of the Japan Service remained lower than those in China.[45] The need to import many goods, the small market for Western-style foodstuffs and other items made Japan expensive. It was argued that servants were essential. Insurance was difficult to obtain – impossible at Hakodate in the 1870s – and costly when it came. Health care was not cheap. Children had to be sent home for schooling at an officer's expense; local schools were thought unsuitable for European children.[46] Leave, especially local leave, was difficult to arrange. The total number of officers available was about 25, and frequent absences on sick leave reduced the pool. Officers had to wait seven years for home leave, and that, too, was often postponed. Before 1874, fares were not paid. Thereafter, officers received half fare, dependants a third. Full salary was paid for the first month; thereafter, officers were on half salary. Inevitably, those on leave from Japan spent most of it on half salary and there were occasionally protests. J.C. Hall, unable to take home leave for 16 years, persuaded the Treasury in 1907 that half pay was not fair in such circumstances. He received an ungenerous five-eighths salary for part of his leave.[47]

Japan was a difficult place to live, and not just in the early years. It was remote and there was the constant fear of assassination. Morrison was not the only man to feel threatened, though most coped better. Russell Robertson's marriage broke down because of his wife's drinking.[48] Even when assassinations ceased in the early 1870s, there were other strains. Hakodate and Niigata were remote and ships were few and far between. Local communities were small and faction-ridden, and there was a widespread sense of claustrophobia. Consular officers found themselves the targets of local jealousies and tensions, to which they sometimes contributed.[49] There was much sickness and a number of officers and family members died prematurely – four officers and a wife, for example, between

1866 and 1869. Others died soon after retirement. There were also mental breakdowns. Kobe (Hyogo), Nagasaki, Niigata and Yokohama were all counted as unhealthy posts, and attracted added years for superannuation purposes. Most officers left well before the official retiring age of 70 – later 65 – with few questions asked about the medical reasons offered.[50]

THE TWENTIETH CENTURY

In 1899, when extraterritoriality ended, the Japan Consular Service was forty years old. It was to survive another forty. When Britain first considered treaty revision in the early 1880s, it was assumed that eventually British consular officers in Japan would become general service officers. But while such views found occasional echoes in subsequent years, nothing happened.[51]

Language training continued to dominate. Although as early as 1910, the Japanese Secretary argued for better teachers, new recruits found that they were left without guidance and expected to teach the teachers how to teach, just as in the 1860s. Satow, in retirement, argued that there was no other way, as did George Sansom, the commercial counsellor, and W.B. Cunningham, the Japanese Secretary, in 1933. London thought this was complacent. It was true that the language skills of many in the service attracted praise and ambassadors argued the need to keep up both the supply of students and the high standards. Officers such as Colin Davidson and Sansom were widely admired for excellent Japanese. Yet others found difficulty in meeting the standards. Esler Dening had not passed the examination after ten years. Not all kept up the language after qualifying. No new system had been devised by 1941 and nobody drew any lesson from the fact that British language students, after four years, were failing to reach a standard others did in two.[52]

After 1900, additional posts were added to the Japan Service. The process began with the Sino-Japanese War of 1894-95, and Japan's acquisition of Taiwan, where Britain had a consulate at Tamsui. Dalian (Dairen) in the Liaotung peninsula was added in 1905, and Seoul and Chemulpo in 1910. Manila (1903) and Honolulu (1904) were also added to the Japan Service, partly to improve career prospects. They were nevertheless something of a mixed blessing. It was not easy to keep up Japanese in either, and different terms of service applied. One new post in Japan was Shimonoseki, opened in 1901.[53]

The cost of living went up steadily after the Sino-Japanese

War. Salaries, however, essentially remained the same, though a system of local and occasional *ad hoc* allowances made things easier. Eventually, in 1913, Edward Crowe, the commercial attaché, prepared the case for across the board increases. The Treasury was not happy, arguing that some posts had received additional allowances as recently as 1912, but in the end accepted the arguments. The increases were nowhere spectacular – the Japanese Secretary got £100, the Yokohama consul general £50, while Manila and Honolulu received nothing – but were nevertheless welcomed.[54] Another grievance was the steady build up of a promotion blockage. Officers still retired early, on health and other grounds, as in the past. But there was also a core of relatively young or apparently immovable senior officers, and by 1913, the ten years minimum of the 1880s had become fifteen years.[55]

The First World War intensified such problems. Leave could not be taken. Some officers left to join the forces, and others were detached for long periods of war work. One resigned because of a German family background. Recruitment stopped. The cost of living soared. Maintenance and construction work halted, even on essential works such as lavatories at Shimonoseki. When peace returned, it took much effort to prise staff out of their wartime slots, and some never returned. Cost-of-living claims and salary increases had to take their turn with those from elsewhere. Recruiting proved particularly difficult. An approach to the War Office failed to produce a single recruit, and it was decided that the universities might produce a better response.[56]

The immediate crisis passed, but the basic problems remained. Promotion continued to be slow. Staff shortages meant posts were left empty or seriously undermanned. Seoul suffered particularly badly.[57] As in the past, pressure took its toll in mental illness, drink and premature retirement. Economic constraints in the 1920s and 1930s hit hard, both in reductions in salaries and in the poor physical environment in which staff worked. The consular premises at Yokohama, destroyed in the 1923 earthquake, were not rebuilt until the late 1920s, and the consular residence not until 1937. There were long delays in providing new accommodation in Tokyo after 1923. At Kobe, the poor state of the consulate was a standing joke. There were battles over minor improvements such as telephones, electric fans and other amenities. Officers in Japan looked with longing eyes on China, where the number of posts seemed to expand and the rewards were high, or on the general service, where promotion seemed faster and more assured. London argued that such impressions were false, but they remained. The Japan Service seemed to be creaking to a halt.[58]

It was not alone. Similar problems existed in all the specialized services. A series of reports and committees in the 1920s and early 1930s concluded that the solution was amalgamation, a decision implemented in 1932. China remained outside the amalgamated service, because of the continued existence of extraterritoriality. Elsewhere, after 1934, all consular staff would be recruited to one service. These arrangements had barely begun to produce results when a new war threw everything into chaos.[59]

When peace returned, there were many changes. The diplomatic and consular services were combined in 1943. Japan was under occupation for several years. In 1952, when it regained its independence, consular posts were re-opened at Tokyo, Yokohama and Osaka, but staffed on a new basis. Many former members of the Japan Consular Service enjoyed successful careers in the amalgamated service, some in Japan. In retrospect, the Service's high reputation for linguistic skills and Japanese scholarship owed more to a few bright stars than to the mass of its members. What killed it, however, was not lack of talent, but the problems of managing a small, highly specialized cadre in a rapidly changing world.

John Harrington Gubbins, 1852-1929

IAN NISH

J.H. GUBBINS was an Old Japan Hand. He went out as a member of the Japan Consular Service in 1871 and stayed till 1908. He was Japanese Secretary at the British legation in the great tradition of Ernest Satow, E.M. Hobart-Hampden and Harold Parlett. His greatest contribution to history was in the British response to one of the major issues of Japanese political and diplomatic history in the Meiji period, Treaty Revision. In retirement he taught Japanese studies in Oxford University, and was the author of several authoritative books. He was the prototype of the scholar-diplomat so often found in East Asia in earlier times who combined a policy-making role with great expertise about Japan. Gubbins was described by a commentator as one of the four (along with Satow, Brinkley and Chamberlain) 'in the firmament of our countrymen who have made themselves masters of the various problems of our Far Eastern Ally'.

Gubbins was born in India, the eldest son of a government officer in the Bengal Civil Service, Martin Richard Gubbins(1812-63). His father was the author of *An Account of Mutinies in Oudh and of the Siege of the Lucknow Residency*, a large book published originally in 1858 and in two later expanded versions. So there was a literary tradition in the family. But his father was forced to leave India and ultimately committed suicide. John Harrington was educated at Harrow. He took the examination for the Far Eastern consular service and was sent out to Tokyo in 1871 as student interpreter in the Japanese language. Like one of his predecessors, Ernest Satow (1843-1929), Gubbins became highly proficient in the language and published *A Dictionary of Chinese-Japanese words in the Japanese language* in 1889. In the compilation of this he worked with Okamoto Jun, who held the post described in old Indian Civil Service parlance as 'writer to HBM's legation'. He became Japanese secretary at the British legation in 1889 to add to his other responsibilities for the language training of new recruits to the legation and the consular service and also to the army and navy language staff. General F.S.G. Piggott, himself an army language officer at the time, makes these comments on Gubbins:

> Behind a somewhat austere manner was a fund of kindliness and humour from which many generations of consular and service language students benefited.[1]

Gubbins seems to have formed a special bond with Hugh Fraser, the minister in Tokyo from 1888 to 1894, possibly because of their family connections with India. In a conversation with Fraser's wife, Gubbins showed remarkable modesty. Mary Fraser reported that he had told her that 'though he has been working at [the Japanese language] for seventeen years, though he has translated three dictionaries and is now publishing one of his own. . ., he feels that many life-times would not put him absolutely in possession of the whole language as it is used by the learned Japanese today'.[2]

Like many of his contemporaries in the consular service, he was expected to undertake the exploration of some untrodden paths in Japan. He made one of the early expeditions in 1875 from Aomori to Niigata and paid a visit to the mines of Sado.[3] Gubbins was a competent horseman and included 'riding' as one of his pastimes in his entry in Who's Who until his death.

ANGLO-JAPANESE COMMERCIAL TREATY 1894

Gubbins became the legation's chief expert on Treaty revision, the central issue in Japan's foreign policy in the early Meiji period. Japan's desire for the revision of her unequal treaties with the various trading powers was a long-standing issue. Indeed it had been raised by the Iwakura Mission in 1871. Japan's complaint was that the treaties provided for extra-territorial rights for foreigners in Japan and fixed low rates of customs duties, while the treaties could only be revised with the consent of both parties. It was, however, a highly technical, legal subject of the kind which could not be fully grasped by diplomats who came to a posting in Japan for a two-year stint. This played into the hands of those belonging to the Japan consular service, some of whom had been in Japan for decades. In 1886-7 Gubbins served as the 'English Secretary' to the conference for the revision of treaties which was held in Tokyo. During this multi-national conference positive progress was made; but the talks had to be broken off because of an explosion of public indignation against the proposed employment of foreign judges in Japanese courts. From this and other experiences Gubbins drew up countless memoranda giving the past history of negotiations on the topic. It has to be said that it was a profoundly boring subject and the conscientiousness with which he mastered it speaks highly for his patience and tolerance.

Treaty revision came urgently on to the political agenda after the creation of the Japanese Diet in 1890. This was because the new parliamentarians were anxious to find an issue on which they could flay the government. Treaty revision was such an issue; they could at once criticize foreigners from the standpoint of xenophobia and Japanese governments for being too compliant with foreign demands and making slow progress. The risk for Britain was that the new generation of party politicians would put so much pressure on the government that it might just cancel the extra-territorial privileges which were at the core of the treaties and leave the foreign commercial communities throughout Japan severely inconvenienced.

Successive governments raised the subject of treaty revision. The British minister, Hugh Fraser, in responding to one such approach in the summer of 1892 said that he was due to return to London on home leave and suggested a resumption of negotiations there. He added that '. . . Gubbins whose help I should like to have in such a matter, wished to go to England as well as myself and could not fairly be detained after his ten years of continuous residence at his post'.[4] Hence Gubbins who was long overdue for leave was to be found in Britain from December 1892, enjoying a busman's holiday.

But first, Gubbins took the opportunity to get married. In his early days in Tokyo he had met the family of Colin McVean, an *o-yatoi* in the survey department of the Japanese government. Colin had gone out to Japan in association with Richard Brunton in 1868.[5] But the McVeans retired to Killiemore House on the Isle of Mull in 1877. Gubbins on leave from Japan visited them several times and fell in love with their elder daughter Helen. They were married in Edinburgh in April 1893, he being 41 and she 24. They took up residence in Thornton Hill, Wimbledon.

The new Japanese foreign minister, Mutsu Munemitsu, who was in office from August 1892, decided to grasp the nettle of treaty revision and dispose of the commercial treaty with Britain first. He agreed to Fraser's suggestion that, in order to avoid the disturbances which had bedevilled previous negotiations, they should move the venue to London away from the hothouse atmosphere of Tokyo politics. Mutsu decided to depute Aoki Shuzo who had been minister to Berlin since January 1892 to visit London briefly in September 1893 in order to talk matters over with Fraser and Gubbins.[6] He was well qualified for this task since he had earlier as deputy foreign minister negotiated with Britain over treaty revision. Aoki, it was felt, had a good rapport with the two British negotiators. But the outcome was disappointing for Japan as Fraser concluded that she was not ready to make enough concessions. Mutsu had, therefore, to go back to the drawing-board and present fresh proposals. These were approved by the cabinet in November. Mutsu took the precaution also of steering his proposals through the Privy Council before presenting them to Britain. He then instructed Aoki to serve simultaneously in London and Berlin for the purpose of the negotiations.[7]

When the terms reached London, Lord Rosebery as foreign secretary wrote: '. . . who on earth in Britain knows about Japan?' – a question that has gone ringing round the Office over the years. Gubbins was the answer. Fraser led the way in the early discussions with Aoki in December and recommended that Mutsu's proposals were a sufficient basis for negotiations. But he set off to return to Japan in the new year. Gubbins was accordingly seconded officially to Whitehall from February to July 1894, working in tandem with the assistant under-secretary, Francis Bertie. He, therefore, took a major part in the talks which Aoki and Bertie held between April and July. His role was all the more vital because Fraser, having returned to Japan in February, died unexpectedly on 4 June at the height of the negotiations, thus depriving Whitehall of one of the few specialists on the topic.

There was, it has to be said, incredible ignorance on the issue in Whitehall. Some of Gubbins' writings of the time set the scene:

> We have nothing to gain in the revision of our Treaties except the goodwill of Japan and the more remote advantage of the establishment of our relations with her

on a more satisfactory and in some respects a more permanent footing. The British communities in Japan are quite aware of this essential weakness of our position as regards negotiation, and the mystery, unsought by us, in which negotiations have been shrouded during the last ten years has, not unnaturally, increased the anxiety with which they contemplate any change in existing conditions. Rightly or wrongly they regard Treaty revision, which they understand to be more or less unconditional surrender to Japanese demands, as an abandonment of their interests by Her Majesty's Government.[8]

Gubbins, therefore, proposed that the mercantile community in Japan should be more fully consulted. But he was nonetheless insistent that it was in Britain's own interest to revise these treaties to put an end to the anomalies.

The *imperium in imperio* which extra-territoriality creates wherever it is exercised exists in Japan as elsewhere, and in a country which has borrowed so much of Western civilization and methods its continued exercise engenders constant friction. The foreign merchants who carry on their trade under the aegis of extraterritoriality are tempted to presume upon their privileges, and to assume towards the Government and people of the country in which they reside a high-handed attitude. This is naturally resented by the Japanese, who lose no opportunity of retaliating, and a bitter feeling is thus created on both sides. Moreover, under Treaties so obsolete as are the existing Conventions, encroachments on the part of foreigners. . . are unavoidable. . .Were Japan an Oriental country, moving as slowly as China, this aegis of extraterritoriality, which covers what the advanced patriot in Japan regards as the insidious advance of the foreigner, would not attract so much attention, but in her assimilation of Western ideas she has far outstripped her more conservative neighbours. . .The new proposals lead us. . .further in the direction of concession to Japanese sentiment but it is not easy to see how this can be avoided. Nowhere is *national sentiment* carried to such extremes as in Japan. [my italics][9]

For Gubbins fear of 'national sentiment' boiling over was the main justification for Britain to sign new treaties. He referred to articles appearing frequently in Japanese newspapers dealing with Yamato Damashii. It was Gubbins who wrote on 16 June 'Ito is cautious in all things but weak in the face of extremist opinion'.[10] London came to the conclusion that Japan's prime minister of the day, Ito Hirobumi, was a more moderate, trustworthy and cautious prime minister than any Japanese politician who was likely to come to power. This judgement was made largely on the basis of Gubbins' advice. It was on this basis that talks were pursued. The doubts were reinforced when a Japanese soldier attacked a British consul in Seoul just as preparations were under way for signature.

But finally the new Anglo-Japanese commercial treaty and protocol were signed on 16 July 1894. Consular jurisdiction was abolished; the whole of Japan was opened to British traders; and new legal codes would be introduced before the treaty came into force. It was to take effect in five years' time during which much additional negotiation had to take place. Gubbins on his return to duty was appointed as British delegate on the Tariff Commission for negotiating the supplementary convention with Japan which was eventually concluded on 16 July 1896.

Shortly after his return to Japan in the unfamiliar role of a family man, Gubbins was delighted to find that Sir Ernest Satow, one of his predecessors as Japanese counsellor, was appointed as British minister to Tokyo in July 1895. His correspondence with Satow which continued throughout his life shows that their style and intellectual interests were very similar. It was probably Satow who secured for Gubbins in 1898 the award of the order of Companion of St Michael and St George for his work on treaty revision. This was a deserved honour and may have atoned for the frequent complaint of British merchants in Japan that the 1894 treaty had failed and that that failure was due to Gubbins. Even Gubbins in one of his writings stated that 'the new treaty was received with a chorus of disapproval by British merchants in China and Japan'.[11] The British merchant community in the East, deprived of privileges it had enjoyed for a generation, was not inclined to see the political advantages.

KOREA AND JAPAN

In 1900, just as he was about to go on home leave, Gubbins was appointed to act as chargé d'affaires in Seoul in the absence of J.N. Jordan of the China consular service. The reasons for this are not wholly clear. Satow on leave in London may have been consulted when the post in Seoul was about to become vacant during Jordan's leave. He may well have recommended that, on account of Japan's increasing interest in the Korean peninsula, it would be appropriate that someone from the Japan consular service should go to Seoul instead of someone from the China service as heretofore. Or again Satow may have thought that Gubbins was in desperate need of a change from Tokyo where he had stayed contentedly since 1871.[12] Revised treaties had come into force in 1899 and Gubbins' presence in the Japanese capital was no longer indispensable.

Gubbins served in Korea from 18 May 1900 to 4 November 1901 when Jordan resumed his position. For the first time in his career he had his own post and was able to report direct to London since Korea was in crisis for most of the time of his tenure. But it was reassuring for him to know that his friend, Satow, was appointed minister to Peking in place of Sir Claude MacDonald who was expected to need a long period of recuperation after the siege of the Legation Quarter there by the Boxers. By a coincidence he was again able to share his problems with Satow.

Gubbins, though he would have liked to stay on in Korea, took a negative view of the country, describing it later as 'an oriental state in complete decay'.[13] He observed the actions of the Japanese and found them to be active in all the aspects of Korean affairs: 'The Japanese legation has the best information in regard to all matters in the peninsula'.[14] He and Jordan fell out over the question of the efforts to be made for British concession-seekers in Korea in imitation of their diplomatic colleagues. Gubbins was distrustful of British merchants and did not want to take an active part in 'the unholy battle of the concessions'.[15]

His wife returned to Scotland with her children, another daughter being born there in September 1901. Gubbins followed on leave early in 1902 and they returned to Japan in 1903. He became secretary of legation which meant being transferred from the consular service to the diplomatic service. This entitled him to one of the houses in the legation compound (soon to be given the status of an embassy). Gubbins naturally became the elder statesman and the voice of continuity in the embassy community.

Family life was not particularly easy. Gubbins had returned with a young wife and a household of small children leaving two young sons behind at school in Britain. In order to avoid Tokyo's heat, the family spent the summers at their house in Karuizawa in the hills to the north, an under-policed area where they were liable to attacks from *soshi* (unruly elements). On life in Tokyo, his son's biographers report: 'He was incapable of relaxed fatherhood, would not brook disturbance when he worked at home and regarded it as his right to shout for silence or service. His inborn irascibility was aggravated by tri-geminal neuralgia. . . and recurring rheumatic pains which were the result of rheumatic fever in his youth.'[16]

In 1908, after a five-year stay, the Gubbins family returned to Britain for good, John having passed the retirement age of 55. He had served in Japan for a total of 37 years.

SCHOLARSHIP AND THE WAR

Gubbins had the reputation in Japan of being a formidable scholar. He had been a founder-member of the Asiatic Society of Japan in 1872. He had contributed an article entitled 'Jasui Shinhei bemmo, being a treatise directed against Christianity' to its *Transactions* in 1875. He had, as we have seen, compiled a substantial dictionary in 1889 which went into a second edition in the year of his retirement, 1908. He had translated the Civil Code of Japan which was in fact a book but it was published in the *Transactions*.[17]

Gubbins' official retirement began on 10 September 1909. At the instance of Lord Curzon, at that time chancellor of Oxford University who may have been approached by Satow, he was made 'Lecturer in Japanese in the University of Oxford'. Since he had gone straight from school into the Japan consular service, he had never attended a university. He had therefore to be given an honorary Master's degree from Balliol College in order to rectify the position, though he was not listed as a lecturer there.

His book on the *Progress of Japan 1853-71* came out in 1911 from the Clarendon Press in Oxford. He writes in the preface that 'six lectures given in the University of Oxford during 1909-10 are the basis of this book'.[18] They still stand up well in relation to the writings of Satow and G.B.Sansom. At a time when history lecturing was not too rigorous, his approach was rigorous. His study included in appendices copious translations of Japanese material which was fiendishly difficult.

But during the next three years the number of interested students declined and the authorities decided to end the appointment. The University decision came as a blow. Gubbins the scholar was well suited to life in Oxford and seems to have spent much time in the Bodleian library. He wrote from his home at 10 Lathbury Road, Oxford on 22 June 1912 to Basil

Hall Chamberlain, a companion for decades in Tokyo, who had just retired to Switzerland:

> Personally I think Oxford should be represented in Japanese, but it is for them to decide and for me to bow to their decision.

The Oxford decision was clearly a disappointment. For Gubbins as for Chamberlain retirement and detachment from Japan were not easy. Their other friend, Satow, who had been less uni-directional in his interests, found it easier:

> Sir Ernest keeps very well and is very busy with local – I had almost said parochial – matters of all kinds. His many-sided-ness comes out in his wonderful adaptation to English modes of life and interests after so many years of foreign experience and official and scholastic activity. I can only look on and admire.[19]

But Gubbins did not have the wide interests of Satow and faced heavy family responsibilities, having two sons and three daughters.

Gubbins had already launched himself on his new book. He told Satow in his Christmas letter for 1912 that he had finished the reading for the first chapter: 'I want to make it a link between old and new Japan, describing the conditions of things politically in some detail, and giving an idea. . .of the international aspect of affairs at the time of the restoration.' But it was to be a decade before it appeared.[20]

When the war broke out in 1914, he took up war work in spite of increasing ill health. He moved to 82 York Mansions, Battersea Park, which he leased for most of the war years. Writing to Satow in December 1915, he said:

> Fortunately for the peace of mind of the War Office I have been able – except for a month in Hampshire – to continue my censorship of Japanese correspondence. Like most work it comes in rushes and during Xmas week my hands were full. It is not always edifying reading. One hears a good deal of sharp comment on English things which one would prefer to criticize oneself.[21]

It is not clear what was meant by this censorship but it raises questions about Britain's confidence in the Anglo-Japanese alliance.

By February 1916 he was complaining of a great increase of

censorship work during the previous two months. But shortly afterwards his work appears to change. He put in 'an hour or so every two or three days dictating translations and memoranda to shorthand typists'.[22] His office was however still at the Postal Censorship, Kingsway WC, though Gubbins by special dispensation still did much of his work at home. In March 1917 John Buchan, the novelist, was given the task of centralizing the whole of the 'newspaper work' on behalf of the War Office, the Admiralty and Foreign Office jointly. Press work was, however, jeopardized by delays in the Far Eastern mails on account of the Russian revolution and loss of mails by the submarine menace. By June Gubbins was writing that 'my position as press reader and memo writer is in course of being regularized but I must go to the department [in the War Office] 3-4 hours daily'.[23] It is not easy to tell exactly what his press work entailed but he did comment that he was much worried by the sentiments being expressed in articles in chauvinist journals like *Nihon oyobi Nihonjin*.

Throughout the war, family anxieties increased. Both his sons were at the front. His second son, Colin, who had joined up in the artillery from the start at 18, experienced war on the western front. Gubbins' letters to Satow show that he was very proud of him ('He is really a good lad and has found, I hope, his *metier*'). But in the same way that he had remained distant from his children in Japan, he still found it hard to show his true feelings. Colin's biographers relate:

> Often, when Colin had returned on leave from France, all his father had done was to glance up from his censorship of Japanese correspondence for the Foreign Office, ask 'What are you doing here?' and return to his work. It was small wonder that the son found it difficult to communicate with the father.[24]

Colin Gubbins survived the war, wounded and gassed, but with a Military Cross for bravery; he lived to become head of Britain's Special Operations Executive (SOE) and to be knighted.

LITERARY EFFORTS

In 1917 John Gubbins was invited to write one of the government handbooks on Japan in preparation for the forthcoming peace conference. Satow was also involved in the writing of one of these booklets. Dr George Prothero was the responsible editor and it was under his editorial pen from the appropriately named Watergate House that they were prepared. The authors gave their services on a voluntary and unpaid basis. Satow's manuscript went in on time, while Gubbins who was fully engaged in war work could not meet his deadline. But the two seasoned authors had a great deal of fun over the good doctor. When the edited version reached him, Gubbins wrote that he felt 'like a school-boy whose exercise is being corrected'.[25] He was able to report to Satow with relief in December 1918 that the draft had been completed. It was ultimately published in 1920 and was a brief and authoritative volume.[26] Like everything that Gubbins turned his hand to, it was a very careful piece of work. It was a very effective summary history, covering a large period of recent history in a relatively short essay. What is important to remember nowadays is that he was writing at a time when libraries on East Asian topics were very poor; and Gubbins had to borrow many of the standard reference books he needed from Satow.

Gubbins had been since 1892 an Honorary Member of the Japan Society of London and occasionally took the chair at its meetings. He delivered to the Society in 1918 an erudite paper entitled 'The Hundred Articles and the Tokugawa Government', giving the findings which were later to appear in his book.[27]

There is a gap of some years in the Gubbins-Satow correspondence at this point. When it was resumed, the discussion was of books and writing. Satow and Gubbins were both publishing major books through the London publisher, Seeley, Service. Satow's book, *A Diplomat in Japan*, was completed in January 1921 and published later in the year. Gubbins produced in 1922 his major work *The Making of Modern Japan*. The Foreign Office tried to prevent the publication of parts of the volume and it required intervention with Lord Curzon, the foreign secretary, before the Office's censors would give way. Responding to Satow's congratulations, he wrote: 'I'm so glad you think I have been just to the Japanese. I have really tried to write with fairness and impartiality but try as one may one does not often succeed.'[28]

1922, however, brought two disappointments. His wife died in Edinburgh in January. Thereafter Gubbins had to follow a solitary existence. He had always rented his houses and found himself with no roots. Instead, he moved from place to place

(Jersey, Kent, Edinburgh, Mull), residing where he could find accommodation close to his daughters and seeing them through exceptional patches of ill health and guiding them into adulthood.

Gubbins' sons were dispersed. He lost track of his eldest son who had emigrated to Canada. His second son, Colin, was posted to the army in India. John Gubbins saw little of that family except when Colin's wife and son visited Mull on a visit home in 1925 and Colin joined them in 1926. These were years of serious illness and considerable loneliness as he confessed in letters to Satow, though he did have the consolation of knowing that he was welcome to stay with Colin's family when they returned from India in 1930.

In some ways it was reading and writing which gave John Gubbins the greatest solace. Of these writing – and with it correspondence – appeared to give him the greatest satisfaction. Satow and Gubbins had both published much during their working lives and were equally industrious in retirement. There was only nine years between them in age; and they shared the urge to write. Something of Gubbins' thinking comes out in this comment to Satow:

> I wish Chamberlain would not follow in Lord Acton's footsteps and keep to himself the wealth of information he has acquired. What interesting papers and books he might have written. All his learning will now die with him. It is the greater pity because he can write so well.[29]

During the 1920s Gubbins spent most of his time in Edinburgh where he belonged to an obscure Scottish body called the National Citizens Union. His task was to make notes on the Socialist press for that body. These were written (as he confessed to Satow) 'for the information – I won't say edification – of the Committee of the Edinburgh Branch'. In due course he addressed the branch on the subject and the lecture was published in pamphlet form under the title of 'Socialism and the Socialist Press'. His appealing message was that 'the whole Socialist-Communist movement has spent its greatest force and is now receding like the tide when the ebb sets in'.[30] It was his only non-Japanese publication.

John Gubbins died in Buckingham Terrace, Edinburgh on 23 February 1929. Fortunately Colin's wife was around. But his family was dispersed, his three daughters being in Hongkong. Gubbins belongs to that group of Japanese well-wishers who first made contact with Japan at an early age, spent their career there and then for twenty years of retirement continued to study and publish about Japan and the Japanese without re-visiting the country. In three important books – and in a large number of scattered articles in specialized journals – Gubbins had passed on the perceptions of Japan which he had gleaned during many decades of hard labour at the British embassy in Tokyo.

9

Hannah Riddell, 1855-1932

JULIA BOYD

ON 16 JANUARY 1891 the SS *Denbighshire* docked at Kobe after a nine-week voyage from England. Among the disembarking passengers were five women missionaries sent to Japan by the Church Missionary Society. At thirty-five Hannah Riddell was the oldest of the group – and the tallest. Accompanied by her pet dog (she would never have considered going to Japan without one), Hannah was a striking figure. A woman whose energy and confidence were apparently un-dented by the formidable setbacks she had already encountered in life.

It is not surprising that Hannah left the impression in Japan that she came from a wealthy and aristocratic background. During the forty years that she lived in the country she maintained a lavish life-style not normally associated with missionaries and which convinced her friends and acquaintances that she was a woman of considerable private means.

Nothing could be further from the truth. Her father, Daniel, was born into a large family of impoverished Scottish weavers and at a tender age enlisted as a private in the British army. He served in India and China and on his retirement took up the post of sergeant in a militia unit in Barnet. Hannah was born in the barracks there on 17 October 1855. Her mother, another Hannah, already 40 when her daughter was born, had been a widow for nine years and was herself the daughter of a farm labourer.

Judging by her subsequent career, the young Hannah received a sound education despite her modest background. Furthermore, Barnet was for the time something of a social melting-pot. The local vicarage, which Hannah may well have visited with her mother, a devout member of the Church of England, was noted as a place where 'noblemen, farmers, bishops and non-conformist ministers could meet and debate on equal terms'.[1] The vicar, William Pennefather, was closely associated with missionary work and his wife, Catherine, founded The Willows, a training-college for women missionaries in north London.

When Hannah was seventeen, her half-brother died leaving a small son and daughter – Samuel and Ada. Ada was only two years old when the children went to live with their grandparents and Hannah soon adopted the role of surrogate mother. Nothing is known of how Samuel fared as an adult but Ada and Hannah forged a close emotional bond that was to last all their lives.

In 1877 the Riddells moved to Oystermouth, a small seaside village six miles west of Swansea. They may have decided to go there because Daniel's health had been precarious since his long years in India and Hannah could support the family by teaching – one of the few careers open to a respectable young woman at that time.

In the summer of 1877 the following advertisement appeared:

Russell House, Castleton, Mumbles.

PREPARATORY BOARDING and DAY SCHOOL for Young Gentlemen conducted by Mrs. and Miss Riddell. Young Ladies are received as day pupils. The House is beautifully and healthily situated in view of the Sea, and close to the ruins of Oystermouth Castle. Special attention paid to the Home comforts and training of the pupils.

For many years the school prospered but, with the death of her parents and increasing competition (the Misses Potts opened a school a few doors away from Russell House and were able to boast that they were the daughters of a clergyman),[2] Hannah ran into serious financial difficulty which culminated with her being declared bankrupt in 1889. Having extricated herself from the bankruptcy court, Hannah found work in Liverpool where she was employed as deputy superintendent in the YWCA. She stayed in Liverpool less than a year but met there a number of philanthropically-minded people who in later years were to prove themselves among her most loyal and generous supporters.

In 1888 the Church Missionary Society (CMS) decided for the first time in its history to send single women into the 'foreign field'. Japan, with her high rate of literacy and recent absorption of Western institutions and technology, was regarded by the missionary societies as particularly promising territory for their

121

efforts and a country where women missionaries could be especially effective. Initially, the most eager response to the missionary call came from middle-class spinsters, many of whom were prepared to contribute to their own expenses. Hannah had no private income but with her obvious drive and long years of teaching experience she appeared to the CMS authorities an ideal candidate to send to their mission in Japan. To leave a sheltered and predictable life in England for an uncertain, even dangerous, one in an alien country required courage. Courage, however, was a quality with which Hannah was amply supplied. For her the CMS represented an opportunity for adventure, achievement and a new start in life.

★ ★ ★

Hannah spent her first two months in Japan at a girls' school in Kobe (still in existence) run by CMS missionaries. She and her companions studied the language, struggled with chopsticks and strange food and watched with fascinated horror the 'heathen' practices enacted in Buddhist temples and Shinto shrines.

HANNAH IN KYUSHU

In April 1891, Hannah and a fellow missionary, the diminutive Grace Nott, set out for Kumamoto in Kyushu, where they had been formally posted by the CMS – the same year Lafcadio Hearn arrived there with his newly-wed Japanese wife. The foreign community in Kumamoto was tiny because, until regulations were eased in 1884, it was generally forbidden for foreigners to live outside the five treaty ports. Despite this stricture a British missionary, John Brandram, had been living in Kumamoto since 1887 and he and his wife found a small house close to their own in which Hannah and Grace installed themselves.

Not surprisingly, the appearance of two such contrasting and independent English women in the midst of a Japanese community that had encountered few foreigners of any description caused a stir. Hannah and Grace, therefore, had little difficulty in attracting to their house curious students from the Fifth Higher School for English lessons. The school was one of the best in the country and both Lafcadio Hearn (arguably the most eloquent foreign writer in Meiji Japan) and Natsume Soseki (the famous writer whose portrait appears on the current ¥1000 note) taught there in the early 1890s. Before long Hannah was even able to claim some converts among her students.

Busy though the two women were with language study and teaching, they found time soon after their arrival in Kumamoto to visit the nearby Honmyoji temple – an experience that was to shape the rest of Hannah's life. The temple had become a mecca for vagrant lepers and it was the sight of these wretched and hopeless people crowding the magnificent flight of stone steps leading up to the temple that overwhelmed Hannah and led her to believe that she had found her life's work.

Leprosy, with its Biblical connotations, would have been familiar enough to Hannah but it is unlikely that before her first visit to the Honmyoji temple she had actually seen anyone suffering from the disease. In Europe leprosy had mostly died out in the late Middle Ages but in Japan it was still a terrible and widespread affliction.

Leprosy is an infectious disease caused by a bacterium which attacks and eventually destroys its victim's peripheral nerves. It can affect the eyes, respiratory tract, testes, muscles and bones causing untold misery for years, even decades. Only a small proportion of the population at large is susceptible to leprosy but it flourishes in over-crowded and unsanitary conditions. Because the bacterium develops so slowly and has for so long resisted culture in an artificial medium, it has proved particularly difficult to study despite the fact that it was the first bacterium to be identified (by the Norwegian doctor, G. Armauer Hansen in 1874) as causing disease in humans.

Hannah died before effective drugs were developed to cure leprosy and like most of her contemporaries she never grasped its pathology. She was, however, only too well aware of the devastating effect it had on human lives. In Japan, as in most societies, leprosy was associated with sin and its victims, in addition to their physical anguish, were often cast out of their homes or kept hidden away as a shameful secret. At the time Hannah arrived in Japan there was almost no provision for leprosy sufferers who were left to wander from temple to temple and beg an existence as best they could.

Hannah was a devout Christian but she was also a pragmatist. At Honmyoji, where she had encountered an appalling situation, she resolved to do something about it. She and Grace at once started campaigning for funds to build a hospital especially for the care of lepers. Confident that she would receive support from the

CMS for such a noble enterprise, Hannah was dismayed but undaunted by the society's cool response to her project. The reason for its indifference was directly connected to its concern over recent reverses suffered on the evangelical front.

Japanese enthusiasm for Christianity so evident during the 1870s and most of the 1880s was on the wane by the time Hannah reached Japan. Like modern economists, the missionary societies anxiously watched and analyzed numbers but their balance sheets recorded converts and 'backsliders'. During the 1890s the figures were not as encouraging as they would have wished. From the CMS point of view, the underlying objection to the leprosy hospital was that, as far as evangelism was concerned, it was a sterile operation. Even if the patients in the hospital were converted to Christianity they could not move freely around in society and could not, therefore, work effectively to expand the Christian church in Japan.

Hannah refused to see the logic in this line of argument believing that, by helping a group of people in such obvious and desperate need, the missionaries would be preaching the most powerful Christian message of all. It was not just Hannah's passionate campaigning for a leprosy hospital that placed her at loggerheads with her fellow missionaries. They disliked her stylish way of living, her social ambition and, above all, her habit of circumnavigating orthodox channels to achieve her ends.

Despite worsening relations with her immediate colleagues (the Bishop of Kyushu, Henry Evington, wrote a vitriolic letter to CMS headquarters in London complaining of her conduct), Hannah's plans for a hospital went steadily forward. She was enthusiastically supported by a number of Japanese including a military doctor, Haga Eijiro, stationed with the Sixth Division in Kumamoto Castle. Dr Haga had seen Wilhelm Roentgen's invention, the X-ray machine, in action in Germany and had bought one out of his own pocket and sent it back to Tokyo – possibly the first to be imported to Japan. He then rode back to his own country across Siberia on horseback. He was precisely the kind of man with whom Hannah felt she could do business unlike the wretched John Brandram to whom Hannah bitterly referred when she wrote '. . . old missionaries seem to have a chronic fear of new missionaries starting new ideas. . .'[3]

KAISHUN HOSPITAL

However, after much wrangling and many set-backs the hospital was finally opened on 12 November 1895. Hannah named it the 'Kaishun' or 'The Resurrection of Hope Hospital' in an attempt to dissociate it from the despair normally attached to leprosy. It was ideally situated near, but not too near, the town and surrounded by the peace and beauty which Hannah considered essential for the patients' welfare.

The first thing that struck visitors to the Kaishun was that it did not look like a hospital. There was a building for the men and another for the women but both were designed to look much like an ordinary Japanese house with tatami-rooms opening out on to a veranda. A larger block contained the consulting dispensary and waiting-room, kitchen and offices. There was also a house for the superintendent doctor, a bath-house and a store-room. Between the buildings there was plenty of space for flowers and plants, while rising behind the hospital were woods of cedar and pine.

The opening of the Kaishun hospital was a remarkable feat. In stark contrast to so many of her missionary colleagues, Hannah had a solid achievement to her credit, one that made a real contribution to a real need and had been accomplished despite formidable difficulties. Professionally Hannah was busy and fulfilled but there remained a big gap in her life – Ada. Ada was the centre of Hannah's emotional life. More like a daughter than a niece, she also filled the roles of companion and secretary to her aunt and it is not surprising that Hannah missed her deeply.

While her aunt was in Japan establishing herself as an authority on the care of lepers, Ada had been struggling to graduate from The Willows, the training college for women missionaries in north London. The CMS authorities considered her to be academically weak but eventually she satisfied their requirements and sailed to Japan, arriving in Kumamoto in 1896 for a joyful reunion with her aunt, just in time for Christmas.

As well as running the hospital, Hannah was busy teaching, translating, studying and proselytising. But despite this laudable industry, the tension between her and the other British missionaries in Kyushu, particularly her immediate boss, John Brandram, grew steadily worse. Brandram was a kind and deeply spiritual man who had lived through difficult times and was already showing symptoms of the illness that eventually killed him. But Hannah regarded him as ineffectual, lacking both foresight and imagination. Furthermore, he had not given the hospital the wholehearted support that she felt it deserved. It was thus an unfortunate twist of fate that brought together these two very different personalities in such close circumstances.

In 1899, Hannah returned to England for her long overdue furlough. But back in London, she soon came under fire from the CMS committee responsible for the Japan mission. After long deliberations over a period of many months, they regretfully concluded that, as Hannah seemed to be the cause of the divisions tearing apart the small CMS community in Kyushu, she must not be allowed to return there. But the CMS had not reckoned with Hannah's determination or her commitment to the hospital. She promptly spiked their guns by resigning and declaring her intention to go back to Kumamoto and run the Kaishun hospital independently.

KAISHUN AS AN INDEPENDENT HOSPITAL

While Hannah was already on her way back to Japan, a tragic event occurred that resolved once and for all her difficulties with Brandram. In 1900, shortly before Christmas, he suffered a complete breakdown. He became so violent that two of his fellow missionaries had to take him to Nagasaki in a strait-jacket where he was locked up overnight in the Bishop's chapel, all the furniture having been first removed. A few days later, on 29 December 1900, Brandram died on board the ship that was carrying him to an asylum in Hong Kong and was buried in Shanghai. There is little doubt that, however unfairly, the Kyushu missionaries blamed Hannah for this disaster.

Hannah reached Kumamoto early in 1901 and on her return entered a new phase of her life. Her old antagonist, John Brandram was dead; Ada, having failed the CMS Japanese exams, had gone far away to Maebashi to work for an American missionary society and her staunch ally, Grace Nott, unable to stand the strains and stresses of recent events, had returned to England. But she could count among her blessings the loyalty of her Japanese friends, a growing network of supporters in England and above all, the hospital and her beloved patients.

Hannah never allowed lack of money to inhibit her standard of living. She moved into a large house overlooking the river in a fine neighbourhood and set about organizing a formal society of supporters for the hospital with president, patrons, vice-presidents and council. Soon, she was even able to expand the hospital thanks to the generosity of the Hosokawa family who leased her the necessary land.

Despite such support and goodwill life was not easy for Hannah. Money – or lack of it – was a constant problem. A woman of less courage and conviction might well have packed her bags and made for home. She was, however, so determined to keep the hospital running that she was even prepared to swallow her pride and write to the CMS, humbly asking them to take over responsibility for the hospital and to re-employ her on whatever terms they chose.

The society's reaction was predictable. They did not want to take over the hospital and they did not want Hannah back:

> . . . her return to us as a Missionary. . . seems fraught with difficulties. It would be practically impossible to accept her and remove her from Kiushiu, as the hospital is so linked with her personally: it would be. . . entirely impossible to reinstate her in Kiu Shiu as our Missionary in view of the feeling of the brethren there.[5]

The outcome of Hannah's latest bout with the CMS proved final and unequivocal. If she wanted the hospital to continue, she would have to rely solely on her own resources and abilities.

Although Hannah's relations with her immediate colleagues were often disastrous, she undoubtedly possessed a flair for public relations and soon put together an impressive network of support for the Kaishun hospital. The first detailed accounts to have survived date from 1903-4 and show that forty per cent of the running costs were provided by English subscribers, the great majority of them women. The rest was raised in Japan both by Japanese and expatriates.

Lady MacDonald, wife of the British ambassador, was listed as a patroness and Count Okuma Shigenobu and Dr Erwin Baelz as patrons. The latter was a distinguished German doctor working in Tokyo who attended many leading figures of the time including the Emperor himself. Baelz's name together with that of Dr Iwai of the Red Cross Hospital added considerable weight to the scientific credentials of the hospital. Although not a patron, Hannah's most effective supporter was another great Meiji figure – Viscount Shibusawa Eiichi, banker and philanthropist.

It was Shibusawa and Okuma (who had already served in the government as finance minister, foreign minister and for a few months prime minister) who rescued Hannah and her hospital from financial disaster. On 6 November 1905, they organized a meeting at the Bankers' Club in Tokyo with the aim of debating the leprosy issue in Japan. Hannah was invited to address a powerful gathering of some twenty-five men from government, business, and journalism on the subject of 'What Should We Do For The Lepers in Japan?'

The sight of this statuesque Englishwoman speaking with such passion and sincerity on a subject that had traditionally been ignored by their fellow countrymen clearly stirred those present and, after this important meeting, events flowed with some speed. A committee was quickly formed to deal with the issues that had arisen and, following its first deliberations, Okuma was able to report to Hannah on 9 December that it had agreed on a number of important measures: the government would submit a leprosy-prevention bill to the Diet; efforts would be made to educate the public about leprosy; government funds would be available for research into the disease; and people of influence would be mobilized to give financial assistance to the Kaishun hospital.

In 1907 these ideas found formal expression in a bill passed through the Diet. For the first time this new law made provision for the construction out of public funds of five leprosaria in different parts of Japan, including the one built in 1909 in Kumamoto, the Keifu-en, which still exists.

The Bankers' Club conference was not only an important landmark in Japan's fight against leprosy but also a vital turning-point in Hannah's own life. Until that occasion she had been a worthy missionary struggling to keep afloat a provincial project. Now, suddenly, she found herself in a leading role centre stage, playing to an influential audience eager to hear her words and act on her advice. On 16 January 1906, exactly fifteen years after she first arrived in Japan, Hannah received the ultimate seal of approval, the Medal of the Blue Ribbon.

HANNAH ON LEPROSY

After a decade of working with lepers, it is not surprising that Hannah had formed strong views concerning their treatment, not all of them correct. Although as early as 1874 Hansen had proved that leprosy was an infection caused by a bacterium, Hannah continued to insist that the disease was hereditary and remained convinced all her life that sex-segregation was the only way to eradicate it:

Despite the many attempts in many countries to cure

leprosy, by medicine and by prayer, no absolutely authenticated cure has taken place since the days of Our Lord.

But why not? His Power is still the same. Sometimes I wonder if it is withheld to compel the nations to take the one plain way open to rid the world of this awful terror: it has been proved that there is one way namely, sex-segregation. There should be *no leper children*. . . An experience of several generations leads us to definitely decide that the disease is both hereditary and contagious but not infectious.[6]

This last sentence expresses muddled thinking. There is no difference between infection and contagion, and a disease that is hereditary cannot at the same time be infectious. But Hannah had a theory, one that she was not prepared to give up easily, even in the face of scientific evidence.

Having decided that a policy of strict sex-segregation was the only answer to the problem, Hannah developed clear views on how it should be implemented in a letter to Okuma who was by then prime minister for the second time:

What I should like to suggest is that . . . two portions of land should be appropriated in each Ken [prefecture] as far apart as possible, and that all the leper men of that Ken should be very comfortably housed and cared for in one place, and the women in the other. . . Another great difficulty is the children of leper patients: and for them special regulations would be necessary. They should of course be allowed every possible chance in life. . . but I think they should not be allowed to marry for two generations, and although that seems a very stringent thing, I believe their patriotism could be appealed to, and boys and girls would grow up with the idea that marriage was not for them, though every other joy and comfort in life might be theirs.

It was true that children born to lepers ran a high risk of catching the disease, and there was the problem of caring for the children when their parents could not or had died. Nevertheless, to deny the comfort of marriage to people who were already deprived of so much in life was an unnecessarily harsh measure in view of the existence of birth control.

Although Hannah enjoyed the company of men, especially when she was teaching them, it is difficult not to gain the impression that the whole subject of procreation was abhorrent

One patient described the Kaishun hospital as having an almost monastic atmosphere.[7] It was observed that Hannah even disliked seeing patients feed a pair of birds in the same cage. Marriage was not allowed under any circumstances and such was the force of Hannah's personality that, despite the fact that the men's and women's wards were separated by only a low hedge, scarcely anyone ever dared to cross the barrier.[8] There were, however, plenty of other places for them to meet and love affairs among the patients were not a rarity.[9]

Despite the 'monastic' atmosphere of the Kaishun hospital, the great majority of patients considered themselves exceptionally lucky to be there. The consensus was that for people who were only lightly afflicted by the disease any sanatorium would suffice but for the seriously ill the Kaishun was unquestionably their first choice.

Hannah's insistence on sex-segregation may have been unnecessarily dogmatic but she was on very firm ground when advocating the vital need for a leprosarium to have a good water supply and drainage system, clean, comfortable quarters for the patients, and a pleasant hygienic environment for them to live in. Leprosy was neither hereditary nor was it sexually transmitted but it did flourish in conditions of poverty, squalor, and deprivation.

As a convinced Christian, Hannah naturally felt that prayer and faith were essential elements in the search for a cure but she did recognize that science had a role. Regrettably, high morals and fresh air were not enough, however sincerely they were served up. During the lean years of the First World War, raising money from England and America was particularly difficult but, with Japanese support, Hannah was eventually able to find enough money to open a laboratory in the hospital grounds.

Over the years, a number of distinguished doctors worked in the Kaishun laboratory and, if none of them achieved a major breakthrough, neither at least did they make any false claims of success. Until effective sulfhone drugs were finally developed in the 1940s the victims of leprosy were constantly having their hopes raised with promises of wonder cures only to have them dashed when the medicines produced no improvement in their condition or, more often, actually made it worse.

Hannah encouraged her patients to think of her as 'Mother'; and when she wrote to a leper, she invariably addressed him or her as 'My dear Child'. Several years after Hannah's death, a number

Hannah encouraged her patients to think of her as 'Mother'; and when she wrote to a leper, she invariably addressed him or her as 'My dear Child'. Several years after Hannah's death, a number of patients recorded their personal memories of her.[10] The fact that she not only cared for them as a collective but was deeply concerned with each individual's welfare emerges very clearly from these reminiscences. But their recollections also invoke the unmistakable image of a traditional English Nanny: 'We were often scolded by Mother... Once she came into the patients' room and said smiling, "Wouldn't you like to see outside?" We didn't understand what she meant... Then she said "wipe the dirty glass door".' One patient recalled being told off for doing her washing when she should have been in prayers and another for letting a piece of pickled radish languish in the kitchen sink.

Hannah was often bossy and overbearing, and her insistence on such high standards of orderliness and dress in the hospital sometimes caused the patients to grumble. Most, however, understood that, by living in such civilized surroundings and by being well turned out, they were able to acquire a new pride and dignity which many of them had lost as a result of their dreadful disease. And, although the Kaishun hospital may at times have more closely resembled a British boarding-school than a Japanese hospital, its patients nevertheless had plenty of agreeable memories of their life there – of games and music, the gardens they themselves cultivated, and the occasions when Hannah would cheer up a sick patient with a special treat such as ice-cream or some other delicacy.

EXTENDING LEPROSY WORK

From as early as 1901 Hannah had nurtured ambitions to extend her leprosy relief work to other parts of Japan. In that year she had visited Kusatsu, a mountain village some 1000 miles from Kumamoto where hundreds of lepers gathered to bathe in the tortuously hot springs thought to be highly efficacious for 'rheumatism, gout, syphilis, leprosy and other loathsome diseases'.[11] It was another 12 years before Hannah had enough money to send a Japanese priest to Kusatsu to pursue missionary work among the lepers. He was apparently so successful that Hannah was able to report with obvious delight that not only had nine of the ten sake shops closed but that the obscene songs habitually sung by the lepers in the hot springs had been replaced with hymns.

It is not Hannah, however, who is chiefly remembered for good works among the Kusatsu lepers but another English-woman and one of a very different temperament and character. Mary Cornwall-Legh was everything that Hannah was not. Hannah had been forced to struggle hard for all that she had achieved in her life but Mary was born into an aristocratic family, had a degree from St Andrew's University, and a substantial private income. She began her missionary work in Kusatsu in 1914 at the late age of fifty-one and over the years built up a leper community that was very different from the Kaishun hospital.

Mary believed that the lepers should live as normal a life as possible. Largely using her own resources, she gradually built several schools, a hospital, and a small library. There were separate homes for men and women and, significantly, houses for couples and families as well. Mary's strategy of encouraging the lepers to marry and work was in direct contradiction to Hannah's strict segregationist policy as well as her view that lepers should live in a calm, protected environment. Hannah had been working with lepers for twenty years when Mary arrived in Kusatsu and she did not welcome any challenges to her authority on the subject. Under the circumstances it was as well that Kusatsu and Kumamoto were a thousand miles apart.

Okinawa was another part of Japan where over many years Hannah tried to establish missionary work among the lepers who lived there under particularly harsh circumstances in crude beach huts, surviving as best they could on seaweed and sweet potatoes.

In 1927 she found just the man. Aoki Kesai, a leper and a devout Christian, had spent a number of years in a state leprosarium before being admitted to the Kaishun hospital. Initially, he had been very happy there but his contentment had been shattered when he fell in love. Well aware of Hannah's rigorous views on love affairs between the patients, he never declared his feelings to the girl although he continued to love her all his life. 'Miss Riddell cared for us as one would a tropical flower in a greenhouse. . . but the hospital had become not only a greenhouse to me but a place of torture. I was so near the one I longed for so much but could not approach.'[12] The last straw for Aoki was the appearance at the hospital of a rival. When Hannah asked him to go to Okinawa to undertake missionary work with the lepers, he thankfully accepted. Aoki carried with him Hannah's parting words: 'Don't visit the women patients and don't get married. . . working as a missionary is your life. If you continue on in faith, keeping yourself pure and remaining single all your life the glory of God will be upon you more and more.'[13]

Aoki worked with great diligence and courage among the lepers of Okinawa in appalling conditions. For five years he regularly received money and letters of encouragement from Hannah until 3 February 1932 when he received a telegram: 'Mother passed into heaven at 1.10pm.'[14]

HANNAH'S DECLINING YEARS

Although the financial problems of the hospital were always present, the last ten years of Hannah's life were lit by the comfortable glow of success and recognition. She had become something of a celebrity who commanded respect and admiration not only in Japan but also in England and America. In 1922 she had been awarded the Sixth Class Order of the Sacred Treasure which underscored just how much her efforts had come to be appreciated by the Japanese.

Despite the diabetes which dogged her old age, Hannah showed great courage by undertaking a long and arduous fund-raising journey to Europe and America in 1927. In an interview she gave to the *Japan Advertiser* just before her departure, it is clear that she realized that this visit to England would be her last:

> I am not as young as I was; time passes fast; whether I shall have another opportunity to visit England I do not know. I have much business to attend to and there are many people I intend to call upon. But then I shall come back here and resume my work.

On 13 November 1931 she was received by the Emperor Showa at the Kumamoto prefectural office. It was fitting that this great event should have been her last major public engagement.

Her funeral, which took place at the church she had designed herself and built in the grounds of the Kaishun hospital, was also a great event. The church was overflowing with flowers and wreaths and some two hundred telegrams and letters of condolence were read out. The coffin was borne to the crematorium and was followed by a long procession of mourners, many of them lepers who were not usually permitted to go beyond the gates. One of whom recorded:

> Despite the mist on the banks of the River Shirakawa, the

setting sun shone on the water. In the west, Mount Kimpo was clearly visible and far away to the east Mount Aso stood as if in silent prayer. At the crematorium the service ended with prayers in English and we looked for the last time on all that was mortal of Miss Hannah Riddell. Loneliness, solitude and silence covered the Hospital that night.[15]

KAISHUN'S SURVIVAL

Hannah's death did not, however, bring about the end of the Kaishun hospital. In 1923 her niece, Ada Wright, had given up her missionary work for the Americans and gone to live and work with her aunt. It was on her shoulders that responsibility for the Kaishun hospital now fell. Ada hero-worshipped her aunt and was much too modest to think she could ever attempt to take her place. (She jokingly referred to herself as the lepers' 'step-mother'.) But she was nevertheless determined not to squander Hannah's legacy and to continue the hospital along the lines that had been so clearly set out.

But times were changing dramatically and for foreigners life in Japan during the 1930s became more and more difficult. As Japan's relations with the West grew steadily worse, donations for the hospital dwindled to a trickle of their former flow and basic supplies of food and medicine became harder to acquire.

Ada was increasingly watched and harried by the police who, anxious to expose her 'espionage' activities, searched her rooms in the hospital. They soon discovered her wireless and at once accused her of using it to receive secret messages. The screw was tightened yet further when the account books were seized and Ada was unable to draw money out of the bank. Finally, the board of trustees met on 13 January 1941 and came to the only possible decision they could – the hospital must close.

On 3 February 1941 – by coincidence the ninth anniversary of Hannah's death – the patients were put into trucks to be transported to the nearby state leprosarium, the Keifu-en. At the very moment the convoy moved off, Ada stumbled forward and, hanging on to the back of one of the trucks, was dragged forward, crying, 'I am so sorry, I am so sorry'. When the vehicle stopped briefly at the gate, her fingers had to be prised off it one by one. As the lepers waved goodbye to the diminutive figure standing forlornly at the entrance they began to sing a hymn, 'God is the Refuge of his Saints'.

Ada spent the war years in Australia sharing a house with

another lady missionary, who had worked for forty years in Japan. When her companion died, Ada was determined to return to Kumamoto despite the refusal of the Australian authorities for a long time to grant her the necessary papers. Finally, on 11 June 1948 Ada arrived back in Kumamoto to be re-united with her Japanese friends.

The Kaishun hospital had been destroyed in the war but Ada was able to live in the grounds in what had once been the doctor's house. The diary that she kept in her last months suggests that she found contentment, one of her chief pleasures being her daily contact with the forty or so healthy children of lepers with whom she often played and to whom she always gave the sweets she received from abroad. She regularly took the bus to the Keifu-en where she spent happy hours with her friends, the former Kaishun hospital patients.

On 21 February 1950 NHK, the national public broadcasting organization, allowed her to send a farewell message to the lepers of Japan:

> I stayed in Australia during the War but my heart was always with you in Japan. I should like to see you, but I am sorry I am too weak to leave my bed. I hope and pray that you will continue to have faith in our Lord's cross and resurrection. Please be good children of God. I am looking forward to seeing you again in heaven.

A few days later, on 26 February 1950, shortly after her eightieth birthday Ada died. According to her wishes, her ashes were placed in the Kaishun hospital mausoleum, close to those of many of the lepers and next to those of her aunt. The two boxes containing their ashes are identical except that Hannah's is twice as big as Ada's.

★   ★   ★

Hannah was a big person – big in every sense of the word – and would have made her presence felt wherever she had chosen to live. God or fate or chance took her to Japan and the fact that she is remembered there with such admiration and affection, when most of her English missionary contemporaries have been long forgotten, speaks for itself.

Hannah was no scientist. She did not find a cure for leprosy nor would her theories on segregation receive any support today. What she did do, despite all the obstacles she faced, both logistic and man-made, was to focus attention on a terrible human tragedy. With the force of her personality she made people sit up and take notice. And by her personal example and sheer determination she compelled them to think more compassionately and constructively about the victims of leprosy. What is more, she achieved all this despite being both a foreigner and a woman.

If today, a hundred years after the Kaishun hospital first opened its doors, there is much in Kumamoto that Hannah would not recognize, there is at least one place that she knew well which is little changed – the Honmyoji temple where she first encountered lepers. These days, however, its splendid flight of steps flanked by hundreds of ancient stone lanterns is no longer defaced by the human misery which affected Hannah so deeply. The very peace and tranquility which now surrounds the temple is in itself a monument to her achievement.

Lafcadio Hearn, 1850-1904

PAUL MURRAY

AT HIS BEST, Lafcadio Hearn was the outstanding Western interpreter of Meiji Japan. Interpretation should not be confused with scholarship: without fluency in Japanese, he could not contribute to scholarly study of that language in the manner of his distinguished Anglophone contemporaries, Ernest Satow, William George Aston and Basil Hall Chamberlain. However, in the wider field of interpreting the culture and polity of Meiji Japan to a Western audience, Hearn was – and, in many respects, remains – superb.

The essential challenge facing Hearn and his contemporaries was to understand, firstly, the fundamental nature of Japanese society; secondly, the dynamic of Meiji transformation; and thirdly, the likely future shape of Japan. Hearn addressed all three of these elements. On the first, he believed that, underneath a layer of Westernization, Japanese society remained essentially unchanged and would continue to do so. On the second, he saw that Japan was modernizing, using Western technology and know-how, but he believed she would take from the West only what was needed for practical purposes. On the third element, the future, he prophesied that Japan would become a world power, not through cheap labour in the economic field or the use of military power, but by the application of unique elements of her cultural excellence to economic ends.[1] His fellow Meiji Anglophone Japanologists, by contrast, believed that Japan would become fully Westernized, adopting the Western value system.

As Hearn was almost forty when he arrived in Yokohama in 1890, he viewed Japan through the prism of experiences and values developed in his life up to that point. Some understanding of his background is therefore essential if we are to place his vision of Japan in context.

There can be little doubt that the multi-cultural flavour of his early life conditioned his exceptional openness to the values of other societies. Up to the time he left for America, Hearn's life had seemed like something from a gaudy popular novel. Materially, it was rags to riches and back to rags again. Psychologically, it was a variegated experience of cross-cultural marginalization and rejection: he was the child of an unwelcome foreign father among the Greeks; the embarrassing Greek offspring among the Hearns, a Roman Catholic affront to their Protestant respectability; a liberal nonconformist affront to the fervent Catholicism of the priests at Ushaw; and, finally, a cast-down public schoolboy among the poor of London. In addition, there was an eye injury which wrecked both his appearance and his self-esteem.

He was, in fact, christened Patrick Lafcadio Hearn in Greece where he was born to an Irish father and a Greek mother in 1850. He was known as Patrick or 'Patricio' until he began to refer to himself as Lafcadio in his mid-twenties. When he came to Ireland initially at the age of two, he accompanied his beautiful, illiterate, Greek Orthodox mother. However, her relationship with her husband rapidly deteriorated and they separated. She returned to Greece where she remarried and had another family before succumbing to the mental illness which had troubled her stay in Ireland. Young Patrick Lafcadio did not fare any better with his father, whom he remembered as a steely, emotionally withdrawn character, who also remarried and went abroad to pursue his army career.

Effectively abandoned by both parents at an early age, Patrick Lafcadio was entrusted to the care of a widowed great-aunt, Mrs Brenane, who did not share the Hearns' rigid Protestantism, having converted to Roman Catholicism to marry a wealthy Roman Catholic. Mrs Brenane was relaxed about religion and put little or no pressure on her young charge in this area. He was allowed very considerable latitude in his reading and had access to a wide variety of books, including many of the great authors in the English language. In the stiffly comfortable middle-class milieu in which he was brought up, his social contact was mainly with his Protestant relations (Mrs Brenane remained on friendly terms with her family, notwithstanding the fact that they had trained their parrot to mock her adopted religion!) An important family source believes that he would have imbibed a generally derisory attitude towards Roman Catholicism in this environment.[2]

The young Hearn was caught between the inflexibility of these two traditions, having left behind a third religion – Greek Orthodox – in which he had been baptised. In his teens, however, he was dispatched to a strictly Roman Catholic boarding school, Ushaw, in the north of England. After possibly going through an early phase of piety, he rejected Roman Catholicism and identified instead with the beauty and values of classical Greece, which he saw as an inheritance from his mother's side. All his life Hearn would be engaged with religion, always as an outsider, and he made it central to his interpretation of Japan, especially in his late book, *Japan: an Attempt at Interpretation*.

His career at Ushaw College came to an abrupt end at the age of seventeen when Mrs Brenane was declared bankrupt and he was sent to London to stay with a former maid of hers in conditions of considerable poverty. At nineteen, he was given his fare to America where he became a journalist and started the career in writing which would dominate the rest of his life.

AMERICA

Given all that had gone before, it is hardly surprising that young Paddy Hearn rejoiced in the marginalized and the dispossessed who were swept his way by his job as a newspaper reporter on the police beat in Cincinnati in the 1870s. Having made his name reporting the most lurid of crimes, he served up an unswerving diet of horror to his readers. He held himself aloof from mainstream, middle-class America, in which he was increasingly welcome as his literary stock soared, and plunged instead into the black culture of the levee. Here he pioneered the appreciation of Afro-American music which would later enter the classical world through Dvorak and the popular rock'n'roll. His defiance of the law to marry a Negro woman was a sad, doomed, attempt to live his ideals but it did provide an early example of his determination to *become* part of the cultures he investigated, to see them from the inside out, eschewing the stance of superiority characteristic of so many of his Victorian contemporaries.

However much he might promote himself as a wild barbarian (exploiting a distinct lack of irony on the part of many of his

American friends), there was another side to Hearn. He had been reared in an upper-middle class world of music and literature in Ireland, demonstrating precocious omnivorousness in his reading from an early age. French culture exercised a powerful magnetism for the Irish intelligentsia of that era – his uncle Richard led the movement of Victorian painters from London to Paris as their centre of influence – and France was the centre of his intellectual focus in America. His claim to have been at least partly educated in France has never been substantiated but it is evidence of his identification with French culture. In Cincinnati and, later, in New Orleans, he immersed himself in the study and translation of his French literary idols, always drawn to their horrific elements.[3]

His move from Cincinnati to New Orleans in his late twenties was important to Hearn in terms of both his life and art. On a personal level, he left behind his failed marriage and completed the move from youthful radicalism to an ever-deepening conservatism. He was no longer working the police beat but found a comfortable niche as an editorialist, translator and *litterateur* on the *Times-Democrat* newspaper of New Orleans.

Intellectually, he became a disciple of the philosopher, Herbert Spencer, whose all-embracing evolutionary system provided a cornerstone of conviction for many Victorian intellectuals. Because of Spencer's relative current obscurity, the totality of Lafcadio's adherence can now appear naive in the extreme but it should be remembered that Spencer influenced many of the greatest writers of the age, including his Irish contemporaries, Oscar Wilde and George Bernard Shaw, as well as others such as Robert Louis Stevenson.

Spencer merged with another great influence of Hearn's New Orleans period, Buddhism, to produce a fusion which would ultimately bring him to Japan and provide the philosophical underpinning for much of his work there. Lafcadio always denied that he was a Buddhist but he was closer to that religion than any other and he set himself the task, in the field of philosophy, of reconciling Buddhism with contemporary scientific thought, represented for him by the work of Herbert Spencer.

The increasing influence of the East on Hearn in his New Orleans period was evident in his literary output. There was a strong Oriental flavour in his books, *Stray Leaves from Strange*

Literature (1884) and *Some Chinese Ghosts* (1887). Attracted particularly to the Eastern aspects of French nineteenth-century literature, Hearn delighted in translating the 'Oriental' fantasies of writers such as Flaubert and followed with fascination the real-life wanderings of Pierre Loti who was, together with Gautier, a key literary influence. Lafcadio translated some of Loti's South-East Asian work but his hugely influential *Madame Chrysanthemum*, based on his mid-1880s experiences in Japan, was not published until after Hearn had arrived there himself.

Lafcadio's first attempt at extended fiction, the novella *Chita* (1889), reflected an aspiration to seek 'the Orient' in America. His second, *Youma* (1890), was a product of the two years he spent in the West Indies in his late thirties and chronicled his increasing sympathy with the paternalist, slave-owning *ancien regime* of the southern USA and the former French colonies in the West Indies. His other book from that period, *Two Years in the French West Indies* (1890), a collection of essays which encompassed observation, analysis, history, autobiography and plain storytelling, formed the prototype of his Japanese books.

JAPAN

When Hearn arrived in Japan in 1890, he was just weeks short of his fortieth birthday. Notwithstanding a largely self-generated myth of failure, he had in fact enjoyed considerable success – both *Chita* and *Two Years in the French West Indies* had been well received. He could probably have become quite wealthy churning out further works of popular fiction; but Hearn was a fiercely committed artist who recognized his imaginative inadequacy and was not content to stand still.

After spending a few early months in Yokohama, Lafcadio moved to Matsue as an English teacher, part of the great influx of Westerners who were aiding the modernization of Meiji Japan; he would remain engaged with this process throughout virtually his whole period in Japan, despite his loathing of it.

In my book on Hearn[4] I disputed the accepted view that Hearn's experience in Japan was essentially a curve, veering from an initial, uncritical, infatuation represented by his early books, to the disillusioned realism of his late work, *Japan: an Attempt at Interpretation*. I maintain that his views were formed early on and did not change in their essence up to his death in Tokyo in 1904. Also, I do not accept that the *Attempt* is necessarily an improvement on the early work; indeed, in some respects it is a regression, an uneven attempt at an academic work for which he was ill-suited.[5]

Hearn's first Japanese book, *Glimpses of Unfamiliar Japan* (1894) was essentially a reflection of his initial period in Yokohama and Matsue; his second, *Out of the East* (1895), a work of his time in Kumamoto; his third and fourth books, *Kokoro* (1896) and *Gleanings in Buddha Fields* (1897), represented his stay in Kobe; and his final eight books were a product of his last years in Tokyo.

I have argued elsewhere[6] that the first four books contain five essays which form collectively the core of Lafcadio's early interpretation of Japan. These are: 'The Japanese Smile' (*Glimpses*); 'Jiujutsu' and 'Of the Eternal Feminine' (*Out of the East*); 'The Genius of Japanese Civilization' (*Kokoro*); and, 'About Faces in Japanese Art' (*Gleanings*). These essays have generally been ignored by the anthologists who have tended to recycle Lafcadio's work along much the same predictable lines, thus helping to perpetuate the erroneous notion that he was a colour writer, not given to serious analysis.[7]

It would be idle to deny that aspects of Hearn's approach to Japan have dated – it could hardly be otherwise – but the critical question is whether the essence of his interpretation remains valid, both in absolute terms and in relation to his contemporaries. The fact that Hearn was a serious writer, whose interpretation was the outgrowth of a deeply intellectual process, has been masked by the ease and naturalness with which he wrote. His philosophical and literary foundations were, iceberg-like, mostly hidden below the surface, leaving on top a seemingly artless, intuitive interpretation, apparently unworthy of serious scholarship.

In reality, a subterranean nexus of literary, political and philosophical influences both impelled Hearn towards Japan in the first instance and underlay the vision he developed there. One of the ironies inherent in Loti's influence on Hearn was that it was not the Frenchman's Japanese books which influenced his vision of Japan but rather his earlier work, *Aziyadé* in particular, where the sympathetic portrayal of a technologically retarded but beautiful Turkish culture contrasts with the predatory intent and military muscle of the encircling Western powers.

HEARN AND HIS CONTEMPORARIES

Hearn's vision of Japan was similar and it was one that he shared, interestingly enough, with his English contemporary, Basil Hall Chamberlain. The latter was, if anything, fiercer in his denunciation of Western imperialism than Hearn.[8] Where they differed – and this became critical in their personal as well as their intellectual relationship – was in their advocacy of how Japan might best safeguard its independence and in their evaluation of the worth of indigenous Japanese culture.

Stated simply, Chamberlain, his contribution to the Western study of the Japanese language notwithstanding, made no bones about dismissing whole swathes of pre-Meiji Japanese civilization out of hand. Japan, he believed, became more civilized the more it became Westernized. To say this is not to caricature Chamberlain: he can be seen as an honourable man, deeply critical of Western 'Christian' imperialism, who believed that Japan's continuing independence depended on her becoming as close to the Western norm as possible.[9] He believed sincerely that Western ways were best and, the sooner Japan abandoned the peculiarities she had inherited from the past, the better it would be for her.[10] Yet he himself was out of tune with the current of his own country's policy, then flowing in Japan's favour. He lauded to the skies what he saw as the strong-arm behaviour of Sir Harry Parkes, a former and, at the time, highly influential British minister to Japan although Ernest Satow, a fellow British diplomat, considered Parkes a bully whose behaviour was inimical to his country's interests.[11] Later, when Satow was about to take up his appointment as minister in Tokyo in 1895, he was being advised by the outgoing Foreign Secretary, Lord Kimberley, that it was no longer possible to bully the Japanese who must now be treated on the basis of equality;[12] Chamberlain, by contrast, was not only contemptuous, in his private correspondence with Hearn, of the notion of his country dealing with Japan as an equal but also publicly vented his fury with the Foreign Office for what he saw as weak-kneed capitulation to the Japanese on the issue of treaty revision.[13]

One of Chamberlain's major concerns was protecting the ability of the Western Treaty Port inhabitants to continue to live outside the ambit of Japanese law. He wanted them to be able to publish their newspapers unfettered by restriction while Lord Kimberley was decrying the harm these newspapers were doing to Anglo-Japanese relations.

Hearn was, of course, an ardent supporter of Japan's right to renegotiate the unequal treaties, which prepared the way for the

Anglo-Japanese alliance – Chamberlain quarrelled bitterly with him on this score – and of her efforts in the wars with China and Russia (although he was critical of the jingoistic excesses to which military fervour could lead and publicly reprimanded the Japanese Minister in London on this score).[14]

Hearn, sceptical of so much of nineteenth-century Occidental development, believed that the Westernization of Japan was regressive socially and morally. From the moment of his arrival in Japan, he developed an extraordinary psychological and emotional empathy with the ordinary Japanese. Basing himself partly on the theories of the French historian, Fustel de Coulanges, he decided that pre-Meiji Japanese culture was at the same stage of societal and religious evolution as ancient Greece. This socio-religious view underlay his interpretive work on Japan.

If his interest in Buddhism had helped direct his path towards Japan, Hearn's mind was gripped by Shintō, the indigenous animistic religion, after he had settled there. His interest in Shintō was shared by his contemporaneous Anglophone contemporaries, Satow,[15] Aston and Chamberlain, and it provides a means of comparison between them. All four had firm, although widely different, religious convictions. Hearn, a determined if ambiguous apostate from Roman Catholicism, remained convinced that religion formed the bedrock of Japanese society and that conversion to Christianity would have catastrophic social and political consequences. Chamberlain was a militant rationalist who saw mischief in all religion and was specifically hostile to the Shintō of Meiji Japan. Satow and Aston wrote from the standpoint of devout Christians who believed that Christianization would be the icing on the cake of Japanese modernization.[16]

Late twentieth-century scholarship tends to be critical of an historical Western tendency to see non-Western religions and cultures through its own value system and to divide religion into a separate or separable domain of human activity. The intertwining of religion, society and politics in the evolution of Japanese polity is apparent in Sansom's monumental synthesis of Japanese history, first published in 1958.[17] Hearn was clearly more in tune with this perspective than were his contemporaries; certainly, his vision that Japanese policy would continue to resist the advance of Christianity has turned out to be accurate and few would seek to advance Christianity nowadays by arguing that it represented a natural societal evolution for the Japanese.

In the wider context, Satow's vision of Japan has been criticized in our own era: according to P.F. Kornicki, he failed to grasp both the meaning of Japan's rise to prominence and to appreciate the changing nature of international society in the twentieth century.[19] This could not be said of Hearn who was arguably the first Westerner to realize the extent of the transformation being wrought around him in Meiji Japan and its implications for the future.[20]

Hearn was familiar with the writings of both Satow and Aston, Satow's diplomatic contemporary and fellow trail-blazing scholar of the Japanese language and customs. Aston wrote far more voluminously on Shintō than any of the others but his two books on the subject – published in 1905 and 1907 respectively – came after Hearn's death.[21] Despite the fact that Aston's first book is the longer of the two, it contains only two passing references, both highly positive, to Hearn's work.[22] He does, however, take issue frequently and vigorously with Hearn's intellectual mentor, Herbert Spencer.[23] Aston's insistence that ancestor worship 'has hardly any place in Shintō' was a demolition of a central plank of Satow's interpretation of that religion, although he did not mention him in this context (Aston's assertion is, of course, strictly true only in relation to the ancient Shintō of the *Kojiki* and *Nihongi*).[24] He did, however, make clear his disagreement with Hearn on this issue in his 1907 book on Shintō.[25] He also dissented from Hearn's claim that Shintō was at one time a religion of 'perpetual fear', stating that his 'interesting and valuable work, *Japan, an Interpretation* [sic], is greatly marred by this misconception'. Aston's contention that, on the contrary, Shintō was 'a religion inspired by love and gratitude' is in line with modern views.[26] On the other hand, Hearn did describe the Japanese as 'a joyous and kindly' race, consonant with the characteristics of Shintō as agreed by Aston and later scholars.[27]

In 1905 Aston stated that Shintō was 'almost extinct' and 'quite inadequate for the spiritual sustenance of a nation which in these latter days has raised it to so high a pitch of enlightenment and civilization'.[28] He was certain that Japan, having accepted European philosophy and science, would convert to Christianity, 'a higher form of faith' than Buddhism, Confucianism or Shintō.[29] Aston could hardly have been more wrong on a point on which Hearn's prediction has proved to be entirely correct.

Hearn not only expounded a far more acute vision but also anticipated and answered his more academic critic quite effectively on the subject of Shintō in his first book on Japan:

> Buddhism has a voluminous theology; a profound philosophy, a literature as vast as the sea. Shintō has no philosophy, no code of ethics, no metaphysics; and yet, by its very immateriality, it can resist the invasion of Occidental religious thought as no other Orient faith can. Shintō extends a welcome to Western science, but remains the irresistible opponent of Western religion; and the foreign zealots who would strive against it are astounded to find the power that foils their uttermost efforts indefinable as magnetism and invulnerable as air. Indeed the best of our scholars have never been able to tell us what Shintō is. To some it appears to be merely ancestor-worship, to others ancestor-worship combined with nature-worship; to others, again, it seems to be no religion at all; and to the missionary of the more ignorant class it is the worst form of heathenism. Doubtless the difficulty of explaining Shintō has been due simply to the fact that the Sinologists have sought for the source of its books: in the Kojiki and the Nihongi, which are its histories; in the Norito which are its prayers; in the commentaries of Motowori and Hirata, who were its greatest scholars. But the reality of Shintō lives not in books, nor in rites, nor in commandments, but in the national heart, of which it is the highest emotional religious expression, immortal and ever young. For underlying all the surface crop of quaint superstitions and artless myths and fantastic magic there thrills a mighty spiritual force, the whole soul of a race with all its impulses and powers and intuitions. He who would know what Shintō is must learn to know that mysterious soul in which the sense of beauty and the power of art and the fire of heroism and magnetism of loyalty and the emotion of faith have become inherent, immanent, unconscious, instinctive.[30]

Modern criticism of Aston's mistaken search for a scriptural and organizational base for Shintō is particularly apposite in relation to Hearn's vision, which, indeed, anticipated the futility of such an approach fully a century before. The poetry of his prose may still militate against scholarly acceptance of the hard core of his meaning: that Shintō was not a religion in the Western sense and so could not be judged accordingly. This is not to denigrate the contribution to scholarship of men such as Aston but simply to recognize that Hearn, with the artist's antennae, transcended their West-centric values and was able to see vital aspects of Japanese culture in terms of what they were, rather than what they should be if they were to conform to Western models. It should also be said, of course, that modern scholarship sees Aston's writings on Shintō generally as fundamentally dated and flawed.[31]

While Aston, as Hearn had done previously, paid tribute to the assimilative powers of the Japanese in his 1899 *History of Japanese Literature*, his description of their 'national character' now comes across as distinctly patronizing:

> It is the literature of a brave, courteous, light-hearted, pleasure-loving people, sentimental rather than passionate, witty and humorous, of nimble apprehension, but not profound; ingenious and inventive, but hardly capable of high intellectual achievement; of receptive minds endowed with a voracious appetite for knowledge; with a turn of neatness and elegance of expression, but seldom or never rising to sublimity.[32]

In other words, the Japanese are a fine people but incapable of competing with their Western counterparts at the highest level, an attitude shared by Chamberlain and reminiscent of Kipling's 1889 view that the Japanese could make the finest troops east of Suez, under British officers![33] On another occasion, less than a decade before the Sino-Japanese War, Kipling was of the opinion that: 'The Japanese makes a trim little blue-jacket, but he does not understand soldiering.'[34] I quote this not to make fun of Kipling, but to show that even as sympathetic and perceptive an observer could be quite wrong. One finds much greater absurdities in the Japanese books of Loti, which, even at the time, infuriated Chamberlain.[35] Compared to his literary contemporaries, therefore, Hearn fares very well indeed.

While Aston was able to accept that Japan had been culturally more advanced than Europe in some respects in the past,[36] he believed, on the other hand, that the fall of the Shōgunate had discredited the 'moral, religious, and political principles on which it was based, and the nation turned to Europe for guidance'.[37] Hearn knew better that Japan was importing only what it needed for material advancement from the West and that the fundamental principles which had guided Japan historically would remain in place: this was his vision of the 'Jiujutsu' principle underlying Japanese policy.[38]

We find in Chamberlain precisely the same attitude towards

Shintō as was evident in Aston, when he complains:

> . . . the religion of the Early Japanese was not an organized
> religion. We can discover in it nothing corresponding to
> the body of dogma, the code of morals, and the sacred book
> authoritatively enforcing both, with which we are familiar
> in civilized religions, such as Buddhism, Christianity, and
> Islam.[39]

I have argued elsewhere that a distinguishing feature of
Hearn's interpretation of Japan was an insistence on accepting
the validity of Japanese culture in its own terms[40] and I will not
repeat these arguments in detail. However, another fascinating
example of the contrasting attitudes of Hearn and Chamberlain
towards the inherent worth of Japanese culture is revealed by
their respective attitudes towards art. Whereas Hearn appreciates – and applauds – the fundamentally different approach of
Japanese art, especially its ability to stimulate the imagination, in
'About Faces in Japanese Art',[41] Chamberlain saw it as
reflecting the inadequacies of the Japanese character which
was neither 'imaginative' nor 'profound':

> We see that the comparative weakness of the feeling for
> colour which characterises Japanese art reappearing here as a
> want of feeling for rhyme and rhythm and stanzaic
> arrangement, for all, in fact, that goes to make up the
> colour of verse.[42]

So even the *haiku*, Chamberlain's most enthusiastic espousal in
the field of Japanese literature, did not, in his view, amount to
much in the scale of civilization generally.

Possibly influenced by changes to the Imperial Rescript on
Education after Hearn's death, Chamberlain came to see Shintō
as a source of great mischief, the basis on which the Meiji
Japanese state was fabricating a religion of 'Mikado-worship and
Japan-worship', to which he objected violently.[43] No one would
deny that Chamberlain was right in that the state Shintō fostered
in the Meiji era was unhistorical and became an important
component of the psychology of militarism which came to
dominate Japanese policy up to the end of the Second World
War. Interestingly enough, Hearn, too, had been critical of the
'Revival of Pure Shintō' movement almost two decades before,
declaring that 'Shintō had been too profoundly modified in the
course of the fifteen centuries of change to be thus remodelled by
a Government fiat'; the only result of this official policy seemed

to him to have been the destruction of priceless Buddhist art – to which Satow and Chamberlain also objected[44] – while leaving the enigma of Shintō's origins as complicated as before.[45] Lafcadio did, on the other hand, consider that the continuance of the 'religion of loyalty', which he believed had evolved from the old religion of the dead and was now transmuted into the modern sense of patriotism, would remain vital to the future of Japan.[46]

Hearn differed from Chamberlain in seeing religion as a vital social force in Japan, entirely different in form from Western norms. Chamberlain did not appear to see that religion had always been a key element of state policy in Japan. Not alone were elements of the various creeds – Confucianism, Neo-Confucianism, Taoism and Buddhism – used to ensure social conformity in the Tokugawa era but the very introduction of Buddhism into Japan centuries previously had been part of a conscious policy.[47] Shintō was not simply 'reinvented' in the nineteenth century but had survived and evolved intertwined with Buddhism, Confucianism and Taoism over the centuries. The idea that it had little or no place in the life of the ordinary people who were clinging stubbornly to their ancestral Buddhism in Meiji times was something of a distortion.[48] To try to define Shintō exclusively as it had apparently existed in the first millennium after Christ was akin to limiting the definition of Buddhism or Christianity to their form in the same era; Chamberlain showed little appreciation that most religions, even the most complex, began simply and grew by assimilation over the centuries.

Modern scholarship is much more in tune with Hearn than Aston or Chamberlain on the issue of Shintō. Sansom's definition of Shintō in the 1950s as not being a religion or system of thought but an expression of national temperament is almost identical to Hearn's conception. Sir Charles Eliot's comment in his *Japanese Buddhism*, on the other hand, that, if considered unsympathetically in the light of pure reason, Shintō could appear as foolish as a fairy-tale could be applied to Chamberlain.

I have focused on the issue of Shintō in some detail as it was central to Hearn's interpretation of Japan and provides a means of comparison between Hearn and his contemporaries suitable to the relatively narrow limits of this essay. Hearn's achievement was, of course, much wider than his interpretation of Japan. As well as wonderful descriptions of the country in his era, its land, people and customs, he explored and illuminated many aspects of its popular culture. He left behind marvellous collections of *kwaidan*, drawn from the indigenous folk tradition of horror (three of which were the basis of a highly effective film in the 1960s).

Japan also profoundly affected Hearn in a personal sense. He began to probe the identity he had so successfully transmogrified in his American years, coming to reclaim its European roots.[49] His late, animated, correspondence with W.B. Yeats underlined their similarity of approach and use of folkloric material.[50] When he talked of leaving Japan, it was increasingly of returning to Ireland or Britain.[51] Indeed, in addition to the tentative arrangements he entered into to lecture to the Japan society in London already known about, he was also dealing with the London School of Economics about lecturing there in his last years.[52]

Hearn never left Japan, dying in Tokyo in 1904. He left behind a huge body of work on his adopted country which was admittedly uneven but on which he had brought to bear great artistic and intuitive gifts. He fell out of fashion for much of this century because the cause he championed, the need for the West to understand Japan in non-Western terms, was drowned by the tides of war and rivalry, as well as by the progressively more hostile campaign waged against his reputation by Chamberlain.[53]

His attempt to live the Japanese experience has been viewed as going native, although his private correspondence reveals that, while he always remained fundamentally loyal to Japan, his attitude towards it was complex and far from the one-dimensional idealism assumed by many commentators. Now that Western attitudes towards Asia are undergoing a fundamental reappraisal, Hearn may well come to be seen as the pioneer of the post-colonial attempt to understand Japan and the East for what they are, not what the West imagined they should be.

11

The Mutsu Family

IAN MUTSU

WHEN MY FATHER'S father, Mutsu Munemitsu, decided to send his son to England for a law degree from Cambridge, the old man, I believe, had no idea of the extent he would be Anglicizing the family for generations to come.

MUTSU MUNEMITSU

Munemitsu's grave is at the ancient Zen Buddhist temple of Jufukuji in Kamakura. Next to his urn stands that of my mother, the lovely, strong-willed British woman who became his daughter-in-law, née Gertrude Ethel Passingham.

The tombstone is housed in a small cave, called a *yagura* (storage for arrows) dug into the hillside. These are peculiar to Kamakura and are said to be the traditional resting-places provided for warriors during the late twelfth-century, when Kamakura was the seat of Japan's first military dictatorship.

Another *yagura* nearby contains a tomb said to be that of Masako, for which the Jufukuji temple is best known. Hojo Masako (1157-1225) was a remarkable woman. Defying her parents' wish she married Minamoto-no-Yoritomo, founder of the Kamakura shogunate which ruled almost all of Japan. She bore him two children, both of whom were assassinated. After Yoritomo's death and the adoption of a two-year-old successor, Masako took Buddhist vows and founded Jufukuji while nonetheless maintaining her political influence as 'ama (nun) shogun'. I have a feeling in my bones that my father's acquisition of the Mutsu *yagura* at this temple was in part motivated by his admiration for independent, strong-willed Masako.

The name of the imperialist Count Mutsu Munemitsu still

seems to be held in high esteem among many in post-war Japan, where almost everybody is a pacifist. This phenomenon may stem from the fact that he was a strong man while modern Japanese society is practically leaderless, and many seem to feel that there is little hope for the future.

I am not infrequently embarrassed by being introduced as the grandson of Count Mutsu Munemitsu and finding the stranger's attitude suddenly to change. Disbelief (How can an obvious *gaijin* – outsider or foreigner – like this claim such a birthright?) is suddenly followed by humble politeness.

Grandfather gained his fame historically on two counts: the revision of the unequal treaties and Japan's imperialist gains after the first Sino-Japanese war – for which he came to be known as the 'Father of Japanese diplomacy'. A very large statue of him on a stone pedestal just inside the gate to the Ministry of Foreign Affairs was designed to impress visitors to that ministry. During World War II the statue, along with other monuments, was torn down, part of the silly campaign launched by the army in order to have the press say that even historical celebrities were contributing to the drive for metal for the war industries. A group at the Foreign Ministry, by pulling strings, managed to preserve just the head and shoulders of their icon. Seventy years after Munemitsu's death, a time to honour the dead, a new statue was made with contributions from citizens and now stands beside the ministry's main entrance.

Munemitsu wrote a masterpiece on the war, *Kenkenroku* (selfless service to the sovereign and the state). It is still on sale at bookstores throughout Japan and is widely read. It is regarded as an achievement in literature as well as an important historical document. An excellent translation into English by Gordon Mark Berger of the University of California was published in 1982 but is now out of print.

Although I never did meet my grandfather in person, his death coming some ten years before my birth in London, I remember as a child I tended to fear him because of the things I heard about him from my father: 'He was a very great man whilst I – due to poor health – have not succeeded as much as I should have done to serve the country. In the years to come it will be a challenge for you.' Most of the time I shrank away and tried to change the subject.

I was told that the popular nickname for Munemitsu 'The Razor Minister' was inappropriate. Yes, he seemed sharp, with bold, quick decisions on matters of state; but these were not impromptu, resulting instead from meticulous research and careful calculation. He was ahead of his time, yes, indeed. And I feel this has been a trend, if I may say so, down to the present generation. I feel that in my life work – communications – I have both gained and lost because of this lineage.

I can still remember the formidable samurai sword which appeared to have been casually left leaning against father's desk in his study in Kamakura. The sharp blade in a long lacquered black sheath had once belonged to Munemitsu. 'The difference between the bureaucrats we now have around us and the old days is this,' my father once told me. 'Your distinguished grandfather was never a soldier. But he was made to train in swordsmanship and to embody the samurai code of honour. In the old days, if a man made a decision for the state and it went seriously wrong he could be called upon to atone for his mistake with death, self-inflicted with his sword.' After World War II, when I worked as a news writer for the United Press, I committed the great mistake of selling the sword. I regret this deeply up to the time of this writing. I do not think Grandpa will ever forgive me for this.

The greatest mistake of Grandfather's life, in his own estimation and on a much higher scale, was his imprisonment for four years, caused by his involvement in a plot to overthrow the cabinet in which he felt power was obnoxiously being usurped by the Satsu-cho (Satsuma and Choshu) ministers from southern Japan. Munemitsu was imprisoned from 1878 until 1882, first at the penitentiary in Yamagata and then in Sendai. The armed rebellion never took place. While in prison he did not waste his time. He studied hard. He achieved an amazing accomplishment: the rendering into Japanese of a most difficult book to translate, *An Introduction to the Principles of Morals and Legislation* by Jeremy Bentham. Soon after his release, his next move was to go abroad to study the governments of 'advanced' European countries.

Munemitsu fathered two children, both boys. The elder boy, Hirokichi, became my father. The younger boy, Junkichi, was destined to be adopted into the wealthy family of Furukawa and eventually to rise to the position of president of the Furukawa Zaibatsu conglomerate.

MUTSU HIROKICHI AND ETHEL

Munemitsu decided to send both his children abroad for education and to broaden their vision. The younger boy, Junkichi, went to America, enrolling at Cornell University in Ithaca, New York. His main course was chemistry, appropriate because the boy was destined eventually to rule over the commercial empire of Furukawa where at first mining was its stronghold. Hirokichi was sent off to England to study at Cambridge.

It had not been so very long since US Commodore Matthew Perry had arrived in his Black Ships to force open Japan's doors to the West. At that time, half the people of class-ridden Japan were farmers; only recently had they started to put on shoes and go about in *yofuku* – clothing from overseas. Only recently had the warrior class of samurai been compelled to cut off their top-knots and give up their swords. Despite the general fear and distrust of foreigners from all the Western countries, the Japanese of the Meiji era held the United Kingdom in highest esteem. The British had been rather sympathetic towards Japan during the recent Russo-Japanese War. England was an island under a monarchy. So was Japan. The Royal Navy ruled the waves – a model for Japan – and the Sun Never Set over the British Empire. British literature was avidly studied and translated by Meiji men of letters. The 'English gentleman' with his moral code and refined rules of conduct was an admirable model for the sons of the new Japanese upper-class whose ancestors were samurai. Hence in post-Meiji history, Oxford and Cambridge were almost exclusively chosen for the schooling of the male offspring of the Japanese court. Much further along in family history my mother, Countess Iso Mutsu, formerly Ethel Passingham, served as teacher of English to members of the Imperial Family, among them the late Prince Chichibu, brother of the Showa Emperor.

It was to the Passingham home in Cambridge that Hirokichi, 24 years of age, found his way, guided by officials of the Japanese embassy in London. They had searched carefully for a most suitable English family which would take the young man in, while he was at college. The day was 23 April 1888. Hirokichi had arrived in England the previous year for intensive study of English at University College, London, and under private tuition.

According to my friend and authoress of non-fiction, Akiko Shimoju, the Passinghams' large house, with some ten bedrooms, was still there when she visited England recently to do her book about my parents called '*Jun Ai*' ('True Love'). The large, dark stone building stood at No 2 Station Road between Cambridge railway station and Trinity College where Hirokichi studied.

Ms Shimoju brought out '*Jun Ai*' with the help of the diary my father kept for 54 years. This book about the instant, irrevocable love between Ethel and Hirokichi and the 17-year courtship preceding their marriage in Japan in 1905 was published in 1993 and became a best-seller. It is my hope, being in the television business, that some day the book will serve as the basis for a docudrama – hopefully a joint Anglo-Japanese production – on my parents' remarkable life together.

A jotting in one of my notebooks says that 'the Passinghams must have come from the old family of Passingham of Henderson Merionethshire Helthstone in Cornwall and Heston in Middlesex.' The head of the family, my maternal grandfather, John Tremenhere Passingham, was a strong, broad-shouldered and broad-minded man, devoted to athletics and outdoor sports. The family lived in Oxford. When he heard that there was a chance for him to run and own his own gymnasium especially for college students in Cambridge, he moved the family there. His younger brother, George Augustus Passingham, was another athletic person and a mountain climber. I have in my possession an article contributed by him to the British Alpine society. The graves of Tremenhere and another brother Harry reportedly lie in Cambridge Cemetery.

Unfortunately, I know little about my maternal grandmother, Mary Margaret, but I possess a small faded photograph of her. With it is a note written by my mother: 'Portrait of my mother, Mary Margaret Passingham, in the year 1858, aged 18, & given to her great friend Louise Baldwin, mother of the Prime Minister Stanley Baldwin. Mrs. Baldwin sent it to me during my visit to her sister Alice Kipling (mother of Rudyard Kipling) at The Gables, Tisbury, Wilts., in February 1898.' Mary Margaret was said to be a strong-willed woman. I remember hearing from my mother when I was a small boy in Kamakura that her mother 'loved to stand in a storm, especially when she was near the sea.'

The eldest of six children, my mother, too, had a will of her own. When Hirokichi arrived in Cambridge, a deep affection sprang up between them. It was instant and without hesitation, and became permanent. Remember, these were the days when international marriages – especially marriages between East and

West – were not the fashion, above all in Japanese diplomatic circles.

Hirokichi started keeping a diary almost as soon as he arrived in London, first in Japanese and then in English. I still have in my possession the 50 volumes of his diary – one page for each day in his life – of which 1800 pages concerned his time as a student. In his final years my father's wish was for me to destroy his diaries. I am glad – and feel sure I am forgiven – that I disobeyed. After consultation with historians, I have made arrangements for father's diaries to go after my death to the National Diet (Parliament) Library in Tokyo.

Student Hirokichi gave his first ring to Ethel barely a month after their first meeting. 'She accepted,' he wrote in his diary. It was a gold ring adorned with a single pearl – a pearl perhaps to signify Japan.

Nearly every page of the diary's early volumes mentions 'E' (E standing for Ethel). They went for long walks together, played tennis, went boating and talked at tea-time. Although they were already living under the same roof, Hirokichi wrote her long letters. She could help him with his English, and seemed to take an interest in what he could tell her about his homeland. She must have been a beautiful girl, gentle and kind and helpful towards Hirokichi who was a lifelong victim of asthma and at times was in need of support. Ethel played the piano and violin well. She loved to read poetry and good books. For her boyfriend she could provide tender care, while at the same time maintaining her strong will.

There was, as expected, quite a difference between the two families' reactions towards the decision of the two eventually to marry and for Ethel to go to live in distant, heathen Japan. After a while, the diary seems to indicate, the Passingham household came to accept the oriental fiancé and to treat him as one of the family. On holidays they would travel to the seaside together. In December 1891 Hirokichi joined the Liberal Club and at a later date he noted that at the club he had 'played billiards with father'.

Hirokichi never dared to mention E to his real father, knowing that it would evoke immediate stern opposition. In July and August of 1889 Hirokichi made a trip by steamship to America to report to his father who had become diplomatic envoy to the United States and Mexico. Munemitsu's second wife, Ryoko, looked smart in foreign dress as ambassadress. Brother Junkichi was a student at Cornell. Hirokichi did not breath a word about Ethel to his father but confided in his brother. His answer was reported to be along the lines of 'Good for you. Best of luck!' Years later, when Ethel published her book *Kamakura Fact and Legend*, she decided to dedicate it to JF – Junkichi Furukawa.

Hirokichi spent approximately five years in England before his return to Japan in 1894. Although he never received a law degree from Cambridge, his was nonetheless a remarkable achievement for a young man from Japan in those days. While still living in Cambridge he was invited to become a member of the first council of the Japan Society of London which was founded in 1891. This was a significant honour for a young man of 28. He moved to London and passed examinations in the Inner Temple. The parchment (still in my possession) reads: 'This is to Certify to whom it may concern that Hirokichi Mutsu of Tokio Japan, the eldest son of Munemitsu Mutsu, of Tokio, Japan, Minister of Foreign Affairs, was generally admitted of The Honourable Society of the Inner Temple in the fourth day of November, One thousand eight hundred and ninety, and was called to the Bar by the same Society on the seventeenth day of November, One thousand Eight hundred and Ninety-three and has paid all duties to the House and to the Officers thereunto belonging.' Certificate in hand, Hirokichi immediately began preparations to leave for home. 'This is the saddest day in my life to have to leave behind my Ethel,' he wrote in his diary. On 18 November 1893 Ethel saw him off in London. Forty-three days later his steamer arrived in Japan.

It was the beginning of a long wait, especially for Ethel. In those days there was no air travel, no international phone calls. Mail might take weeks. Japan seemed far, far away. Things could not wait much longer. Hirokichi had to inform his father of his intentions and ask permission as soon as possible, so as to send the good news to Ethel. Grandfather's reaction was as anticipated: 'Sheer nonsense. Get rid of the girl immediately. It would be ruinous for your career as diplomat to have a foreign wife. Besides which, she would never find happiness in Japan.' Nobody was around to record Munemitsu's words, but this is how I heard things went. Munemitsu demanded immediate action. There were more important matters demanding attention, like the war with China.

Hirokichi did not comply. His father was already weakened by his prolonged pulmonary illness and stress; and death was not far away. It was fortunate for my father, a rising diplomat, that the post-war conference in 1895 in Shimonoseki was conducted in English. Here his skill with the language, which he had acquired with help from Ethel, proved to be of immense value. Soon afterwards, Hirokichi received a citation for his meritorious services to the state from the Imperial Court, an auspicious start for a young diplomat.

Hirokichi passed the difficult foreign service examination and began his diplomatic career which included postings in China, the US, Italy and, finally, the UK. His first appointment to the consular service in Peking must have seemed an appropriate training ground in view of the prominent role his father had played during the Sino-Japanese War, although the assignment lasted only a few months.

From Peking, Hirokichi was posted to Washington, D.C. This was useful experience for the young diplomat, now nearing 30. While he was in Washington, word arrived from Tokyo that his father was gravely afflicted, having soldiered on long enough to complete his famous *Kenkenroku*, which related the inside story of the Sino-Japanese War and how he had coped with the triple intervention by Russia, France and Germany. Hirokichi returned to Tokyo a month before the grand old man's death on 24 August 1897. Hirokichi became a count, his father having been given the hereditary title in recognition of his distinguished service to the state.

Hirokichi later took up his posting to San Francisco, where he anticipated the next great event in his life: a reunion with Ethel Passingham. Making the long journey by sea, Ethel left Britain for the first time in her life. Hirokichi met her in San Francisco on 9 April 1899, five years and five months since they had last seen each other at King's Cross railway station, and twelve years since they had first met.

They set up home at 1714 Van Ness Avenue, again under the same roof. Lawful matrimony remained out of the question, however. Members of the peerage required permission from the Emperor to marry, and Hirokichi was now a count. Furthermore, this was an era of intense nationalism in Japan. An Occidental bride in the Mutsu family was bound to stir up all sorts of opposition; and the issue would also have to be taken up in the foreign service, where Hirokichi was endeavouring to follow in Munemitsu's footsteps up the ladder. The two worked out a clever strategy so that they could stay together: Ethel agreed to enter Japan in the role of governess and English teacher to one of Hirokichi's children. He had none.

A nine-year-old illegitimate Mutsu offspring was found at Gion, Kyoto, in one of the exclusive geisha houses. The beautiful child Fuyuko – 'Miss Winter' since she was born on 15 December – had been begotten by the old Machiavelli, my grandfather, in one of his more playful moments. A huge sum – because she was expected to be groomed into a top-ranking entertainer – was paid in order to bring about her adoption into the Mutsu family. There is evidence that Munemitsu's second wife, Ryoko, liked the idea and lent a hand with the adoption herself.

A year later, Ryoko died and Hirokichi returned to Japan for the burial. It was then his turn to suffer a prolonged illness which prevented his return to San Francisco. Once recovered, he called for Ethel to sail to Japan as English teacher. Ethel's steamer, *The Gaelic*, reached Yokohama on 19 April 1901. Hirokichi and brother Junkichi travelled with Ethel by train and escorted her to the large Mutsu mansion in the suburb of Nishigahara in Tokyo.

The big house standing in some five acres of land is no longer in the possession of the family. The grounds are now shown on the map as Furukawa Gardens, and tourists pay admission to admire the English rose garden and walk through the English-style mansion designed by Josiah Conder (1852-1920), a British architect who spent most of his life in Japan and created many landmark structures that are still respected and admired today.

Ethel became immediately fond of Fuyuko. On the day after her arrival, they went together on a long drive in the carriage to see what the city was like. The next day they went to the zoo, to a museum and then shopping at one of the department stores. Ethel and her adopted daughter got along extremely well, much to the satisfaction of Hirokichi and his brother. The newly-formed family of three now travelled together to Italy and the United States where Hirokichi assumed new posts. Fuyuko was a beautiful but ill-fated child. In her 14th year she died aboard ship on its way from Honolulu to Yokohama, having fallen prey to a sudden violent attack of malaria while the family was sightseeing in Hawaii.

The time seemed to be growing ripe for both the legalization of the marriage and a posting to the embassy in the UK. Hirokichi, deftly, had been pulling strings. Finally in 1905, imperial sanction for the marriage was secured, and many well-wishers offered their support. The legalization itself was a simple matter: registering formal documents, signed and sealed at the ward office where the Mutsu mansion was situated. There was no religious ceremony. A banquet took place attended by a dozen or so close friends and relatives.

Ethel was now a Japanese citizen and a countess to be. She was given the Japanese first name of Iso – 'the seashore' – because, voiced in Japanese, it sounded a bit like Ethel, because Ethel loved the sea and perhaps also because the matrimony was trans-oceanic.

It was most logical and fortunate that Hirokichi was shortly appointed to the Imperial Japanese Embassy in London, as first secretary. They sailed to London and took up residence in a large, comfortable flat in South Kensington.

Two major achievements mark Hirokichi's five-year term in London. On the political side there was the Japan-British Exhibition of 1910, while on the personal side there was my birth on 14 January 1907 as the one and only Anglo-Japanese grandson of Count Mutsu Munemitsu. Mother was already in her 39th year. I was christened Yonosuke ('son of sun') in honour of the same boyhood name given to Munemitsu and it was so recorded on my British birth certificate.

The exhibition ran for six months at White City, Shepherd's Bush (near where the BBC Television Centre stands today). The exhibition was carefully prepared by father and ambitiously staged. For the British to see were reproductions to scale of magnificent Japanese temple architecture, the tea house, replicas of gardens as well as examples of art. Japanese sports such as judo, kendo, karate and sumo were demonstrated. Also on display were examples of science and technology to show visitors that Japan, now an empire of its own, had already achieved much in the short time since its opening to the West. Japan came to London to show itself at its best.

My very first childhood memories are of scenes at the exhibition: paintings of Japanese scenes fitted into the windows of a stationary passenger train, people in rowboats on the illuminated lake and, above all, the Flip-Flap. This was a giant pair of observation towers that functioned like scissors, In its horizontal position people were locked into a pair of observation cages. The giant scissor closed and raised the riders to a tremendous altitude from which they could take a bird's-eye-view of their capital city. Years later in Kamakura as a small boy,

I would tell my friends how great it was in England to go up into the sky on a Flip-Flap.

After the family's return to Japan in the autumn of 1910, at the conclusion of the Exhibition, Hirokichi did not feel fit enough to take up a new appointment straightaway though he was nominated as Counsellor at the Rome embassy in 1912. But in June 1914 his appointment was gazetted as minister to Belgium. He took preparatory instruction in the French language. He set off for his new post but fell seriously ill at Kobe. He then decided to quit the diplomatic service and move the family home out of Tokyo to Kamakura.

The British ambassador reporting to London stated that

> Count Mutsu is a charming and distinguished-looking diplomat, son of the late Count M. Mutsu. His wife who is English shows a disposition to keep in the background. Count Mutsu himself, owing to ill health – he suffers from asthma with consumptive tendencies – has lived in such retirement during the last four years as to have been almost forgotten, according to the newspapers.

Father's motivation for the move was mainly his delicate health, due to asthma, and the resulting impossibility of continuing in the diplomatic service. I suspect there was also another reason. I have only one or two photographs that were made of mother sitting on the matted floor of a Japanese room wearing kimono. She looks extremely uncomfortable. Though everybody was polite to her, it must have been cruel compelling her to bear the discomforts of a traditional Japanese home and to submit to the rigid codes of the day.

In 1924, when Hirokichi was 55, he was visited by Baron Shidehara Kijiro, then the foreign minister, and asked to serve as ambassador to the United States, one of the senior diplomatic posts. After due consideration, Hirokichi declined because of his continuing poor health.

Father purchased a choice area of land near the sea in the resort town, built a British-style home with ample room for the servants, and the family blissfully took up residence there. Fresh vegetables and fruit as well as poultry and eggs were in constant supply from our own miniature farm, adjacent to the garden and in the garden of our professional farmer with his cottage in the grounds. Fish was abundant from the sea less than a mile away. Life was easy, healthy and just right for all three of us.

Mother was immediately enamoured of Kamakura, and grew

very interested in its history. Many times she made the rounds of the temples and shrines; and as a boy I would accompany her on my bicycle. She probably was not only the first English woman to become a Japanese countess, but also the only Japanese countess of the era to move around astride a bicycle.

As a result of her visits to the temples and historic findings, she decided to write a book of her own. Since she had very little Japanese, it was now her husband's turn to help her with her research. *Kamakura Fact and Legend* came out in 1918. Now in its fourth edition, it is still widely read and admired. As she grew fonder of Kamakura, I believe she came to think that the long wait and the long journey from her homeland had all been worthwhile.

Mother's next and last visit to England, with me, was in 1925. I had graduated from Gyosei Middle School, run by French Catholic priests in Tokyo. Mother had taught me to play the violin, and I was aimless but wished vaguely to study music further – to go into conducting if I could – and to polish my English with a view to reportorial work. The NYK liner, *Atsuta Maru*, sailed out of Yokohama bound for London on 12 March with both of us aboard, carrying our fiddle cases.

In Birmingham, we were fortunate, by prearrangement, to live with the family of the famous composer Sir Granville Bantock. Some time later, I attended classes both at the Midland Institute of Music, which Sir Granville headed, and the University of Birmingham, where I read English. Like my father, I spent about six years in England as a student and it was similarly a most enjoyable and fruitful time of my life.

Mother missed both her husband and the sea at Kamakura. She 'left for home' within eighteen months. But a message was brought to me by a Salvation Army officer from London – so that the news could be conveyed as gently as possible – of mother's death on 8 June 1930. I, too, returned to Kamakura. When mother's funeral took place at the modest Methodist church in Kamakura, a remarkable incident occurred – an apt sequel to her visits to the Buddhist temples to research her book. As the service progressed, the vice-abbot of Engakuji Temple, resplendent in his gold and scarlet brocade surplice and attended by an acolyte, ascended the pulpit. On the Bible he placed the Buddhist sutras, then spoke words of praise and uttered an incantation of solace for the departed soul. A lead article in the *Japan Times* of 1 July 1930 said: 'And of all the body of mourners

– among whom were many from the business activities of the Capital – not one but felt that the words of the Buddhist priest were as they should be even in their strange surroundings.'

Although mother had thrived in Kamakura, father's health did not improve much. Now and then he would go up to Tokyo by train (two hours then, one hour now) and counsel his friends at the Foreign Ministry. At one point he was offered the position of ambassador to Washington but he decided not to take it. He devoted most of the rest of his life to serving the country with philanthropy and education.

With funding from Furukawa and in memory of Junkichi, father set up a large foundation called Ujunkai which he ran for 25 years. Donations were made to such activities as the advance of Western music in Japan, earthquake-proof buildings, modern woodblock prints, medical research, and education for women. Help was given to leper colonies and a hospital was built for the Salvation Army. Father was moved by their work and extended help on the condition that their activities in Japan remain under control of the Salvation Army headquarters in London. Kamakura Jogakuin, the middle and high school for girls which father established, recently celebrated its 90th anniversary. He also built a museum, still very much in business, to protect the sculpture, paintings and other historical treasures of Kamakura temples from quakes and other natural calamities. As war clouds thickened in the 30s and military rule took a grip on state affairs in Japan, none of the Ujunkai money could be diverted to such avenues. Father died at 72 in November 1942, surviving mother by 12 years. Before his death, however, he dissolved Ujunkai and distributed its capital to various worthy social and non-militaristic causes.

YONOSUKE IAN MUTSU

In 1931 I started my life's work as a journalist. The Mutsu genes, no doubt, prompted me to go into international reporting of what goes on in Japan. I have persisted in this field of activity for approximately half a century, first with the typewriter and later with the film and video camera.

I first found an excellent training ground as a journalist for the *Japan Advertiser*, the American-owned liberal newspaper in Tokyo. Soon I picked up a side-job as Tokyo correspondent for the London *Daily Express*. This was the beginning of a dark period, dominated by control of the state by the army, starting with the invasion of Manchuria. The *Advertiser* had a small circulation, the *Express* a big one. Both paid badly. After some six years in search of wider audiences, I moved over to the Domei News Agency, internationally transmitting news stories on Japan by morse signals to Domei bureaux overseas. The news was then distributed to the local media. World-ranking news services like Reuters, Havas, AP and UP used the material as background. From a small start I managed to build up Domei's world service to a department of about fifty news-writers and served for a while as its chief.

One morning the office was boiling over with excitement as I arrived at work. The Emperor had declared that war had begun between the countries of my parents. The year after Pearl Harbor my father died. I spent the rest of the war years at the family villa in Karuizawa, in the mountains north of Tokyo.

Soon after the war I was employed by United Press (now UPI) as a news writer. I gained the position of news reporter accredited to General MacArthur's headquarters. Watching, at the Foreign Correspondents Club, scenes of the war shot by US newsreel cameramen, motivated a change in my career from print to photo journalism. With the help of an American news cameraman, the late Gene Zenier, my first documentary film, 'Japan Awake' – mostly a compilation of news footage – was put together and sold to the Toho Motion Picture Company. The film's message to the Japanese people was not to be led sheep-like, not to be gullible and never again to allow dictatorial rule of their country. It reached a large audience and it was a financial success.

In its wake, I made half a dozen more documentaries, and this led to my resignation from UP to take up a new occupation: Tokyo Bureau manager of the US Newsreel Pool. The pool comprised MGM News of the Day, Paramount News, 20th Century Fox, Universal International News and Movietone News – the bulk of the world's newsreel companies – in an age when one could see moving picture news only by going to a theatre. Though news clips from Japan were infrequent, the audience was enormous.

With the rise of television, the theatre newsreels gradually disappeared, and in 1952 I established IMPC – International Motion Picture Company – with the object of producing and distributing documentary films and video on Japan for audiences overseas. IMPC also lends a hand to production teams from abroad coming over to film in Japan. Since its inception, IMPC has produced or has helped to produce well over a thousand documentaries for audiences overseas. There must be countless numbers of people who have seen them and come as a result to understand Japan better. Some of the productions have had long lives, especially the historical ones.

Many years ago, IMPC collaborated with Thames Television, London, during production of the 'World at War', a series in 13 parts. I was compelled to play a small role in one of the episodes on Japan. The famous series is still showing on TV around the world and at totally unexpected moments, people call up to say, 'Hey, I saw you on television last night.'

I have also worked closely with the BBC in the field of sales-distribution of programmes to network television in Japan, first for a dozen years through IMPC then through the agency of a new company, British Television Inc., which I formed with my associate Sugiyama Jiro. BTI is still vigorously carrying on its work. Trying to determine the size of audience of a programme just aired is never an easy task. All the same, I believe I can say that my colleagues and I have managed to present BBC programmes to Japanese audiences cumulatively of astronomic proportions – many times the size of the entire British population – during the past near-quarter century.

Among the programmes sold to NHK was, of course, Sir Kenneth Clark's famous 'Civilization' series. The very fine conversion of this series into Japanese and local presentation was of particular importance to me. I had met Sir Kenneth in Japan some time previously and, for a week, filmed him in the temples, museums and gardens of Kyoto for a programme he would be doing for British viewers. He had been invited over by the Japanese government. Wherever we went to film he was a VIP and treated with great respect for his deep knowledge about the art treasures brought out for him to see – although it was his first visit to Japan. I came to admire him greatly and we got along well. Over lunch one day I put to him the question of when, where and how his interest germinated to turn him into such a great scholar on Japanese art? His answer astounded me: 'Whenever I'm asked that, my answer is "At the British-Japanese Exhibition of 1910 at White City".'

Father had done it.

J.W. Robertson-Scott and his Japanese Friends

MARI NAKAMI

JOHN W. ROBERTSON SCOTT (1866-1962), a British journalist who resided in Japan during World War I, made a profound study of Japanese rural society as well as being actively engaged in Tokyo in editing the English-Japanese bilingual magazine *The New East* (*Shin-Tōyō* in Japanese). While in Japan, he became acquainted with many Japanese and made some lifelong friendships.

In a lecture at Ōsaka in November 1989, Dr Ian Nish pointed out four important Japanologists who had influenced him. Along with Sir Ernest Satow, Sidney and Beatrice Webb and Richard Storry, he named Scott. Nish explained that Scott began his career in journalism but, after studying Japanese rural society, was recognized as a Japanologist. He also explained that Scott had a strong interest in Anglo-Japanese relations during World War I, and had published a pamphlet entitled *Japan, Great Britain and the World: A Letter to My Japanese Friends.*[1]

Although Scott seems worthy of study, there is neither an article nor a book on him either in Japan or Britain. In Japan, moreover, he has now fallen into oblivion. Few specialists in Japanese studies know his name. this is a situation quite different to that of such Englishmen as Lafcadio Hearn or Bernard Leach who are perennial favourites with the Japanese. What kind of personality was Scott? Did he play an important role of any kind in Japan-British relations while he was resident in Japan? Did he exert any influence on his Japanese friends?

BIOGRAPHICAL SKETCH

Scott was born on 20 April 1866, in Wigtown, Cumberland, of Scottish extraction.[2] The surname Scott was taken from his father's stepfather, and Robertson came from his maternal grandfather. When he decided to make his career in journalism, he found there were other J.W Scotts. So, after that he prefixed his mother's name to Scott. His origins were 'wholly rural'[3] and his family came from farm workers. His father, besides his regular work, had a passion for public service and occasionally made speeches and sermons which he could do convincingly.

When Scott was seven or eight, he became 'an assiduous reader' of newspapers,[4] and was attracted by pictures of the Franco-Prussian War and the Russo-Turkish War that he saw in the *Illustrated London News*, and felt the miseries of people involved in a war.[5] Then, at the age of sixteen, after being educated at grammar and Quaker schools and having one or two years' experience at secretarial work, Scott set up as a freelance journalist in Birmingham and in London. From 1886 to 1899, he worked for such newspapers as the *Birmingham Daily Gazette* (1886-87), *Pall Mall Gazette* (1887-93), *Westminster Gazette* (1893-99) and *Daily Chronicle* (1899). At that period, Scott had already become interested in foreign and colonial politics. In regard to Far Eastern problems, he adopted a stance that would later be regarded as supporting the 'Japanese during the Russian [Russo-Japanese] War and in favour of the abolition of extraterritoriality'.[6]

When the Boer War broke out in 1899, he left daily journalism and concentrated on writing for himself. In 1900, he published pamphlets against the South African War and a book entitled *The People of China*. In the latter, although Scott had never visited China, he tried 'to gather facts, incidents and opinions from as many sources as practicable', and 'to supply . . . the kind of information . . . which an intelligent newspaper reader would be likely to seek from a friend who had lived in the Far East'.[7] However, he does not seem to have made much of a success in the field of foreign affairs.

Then Scott went into 'retirement'[8] in Essex as 'a cottager' and began to write on rural subjects. He settled down to the study of agriculture and wrote more than ten books relating to it during his life. The reason why he became interested in agricultural problems was that he regarded agriculture and rural life 'as a means' of establishing a sound society, 'the touchstone of a healthy State'[9] and even went so far as to say that it was 'the foundation of everything'.[10] Besides, by discussing them, he wanted to criticize the British tendency of being 'too much wrapt up in urban problems'.[11]

When World War I broke out, Scott having recognized that he was too old to be enlisted in the army, decided to pursue a theme which seemed to him likely to be useful for Britain after the war. His decision was to investigate Japanese agriculture from a sociological perspective and to write a book on it. He thought it important to make a reconstruction of the rural areas of Britain. But why Japan? It was because, when he visited the large library of the International Institute of Agriculture in Rome early in 1914, he found that there was no study in English dealing with the agriculture of Japan in spite of the fact that it seemed very suggestive for British agriculture.[12] In March 1915, Scott left for Japan 'with a round the world ticket available for two years',[13] although, after all, he stayed in Japan for four-and-a-half years.

In his first year in Japan, Scott spent most of his time in rural areas, closely investigating its agricultural system and obtained enough material for the book. However, before completing his book, Scott turned aside from his studies to attend to 'the more immediately useful task' and 'the issues at stake'.[14] For him, 'it could not but seem poor work at times to be studious of rice and *daikon* while Europe was dripping with blood'.[15] The unexpectedly long war and the anti-Allied campaign which broke out in Tokyo at that time, in addition to the Japanese ignorance about the war, irritated him. He felt it necessary to explain to the Japanese why Western nations in pursuit of peace must fight against Germany. Consequently, Scott published two bilingual books in 1916. One is a little book entitled *Japan, Great Britain and the World*, and the other, *The Ignoble Warrior*. These books achieved a fair degree of success, each having a circulation of about 35,000 copies.[16]

Before long, Scott engaged in the task of founding and editing a monthly review *The New East* in Tokyo. However, soon after the end of the war, the financier stopped providing further funds, and *The New East* had to cease publication. After that Scott tried to start a new periodical dealing with Asian problems, the *Asiatic Monthly*, but this did not succeed.

He then returned to Britain and reverted to the study of rural subjects. In 1922, he completed his socio-agricultural studies on Japan, and published his findings under the title of *The*

Foundations of Japan. Thereafter, because he did not feel at ease being 'away from "printer's ink on paper",'[17] he started a quarterly magazine, *The Countryman* which ran until 1947 'with a rising circulation of 58,000'.[18] Scott, as editor as well as proprietor, achieved a great success. Spending his remaining years in writing several retrospective books, he died on 21 December 1962.

STUDY OF JAPANESE AGRICULTURAL SOCIETY

Scott thought that previous books by foreigners on Japan were either 'fervid "pro-Japanese" or determined "anti-Japanese" romanticism',[19] and still they exerted influence in forming public opinion. Therefore, what Scott tried to do was to write on Japan as objectively as possible. Besides, in spite of the fact that more than half the Japanese population at the time was rural, Scott considered that the world mainly knew the Japanese as 'townified, sometimes Americanized or Europeanized' and that it appeared that they 'stand for a great deal in modern Japan',[20] but that the countryman who composed most of the population was not given due attention. For Scott, 'the basic fact about Japan is that it is an agricultural country'.[21] He thought, in so doing, 'it is possible to find the way beneath that surface of things visible to the tourist'.[23]

To gather information, Scott made rural journeys of 6,000 miles, which took almost twelve months, to explore all the areas except for Kyushu, the southern island. As a rural sociologist, to find out the socio-political and moral backbone of Japan, he talked with many Japanese people from all walks of life not only on agricultural problems but also on religion, morals, life and the future of Japan. He also took part in shows, fairs, *Bon* dances and public meetings. He was asked to plant commemorative trees and to write many wall writings for schools etc. It is noticeable that he talked with the Ainu people, too. By talking, eating, bathing and sleeping with many Japanese, Scott observed the Japanese way of life with his own eyes; and hence obtained first hand knowledge about Japan. In his view, Japan 'has always been a more democratic country than is generally understood',[24] although the 'average Japanese do not yet conceive the Government as something which they have made and may unmake'.[25]

It is not clear how well he could speak Japanese, but the following fact gives some evidence of his ability in the language.

After the Australian Army's decision to embark on the serious study of the Japanese language in 1916, Sydney University invited applications for a part-time lecturer in the Japanese language. At that time, Scott was, at the suggestion of the British Foreign Office, considered as one of the four candidates for the lectureship. Although he did not get the job (James Murdoch was appointed), he was regarded as having a sufficient knowledge of Things Japanese.[26]

In his letter of 22 November 1915 to Mr Thring of the Society of Authors (London), Scott said that, living in Ōmori, Tokyo, he was writing a thick book on 'the rural Life and Agriculture of Japan' which 'will be my best book'.[27] However, as we have already noted, he did not complete it before his return to Britain.

Among his books relating to Japan, *The Foundations of Japan* is the most important for students of Japanese Studies. It is still available as one of the 'Books on Demand Reprint Series' reproduced by University Microfilms International, which proves its academic value. Scott got the title of the book from a phrase of one of his Japanese friends, Uchimura Kanzo. Uchimura said 'as you penetrate into the lives of the farmers, there will be laid bare to you "the foundations of Japan"'.[28] Uchimura was a well-known Christian preacher and there is a chapter in *The Foundations of Japan* on Uchimura in which he is described as 'the Japanese Carlyle'.[29]

THE NEW EAST

When Scott began to study Japanese agriculture and society through travelling in the Japanese countryside, he had not made contact with the British Embassy. However, about one year later, Scott was 'summoned to Tokyo' by the Embassy.[30] The Embassy, being annoyed by the strong German influence over the Japanese, felt it necessary to take measures to meet the situation and asked London what they could do to improve it. Answering by telegram, Sir Edward Grey, the Foreign Secretary, suggested they should 'try to get in touch with Robertson Scott'.[31] This suggestion finally brought forth the bilingual monthly magazine *The New East*. When approached, Scott thought that there was no English magazine in the Far East or India of a London or New York standard,[32] and wanted to publish one.

The money for its publication came from a London

committee composed of Lord Burnham (the proprietor of the *Daily Telegraph*), C.V. Sale (head of a well-known City firm long established in Japan), J.St.Loe Strachey (the editor of the *Spectator*), and Sir G.W. Prothero (the editor of the *Quarterly Review*).[33] The British commercial community paid for the advertisements, in Scott's later conjecture, with an expectation of getting from him 'a kind of "pro-British" tract'.[34]

With Scott as the editor, and Hugh Byas, formerly the editor of the *Japan Advertiser*, as the associate editor and business manager, and an American woman who was once Mrs Yonejirō Noguchi, as a secretary, the bilingual 200-page monthly magazine, *The New East*, started in June 1917. The Japanese section was set up on the pattern of his bilingual books. But the English and the Japanese sections do not necessarily correspond to each other. Scott soon found that it was a mistake because there were few English or Japanese who could read both languages and 'it was impossible to give under one cover at a moderate price a good Japanese magazine as well as a good English one'.[35]

In its initial number, the objects of *The New East* were expressed as follows: '1. to interpret to the West the best in the thought and achievement of Japan, and to Japan the best in the thought and achievement of the West. 2. to develop, by better acquaintance between the Brutish and Japanese peoples, the good relations which so happily exist between Japan and Great Britain.' The magazine was composed of all sorts of writings: editorial notes; articles on domestic and foreign affairs; essays dealing with art, religion and daily life; extracts from Japanese as well as English newspapers; book reviews, poetry, cartoons, literature and English competition for Japanese students.

Scott's American friend, Langdon Warner, as well as his intimate British friends, Ashton-Gwatkin and Sir Edward Crowe were regular contributors. Japanese supporters were Nitobe Inazō, Inouye Junnosuke, Yanagi Muneyoshi, Yanagita Kunio, Tokugawa Iesato and Makino Nobuaki. The following articles or essays by the Japanese came out: articles on the Anglo-Japanese Alliance by Prime Minister Terauchi Masatake and by Foreign Minister Motono Ichirō, articles on foreign affairs and others by Ōkuma Shigenobu, Yoshino Sakuzō, Nitobe Inazō, Tsurumi Yūsuke, essays by Yanagi Muneyoshi and Arishima Takeo, the English translation of the novels written by Mushanokōji Saneatsu, Shiga Naoya, Suzuki Teitaro's (later known as Daisetsu) articles written on Zen, etc. The English section included articles by such prominent writers as H.G. Wells, Lord Curzon, Havelock Ellis, Tagore, Theodore Roosevelt, George Ernest Morrison, Sidney Webb, and Bernard Shaw.

Aside from the copies for free distribution, the average circulation for sale was 3000. It was distributed not only in Japan and Britain, but also in China, the USA and other areas within the British Empire. However, after one-and-a-half years of publishing, the magazine came to a stop in December 1918[36] because the financial backers of The New East stopped providing funds.

Although the British Foreign Office as well as Scott had made efforts to try to sweep away its propagandist taint,[37] The New East was no doubt 'a propaganda journal for the British government'[38] and was regarded by the Japanese as such.[39] It appealed only to a small section of the Japanese, especially to the Anglophiles.[40]

DEFENDING BRITISH WAR ACTIVITIES DURING THE WAR

Japan, Great Britain and the World was an expansion of an article by Scott which came out in the prominent Japanese magazine Taiyō in April 1916. The article was written 'prompted by the article by Mr Kōson Asada on the Anglo-Japanese Alliance which appeared in the March Taiyō'.[41] Scott, evaluating Asada's article as serious and considered, refuted his argument in favour of asking for 'the immediate and radical revision or the immediate or early abrogation of the Anglo-Japanese Agreement'.[42]

In this book, Scott called Japanese attention to the fact that the agitation for the radical revision or abrogation of the Agreement had made people round the world distrustful of the Japanese, because Japan seemed to want to get rid of the Agreement long before its expiration and to enjoy a free hand in China, while Britain was engaged in a life and death struggle in Europe. Then he asked whether such criticism would not impair the national interests of Japan in the long run and suggested that, if Japan wanted to hold a good position in the world, Japan should consider its good name before everything else.

Another point which Scott emphasized was that the Japanese had criticized Britain without realizing concretely what was happening in Europe, the capacity of the British navy and army, and the fact that Britain was in a strong position in the fighting and was likely to win the war. Therefore, Scott continued, if Japan neglected these facts, it would lose out in the end. Finally, Scott said, Japan should act with prudence towards Britain because 'nowhere in the world is there greater capacity than in Great Britain to understand and appreciate the very highest aspirations of which Japan is capable, or less desire among responsible people to thwart the just and special ambitions of Japan'.[43]

In conclusion, Scott demanded Japan's cooperation with Britain on one hand, and tried to keep in check Japan's move closer to Germany, on the other. For Scott, the value of Germany was exaggerated in Japan. From his study of Japanese society, Scott had already recognized that 'not only Japanese soldiers but many administrative, educational, agricultural and commercial experts had been to school in Germany. There was much in common in the German and Japanese mentalities, . . . regard for the army and for order, devotion to regulations, habit of subordination and deification of the State.'[44] But, at the same time, Scott thought 'what may be said with certainty is that there is little enough just now and is likely to be little enough in the immediate future, worth Japan's having, in Germany at the present stage of her development, a Germany brutalized and brutalizing'.[45]

Scott's standpoint was fundamentally a justification of British government policy towards China and India. He thought it important to protect the interests of Britain as an imperialist power through cooperation with Japan. For Scott, 'cooperation' meant that Japan should not establish control over China exclusively while disregarding British commercial interests, nor take the part of Indian revolutionists. He said 'the Indians knew that under no Power in the world could they have greater freedom in the future for working out their destiny than under Great Britain'.[46] As to Korea and Formosa, he said, 'the Koreans are backboneless and the Formosans seem to be half of them savages. In this fact is the justification for Japan's presence in Korea and Formosa, and no instructed person denies that the Koreans and the Formosans have benefited to a considerable degree by Japan's exertions'.[47] But, Scott went on, China was different from Korea and Formosa. There, the Powers should respect the desire of each to preserve their respective interests.

After writing in his first publication relating to Japan that he had been 'troubled by continually meeting with incredible ignorance about the War'[48] among the Japanese, Scott published his second bilingual book, *The Ignoble Warrior*. In it, by exposing Germany's atrocities, asserting that Germany was solely responsible for the outbreak of war and defending British war aims, Scott asked for Japanese better understanding of the situation.

Scott at the time was like a government agent who was interested in how to exert influence, rather than as a sociologist who attached importance to objectivity. He was even financially supported by the British government.[49] Therefore it is not surprising that he is now described as a personality who was 'in charge of Britain's wartime propaganda in Tokyo'.[50]

In 1947, Scott said retrospectively: 'Had I returned to Japan, as I was set on doing, I might have survived long enough to give the *Asiatic Monthly* a vigorous and widely influential life in the Far East and beyond it, and to help a widening section of Japanese, in need of understanding and timely encouragement, to bring about a state of things in which their country would have thought twice about siding with Germany in the Second World War. Events in China, . . . might too, have taken another course.'[51]

SCOTT AND YANAGI

One of the Japanese who had close contacts with Scott was Yanagi Muneyoshi (also known as Sōetsu), who is known as the initiator of the Mingei Movement. In *The Foundations of Japan*, Scott allotted a chapter to Yanagi and described him as an anti-militarist as well as a thinker who tried to harmonize East and West. Yanagi was especially influenced by Scott in his speculation on the problems of war and peace, although often in a negative way. Their exchange of opinions also sheds light on Yanagi's still unknown standpoint as a pacifist.[52]

Yanagi became acquainted with Scott in June 1915, through an introduction by Bernard Leach, one of Yanagi's best and lifelong friends. In his letter of 2 June 1915, to Shiga Naoya, Yanagi said, 'I have decided to visit your place on the 10th. I may go along with Mr. Scott who is around fifty and has stayed overnight with me. Leach introduced him to me. Scott is said to be a well-known writer in Britain. . . Bernard Shaw is his favourite and like Shaw, he is also a pacifist. . . Scott is anxious to talk with you.'[53]

In his English letter of 7 June 1915 to Leach, Yanagi gave his impression of Scott as follows:

> About Mr. R. Scott. Is he not one of the typical sound Scotchmen? He seems to be open-hearted for every man & thing. Was it not the reason why I could talk to him like a familiar friend in spite of a new one? When I saw him first at the station, he reminded me intuitively of Edward Carpenter. Am I not right? You see is it nearly hopeless to find out such a man among our old people here. . . Thanks for your kind introduction of him to me. It gives great pleasure & lesson that I learnt something of the best English quality from him, as well as indeed from you.[54]

Yanagi visited Shiga with Scott in June, and introduced Scott to Shiga.[55] Through the channels of Leach and Yanagi who were the members of the Shirakaba (Silver Birch) literary group, Scott had access to the most promising young literary men at that time in Japan, such Shirakaba members as Shiga, Mushanokōji Saneatsu and Arishima Takeo, and was about to enlist contributions from them in *The New East*.

What Yanagi discussed with Scott most frequently was the problem of war and peace. Yanagi had probably been given information about Scott's belief in Quakerism. When Scott was a child, he was interested in Friends and his family went to the Friends' Meeting on Sunday mornings, although he did not join the Quakers,[56] and, as noted above, he had been educated at a Quaker school. Yanagi said in his English letter to Leach, in November 1915, that he had become 'acquainted quite recently'[57] with Quakerism and in the same letter he continued: 'Who is Mr. Gilbert Bowles? Do you know him? He, through the introduction of Mr. Scott, kindly sent me the books on Quakerism. I know only he is the secretary of the American Peace Society in Japan. I look forward the day to call on him in order to know his ideas on war.'[58]

Yanagi, after he became enlightened by Quakerism, became enthusiastic in reading books on the subject and in speculating on war and peace. Yanagi's personal library includes about 40 volumes of books relating to Quakerism, with *Passages from the Life and Writings of George Fox*, one of the books Bowles had sent.

Yanagi had been impressed by pacifism as advocated by Tolstoy at the time of the Russo-Japanese War and, when World War I broke out, he had shown his anti-war sentiment in his letter to Leach. However, it was just a naive feeling rather than deep thought. Influenced by Quakerism, and through his opposition to Scott's attitude towards World War I, Yanagi's pacifism took strong root.

In his draft letter to Scott written in English on 12 February 1916 (whether it was sent to Scott or not remains uncertain) Yanagi, distinguishing his attitude from that of Scott's, criticized him as follows:

> Unfortunately, I found out that the point what you defended and what I pursued is not the same thing. What you apologized and explained is the English attitude against the German military atrocity, but what I wished to inquire and obtain is the human attitude based upon the first principle of our being... Mine is neither English nor Japanese standpoint, but of human being... Before anything else, your people must become man before he becomes an English... She [England] said she rose against German militarism in honor of moral victory. But alas! she is going to buy much moral victory with military power!... Let us be a human hero, not a sworded hero![59]

Judging from Yanagi's follow-up postcard of 18 December, sent to Leach, Yanagi seems to have been asked by Scott to join in Britain's anti-German campaign which Scott was at that time carrying on enthusiastically. Yanagi said in English:

> S. [Scott] came here yesterday & we had much talk about his plan... I am thirsty [for] what is radical, but he is apt to pull me to what is practical... His plan is hardly a movement in the sense we require. You will understand what I mean. Please help me in your advice morally as well as spiritually for the attitude I ought to take. I want to see you as soon as possible in order to discuss the subject, because it is serious.[60]

Then on 23 December, Yanagi wrote to Leach in English as follows:

> Since I met S. the other day, I have read his new work entitled 'The Ignoble Warrior' with much attention. So sorry to say that it entirely puzzles & boils my head. I am about to attack him in the expense of our friendship. I shall never forget his good character from which I have learnt many things. His thought, however, seems to me more & more conventional & even quite useless especially for those who desire to create future Japan. How I could bear in such an idea that our attack on Tsintau was our moral duty! He

seems to have no clear understanding of the spirit with which our young people are moving.[61]

The copy of *The Ignoble Warrior* in Yanagi's personal library shows that Yanagi had read the Japanese section of it, making marginal notes in Japanese on several pages. Those notes are important as evidence of Yanagi's thought on war and peace, supplementing his draft letter to Scott. In his book, Scott defended British activities against barbarous Germany, saying that Britain was playing the role of the world's policeman. Rejecting Scott's ideas, Yanagi wrote in the marginal notes: 'There seems to be no room to approve a just cause in the German war effort, yet this can never lead a conclusion that British action is absolutely right' (notes on page 15). 'I can not accept the British assertion that she declared war against Germany exclusively for the public interest... Every proclamation of war craves for a moral pretext' (notes on pages 18-19). Regarding Scott's statement that Britain many times proposed to Germany to limit naval shipbuilding mutually but was rebuffed, Yanagi responded as follows: 'British proposals sound egocentric, because they aim to keep Britain's command of the seas eternally, checking the rise of German power. Its object is not to improve mutual relations but to oppress Germany. Germany has good reason not to accept such proposals (notes on page 145).

As he noted on page 203 that 'no war can claim justice', Yanagi's pacifism had been clarified through conversation with Scott. On 23 August 1918, Yanagi wrote to Leach in English:

If there is anything to be done for this foolish disastrous war, it must be some spiritual work against the war. I believe, as you know, what England or France requires is a Russell, or a Rolland, or a quaker... You will say that I have no real knowledge about true England, & never been in real war atmosphere and you will say any opinion by such one is superficial and out of sound reason. But I never believe fighters are the only true observers of fighting. No, they fight very often because they have never true observation... I do not do any work concerning the war, simply because it is not so urgent as for your people. But if it becomes so urgent, I must do some spiritual work against the war. This is my position, immovable position.[62]

Scott was not a pacifist who denied every kind of war, but it was true that he was an advocate for peace. What he tried to do was to distinguish a just war from an unjust war and to caution against the pursuit of irrational goals. Therefore, he was critical of excessive Japanese expansionism[63] and suggested the necessity of drawing a sharp line between ardent and true patriotism.[64]

Although Yanagi and Scott differed in their opinions about war and peace, their friendly relations were not broken off as a result. Even after Scott returned to England, their correspondence continued, although not very often. In Yanagi's personal library, there is a pamphlet entitled *The Quaker Bookshelf*, which was presented by Scott in 1921. Moreover in June 1929, when Yanagi stopped in England on his way to the USA, he visited Scott in Idbury and stayed there with him.[65]

CONCLUSION

How did Scott correlate his study on rural problems with his interest in journalism? In his words, 'throughout my life my chief interest has been foreign affairs, with the study of rural life as recreation',[66] and he also said 'for me journalism was . . . "a natural profession"'.[67] When he wrote on foreign affairs, he did so as if he was an agent of the British government. However, on the other hand, Scott wrote:

> The promotion of a better understanding between the West and East . . . can never be done merely by fervent addresses to the East by the West, particularly when these addresses are suddenly arranged for at a time when the West has especial need of the goodwill of the East. The East will begin to listen attentively to the West as soon as the West begins to listen attentively to the East. . . The condition of successful Western preaching to the East is that the West should be as diligent in hearing as in preaching.[68]

Scott even recognized that 'the Japanese justly resent being lectured'.[69]

In his above-mentioned draft letter to Scott written in English, Yanagi criticized Scott for his posture as a preacher and distinguished him from Hearn and Leach, in the following words:

> Very unfortunately, almost all of the foreigners come to Japan with a spirit of preacher. To preach, to teach and even to educate are their first work to do for us, and scarcely live in the inside of our minds with love. . . Most of you, have high self-praised spirit of your civilization, but seldom a love. How can you preach us without

understanding us! Hearn never praised or boasted of his European culture, but simply loved & lived in Japan and finally became himself a Japanese in his spirit as well as nationality. Our Lafcadio never preaches once, that is the very deepest reason that he became the best preacher in Japan in its truest sense. . . Young Leach was loved by all of those who knew him in Japan, for he never preached but showed us his warm study of oriental spirit in his art. At all events, your assumption as to our ignorance of your civilization may be right. Indeed our understanding of European culture and its reality may still be very poor in spite of our more familiarity from our childhood about your civilization, in its spiritual as well as material sides, than you are to our culture. (In this sense we are poor, but you are still poorer.)[70]

It must be noticed that Yanagi wrote this draft letter after he had completed his voluminous book on William Blake who was still underestimated in Britain.

Scott also highly appreciated the attitude of Hearn in his book, saying that 'what mattered was that the mental attitude of Hearn was so largely right. He did not approach Japan as a mere "fact" collector or as a superior person. What he brought to the country was the humble, studious, imaginative, sympathetic attitude; and it was only by men and women of his rare type that people were interpreted one to the other.'[71] But Scott could not take such a posture, especially when he discussed the problems of foreign affairs. In foreign affairs, he was too impatient to avoid preaching. Besides, like his father, he was a man with strong sense of mission. Do these facts not explain why Scott was not loved by the Japanese and is now forgotten, in spite of the fact that he had produced excellent results in the study of Japan's agricultural society?

Lionel Berners Cholmondeley: A Chaplain in Tokyo, 1887-1921

HAMISH ION

> He is known to be a noble man of the Cholmondeley
> Palace in England, but came out to Japan over twenty
> years ago, with plenty of money, to preach
> Christianity. Spending much for that object and also
> for purposes of charity anonymously, his bank
> deposits are understood to be still enormous. One
> day he watched a 'prentice boy steal his watch, but
> would say nothing, and on the following Sunday the
> young thief and other urchins of the neighbourhood
> were treated to the side-shows of Asakusa. Such a
> peculiar man![1]

EVEN IF there was a smack of ridiculousness and caricature
about Lionel Berners Cholmondeley (1858-1945),[2] which
would have passed unnoticed in his native Adlestrop in
Gloucestershire but was evident in Tokyo, many Japanese still
viewed him with favour as a stereotypical English gentleman.[3]
That he was such helped his missionary work as the interest of
many Japanese enquirers in British Anglicanism was intimately
connected to their broader Anglophilia sentiments. Lionel
Cholmondeley first came out to Japan in 1887 under the
auspices of the Society for the Propagation of the Gospel in
Foreign Parts (SPG)[4] to serve as chaplain to Edward Bickersteth,
the first Bishop of South Tokyo, and to become a founding
member of St Andrew's Mission and its celibate Missionary
Brotherhood.[5] To the SPG, it was a necessary Christian duty to
provide for the needs of Anglicans abroad as well as to convert
non-Christians to Christianity. From the late 1880s until his

retirement in 1921, Cholmondeley's activities reflected this dual SPG concern.[6] He and his colleagues at St Andrew's Mission House in Shiba, Tokyo were part of the gel that helped to hold the British community together.[7] As well as being chaplain to successive Bishops of South Tokyo, Cholmondeley taught during the 1890s at the Senmon Gakko (later Waseda University), served for most of his career as priest-in-charge of St Barnabas' Church, Ushigome, Tokyo, and engaged in literary work, both Christian and historical. He was responsible for opening Anglican work in the Bonin Islands and is best-known for his history of the original English-speaking settlers of those islands.[8] Importantly, in 1902 Cholmondeley succeeded Archdeacon A.C. Shaw as honorary chaplain of the British legation in Japan. This latter post, which he took seriously, allowed him entry to the private world of British diplomats in Tokyo.

In exploring Cholmondeley's work and life in Japan, one is investigating the personalized foundations of Anglo-Japanese goodwill. Cholmondeley himself was clearly one of the myriad lesser names in Anglo-Japanese relations, but he had friends who were greater names. Indeed, one of the attractions of looking at Cholmondeley is that his experience gives the opportunity to investigate the links between Britain and Japan at a different level from those provided by important diplomats, government officials or cross-cultural icons. The views revealed in his published writings and letters to friends reveal a strong sympathy for Japan and the Japanese of the Meiji era, but a growing disenchantment with the modern Japan and the Westernized Japanese of the Taisho period. While Cholmondeley's increasing dissatisfaction with the new Japan was evident after the Russo-Japanese War, it was the Great War which proved to be a watershed in terms of his changed attitude. Always conscious that Japan's actions reflected upon Britain's reputation as a result of the Anglo-Japanese Alliance, he firmly believed that Japan had not been wholehearted in her support of Britain during World War I. The feeling that Britain was let down by Japan during the war was not the only reason for his changed feelings. There were others, not the least of them being that he felt modern Taisho Japan was destroying the good manners and ordered hierarchical society (reminiscent of home) that had first attracted him to Japan in the late 1880s. Just as the Cotswold world or the rural gentry into which he had been born was fast disappearing under pressure from industrialized and urbanized England, a similar

181

phenomenon was changing Taisho Japan. Importantly, however, this nostalgia for a disappeared Japan and its conservative values reflected not only his own upper-class prejudices but also mirrored the changing view of Japan held by the other old Japan hands of his generation.

Cholmondeley's growing unease with Japan and Anglo-Japanese relations largely parallel both the changing fortunes of his own missionary work among the Japanese and his increasing disquiet about the state of Christianity in Japan. Cholmondeley held strong views about the nature of Christianity in Japan, and the religious policies of the Japanese government. The decline of British influence in the religious sphere, as illustrated in microcosm by Cholmondeley's example, can be taken as a harbinger of a broader decline of overall British influence in Japan during the last years of the Anglo-Japanese Alliance. Owing to space, however, this paper will concentrate on Cholmondeley's missionary work.

TOKYO MISSION

In his first years as a missionary, like many others before and after him, Cholmondeley did much teaching of English. During the 1890s, he taught at the English Night School attached to St Andrew's Mission, and also at the Senmon Gakko (later Waseda University).[9] Central to his missionary activities, however, was St Barnabas' Church, Ushigome, which Cholmondeley built in 1897.[10] He served as priest-in-charge at St Barnabas' from then until he retired from Japan in 1921. Many of the congregation were associated with the Senmon Gakko, and there was a steady flow of young Japanese students and friends visiting him at his Japanese house close to the church.[11] He was acutely aware that some of them simply wanted to meet him out of curiosity or for English practice. In an occupation which required a thick skin, Cholmondeley was remarkably thin-skinned. However, fortunately, he was ably assisted at the church by an SPG woman missionary, Susan Ballard, whose brother was a vice-admiral. He was further helped by Japanese church wardens elected from the congregation. Among these was Philip Hatoyama [Hatoyama Hideo (1884-1946)], the younger brother of Hatoyama Ichiro (1883-1959), the post-war prime minister. Cholmondeley's initial connection with Hatoyama Hideo was through his father, Hatoyama Kazuo (1856-1911), the Principal of the Senmon Gakko.[12] Another important church warden was Saeki

Yoshio (1871–1965), who had studied at Toronto University and became an authority on Nestorian relics in China.[13] Both Hatoyama and Saeki could speak English fluently. Cholmondeley's diaries reveal that, other than Hatoyama and Saeki, he had two other main Japanese friends, Joseph Gonzales, the priest-in-charge of St George's, Chichijima, Bonin Islands, and John Imai [Imai Toshimichi (Judo)], the senior Japanese priest in the South Tokyo diocese. For those missionaries who were not particularly fluent in Japanese,[14] the Japanese Christian worker or clergyman served as a bridge between the missionary, remote in his Western way of life, and Japanese society. Indeed, the success of a missionary often depended on having talented Japanese assistants. This was certainly true in the case of Cholmondeley at St Barnabas'.

By 1914 St Barnabas' was beginning to decline. This cannot be ascribed to any single factor, such as Cholmondeley's deafness, as after his return to England in 1921 he served over ten years as the vicar of a Gloucestershire country parish.[15] During his last decade in Japan, nevertheless, it was evident that he frequently missed attending Sunday services at St Barnabas' and left the Japanese catechist to conduct them. Cholmondeley had difficulty in keeping Japanese catechists for any length of time. In its turn, this was largely because he did not give enough direction to church administration. Plainly, his own enthusiasm for St Barnabas' was also waning, and undoubtedly this was a result of the church's decline and also a contributory factor to its growing weakness.

BONIN MISSION

As well as St Barnabas', Cholmondeley was also responsible for the building of St George's, Chichijima, Bonin [Ogasawara] Islands.[16] He had a particular affection for the Bonin Islands which he first visited in 1893, and regularly visited them from then on. In explaining why the SPG began missionary work in a group of little islands some five hundred miles off the Japanese mainland, Cholmondeley wrote in 1907:

> When on an island belonging to Japan there are found to be among the Japanese inhabitants some families, descended from settlers of former days, who are of western extraction, speak English and are professedly Christian, such an island would make an immediate claim upon us; and these were the peculiar circumstances that led to a link being established between the Bonin Islands and ourselves.[17]

Fittingly, Joseph Gonzales (1870-1943), the priest-in-charge of St George's, was a member on his paternal side of a Portuguese settler family which had come to Chichijima in 1831, and his mother was the eldest daughter of Nathaniel Savory, the first white settler.[18] Cholmondeley thought highly of Gonzales, and had helped to train him as a priest at St Andrew's in Tokyo. As well as his parish duties, Gonzales also ran a small English mission school. Teaching English and Christianity went hand-in-hand together, even in the Bonin Islands. Most of the third generation of English-speaking settlers, including Gonzales himself, however, married Japanese wives and were assimilating into the ethnic Japanese population. Indeed, Cholmondeley noted in his history of the Bonin Islands that 'the children of such marriages are hardly distinguishable from the Japanese' and were educated at the Japanese elementary school.[19] Despite this, his concern with the Bonin Islands and its English-speaking settler families reflected a nostalgia for a pure and innocent time before the arrival of the modernized Japanese. In that sense, Cholmondeley found escape from the modern face of Japan in the remnants of a more convivial past still evident in the remote Bonin Islands. Similarly, Walter Weston, the Church Missionary Society missionary who popularized mountain climbing as a leisure sport in Japan, discovered in the high valleys between the peaks of the Japan Alps a hardy unspoilt people who still kept to a traditional way of life and value system which no longer existed among the masses of modern urbanized Japanese. Likewise, Archdeacon John Batchelor in Hokkaido studied the dying language and culture of the Ainu which was threatened with extinction. All three missionaries were chronicling disappearing societies.[20]

While the literary output was not large, Cholmondeley wrote, as well as his history of the Bonin Islands, a number of shorter articles on Christianity in Japan and his strong views have attracted some attention from Japanese Anglican historians.[21] Indeed, Professor Tsukada Osamu has argued that one important legacy of the attitude of British High Anglican missionaries, including Cholmondeley, towards the Japanese state was the ready acceptance of *tennosei* by Japanese Anglicans.[22] Certainly, it is clear that the SPG missionaries thought that Japanese Anglicans should give to the Meiji Emperor the same respect which British Anglicans gave to the British monarch. What the missionaries did not foresee or fully appreciate was that cultural differences between Britons and Japanese were such that this British view would lead many later Japanese Anglicans to accept uncritically the cult of the Emperor system. Be that as it may, Cholmondeley did show a deep concern about the deliberate fabrication of falsehoods by Japanese concerning their traditional values as it applied to religion. This was especially true in the years immediately following Japan's victory in the Russo-Japanese War. Cholmondeley, not without some self-interest as he did not want to see any decline in British support for the SPG mission in Japan, was particularly worried about the vogue for things Japanese which gripped Britain after 1905. He was concerned that this would lead to ready British acceptance of the idea, propounded by the American-educated Japanese Quaker, Nitobe Inazo, that bushido was the soul of Japan.[23] The *South Tokyo Diocesan News*, which Cholmondeley edited, contained articles by Saeki Yoshio and Imai Toshimichi that underlined the limitations of bushido and stressed the need for it to be transformed by interaction with Christianity in order to be meaningful in the New Japan.[24] So important was this issue that Imai expanded his ideas into a book *Bushido in the Past and in the Present.*[25]

Cholmondeley's disenchantment with new religious developments in Japan went beyond the bushido debate. In June 1913, in a letter to Sir Ernest Satow, he noted that for the Japanese, 'Christianity must be a Japanese Christianity, Christianity must not supersede but must find a modus vivendi with Shintoism, Confucianism and Buddhism.'[26] In 1914, in a perceptive survey of Japan's attitudes towards Christianity, Cholmondeley noted that paradoxically 'Japan has rejected Christianity while saying too that Christianity is making wonderful progress among the Japanese people.'[27] By this time, Cholmondeley had correctly come to the conclusion that Japan was not going to embrace Christianity, a reality which he believed that many missionaries and their supporting societies still had not yet accepted. The reason for the failure of Christianity in Japan was not, in his opinion, because the Japanese people were particularly adverse to the Christian message but rather a result of deliberate policy by the Japanese government which played on the fact that the Japanese people 'have been content that the men at the top should understand and know what ought to be done'.[28] When it suited the government, according to Cholmondeley, it was quite prepared to take advantage of Christianity and Christian missionaries. During the early Meiji period, he noted that Japan had recognized in missionaries ' a force of voluntary workers, all anxious to court her good will, whom she could turn to account as powerful assistants in promoting the cause of Western civilization', but it was also true, Cholmondeley contended, that 'Japan had, nevertheless, implicit trust in the patriotism of her people; and, whatever line she might eventually determine to take on the question of religion, counted on the people's obediently following her directions'.[29] Moreover, he believed that Japan had granted religious tolerance only to gain kudos from civilized nations, and that Japan's 'non-Christianity became rather a source of pride to her than otherwise, and this pride her subsequent alliance with England did much to increase'.[30] However, what was even more disagreeable for Cholmondeley was that 'Japan not only continued resolutely non-Christian, but had been determining, even before the war with Russia, to put forth a religion of her own. That she had a religion of her own she was fully persuaded. To discover it, and bring other nations to the respectful recognition of it, in return for the due respect she on her side was prepared to accord to Christianity, became one of her chief endeavours.'[31] This was exceptionally difficult, in Cholmondeley's opinion, because he believed that Buddhism and Confucianism had been the primary religious and moral influences on traditional Japan, and neither of these were of Japanese origin. There was, however, Shintoism, which he considered 'the vaguest and most indefinite of cults, which had become inextricably entangled with Buddhism as far as its religious rites and ceremonies were concerned. It had, however, the required merit of being indigenous'.[32] He went on to speak of 'the revival of Shintoism, with Bushido as its helpmeet [sic], to which the energies on the part of the Japanese authorities were from this time directed. Results manifested themselves in the extravagant development of Emperor worship, in newly encouraged reverence for Shinto shrines, and in elaborate festivals in commemoration of national heroes and of the soldiers who had fallen in the wars'.[33] In his dislike of the development of Emperor worship, it is important to stress that Cholmondeley's ideas resonated with similar ideas expressed by Basil Hall Chamberlain in his classic diatribe, *The Invention of a New Religion*.[34] In that sense, Cholmondeley was expressing ideas which reflected a growing dissatisfaction with trends in Modern Japan which other old Japan hands clearly also held.

EMBASSY CHAPLAIN

Cholmondeley's major connection with other old Japan hands came from his ties with the British legation. From 1902, in addition to his missionary responsibilities, Cholmondeley also served as honorary chaplain to the British legation (later embassy) in Tokyo which brought him into close contact with the private world of British diplomats and the public world of Japanese official receptions. Part of his relationship with the embassy was of the baptism and burial variety; he was called upon, for instance, to baptize successive generations of Piggotts[35] and, as early as 1894, was present when Hugh Fraser, the then British minister, died.[36] Yet, Cholmondeley's friendship with other diplomats went deeper. Cholmondeley had a somewhat adversarial relationship with Sir Claude Macdonald, who was responsible for his appointment as chaplain[37] and also a fellow graduate of Uppingham School.[38] He was particularly fond of Sir Conyngham Greene, his wife and daughters. As well as ministers and ambassadors, Cholmondeley was friends with many of the more junior members of the embassy staff. Among these was Sir Harold Parlett,[39] who remained his lifelong friend, Everard Calthrop,[40] the military attaché who died tragically young in the Great War, as well as Hobart Hampden, J.H. Gubbins, Robert Clive and their families. He was friendly also with George Sansom, when Sansom first came out to Japan as a student interpreter in 1904. The most intriguing of Cholmondeley's diplomatic friendships, however, was undoubtedly with Sir Ernest Satow,[41] whom Cholmondeley very much revered.[42] Their friendship was cemented between mid-August and mid-September 1896 when Cholmondeley, Parlett and, for a few days, Isabella Bird Bishop spent at Tozawa, Satow's newly built summer cottage on Lake Chuzenji.[43] In later years, after Satow had left Japan, Cholmondeley corresponded with him and kept him informed about happenings in Japan. Cholmondeley also kept an eye on Satow's Japanese family.[44] There was a quid pro quo for this, Satow's support for missionary work in the South Tokyo Diocese.[45]

While he had already expressed misgivings about the Japanese on religious issues before 1914, World War I greatly altered Cholmondeley's overall attitude towards Japan. His suspicions about the motives behind the Japanese government's religious policies clearly extended also to Japan's attitude towards the war against the Central Powers. Initially, the beginning of the war marked a high point in Cholmondeley's feelings of pride in the Anglo-Japanese Alliance and good feeling towards the Japanese. He shared Satow's enthusiasm for Japan's declaration of war. In October 1914, Satow pugnaciously wrote about the ongoing Tsingtao campaign in China that 'if I had still been in Peking I would have sent every man of the Legation guard and the whole of the troops at Tientsin and on the railway to join in the attack!' and added: 'how brilliantly the chivalrous Japanese way of fighting distinguishes itself from the mean and shabby way in which the Germans bombard towns and cities full of non combatants without giving them a chance of escape'.[46] Satow even wished that he was back in Tokyo, stating that 'I wish I were in command of the British Legation at Tokio now. How many Japanese between 1895 and 1900 talked to me of their desire to see an alliance between England and Japan and I had nothing to offer them'.[47] While Satow might remain positive, Cholmondeley's sense of isolation from Britain during a desperate time, the deep sorrow he felt over the loss of relatives and friends in battle, all contributed to heighten a very strong feeling that the Japanese were only lukewarm allies. He spent his spare time rolling bandages for those bleeding in Flanders. Conscious of his own feeble efforts to help the war effort, Cholmondeley was increasingly aware, especially after the Battle of the Somme, that the Japanese military were becoming more pro-German despite the Anglo-Japanese Alliance. In August 1919, writing to Joseph Gonzales, Cholmondeley bitterly noted that 'it is a fine thing for the Japanese that they have been the allies of England. They were not very proud of being so while the war was in progress'.[48] In sharp contrast to Cholmondeley who did not want Japan rewarded by mandates from the League of Nations, Satow took a more charitable view. The former diplomat thought that Japan 'helped us so much in our naval operations in different parts of the world that we were obliged to do something for her in return' and so deserved to hold onto the German concessions in Shantung.

It was perhaps fortunate that Cholmondeley did not remain in Japan for long after the Treaty of Versailles. He had spent over thirty years working in Japan, a period which had seen the rise and wane of the Anglo-Japanese Alliance. During these years, Japan and her society had changed profoundly. In his opinion, clearly for the worse. After leaving Japan in 1921, Cholmondeley remained in touch with events through letters, from among others, Hugh Byas, the longtime Japan correspondent of both the London and the New York *Times*. In August 1932, at the end of a long letter Byas noted:

> Have you read Sansom's History? I confess I take up any Japanese history with some reluctance, but I have found Sansom's astonishingly interesting. The more one gets into it the better it becomes. What a pity Parlett has evaded the temptation to write a book. It is not too late. You should set him on to it. The age he knew in Japan is rapidly becoming a thing of the past. I am afraid that applies to the 'age' of all of us who are Victorians. The world is rushing into something new. No doubt it will be better but I have no great desire to hasten it.[49]

Indeed, for Cholmondeley also, the world of late Meiji Japan that he knew had long since become a thing of the past.

14

Richard Ponsonby-Fane: A Modern Scholarly William Adams

DOROTHY BRITTON

SURPRISINGLY LITTLE seems to be generally known nowadays about this remarkably industrious and talented scholar/eccentric who visited Japan in 1901 and shortly thereafter made that country his second home. A prodigious writer, Richard Ponsonby-Fane, 1878-1937, left enough published works to assure himself, one would think, a noteworthy place in the history of Anglo-Japanese relations but, strangely, his name is hard to find in encyclopaedias or bibliographies.

The mark he made – and it was considerable – was in people's hearts. And not just ordinary people. Prominent Japanese and members of the nobility. The impression he made on them of a fine English nobleman with a deep admiration for their own country would stay with them all their lives, warming their hearts, and sowing true seeds of Anglo-Japanese friendship, ephemeral though this necessarily was. It is high time that we remembered him.

He was an immensely modest and private man, who, as his Japan-based bosom-friend, Dr Thomas Baty, writes, 'disliked all invasions of privacy'.[1] Ponsonby-Fane would no doubt have felt with Virginia Woolf that 'Better was it to go unknown and leave behind and you an arch, a potting shed, a wall where peaches ripen, than to burn like a meteor and leave no dust.'[2] He left, indeed, a wall where peaches ripen in Somerset, England. And in Japan, he left a beautiful Japanese garden where plum-trees blossom, and a house exquisitely wrought in pure, authentic Japanese style.

Japanese circles knew him as an English teacher of influence

190

and renown, as well as a respected lecturer in fluent Japanese on Japanese institutions and culture to prestigious organizations such as the Meiji-Japan society – a considerable achievement. To be able to lecture and write articles in Japanese as well as carry on correspondence in that language is no mean feat, especially in those days, when foreigners mastering that difficult language were few and far between indeed. The late Sir John Pilcher once referred to him as 'a modern scholarly William Adams'.[3] In many ways he did resemble his seventeenth-century predecessor – the first Englishman in Japan. Like Adams, he paid the Japanese people the compliment of unreservedly adopting their life-style, and revelling in it.

The Japanese seem never to have quite recovered from the shock of finding themselves and their seventeenth-century culture suddenly thrust into a nineteenth-century world. Therefore, they seem to thrive on any reassurance that people from Western nations find their native culture and life-style worth emulating and not horribly primitive and out-of-date.

It is hard to believe in this day and age, when Japan leads the world in so many spheres; but only this year, the editor of a bi-weekly comic-strip magazine aimed at business people and housewives over 30, is quoted in an interview in *The Japan Times*[4] as saying: 'I think many Japanese are ashamed of being Japanese and think Japanese culture is *dasai*' – a disparaging modern slang word meaning 'un-cool'. He went on to say: 'We are all too ignorant of the wonderful culture of our country and discard it without knowing much about it.'

His magazine features a popular comic strip character – a Westerner who speaks flawless Japanese – complete with honorifics – dresses in kimono when at home, is a dab hand at cooking traditional Japanese food, and, a lover of the old Japanese crafts, tries to encourage dispirited craftsmen while at the same time doing his utmost to inspire the disaffected youth of today to appreciate the beauty and worth of Japanese arts of yore.

One could almost say the character was a modern proletariat remake of Ponsonby except that Ponsonby went one better and not only wore kimono at home, but all the time when in Japan, except, appropriately, for his infrequent visits to the British Embassy. When in Rome he did as the Romans did, but the embassy, after all, was British soil. He also changed into Western clothes when he went back to England, but not until he neared its shores, since he always travelled in Japanese ships. As I remember, John Pilcher said the sartorial change-over took place around Port Said.

When, as the representative of the Japan Society of London, Ponsonby was invited to stand in front of the Kenrei Gate of the Imperial Palace in Kyoto for the Enthronement ceremony of Emperor Showa, he insisted on wearing Japanese formal dress, against instructions. Aida Yūji, Professor Emeritus of Kyoto University, recalls that his former Kyoto First Middle School teacher retorted: 'It's scandalous for *montsuki* and *hakama* not to be considered sufficiently formal. I shall certainly go in mine.' Aida relates that, when the Imperial procession came in sight, Ponsonby made his way through the crowd to the front row, took off his *geta* and prostrated himself, with his forehead on the wooden clogs. Bystanders were so amazed at the action of the very conspicuous six-foot, bearded Caucasian that he became known as the English Takayama Hikokurō, a legendary samurai famous for his extreme loyalty to the emperor.[5]

Ponsonby was disappointed in the apparel of most of the other guests: 'Some two thousand citizens of the Empire were gathered in the Shishin-den and Nan-yen, and the great majority were in western uniforms. I confess I should like to see them all arrayed in national robes, preferably in the fashions of Heian; but if that is impossible, then in the dignified *hakama* and *mondzuki* of today.'[6]

FAMILY

Richard Ponsonby-Fane was an English aristocrat of highly noble lineage. Ponsonby was the family name of the Earls of Bessborough and, when Richard's great grandmother, Lady Maria Fane, daughter of the 10th Earl of Westmorland, married Richard's great-grandfather, the 4th Earl of Bessborough (whose family name was Ponsonby), their son Spencer (Richard's grandfather) eventually became the Right Honourable Sir Spencer Ponsonby-Fane. This caused someone in the pavilion at Lords, London's famous cricket ground (whose foundation-stone Spencer, in fact, had laid) to quip, in rhyme:

> He who (why I can't explain)
> To the honourable name of Ponsonby,
> Has added that of Fane.[7]

It is the Fanes who provided Richard with his English 'arch and potting shed, and wall where peaches ripen'.

Francis Fane, brother of the 8th Earl of Westmorland, was a

prosperous barrister and a member of parliament. It was Francis who bought, in 1731, the spacious Somerset estate called Brympton d'Evercy. In his book on Somerset, Arthur Mee called it 'Paradise':

> We ride through a long oak avenue and come by a drive lined with shrubs to this little paradise, which breaks upon us suddenly so that we feel we have seen nothing quite like it. We turn a corner and, lo, there is something not of the everyday world. It is one of the surprises of Somerset, unexpected and unforgettable, a group of buildings round a green forecourt, stables, church, dower house, and the manor house itself, one of the most beautiful of Somerset's country homes. This great house, with its exquisite Tudor front, sculptured and battlemented and 130 feet long, is England as she was, quiet and far away and something like a dream. Its grey-gold walls are set in a lovely park with grand old yews and a lake like a mirror for all the beauty round about.

One approaches it from Yeovil through T.S. Eliot country where 'Now the light falls/Across the open field, leaving the deep lane/Shuttered with branches, dark in the afternoon,/Where you lean against a bank while a van passes. . . .'[8]

It was not until Richard Ponsonby inherited Brympton d'Evercy that he added Fane to his name. Richard Arthur Brabazon Ponsonby was born on 8 January 1878, to John, son of Sir Spencer Ponsonby-Fane, at Gravesend. John was presumably residing at the then fashionable Thames estuary yachting resort on the outskirts of London on account of his poor health, which the boy unfortunately inherited. John had married Florence Farquhar, daughter of a wealthy banker; and ailing father and son often sailed together in the Farquhar steam yacht, the *Wakasa Maru*, which had been bought from the Japanese. Its bell, inscribed 'Tokio, 1897' hangs at Brympton, to be rung by visitors. The family kept the bell when the ship was requisitioned by the War Office at the time of World War I, when its name was changed to HMS *Albert*. It was sunk off Liverpool.[9] Later, visiting from Japan, Richard sometimes joined his Farquhar relatives in cruises to European ports in their second yacht, the *Medusa*. The *Wakasa Maru* must have been Richard's first and prophetic acquaintance with Japan. How little did he know then how many ships he would be travelling in with names ending in 'Maru'.

In September 1889 Ponsonby entered St Neot's preparatory

school which was near the Farquhars' Thames-side residence in Sunningdale, where he stayed during his many bouts of bronchitis. His studiousness, excellent memory, and aptitude for writing and mathematics kept him from lagging behind in his studies, and he entered Harrow in 1891, placed in the special care of the headmaster, with whom he lodged. Richard suffered from so many bronchial attacks that he had to leave Harrow when he was 16. But not before having distinguished himself at cricket. Cricket was a great family tradition, and it was his paternal grandfather, Sir Spencer, who had founded, on 4 July 1845, the still famous and most prestigious of wandering amateur cricket clubs in England called 'I Zingari' (The Gypsies).[10]

Doctors recommended sea travel for young Richard, as they often did in those days, and so Ponsonby began the first of his many long sea voyages by travelling to Australia in 1894 whence he returned in a sailing vessel. In later years he once totted up all his sea trips and they came to a total of 600,000 nautical miles![11]

On his return from Australia, he spent the winter in Cannes, Madeira, and the Canary Islands. It was obvious to his family that he must avoid the English climate, so positions were found for him as private secretary to governor generals in various parts of the British Empire. His first posting was to Natal, in South Africa, where he went in 1896. From there he moved to Trinidad in 1898, after wintering in New Zealand, and then he moved on to Ceylon in 1900.

It was in August, 1901, that Ponsonby first set eyes on the island kingdom which he would find to be his perfect spiritual home. He had not been well while in Ceylon, and had taken a trip to Hong Kong and Japan, hoping the change would improve his health. There is no record of his first impressions.

After a furlough in England from June to October the following year, he decided to leave Ceylon that December and take up an appointment in 1903 as Private Secretary to the Governor of Hong Kong. That July, he visited Taiwan, as well as Japan, and he continued to visit the latter every summer thereafter for the next three years.

He made many Japanese friends while in Hong Kong, especially Mihara Shigeyoshi of NYK, Japan's leading steamship company, and he also found himself teachers of the Japanese language, with whom he studied assiduously, even committing to his phenomenal memory the *Kojiki* and *Nihon Shoki*. One outstanding teacher was Sano Yoshitsugu, 'a samurai of Mito', who had been General F.S.G. Piggott's teacher when he was a language officer in Tokyo in 1904. 'Sano', writes Piggott, 'had decided to seek his fortune abroad, and accompanied me to Hong Kong, where he earned a living teaching Japanese to officers of the garrison. He was subsequently employed by the governor's private secretary, Richard Ponsonby, who was anxious to learn Japanese; Sano eventually accompanied him to England, and later to Natal and the Fiji Islands. One result of Ponsonby's long association with Sano was a series of scholarly articles on the history of the Japanese Dynasty, and on Shinto Shrines.'[12]

Ponsonby-Fane's second posting to Natal was in 1907. He went to Fiji in 1910 and during his tour of duty accompanied the governor to the Solomon Islands and the New Hebrides. After two more visits to Taiwan and Japan, he returned to Hong Kong in 1915.

It was in December, 1915, the year of the enthronement of Japan's 122nd sovereign, Emperor Taisho, that the Kobe Chronicle Press brought out his possibly most interesting opus, 'The Imperial Family of Japan'.[13]

He spent the next four years in Hong Kong, where, besides being private secretary to the governor once more, he donated his services to Hong Kong University as honorary lecturer in English and history from December to March each year. He went on lecturing there, while wintering in Hong Kong's milder climate, until 1926, although in 1919 he had relinquished his colonial government post and taken up permanent residence in Japan. The University rewarded him for his work with an honorary Doctor of Laws degree.

Ponsonby refused to accept remuneration for any of his writing, lecturing or teaching – and no doubt his colonial, work too. His private means must have been substantial enough for him to consider it wrong to do so. Some have assumed Brympton provided an income,[14] but the estate was beset with financial difficulties. It was leased to Clare School from 1959 to 1974, and finally had to be sold in 1993.

Dr Thomas Baty writes of Ponsonby's generosity: 'The way in which he put his great resources, in the quietest and most delicate fashion, at the services of those in whose careers he took an interest, was a lesson in philanthropy. There must be not a few of the younger generation in Japan who have cause to regard him as the architect of their fortunes.'[15]

He was now Dr Richard Ponsonby-Fane. In quick succession, the ownership of the estate of Brympton d'Evercy had become his in 1916, when his frail father, John, died only eight months after inheriting the property from the redoubtable and venerable Right Honourable Sir Spencer Ponsonby-Fane, aged 91.

But Richard had no intention of hurrying home to claim his inheritance and set up housekeeping there, although he loved the beautiful estate set amid the green rolling hills and apple orchards of England's lovely west country. Seldom had there been a year when he had not visited it for a game of family cricket and to see his beloved sister and aunt. He planned to do so regularly in future, and in the meantime the property was safe in the capable hands of his sister Violet and her husband Edward Clive. Just the place to bring up their three-year-old son Nicholas. What was more, Violet was an expert landscape gardener and revelled in the idea of carrying on the loving care that had been put into Brympton's gardens by the remarkable Lady Georgiana Fane. these gardens are in great part the glory of this gem of an English stately home. It was she who created the delightful pond in front of the house, later embellished by Ponsonby-Fane's addition of a handsome, large stone lantern from Japan.

Georgiana was the daughter of John Fane, 10th Earl of Westmorland and his second wife with whom he did not get on, and she and her mother had been encouraged to live by themselves at Brympton. Georgiana never married. When her father, the earl, was Viceroy of Ireland, Georgiana had lost her heart to his ADC, but had not been allowed to marry the 'lowly subaltern' – who, the story goes, went on to distinguish himself and become the Duke of Wellington! But it was lucky for Brympton that the love-lorn girl had to sublimate her home-making talents. The last owner, Richard's great-nephew Charles writes: 'Everything of beauty and good taste that the family now owns originates from this time. Pictures, jewellery, furniture, even the marble fireplaces, and most of the formal layout of the gardens. She planted thousands of oak trees round the estate.'[16]

Georgiana had eventually inherited Brympton, and when she died, had left it to Spencer, her nephew and godson. He had never seen Brympton before inheriting it at the age of 51 in 1875, but was so taken with its charm that he lived mainly there for the remaining four decades of his long life.

It was during those years that young Richard used to visit his grandfather – the famous founder of I Zingari – never failing, if at all possible, even when living abroad, to show up in August for Brympton Cricket Week to keep wicket in the family XI, consisting of 10 Ponsonbys and the butler. It is said that Richard used to stop the ball with his shins, refusing to wear pads because he maintained they got in his way. He did his best to encourage his Japanese students to take up the game, especially if they were studying at Oxford or Cambridge, and one of them Hachiuma Senzō, apparently showed so much promise that he might well have succeeded in popularizing the game in Japan had World War II not intervened.[17]

Ponsonby was 38 when he inherited Brympton d'Evercy. He kept it for 16 years, visiting often from Japan, happy that his sister and brother-in-law, Violet and Edward Clive, were living there. He watched with interest their son Nicholas grow up, and liked what he saw. In 1932, when Nicholas was 19, he decided to make ownership of the estate over to him. Ponsonby had no intention of ever marrying and producing an heir. He was what was called in those days a 'confirmed bachelor'. He was also something of a misogynist. '"Cherchez la femme"', he writes, 'is an idea that instantly springs to the mind when the affairs of man are seen to have gone awry, for there can be no doubt that woman has played and will continue to play an important part in the downfall of man.'[18] One reason for his feeling so comfortable in Japan may have been the absence in that country of a Western-type social life with its constant partying and pressure on young men and women to marry, as well as the fact that homosexuality has never been considered a sin there or looked upon askance.

RESIDENCE IN JAPAN

Ponsonby found Japan utterly congenial when he made his home there in 1919. The main reason seems to be that it appealed to his extremely reactionary disposition, which he admits himself. He was outrageously old-fashioned, and disliked everything modern. He hated concrete buildings, telephones, radios, trams, trains, and even electric lights.

He firmly believed in Shakespeare's 'divinity that doth hedge a king'. He writes: 'I myself am a most pronounced royalist; I belong indeed to that now obsolete body of people who hold to the doctrine of the divine right of kings. It is indeed a pleasure to come to a country whose people have never doubted that their sovereign ruled by the will of heaven.'[19] He expressed his fervent thoughts on this subject in his address in Japanese at the annual general meeting of the *Meiji Seitoku Kinen Gakkai* (literally 'Learned society commemorating the Meiji virtues'), whose English name was the Japan Meiji Society. His talk was entitled 'Sovereign and Subject', and the gist of it was later incorporated in '*Tōgū Rinri Goshinkō Roku*', a collection of lectures on ethics given before Crown Prince Hirohito by his tutor Sugiura Jūkō. An article based on Ponsonby-Fane's English notes for the talk appears in his collected works.

Not only was he a royalist, but he disliked the conception of 'government of the people, by the people'. He contributed an article in English entitled 'The Fallacy of Democracy' to Volume 20, No. 6 of the Japanese publication *Rekishi to Chiri* (History and Geography). It begins with the doctrine of the divine right of kings, and concludes by deploring the fact that 'the governing power the world over is passing out of the hands of those who have the real welfare of their country at heart and whose position and training fit them to govern into the hands of the ignorant and self-seeking mob'. He concludes with the hope 'that in Japan at any rate there may be one corner of the world which is *free from* democracy'. (his italics)[20]

He also believed in empire, and the benevolent and wise rule of countries not yet able to govern themselves. Having spent over 20 years connected with the administration of the British colonies, he was in a position to judge and, while he felt that for the most part Britain was a good coloniser, he came to the conclusion after visiting Korea in 1920 that Japan was even better. Anxious, therefore, to refute the very adverse criticisms expressed by many Western residents of Korea, especially missionaries, he sent an article to the *Japan Advertiser*. He admitted that he does not consider the Japanese administration to be perfect, but said he had yet to meet one that was. Hong Kong had seemed to him at first eminently successful, but even it, too, was unjust.[21]

Ponsonby-Fane is shrewd in his grasp of self-respect as the key to successful colonization. The first essential, he felt, was that all classes of the population should be made and kept contented, and he had come to the conclusion that he would rather be a Korean under Japanese rule than an Indian under Great Britain or a Zulu or Kafir under South Africa. He was convinced that, since the reorganization by Governor General Baron Saitō, there was absolute equality between Japanese and Koreans. Koreans, for instance, were eligible to join social clubs and mix in society. 'Anyone who knows India at all', he wrote, 'knows the very strong feelings that the average Anglo-Indian has on this point.' However, he does admit that in Korea not all public baths were open to both peoples!

The *Kobe Chronicle* published an article in which he discussed the eligibility for independence of three countries where independence movements were afoot – the Philippines from the USA, India from Britain, and Korea from Japan. His conclusions regarding the first two have been borne out – namely that the Philippines would lose their considerable US-funded prosperity, and that independence in India 'with its many races, castes and creeds, . . . would result in anarchy' owing to 'the conflicting desires of the various sections of the population'. There is no denying his claim that 'it was only the sovereignty of Great Britain that rendered a united India possible', although his further claim might be open to contention – that a united India was necessary for the welfare of the world.[22]

What Richard Ponsonby particularly deplored was the habit outsiders had of advocating and supporting movements of independence, and urged them to confine themselves to 'pointing out necessary reforms and exposing cases of properly authenticated misgovernment'. This advice was presumably not only directed towards those carping foreign missionaries in Korea, but also to the Japanese themselves for the bitter criticisms of British rule in India expressed in the Japanese *Asian Review*, to which Ponsonby first submitted his article, and which refused to print it unless he altered his implications that even the Japanese were not above criticism in their colonial policy![23]

This apologist for Japan was surely too intelligent and well-travelled to be completely blinded by their pre-war propaganda as some have contended. According to Baty, 'He was by no means easy to delude'. Ponsonby himself writes:

> I do not pretend that there have not been incidents, particularly in Chosen, where a mistaken and over severe policy was pursued, but such incidents have been magnified out of all reason, and could, moreover, easily be paralleled in the annals of the Colonies of every nation, whether eastern or western. For myself I long ago decided that, provided I was a law abiding citizen, I would as soon be

under the domination of Japan as of any country in the world, but if I were an evil doer or 'disaffected' I would prefer to go elsewhere, and that quickly, but the punishment of the malefactor is one of the duties of a Government.[24]

Well-travelled he most certainly was. The habit of getting away for the sake of his health was ingrained in him from an early age, and hardly a year passed that he did not take a sea-voyage somewhere. One of the few he wrote about was a trip to the Japanese Pacific Mandated islands, which he describes in one of the series of articles he wrote for the NYK's *Travel Bulletin*.[25] What interested him there were Japan's colonial methods, a subject on which he felt himself qualified to write. His personal impressions are always a good read, but they are few, since it was a form of writing he disliked. He begins, 'My Reflections of the Recent Enthronement' with the disclaimer that, 'Dryasdust historical details are more in my line than impressions.'[26]

Unfortunately, most of his writings might well have been written by the imaginary Dr Dryasdust, the dull, laborious antiquary and historian to whom Sir Walter Scott dedicated novels. It is a great pity, for Ponsonby amassed with almost superhuman industry a tremendous wealth of valuable material on the Shinto Shrines, Imperial mausolea, Imperial Family, as well as many important historical personages, and accounts of famous campaigns. His research must surely still be definitive, and the facts are there in minute detail, but in a form that is for the most part reader-unfriendly. One feels he was working against time to get it all down. One hopes that perhaps one day someone will feel the urge to edit his extraordinary oeuvre.[27]

Admittedly, most of his writings were papers published in the transactions of learned bodies such as The Japan Society of London, The Asiatic Society of Japan, The Meiji Japan Society, and the Royal Anthropological Institute, so perhaps he did not deem readability necessary. But one might have expected a lighter touch in his articles on Shinto Shrines contributed regularly to the NYK monthly magazine *Travel Bulletin*, but alas, they, too, make heavy reading. His choice of Shinto Shrines for that publication was apt, for most of their ships, passenger liners and freighters alike, were named after them.[28]

When Richard Ponsonby decided to make Japan his home in 1919, he had initially settled in Tokyo, where, besides scholarly research, he offered his services as English teacher to the prestigious Seikei Academy. However, less Europeanized Kyoto exerted a far greater charm, and so he moved there in 1924. He eventually obtained some land in Kamigamo in the northern suburbs of the city, not far from the Shinto shrine of the same name, and built himself a gem of a Japanese-style home. The traditional ridge-pole raising ceremony took place in April 1929, and he moved in that September. The house, quite remarkable architecturally, was erected by a carpenter specializing in the building of Shinto shrines; and Ponsonby supervized the design himself, incorporating many shrine features. It has a handsome lacquered *tokonoma* (alcove); and a variety of fine and rare woods, such as Taiwan cypress, were used throughout. The eaves-end tiles of the roof were specially decorated with the Ponsonby crest. The garden was beautifully landscaped in traditional Japanese style, and contains an interesting seventeenth-century milestone.[29]

He lived out his final eight years there. When he was not trekking about the country visiting shrines or researching in libraries, he would be hard at work upstairs, seated with his legs folded under him on the tatami at his low, Japanese-style desk. That is, when he was not teaching at Kyoto's First Middle School, where he was affectionately known among the pupils as *o-fuda hakase*, 'Dr Talisman' – because of his avid collecting of the various talismans sold at Shinto Shrines.

PARTNERSHIP WITH SATO

Ponsonby-Fane was fortunate in finding the perfect secretary and personal assistant in the person of Satō Yoshijirō, a talented young man who rendered devoted service to Ponsonby-Fane and lived with him for sixteen years. Sato told Dr Carmen Blacker, who visited him in March 1977, that Ponsonby-Fane had not only been his master, but father and teacher to him as well. During part of that time Sato was attending Otani University, probably paid for by Ponsonby, who refers to his attendance there in a letter written to him from shipboard in 1926 as well as to the fact that he is responsible for the cook/ housemaid Tomiko-san's school fees. He also paid Sato a salary, for Dr Blacker noted in her diary that Sato told her that Ponsonby so hated any compromise with Western ways that he would go red in the face with fury at the very thought, and said he would stop Sato's salary if he ever made any such compromise.

Sato's devotion did not end with Richard Ponsonby's death in 1937. Richard must have left him the house, which he maintained as 'Ponsonbi-kan' (Ponsonby House), and, with whatever funds he inherited, he founded the Ponsonby Memorial Society and set about collecting Ponsonby-Fane's writings together in order to publish them in book form.

Sato also published, on his own initiative, a small paperback in 1958 (reprinted in 1961) entitled *Ponsonbi Hakase no Shinmenmoku* (The true character of Dr Ponsonby). His aim was to introduce Richard Ponsonby-Fane to Japanese readers, since most of the scholar's publications were in English. The book was in two parts. Part I, entitled 'His Convictions' comprised Japanese translations of published articles airing his views on kingship, democracy, modernization, etc., and Part II 'His Character' contained reprints of some of the sixty-eight contributions to a collection of eulogies entitled 'Memoirs of Dr Ponsonby-Fane' published in 1939. There is also a short biographical sketch of the scholar which had been specially written by Yamada Shinichiro, a Shinto High Priest, for the Japanese translation of his papers on the Shinto Shrines of Kashima and Katori brought out to commemorate the erection of the Ponsonby memorial stone in the precincts of Saiho-ji temple in Nishigamo in 1939.

There is an account by Matsudaira Ichirō of a visit to Brympton d'Evercy in 1930 with two other former Seikei Academy classmates who were then up at Cambridge. His father being Ambassador in London at the time, Ichiro was in England visiting his parents. Two years previously, his sister Setsuko had married Prince Chichibu. Ichiro describes the visit engagingly. The entrance hall at Brympton, its walls decorated with weaponry, reminded the three youths of the Tower of London, and the elderly white-haired lady who received them in the drawing-room looked 'as if she had just stepped out of one of the oil paintings on the wall'. Miss Farquhar, Richard Ponsonby's aunt, showed them round the great house until Richard appeared, 'shoulders hunched against the cold just as in the old days at Seikei Academy', when the conversation lapsed into easier Japanese. That night, after a black-tie dinner, they wended their way to separate bedrooms by candlelight, which was all rather creepy,and when he blew out the candle in his, with its canopied four-poster bed, 'the deep silence was not even relieved by the sound of a single insect, and I felt as if I had been reborn in a faraway land 500 years ago'.

Part I also includes an article Ponsonby was once persuaded by Ichiro to write for the Seikei Academy magazine. Young Matsudaira had asked for something about his former professor's life in Kyoto, but got instead a diatribe entitled 'Abolish double lives!' inveighing in no uncertain terms against the Japanese predilection for adopting Western food, clothing, customs and other dreadful innovations when the Japanese equivalents were so much better in every way!

Sato finally added a chatty essay of his own on Dr Ponsonby's daily life, describing his master's meticulously ordered existence, 100 percent *a la japonaise*. The only foreign things in his own life were two: his omnipresent woollen scarf, reaching down to his knees, for warding off the chills, knitted by his beloved aunt Helen Farquhar – to whom he wrote every single day of his life – and a cane on the handle of which his sister Violet had carved for him a life-like chameleon. He took these with him wherever he went, always dressed in *haori/hakama* emblazoned with the Ponsonby crest.

The scarf raises a mystery. It is visible in every photograph, and according to Brympton d'Evercy family tradition – and even John Pilcher – it was knitted for him by the Empress Dowager. I have come to the conclusion there must have been two scarves. Her Majesty Empress Teimei, the widow of Emperor Taisho, was a most remarkable lady. She had a lively mind and took a great interest in everything, especially international friendship. It is quite conceivable that she might have presented Richard with a new one, either knitted or not by herself, perhaps noticing that the scarf he habitually wore was old and worn.

Ponsonby was on friendly terms with Japanese royalty. He had interpreted for the Governor of Hong Kong when Hirohito, as Crown Prince, visited there on his 1921 European tour. Crown Prince Hirohito had been impressed by his fluency in Japanese, and granted him an audience on his return, as well as investing him with the Order of the Sacred Treasure, Fourth Grade. Ponsonby had also made the acquaintance of Prince and Princess Takamatsu when they happened to be travelling to England on the same ship in 1930, and had consequently attended most of the receptions for them there.

Richard had made his last visit to England in 1936 and, although ill with a stomach ulcer, he insisted on returning to Japan, against the advice of his doctor and his sister Violet, who wrote to Sato that her brother insisted on dying in Japan. In spite of his failing health, Ponsonby-Fane spent the following year travelling indefatigably to collect material on more Shinto shrines. His last excursion was in September to Nagoya to visit several in that area.

Death came on 12 December 1937. He was only 60, but he looked a good deal older. With him at the end were a number of his devoted Japanese friends and students, as well as Dr Baty, and John Pilcher, then a young diplomat studying Japanese in Kyoto. A funeral service as held on the 15th at St Agnes Church, and the following year his sister Violet came to Kyoto and took his ashes back to Brympton for burial in the little family churchyard on the estate.

On the 5th anniversary of his death, and in spite of great difficulties owing to the war, Sato and his Ponsonby Memorial Society managed to collect together most of Richard's papers on the subject and publish them in a volume entitled *Studies in Shinto and Shrines*. When things had eased up somewhat in 1954, plans were made with Kenkyusha – with the help of the Ministry of Education[30] – to publish his complete works in six volumes. A revised version of the 1942 book was re-issued as Volume 1.[31]

Chief High Priest Yamada wrote in Sato's book that many foreigners had taken up residence in his country and become Japanized, but none so thoroughly as Ponsonby, not only in mastering the intricacies of the language but achieving an understanding of their ethos surpassing that of many Japanese themselves. And Dr Baty, the friend who knew him best of the foreigners in Japan, wrote: 'He found here a real religion, real devotion to the ideal, and the ever-present consciousness of the Divine. This is not to say that Ponsonby was not a Christian. He was, and an uncompromisingly High Churchman. Heartfelt, genuine Sintau, (Shinto) he seems to have felt, was better than a watery Christianity. No more high-minded thinker, no more encyclopaedic worker, ever landed on these shores.'

Crown Prince Hirohito in Britain, May 1921

IAN NISH

THE VISIT of the Crown Prince to Britain in May 1921 occupies an important place in Anglo-Japanese relations. In Japanese history it was a new thing for the heir to the throne to go abroad and all manner of objections – political, constitutional and emotional – were raised which threatened the cancellation of the journey. It was significant for Japan that a person who was to occupy the throne for 63 years should at a formative time of life be able to observe the processes of government in some of the world's democracies. Britain, like other countries of Europe which he visited, could not fail to recognize its significance in political terms. She was being visited by the heir apparent to the throne of a country to which she had been linked for two decades in the Anglo-Japanese Alliance. While she was grateful to Japan for her efforts for the common cause during World War I, she was aware of the rumblings of opposition in Canada and the United States to the renewal of the alliance which was under consideration. [1]

This is not an attempt to retell the story of the Crown Prince's mission. The official account by Count Futara of the Imperial Household Agency and Sawada Setsuzo of the Foreign Ministry who had stayed in England when she was engaged in 'her brave struggle against the Central European powers'[2] gives a detailed, if cautious, description of the mission. The intention here is not to duplicate the account given in their diary but to discuss the highlights of a crowded trip in a broader historical context.

PREPARATIONS

Hara Kei who took over as prime minister in September 1918 had a major court problem on his hands. The Taisho Emperor (1912-26) had since the 1900s when he was heir to the throne given grounds for anxiety. From Hara's appointment onwards the Taisho Emperor's mental state markedly deteriorated. Hara's vision was that his son (b. 29 April 1901) who was later to be known as Hirohito, the Showa Emperor, should be trained as an international monarch both for his own good and for the sake of the country. Since he might have to take over as regent (*sessho*) if there was a further deterioration in his father's health, the sooner that the Crown Prince completed his education the better. From November 1919 Hara discussed the issue of capping his education with a journey overseas with the elder statesmen, who were an essential part of the decision-making process. Yamagata Aritomo, Matsukata Masayoshi and Saionji Kimmochi who had travelled abroad in their youth were all supportive. Such a trip was all the more necessary because Europe had changed since the war and it was desirable, they thought, that the heir to the throne should see it at first hand.[3]

The position of the prince was that he had been educated privately by Sugiura Shigetake (Jugo)(1855-1924), a professor of ethics from Kokugakuin. His subjects of study had been traditional and narrowly conceived. He had been invested as Crown Prince in November 1916 and been engaged to Princess Nagako, daughter of Prince Kuni, in January 1919. The royal match was not universally popular; and Genro Yamagata in particular deplored it because it seemed to favour the Satsuma clan rather than his own clan of Choshu. The issue assumed crisis proportions and distorted the decision over whether the prince should go overseas. The matrimonial party wanted him to complete the wedding ceremonial without delay, while Yamagata seems to have wanted him to go overseas in order to allow a cooling off period.[4]

Hara's idea of an overseas journey may have been influenced by the prospect of a visit to Japan by the Prince of Wales. But it had already taken shape in his mind. He records in his diary in June 1920 that he was aware of the Rumanian Crown Prince and the King of Thailand making such trips and that it was appropriate for Hirohito to do so also.[5] The Prince of Wales who was 26 years of age was due to pay an official visit to Australia, New Zealand and India in 1920. Japanese statesmen considered that there were strong grounds for inviting the prince to visit Japan as part of his official itinerary. It was proposed that the Japanese emperor should issue a warm invitation in order to assure Britain of Japan's goodwill towards her British allies. In London the Foreign Office was pleased to receive the suggestion on the ground that such a visit 'would greatly facilitate our task if we decide to negotiate for the renewal of the alliance'. King George V sanctioned the proposal; but, while the visit to New Zealand and Australia took place between March and October 1920, the idea of a side-trip to Japan was declined because the prince was suffering from the after-effects of a strenuous, but popular, visit to the United States and Canada in 1919. So long as the Prince of Wales's visit was a possibility, there was less pressure for a decision over the Crown Prince; but, when it was postponed, the way was open for the Japanese to send their own prince abroad.[6]

Hara reintroduced the matter in October. The matter was allowed to trickle out to the press. On 27 December the *Times'* correspondent in Tokyo reported on the widespread coverage of the story in the Japanese newspapers, adding

> A formal announcement would electrify Japan, and deeply touch national sentiment, crowning the alliance with the bond of human fellowship at present lacking in the relationship of the two island Empires.[7]

In other words, the presence of a Japanese royal personage in Britain would perform a role similar to that which King Edward VII had performed in Paris two decades earlier. The Crown Prince could supply an element of goodwill and cordiality to the relationship with Britain which was becoming rather distant. Eventually, on 16 January 1921, Matsukata as lord keeper of the privy seal managed to get the Taisho Emperor's permission to his son going overseas. Thereafter the arrangements were rushed through by cabinet, court and genro.[8]

Hara was opposed from various quarters. The empress, relying on the advice of the prince's tutor, Sugiura, who had in fact been instrumental in bringing the young couple together, doubted whether it would help Hirohito in any way with his education to go overseas. Was there a need for a monarch of a country as ancient as Japan to go abroad to pick up alien notions? Those from the right wing like Toyama Mitsuru and Uchida Ryohei formed an association to prevent the Crown Prince departing from Japan's sacred soil.[9] There were of course arguments galore against the mission which were fed into the press: the sea journey to Europe was a hazardous one; there was an element of risk to the person of the prince in sending him abroad; there was the inconvenience if an emergency occurred and he had to be recalled at short notice.

The opposition launched a movement to stop the prince's European journey *Kotaishi yoko chushi undo*.[10] It drew up a petition, calling for the cancellation, or at least the postponement, of Hirohito's departure. It professed to see behind the speed with which the preparations were being made a sinister plot to prevent the proposed marriage to Princess Nagako or at the least to divert public attention from the issue. Calling for swift progress over the wedding ceremony, the movement threatened to use force and in the last resort to lie down on the tracks in front of the royal train. Members of the government who had to make an agonizing choice were placed under special protection; but they persisted and steered through the Diet a bill to earmark the expenditure needed for the journey, which was immense, considering the post-war recession which was then afflicting Japan. There was a formidable demonstration in Tokyo on Kigensetsu, National Foundation Day (11 February 1921). When Hara was confronted on 21 February by a delegation, demanding that the trip be cancelled, the prime minister announced that it was too late for any changes to be made. Hirohito's departure passed off without a hitch. He was seen off at Tokyo station by cheering crowds and there were more demonstrations of public goodwill when he embarked at Yokohama on 3 March. The engagement was, however, officially confirmed.[11]

Japan's decision to send the Crown Prince was taken with the backdrop of World War I very much in mind. He was only to visit countries which had been on the allied side. It is of course true that the prime destination was Britain, which was the long-term ally of Japan and a monarchy. But it is well to remember how much life and thinking in Britain were still affected by the harrowing experiences of the war which had so recently finished. The speeches made and the addresses of welcome received by the Japanese delegation confirm strongly the military-naval content of the mission. Hirohito was to dress, sometimes as general, sometimes as admiral. He had a full complement of senior military and naval officers to accompany him, Lieutenant-general Nara Takeji for the army and Admiral Oguri for the navy.

Moreover, the British welcoming party was similarly constituted: Admiral Sir Stanley Colville and General Sir Charles Monro with General Woodroffe and Lieutenant-colonel F.S.G. Piggott as well as civilian officials like Miles Lampson and Frank Ashton-Gwatkin.

Hirohito was to be conveyed to Europe by the cruiser *Katori* with the cruiser *Kajima* as escort. The choice of these ships which had been built in British yards some fifteen years earlier was intended as a compliment to Britain and as a reminder that Britain was the major port of call for the royal visitor. This was in any case not seriously in question for the expedition sailed from colony to colony: Hong Kong, Singapore, Ceylon and Malta. At each port the prince received a naval salute and was lavishly entertained by the colonial authorities.

The stopover at Malta was rather special. For one thing, the prince attended a theatre for the first time in his life and heard the Italian opera, Verdi's *Otello*. More seriously, Malta had been the base from which the Japanese second squadron on special duty in the Mediterranean had operated during the war as part of the allied anti-submarine campaign. On 25 April the prince visited the Royal Naval cemetery and paid tribute to the 77 naval ratings who had lost their lives in battle. They had been members of the crew of the frigate *Sakaki* which had been sunk with her captain and crew while escorting allied military convoys. This was to reinforce the message which, in Japan's view, the allies had been inclined to forget, namely, that the Japanese had played a substantial naval role in European waters and had suffered loss thereby.[12]

At the next port of call, Gibraltar, the prince was met by Admiral Takeshita Isamu, naval attache at the London embassy, who was to accompany him until he left European waters again and to serve as one of his interpreters. From the London embassy also came Yoshida Shigeru, then a first secretary of 42 years of age and later to become post-war prime minister. It was his task to devise, explain and get the approval of the prince's entourage for the elaborate programme of festivities which had been mapped out for him. An ancillary task was to supply the wardrobe needs of the prince in London which was then sartorially the world leader – for men! The problem was that the Crown Prince would, as soon as he arrived in the capital, take up residence in Buckingham Palace and so it was necessary to establish his requirements beforehand. Yoshida had, therefore, rushed to Gibraltar via Paris with a cutter from MacVickers, the tailor thought to have the highest reputation in London, to take his measurements. [13]

At Gibraltar Hirohito also met Admiral Black, commander-in-chief of the US European squadron in his flagship *Pittsburg* who passed on the respectful greetings of the US president and invited him to visit that country on his return journey. Such had been the haste of the departure from Japan that this point had not been clinched. Though the prince was very attracted by the idea of returning by way of the United States and the Panama Canal, it was not to be. He replied diplomatically that he looked forward to visiting the United States on another occasion. It was to be 1975 before that took place.

TRAVELS IN BRITAIN

On arrival in British waters, Hirohito was accorded a naval review at Spithead. He disembarked at Portsmouth on 9 May, accompanied by his uncle Prince Kan-in and Count Chinda Sutemi, his political adviser, who had previously served as ambassador to Britain (1916–20). He was met by the Prince of Wales and travelled to Victoria Station where he was welcomed by King George V. Japan had timed the visit well. It was the beginning of summer and the start of 'the London Season'. Since the war London had been sparing in putting on ceremonial spectacles and this was almost the first of its kind. As against that, Britain's most important industry, coal, was at the time paralyzed by a protracted strike and the cabinet was frequently in emergency session to deal with the matter.

For three days Hirohito was the guest of the sovereign at Buckingham Palace. On 9 May he was given an official welcoming banquet there which was described in the Japanese press as a diamond-studded occasion and in terms of sheer brilliance unprecedented since the outbreak of the war. The king in his speech referred to his visit to Japan as a young naval officer, saying that he could not 'forget the warmth of the reception given to my brother and myself by the Japanese people'. [14] George V as the father of children roughly comparable in age to the prince was anxious to make him feel at home. Nonetheless, the emperor found that the informal atmosphere inside the palace gave him a profound cultural shock. The following day a more idiosyncratic dinner-party was given by the foreign secretary, Lord Curzon, in the authentic Curzon style. No other member of the cabinet had been invited; and it was not altogether concealed that the foreign secretary had only with difficulty been able to spare the time from all the pressing diplomatic problems with which he was faced. At the customary lord mayor's banquet at the Guildhall, Prime Minister Lloyd George said that as an ally Japan had remained steadfast and true and that the Allies had deeply appreciated the sacrifices made during the war by Japan. He promised to do all in his power to see that the friendly relations between the two nations were long maintained in the future.[15] With this, the state visit came to an end. The Crown Prince moved from the palace to Chesterfield House in South Audley Street and became the guest of the government.

Hirohito acquired high reputations. He was saluted by *The Times* as 'a modest and gentle prince' and 'a courier of friendship', while *The Observer* remarked that the Crown Prince 'is extremely popular in his own country'. Lord Curzon described him as showing 'intelligence, amiability, dignity of demeanour and anxiety to please'.[16] Accompanying officials were in their letters home expressing their anxieties that their prince, a young man of 20 from a narrow court background, might have difficulty in hobnobbing with statesmen of international calibre (Asquith, Milner, Lloyd George). They were relieved that he did not appear to be over-awed by these nerve-racking encounters. He had, of course, been well-briefed; but he had nevertheless carried off his public appearances well.[17]

Hirohito may have looked towards the Prince of Wales – mildly nonconformist, individualistic and young at heart – as something of a role model. At all events there were those in his British escort who were anxious to 'modernize' the Crown Prince while he was in London, even suggesting that he should travel on the underground. Miles Lampson, one of his organizers from the Foreign Office, stated that he was 'told off to run the visit, and derived a great deal of fun and amusement from it'.[18] Fun and amusement were, however, rather remote from the thinking of the prince's large Japanese entourage who were jealous of his image and sought to keep it under control. Hirohito's reactions are not clear.

The functions which Hirohito had to undertake were of various kinds: military and naval; ceremonial and social; and educational. The military aspect had always been stressed throughout the alliance and should not be down-played. While he was in London, Hirohito was made a general of the British army (his father was an honorary field-marshal) and appeared at Aldershot, Sandhurst and Camberley in the uniform of that rank.[19] To conciliate the other British services, he also had to appear at Greenwich and Kenley. On the social side, he attended a multitude of luncheons and dinners including that given by the Japan Society at the Hotel Cecil when the Society promised to continue its efforts to bring the two nations into 'a still closer alliance'.

On the educational side he visited colleges and universities. Visiting Oxford University on 14 May, he inspected the Officers' Training Corps and watched a regatta on the river. On 18 May he visited Cambridge University and looked at the Aston collection of classical Japanese books in the University library. He received an honorary degree as Doctor of Civil Law and attended a lecture by Professor J.R. Tanner, professor of constitutional law, on 'The British monarchy and the people'. After meeting Japanese students, he visited Newnham College. On the following day he reached Edinburgh and there, too, received an honorary doctorate (LL.D) from the university which he described in his response as 'the university of the North'[20]. In Edinburgh he was again put up in a royal residence, Holyrood Palace. He not only visited Rosyth naval dockyard but also visited Redford barracks – not, alas, Retford barracks as the Anglocentric London newspapers would have it.[21]

Then followed what must be described as the most imaginative part of the programme, the visit to Blair Castle in Perthshire. It had been arranged that he would stay for three days as the guest of the Duke of Atholl. It seems to have been a combination of the ideas of Miles Lampson as escort and Lord Curzon as foreign secretary. Lampson records in his diary: 'After the usual few days in London I remember that we took him for a trip round the North and, incidentally, stayed up at Blair with the late Duke of Atholl when we inducted the Crown Prince into the gentle art of snouking salmon'.[22] The Duke, a former soldier, was a staunch member of the Conservative party and had recently been in close touch with Curzon on various Balkan matters. Driving from Perth station to Blair Atholl, an interesting contrast to the urban environments the Crown Prince had passed through earlier, his diarists recorded that:

> . . . he received a rousing welcome from the people along the route, who for the first time in their lives set eyes on Japanese people in the person of His Highness and his suite.

At some of the villages he passed through, he was requested to stop to permit them to read a message of welcome. At other places, lovely country lassies presented him with garlands of flowers.[23]

Contrasted with the hectic schedule in London, this was a relaxing long weekend. In the evening the Duchess who was a talented pianist and was later to become a distinguished lady member of the House of Commons, played a transcription of Japanese airs for the piano. She says in her autobiography that she also transcribed the national anthem, *Kimigayo*, during the performance of which one of the visiting party, Mr Toda, was instructed to sing the words. The anthem was also played on the bagpipes.[24]

What was the message intended to be projected by this strange visit? Was it to show that Britain was a country like Japan, part feudal and part industrial? Whatever the message, the Crown Prince often referred later in his trip to the bizarre experiences he had had in the highlands.

On his journey south he visited factories in the Manchester area. He called on Eton College and received the *banzais* of the assembled students.[25] On 27 May he was present at a commemorative dinner in London for Japan's naval victory over the Russians at the Battle of the Japan Sea in 1905. Leaving Portsmouth the following day for the continent, he was accompanied into the English Channel by Royal Navy destroyers. He visited France, Belgium, Holland and Italy, all countries chosen for being on the allied side during the war of 1914–18. He had expressed an interest in visiting the battlefields of Europe and was escorted round some of them. On 18 July he joined the *Katori* once again at Naples for his return by way of the Indian ocean.

The Crown Prince reached Japan's shores again on 3 September, exactly six months after his departure. The prime minister went to greet him at Yokohama with the imperial household minister and the navy minister. They led the shout of three *banzais*. Asked how the trip had been, the prince replied that he had not liked the heat of the return journey. It was recorded that *banzais* greeted him all the way from Yokohama to Tokyo, showing him the people's happiness at his return.[26]

After the prince was safely back, Hara offered his resignation because he was exhausted and felt that his work was done. This shows how far Hara saw his own career as being tied up with the prince's educational travels. Yamagata who found that he could work with Hara despite the fact that he was a party politician persuaded him to stay at his post. Within two months, however, Hara was dead, the victim of an assassin's knife wielded by a right-wing youth.

ASSESSMENT

It had been a successful trip, both politically for Japan and personally for the prince. Admiral Kobayashi, writing to the Navy Ministry, said 'it has been a great success for throne and country'. Count Chinda confirmed this when he reported to his prime minister on 20 September. In Britain, Curzon said that the visit could not but have 'the happiest results' in concentrating attention on Japan at an important juncture.[27]

But a mission of this kind is inevitably many-sided. Like the Japan-British exhibition of 1910, this mission had its commercial side, though it had no commercial members. *The Times* issued a trade supplement of about 40 pages associated with the prince's arrival. The foreword was written by Ambassador Hayashi Gonsuke. A good deal of government money was being spent for the purpose of promoting Japan.[28]

Futara and Sawada wrote that Hirohito's visit was 'entirely unconnected with any political considerations'. They went on to say that this was true in respect of the Anglo-Japanese Alliance which was 'being discussed in the press at the time'. So far as we are aware, there were no special political overtures associated with the mission. Indeed, the empress had insisted that Hirohito was too young to undertake any diplomatic mission. But May was an important juncture in the story of the Anglo-Japanese Alliance when Foreign Secretary Curzon asked Japan to agree to a prolongation of the alliance, but only for three months.[29] This was surely an indication of Britain's doubts about the long-term future of the alliance; and Japan was slow to respond. The presence of a visiting delegation in London at this very time was largely coincidental but it must inevitably have had political overtones. Royal missions are highly symbolic and are intended to create good relations between countries. It was natural, therefore, that many involved should assume that the 1921 mission was at least in part an attempt to secure the continuation of the Anglo-Japanese Alliance whether this was the intent of the Japanese government or not.

For the prince himself, it was an important educative

experience. Inevitably, it is hard to find a totally objective assessment of the mission. Nothing serious had gone amiss. The prince had been studious, dedicated, loyal and hard-working. He had socialized ably with the top statesmen of his day. It prepared him for the next stages of his career : becoming Regent (*sessho*) in November 1921; marrying Princess Nagako in 1924 (after Yamagata's death); and becoming emperor on Christmas day, 1926. In his new capacity, he acted as host for the Prince of Wales when he paid his postponed visit to Japan in April 1922. It would appear that he came into close contact with his visitor, both formally and informally (for example) on the golf links.[30] Who knows but that these experiences may have persuaded Hirohito to break loose from some of the confining restrictions imposed by Japanese court tradition.

The 1921 mission gave further impetus to royal diplomacy between Britain and Japan. There had been exchanges of visits in the past; but they were stepped up in the 1920s. The Regent's brother, Prince Chichibu, stayed in Britain in 1925-6, spending a term at Magdalen College, Oxford. It is striking incidentally that he should also visit Blair Atholl where the duke and duchess 'liked him very much'.[31] In the summer of 1929 the Duke of Gloucester paid a visit to Japan in order to confer the Order of the Garter on the Emperor Hirohito. A reciprocal mission of thanksgiving was led by Prince Takamatsu in 1930. Seven years later at the coronation of King George V and Queen Elizabeth, Japan was represented by Prince and Princess Chichibu. These exchanges probably had less political significance than the mission of 1921, despite their symbolism.[32]

The Crown Prince had followed an itinerary strikingly similar to that of the mission of Prince Iwakura half-a-century before. We have no way of knowing whether Hirohito enjoyed his trip. But when the compilers of the history of the Japanese Foreign Ministry presented him with their two-volume work to mark the centenary of the ministry in 1969, he first looked at the account given of his mission to Europe almost seven decades earlier. Presumably this was an indication of the enjoyment and pride which he still felt. It is fitting to conclude with the remark at the state banquet to the Duke of Gloucester at the imperial palace on 3 May 1929, when the Emperor said in his address of welcome that 'this gathering recalls one of the happiest experiences of my life, my visit to England'.[33]

16

John Batchelor, Missionary and Friend of the Ainu

SIR HUGH CORTAZZI

JOHN BATCHELOR, 1855-1945, devoted his life to missionary work among the Ainu in Hokkaido. He studied their language and customs and worked hard to help them to survive. He was a pioneer whose contribution to Ainu studies is impressive. He was not an expert in linguistics, ethnology or folk lore and inevitably some of his conclusions have been questioned by later scholars, but this should not belittle his achievements.

THE AINU

The Ainu among whom he worked have continued to suffer discrimination, but a vigorous ethno-political movement has helped to boost their position. There were reported to be 23,830 Ainu in Hokkaido in 1993 (there were 863 Ainu in Tokyo according to a 1989 survey). The Ainu language and culture must be regarded as endangered. Japanese governments since the Meiji Restoration and the Japanese colonization of Hokkaido in the latter part of the nineteenth century must bear the main responsibility for this situation. The Ainu were regarded by many as the descendants of the Ebisu (barbarians), who were largely expelled from northern Honshu in the latter part of the Heian period. They were accordingly treated as an inferior race and exploited by the Japanese colonists in Hokkaido in the nineteenth century.[1]

In April 1995 it was reported[2] that an advisory panel to the Chief Cabinet Secretary had begun debating the longstanding issue of protecting the rights of the Ainu as an indigenous people of Hokkaido, but 'a resolution of the problem still appears as elusive as ever'. The Japanese Government were said to have maintained the stance that there is no strict definition of 'indigenous people' under the United Nations and that even if the Ainu were so recognized, it is doubtful whether they could be given preferential treatment under the Japanese Constitution of 1946 which states that all people are equal before the law. Ainu rights, in so far as they have been recognized under Japanese law, depend on 'The Hokkaido Former Natives Protection Law' which came into force during the Meiji period, but it is said to have discriminatory overtones and to have done little if anything to improve the position of the Ainu. In 1984 the Ainu Association of Hokkaido drew up draft new legislation calling for government help to preserve the Ainu language and culture and set aside a number of seats in local and national assemblies for Ainu representatives.

In 1994 Kayano Shigeru, the author of a memoir of Ainu life, published in English in 1994 under the title 'Our Land was a Forest',[3] became the first Ainu member of the House of Councillors as a member of the Social Democratic Party of Japan (SDPJ). Kayano has argued plausibly that government reluctance to address the issue 'stems from fears of apologies and redress'. The Japanese attitude towards the Ainu compares unfavourably with the attempts to make amends in other countries such as Australia towards indigenous people[4]. Fortunately, there has in recent years been an attempt, with the support of some Japanese scholars, to revive Ainu traditions and Ainu studies.

BATCHELOR'S LIFE[5]

John Batchelor was born on 20 March 1855 in Uckfield, East Sussex, where his father was the parish clerk. In 1873 he heard a sermon which determined him to become a missionary. He studied briefly under two clergymen and at the college of the Church Missionary Society (CMS) in Islington, London, but was not ordained at this time. On 22 September 1875 he joined a group of young missionaries bound for the Far East. After an uneventful but uncomfortable journey he reached Hong Kong on 11 November 1875, where he was placed under the tutelage of Bishop Burdon and began the study of Chinese. The Hong Kong climate did not, however, agree with him and he found that he could only breathe properly when he was up on the peak. He suffered from boils and malaria. In March 1876 the missionaries' doctor said that he must leave as soon as possible for a cooler climate. Some three hours later he was placed on a French ship bound for the treaty port of Yokohama which he reached on 21 March. He was sent from there to Tokyo to stay with the Reverend John Piper, the secretary to the CMS in Japan. Following a further medical examination it was considered desirable that he should live in a more northern climate and plans were made to send him to Hokkaido. On 10 April he sailed for Hakodate on a small American schooner which only reached Hakodate on 1 May. Batchelor stayed in Hokkaido, apart from brief intervals of home leave and visits to Tokyo, until he was forced to quit Japan for ever in 1941 following the outbreak of war.

At Hakodate he was taken under the wing of the Reverend James Williams of the CMS. Among his acquaintances in Hakodate at this time were Eusden, the British consul, and Bishop Nicolai of the Russian Orthodox Church whose bells reminded him of home. He quarrelled with another Orthodox priest who asked him to climb to the top of the nearby mountain and cast down the stone idols there into the sea. Batchelor refused, asking the priest how he would like it if someone broke into his room and destroyed his icons of the Virgin.

Batchelor immediately began to study Japanese. His first teacher was a Mr Terata who had been a member of the Hakodate garrison during the troubles in Hokkaido after the Meiji restoration of 1868. Terata had hated the Christians and had planned to murder the missionary in charge at Hakodate at that time. Another of his teachers was a Mr Ogawa, a refugee from Aizu (Fukushima) which had put up a fierce resistance to the imperial forces in 1868/9. Batchelor recalled that he once rebuked Ogawa for resting his head on a Chinese bible: the teacher riposted that there could not be a better pillow.

Batchelor was shocked by some Japanese attitudes. He could not accept that '*uso wa Nihon no takara*' (lies are Japan's treasures). He was also horrified when he heard a mother tell her maid who was having difficulty in getting her child home: '*Damashite tsurete koi*' (deceive the child and bring it back).

Batchelor soon made the acquaintance of some Ainu. He and Ogawa met two Ainu bear-hunters in 1876. They had just sold the meat and the skin and wanted Batchelor to buy the gall-bladder which they declared was good for stomach troubles. They came from the village of Piratori which Batchelor promised to visit as soon as he could. He described the two Ainu in these words:

> They wore no head or foot gear and were dressed in coats woven from elm bark reaching just below the knees. They had well developed calves and stout arms well covered with hair. Their voices were gentle and their faces good-tempered and well pleasing to look at. Thus began Batchelor's affection for the Ainu.

Batchelor made reasonable progress with his Japanese although he confesses that he once asked a lady how many children she had using the numeral classifier for animals.

In 1877, he determined to visit Piratori as he had promised. In order to do so he had to go outside the limits of the treaty port of Hakodate and this required a passport from the Japanese authorities. He gave as his grounds for requesting permission that he intended to study the Ainu language. (If he had declared his purpose as being to try to convert the Ainu to Christianity the Japanese authorities might have been less willing to grant a permit. Undoubtedly, this was his long term intention but he realized that, if he were to make any progress with the Ainu, he would need a good understanding of the Ainu language. The reason given in his application was not, therefore, deceitful even if it was not the whole truth.) He set out on his own over the rough roads first by cart and then by pony. He made slow progress breaking his journey in Sapporo. From there it took him three further days to reach Piratori where he was warmly received by the local 'Chief' (as Batchelor always called him, although the title was hardly justified) Penri and his wife. Penri's dwelling was primitive and he had to sit on an empty sake tub and sleep on a small platform by the hearth where he used a bear-skin full of fleas. Later, he had some mats hung round his 'bed' to give him some privacy. Over the years which followed Batchelor developed respect and affection for Penri who died in 1903 aged about 85. Penri was, Batchelor declared, his greatest friend among the Ainu although Penri never became a Christian and adhered to the traditional practices of the Ainu. He loved sake while Batchelor was a life-long teetotaller.

Penri's wife Crosia was 'of a very gentle disposition'. It was her job to provide the family with vegetables and cereals while the husband did the hunting and fishing to obtain animal food. She eventually became a Christian.

Batchelor worked hard to learn the Ainu language beginning

by asking the names of objects around him. After about two months he found that he could understand most of the stories told around the hearth. While he was studying one day a man who was apparently deranged came to see him and asked Batchelor to find his lost soul and hang it up in the right place. Batchelor said that this helped him to understand the Ainu belief in devil possession.

Batchelor recalls that one Ainu named Tunkamarek whom he met while he was at Piratori wanted to be baptised but was worried that his beloved dogs might not go to the same heaven. Batchelor who had a favourite pet dog recorded that he told the Ainu that if for his happiness dogs were really needed in heaven then he was sure that God would ensure that dogs were there.

After some months at Piratori Batchelor returned to Hakodate to continue his mission work there. But in the summer of 1878 he set out once more for Piratori. At Oshamambe he met two Ainu elders who were not allowed to enter the inn where he was staying. They had brought him two bottles of *shōchū* (a cheap white spirit made from sweet potatoes or grain) as a welcoming present. As a teetotaller he had to refuse these gifts but he was pleased by the warmth of their welcome. At Sarubito he found many Ainu suffering from malaria and used up his stock of quinine in treating them.

At Piratori Batchelor found that a tiny cubicle nine feet by six feet had been put up for him to use. He stayed for some months before returning to Hakodate.

In 1879, Batchelor was accepted as a member of the CMS mission in Japan and was asked to pay special attention to the Ainu. He was in Hakodate for the opening of a new church that autumn but it and the house occupied by the Reverend Walter Dening, then head of the CMS mission, were burnt down two months later. In 1880, he made another visit to his Ainu friends. Dening had himself begun to study the Ainu language and no doubt encouraged Batchelor in his endeavours.

Early in 1882, Batchelor returned to England for further training. According to Professor Nitami Iwao, Dening considered Batchelor uncouth and uneducated. While in England he studied at the CMS colleges at Islington and at Ridley Hall in Cambridge.

Batchelor was back in Hakodate in 1883 where the mission had been taken over by the Reverend Walter Andrews. Andrews' wife had died leaving him with three children who were looked after by his sister Louisa. Louisa was eleven years older than Batchelor but they were soon engaged. On 31 December 1883 Batchelor married Louisa at a ceremony at the British legation in Tokyo. After two nights at the Grand Hotel in Yokohama they spent a week's honeymoon at Atami. On their return to Hakodate they were unable to go straight to Piratori as they would have liked. It was the middle of the winter in Hokkaido and very cold. Moreover, the rules at that time forbade foreigners from renting houses outside the settlements and passports for travel outside the settlements were difficult to obtain. Batchelor accordingly sent to Piratori and persuaded Penri to come to Hakodate so that he could continue his Ainu studies. He began to translate portions of the New Testament and the Psalms into the Ainu language while at the same time helping the Reverend Andrews with the work of the mission.

Batchelor again applied in the spring of 1884 for a passport to revisit the Ainu. But on this occasion a passport was refused as a law suit had been brought against him in the Consular Court under whose jurisdiction Batchelor came through the extra-territorial provisions of the 'unequal' treaties of 1858. Batchelor was accused of having built a home in the interior contrary to Japanese law (his tiny room at Piratori), having shot outside the treaty limits (he had both a gun licence and a passport and only shot game for food on which to live) and having outstayed the time limit on his permit. The third charge was the only substantial one but it was based on a linguistic misunderstanding. When the Ainu witness said he had been in the house '*hito tsuki hambun*' this had been interpreted as meaning 'a month-and-a-half' rather than as it should have been as 'half a month'. Batchelor accordingly protested against the trial being conducted in Japanese and asked that the trial should be either in Ainu or in English, but he was persuaded against pursuing this request, presumably in order to avoid offending Japanese susceptibilities. The trial was, however, adjourned for three weeks while a better interpreter was found. Batchelor's interpretation was proved correct and the charge was shown to be without substance. When the consul asked the Japanese official why he had brought the case, the official replied that the reason was that 'Mr Batchelor is trying to make the Ainu language live while we desire it to die out.' The official was displeased at losing the case and asserted that this was because the case had been brought under British law and not Japanese law. He also asked if Mrs

Batchelor could be charged with contempt of court because she had sat knitting while the case was being argued.

This was not the only occasion on which the Japanese authorities showed their opposition to Batchelor's efforts to study the Ainu and their culture. On one occasion when Batchelor wanted to visit neighbouring Ainu chiefs Penri said that this was forbidden although Batchelor's passport permitted him to visit the whole district. Penri who had received his orders from the Japanese authorities to watch Batchelor and limit his movements eventually agreed to take Batchelor by boat, arguing that the orders referred only to preventing Batchelor going by the path. Batchelor also encountered a good deal of opposition from Japanese in Hokkaido to his efforts to preach Christianity.

After the law suit had been settled, the Batchelors reapplied for passports and these were granted. At Piratori Mrs Batchelor found the rooms too small and the smoke hurt her eyes. They accordingly went on to Nikap where an Ainu had two Japanese-style rooms which they hired for a month. Here they made new friends and eventually more than fifty converts. On their way back to Hakodate they called at Horobetsu where the Ainu chief offered to make a lean-to at the end of his house for the Batchelors. They accepted, and having obtained new passports, returned to Horobetsu in March 1886. They found their lean-to a great improvement on Penri's smokey hut where, as a result of talking in a smokey atmosphere, Batchelor had begun to suffer from laryngitis. Horobetsu at this time was, Batchelor said, 'a mixed village of Ainu and Japanese fishermen with a shop or two and a doctor. They were also not far from Muroran where there was a ship's chandler'. Another nearby settlement was Shiraoi where Batchelor was soon active as a preacher.

It had only been in 1885 nine years after he had started work that he had made his first convert, but he was still not ordained as a priest and baptism was given in Hakodate by the Reverend Andrews. Finally, in 1887, he was ordained as a deacon by Bishop Bickersteth at St Andrews Church in Tokyo. On his return from Tokyo in 1888, Batchelor worked in Hakodate, Horobetsu, Piratori (where a Christian meeting house was established), Nikap and Kushiro. In the next year he was finally ordained as a priest and left for England on leave. It is not clear why Batchelor delayed so long before he was ordained. One possible reason adduced is that he wanted to devote his life to the Ainu and may have feared that as an ordained priest he would be more restricted. While in England on this occasion Batchelor translated the first three gospels into Ainu.

In 1891, the Batchelors returned to work in Hokkaido where they made their headquarters at Usu. Converts remained few and Batchelor recorded that it was only five years later that his two servants and Yaeko, the daughter whom they had adopted, were baptised by Bishop Bickersteth.

In 1891, at the request of college students, Batchelor was given permission by the Japanese authorities to reside at Sapporo to do temperance work. The Batchelors arrived there in January 1892 and took up residence near the University gardens. Their first Japanese congregation assembled in July that year with three Ainu and 14 Japanese present. Batchelor continued to travel among the Ainu whom he found 'in a very sorry plight. They were poor and with no legal standing'. There were, he noted, no schools in the villages, nor were there doctors, medicines or hospitals.

In 1895, he managed to hire a plot of land near his house and built a small rest-house so that such of his Ainu friends as were sick could come in from the mountains and get medical treatment. Batchelor particularly commended the work of a Japanese doctor, Sekiba of the Sapporo City Hospital, who attended the patients free of charge. It was not an easy task, Batchelor noted, to treat these Ainu patients as they lacked the basic education needed to understand the way medicine worked and some would try to combine Western medicine with traditional remedies. Soon after the rest house had been established Mrs Batchelor set up a school for Ainu girls.

In 1896, the Batchelors were joined by a Miss E.M.Bryant, an Australian, who had trained as a nurse at Guy's hospital in London. After studying the Ainu language for 18 months with the Batchelors, she moved to Piratori where she established a bible class. She remained in Hokkaido until 1922 when she was 65. She then retired to Britain where she died in 1934.

Batchelor's translation of the New Testament appeared in 1897. In 'Steps by the Way' he sadly recorded that his translation had become obsolete as the Ainu language had ceased to be used and had been superseded by Japanese.

In 1903, at the request of Professor Starr of Chicago and Baron Sonoda, then Governor of Hokkaido, the Batchelors got together nine Ainu to attend an exposition in St Louis. In 1907, Batchelor was given permission to visit the Ainu in Sakhalin. He recorded that on his return the Governor asked him to address the judges and police at Otomari on matters Ainu and how they should be treated. Batchelor's work was now beginning to receive the recognition it deserved and in June 1909, while on home leave in England, he was awarded the Order of the Sacred Treasure, fourth class. On his way back to Hokkaido the following year he was presented to the Emperor Meiji at an Imperial Garden Party in Tokyo. He recorded that he felt a thrill of excitement running through his hands. He appears to have had a special sensitivity in his hands which, he thought, gave him an ability to treat sufferers from migraine and stomach disorders.

In 1911, Bishop Andrews was appointed to the diocese of Hokkaido and decided to move from Hakodate to Sapporo. The Batchelors then gave up their house in Sapporo and moved to Usu where a new house was built for them. The Bishop found that Sapporo was less convenient than Hakodate to which he returned, but the Batchelors stayed on at Usu where Mrs Batchelor ran a bible class and sewing school, although a few years later they returned to Sapporo.

Batchelor retired from missionary duties in the early 1920s.[6] But he continued to work for the Ainu, being appointed a member of the Ainu Protection and Social Service. In 1923, he was received by the then Crown Prince (later the Emperor Shōwa). In 1924, he built a dormitory in Sapporo for Ainu students. In 1932, the late Prince Takamatsu, younger brother of the Shōwa Emperor, granted Batchelor one thousand yen to further his studies of the Ainu. In 1933, he was promoted in the Order of the Sacred Treasure to third class and, in 1936, he dined with the Emperor and had the honour of addressing His Majesty on the Ainu. In 1937, he was made an officer of the Order of the British Empire (OBE).

Mrs Batchelor died in 1936 at the age of 93 and was buried in Sapporo. Despite the difference in age between Batchelor and his wife and the absence of children, John and Louisa Batchelor appear to have had a happy marriage. She was clearly a tough and intrepid lady, putting up with many discomforts and difficulties in supporting Batchelor in his endeavours on behalf of the Ainu.

After her death Batchelor brought out to Hokkaido in 1937 his niece Miss Andrews to help him with his scholarly work. He remained in Japan until 1941 when, because of the worsening situation in World War II, he was forced to leave the land he had come to love. He and his niece went first to Canada where they hoped that the war would end and enable him to return to Japan. Their hopes being disappointed, they were flown home to England via Portugal. Batchelor died at his old family home in Hertford on 2 April 1944 aged 90. He was buried at Uckfield, East Sussex, his birth place.

★　★　★

BATCHELOR, THE STUDENT OF AINU CUSTOMS

Batchelor's first substantial book on the Ainu was *The Ainu of Japan: The Religion, Superstitions, and General History of the Hairy Aborigines of Japan*, published by the Religious Tract Society in London in 1892. In the preface he said that the book was based on letters to relatives who were interested in the work of the mission. The book which contained eighty illustrations including photographs and sketches produced by his wife, describes Ainu customs and folklore. He noted the decrease in the Ainu population. Among the causes for this were, he thought, the wars of extermination carried on by the ancient Japanese against the Ainu, their exposure to the climate of Hokkaido and to diseases such as small-pox, and indulgence in intoxicating liquor. Batchelor affirmed from his acquaintance with the Ainu that 'a more kind, gentle, and sympathetic people would be difficult to find'. 'The Ainu is very much what others make of him. Treat him as a man and he will show himself to be a man.'[7] Batchelor, after commenting on the fact that the Ainu living near the Japanese 'have an air of slavishness, slovenliness, and general depression. . .apt either to excite contempt and disgust, or to arouse one's pity' added that this state of things was only to be expected as the Ainu 'have been conquered and crushed under foot' by the Japanese'.

Batchelor's main work on the Ainu was, however, *The Ainu and their Folklore*, published by the Religious Tract Society in London in 1901. It was later reissued and revised. This was accompanied by 137 illustrations including photogaphs and sketches. It deals in much greater detail with Ainu customs and folklore and demonstrates the care with which Batchelor had observed the Ainu and recorded Ainu life. In the preface Batchelor admitted that many matters contained in his first work needed modification and some points in it were misleading. He explained that his aim had been 'to let the Ainu themselves speak'. He wanted the ethnologist 'to have materials for purposes of comparison with the lore of other races'. The book of 51 chapters and some 600 pages is a comprehensive compendium of observations and accounts of the Ainu and their folk-lore.

Ainu Life and Lore: Echoes of a departing race, published by Kyobunkan in Tokyo in 1927, was based on articles contributed by Batchelor to *The Japan Advertiser*. It is primarily a collection of folk stories. Batchelor's little book *Sea-Girt Yezo: Glimpses at Missionary Work in North Japan* was published by the Church Missionary Society in London in 1902. It was intended for children and is a Christian tract.

Neil Gordon Munro[8] was another conscientious student of the Ainu. In his book *Ainu Creed and Cult*, published posthumously by Kegan Paul in 1962, he takes issue with Batchelor on a few points. In particular, he expresses doubt[9] about Batchelor's interpretation of '*Pase-kamui*' as the 'one true God' of Ainu belief. Munro thought that Batchelor 'in all sincerity adapted Ainu beliefs to his own'.[10]

Batchelor's prime aim was to spread Christianity and his study of the Ainu and their folk-lore were a secondary consideration although, at times, his interest in the Ainu people and their ways must have dominated his life. Munro was a doctor and an ethnologist and historian even if he did not regard himself as a specialist in these fields. Munro lived at Nibutani in Hokkaido from 1932 and in 1933 he made an amateur film of the Ainu bear festival. Batchelor denounced Munro for producing this film, declaring Munro's behaviour to be cruel, barbarous and shameful.[11] Munro riposted that Batchelor, despite his many years of study of the Ainu, simply did not understand them and that his only interest was in converting them to Christianity. This led to a breach between the two which was only bridged some years later in 1938 when Batchelor who was suffering from a boil on his cheek was taken by his niece to Munro's clinic for treatment.

Professor Nitami Iwao[12] quotes the Japanese historian Umehara Takeshi in praise of Batchelor's achievements in recording and interpreting the Ainu and their folk-lore. Umehara deplored the neglect by many Japanese scholars of Batchelor's works.

However, some modern ethnographers inside and outside Japan have expressed doubts about the value of Batchelor's observations. Hans Dieter Oelschleger in his essay on 'John Batchelor's Contributions to Ainu Ethnography'[13] has argued that, although Batchelor tried to allow the Ainu to 'speak for themselves', his observations tended to be distorted by his prejudices. Oelschleger admits that Batchelor's 'acquaintance with the life of the Ainu seems to have surpassed any other ethnographers in the same field – actually in any other region of the world. He spent 63 years of his life in Hokkaido, he lived in direct contact with the Ainu for most of his time, he spoke their language fluently and he gained their confidence – at least this is what he tells us'. Oelschleger notes that Batchelor found the Ainu 'much less thoughtful for the future' and thus compared them unfavourably with his own countrymen and with the Japanese. As a result 'the Ainu are slowly dying out. . .[This] is part of God's plan which human beings cannot understand'. Batchelor's Christian beliefs led him to identify the Ainu's supreme god with the Christian God: he 'sees what he wishes to see'. 'Many further contradictions, along with conceptions that bear a strong resemblance to Christian belief, can be found in Batchelor's works'. This led Oelschleger to ask: 'What should be done with the works of John Batchelor?' He concludes 'the greatest possible caution is, therefore, necessary in making use of data taken from the works of John Batchelor'.

Oelschleger is an ethnologist who has been trained to make objective observations. Objectivity is, however, not at all easy to achieve even by the trained ethnologist. The fact remains that Batchelor's observations and accounts, even if tinged by his own prejudices, remain the single most valuable source of information about the Ainu and their folk-lore which for the most part can no longer be observed in a natural setting. Students of the Ainu have, therefore, no alternative but to rely to a considerable extent on Batchelor's accounts. Of course they must exercise caution in using these accounts but 'greatest possible caution', as recommended by Oelschleger, might lead them to dismiss some of the only real evidence remaining.

BATCHELOR AND THE AINU LANGUAGE

Batchelor was not the first foreigner to study the Ainu language, but he was the first to make a comprehensive study of Ainu grammar and Ainu vocabulary. His Ainu-English Dictionary was first published in 1889 together with notes on Ainu grammar. A second edition of the dictionary appeared in 1905. In this was included 'A Grammar of the Ainu Language' which had first appeared in that form in 1903. (A version had first appeared in

1887.) This also covered Batchelor's studies of Japanese place names and Ainu origins. He had first dealt with this theme in his essay 'The Pit Dwellers of Hokkaido and Ainu Place Names considered' in 1884. This was a subject to which he reverted in 1929 and which he further revised in 1935. A third edition of his dictionary appeared in 1926 and a fourth in 1938.

Batchelor's dictionary (1905 edition) of 525 pages first gives the Ainu word in romaji. This is followed by the *katakana* pronunciation and a translation into *kana-majiri* for the word in question. Finally, there is an English translation sometimes together with example(s).

In his introduction to his dictionary Batchelor acknowledges the efforts of previous scholars to put together collections of Ainu words. One of those mentioned is the Rev Walter Dening of the CMS in Hakodate who put together a vocabulary of 925 words and 38 phrases. Another was the British Japanologist Basil Hall Chamberlain who had stayed in Hokkaido with Batchelor. He also mentions the early Japanese vocabulary entitled the *Moshiogusa* which had been studied by the Austrian scholar, Dr August Pfizmaier.[14]

Batchelor's Grammar of the Ainu Language which runs to 159 pages and deals in 14 chapters with orthography, the various parts of speech and syntax, is comprehensive. It is inevitably based on Western views of grammar. In his introductory chapter Batchelor noted that 'grammatically speaking, the Ainu language has no general affinity with present Japanese'. However, he affirmed that 'there is certainly a root affinity' between ancient Japanese and Ainu. He was 'struck at times by the great similarity found to exist between certain Ainu and Hebrew words' but he had to admit that 'as far as grammar is concerned no analogy has been found to exist between the two languages'. He also, however, found some resemblance between some Basque and Ainu words and even between Ainu and Welsh and Cornish words. He concluded that the chief argument 'for an Aryan origin of the Ainu language will be found to lie in the grammar rather than the vocabulary'. His thesis about the Aryan origin of the Ainu language seems far-fetched and has been widely disputed by later scholars.

Batchelor's pioneering efforts to study the Ainu language were followed up by Japanese scholars including Kindaichi Kyosuke (1882-1971), Hattori Shiro, who produced an Ainu dialect dictionary, and Chiri Mashiho, an Ainu who was not however a native speaker (1909–1961). Chiri was particularly contemptuous of Batchelor's efforts.[15] He declared: 'Quite contrary to the trust which is generally placed [in Batchelor's dictionary], I must say that I have never in my life seen a dictionary with so many flaws. Nay rather than say that it has many flaws, it would be closer to the truth to say that it consists solely of flaws.' Kirsten Refsing commented:

> While the dictionary cannot be relied upon as a primary source for the study of Ainu, nevertheless, considering the scarcity of sources and the generally poor quality of any material published before the works by Kindaichi and Chiri began to appear, Batchelor's dictionary should not be dismissed altogether. It contains valuable material which can certainly be used with a critical and cautious approach. The dictionary gives both Japanese and English translations for the Ainu entries and perhaps Batchelor's knowledge of Japanese was more at fault than his knowledge of Ainu, since in a number of instances one finds that while the Japanese translation is totally misleading, the English one is much closer to the point. Perhaps one may question whether Chiri actually bothered to read the English translation as well.

Kindaichi and Chiri cooperated in the production of a new grammar of the Ainu language in 1936[16]. Chiri claimed that he was the main author of the work[17]. There seems to have been an unwillingness on the part of Chiri to acknowledge the work of others and this may have been one reason for his outspoken contempt for Batchelor. Hans A. Dettmer[18] declares that Batchelor's Grammar was in its time a remarkable achievement and remained for a long time unequalled. However, its contents changed very little in the six editions published between 1887 and 1938.

Katarina Sjoeberg[19] from the University of Lund says in her recent book *The Return of the Ainu: Cultural Mobilization and the Practice of Ethnicity in Japan* that '. . . in the event of uncertainty [in relation to Ainu words] I have turned to Batchelor. This is not a random choice. Batchelor's work with the Ainu langauge is highly appreciated among the Ainu who say: 'he could make himself understood among our people, which is more than one can say of linguists of today'.

Dr Lone Takeuchi, an expert linguist, whom I consulted, considers[20] that '. . . with Ainu now having become extinct – for all good linguistic, if not political, purposes – there is among present-day linguists (rather than Ainu scholars?) a recognition of Batchelor's work as an extensive source, which can be used with caution'. 'Unfortunately, Batchelor's dictionary for the most part fails to deliver the kind of information that is crucial in internal reconstruction [of Ainu], e.g. which dialect a word form belongs to etc.' Dr Takeuchi says that Batchelor's rival as the father of Ainu language studies is the Polish scholar, who spent time in Sakhalin in a Russian prison camp. The Ainu scholarly community is now awaiting publication of his phonographic records of Sakhalin Ainu from the turn of the century.

All in all, it seems clear that, whatever the limitations and errors in his Ainu dictionary and grammar, Batchelor made a unique contribution to studies of the Ainu language.

BATCHELOR AND THE JAPANESE

At first, Batchelor's efforts to learn the Ainu language and to preach Christianity to the Ainu were treated with hostility by the Japanese authorities who attempted, not always successfully, to put obstacles in his way. The authorities were no doubt constrained by the 'unequal' treaties of 1858 and by the presence in Hakodate of a British consul.

In his letters to the CMS in London Batchelor was often outspoken in his criticisms of the Japanese authorities. Professor Nitami Iwao's collection of Batchelor's letters[21] includes many critical comments. For instance, in a letter of 10 November 1893 to C.C.Fenn at the CMS, Batchelor wrote that, while Japanese in general were sympathetic to the Ainu and it was reported that much was being done for them, in fact the Ainu were afraid of the authorities. The Ainu had no recognized rights to their property. Despite the constitution they were subject to many punishments and had few rights. In the same letter, he recorded that, while living that year in Piratori, he had been required to submit his passport each week to the authorities. He had complied but on one occasion he had been a day late in submitting his passport to the authorities who were 12 miles away. Penri, with whom he was staying at that time and who was considered to be responsible, was hauled before a local court and fined one yen (a not inconsiderable sum in those days for a poor Ainu). Opposition to his attempts to convert the Ainu still continued. After 11 inhabitants of Nibutani, which lay one-and-a-half miles away from Piratori, had been baptised, the local village head and the police came to investigate, called a meeting and took down the names of those who had received baptism. This naturally aroused the fears of those concerned that they would be persecuted.

In another letter to Baring-Gould, dated 14 September 1895 from Sapporo, he said that at a meeting in Hakodate in August three representatives had raised various questions. The first question was why could not the Ainu language cease to be used in church and church documents. Batchelor in his reply had noted that the Ainu language was not recognized by the Japanese government and was not to be used in speaking with the Ainu. Legally the Ainu did not exist, but he firmly defended the use by the church of the Ainu language.

Batchelor's attitude towards the Japanese authorities softened as he got older or perhaps his attitude was softened by the attentions increasingly paid to him by Japanese officialdom. In 1904, he cooperated with the authorities by organizing a concert and a collection at the time of the Russo-Japanese War. In 1905, he dedicated the second edition of his Ainu-English-Japanese dictionary to Baron Sonoda Yasukata, then Governor General of Hokkaido, 'in grateful remembrance of sympathy shown in the publication of this work'. As recorded above, he accepted in 1909 the Order of the Sacred Treasure (fourth class) and in 1910 attended a cherry blossom party at the Imperial Palace where he shook hands with the Emperor Meiji. During the Taishō and early Shōwa era his relations with prominent Japanese deepened and he maintained a regular correspondence with Prince Tokugawa Yoshichika after they met in 1920.

The Japanese authorities had for their part softened their opposition to Christian missionary efforts and their attitude towards the Ainu. Perhaps this was, to some extent at least, due to Batchelor's efforts?

It is impossible to quantify Batchelor's achievements as a missionary. Even if there were figures for the number of baptisms at which Batchelor officiated, it could not be argued that those baptised owed their conversion solely to Batchelor's efforts. Rather we must look at his achievements from a broader perspective. He worked hard for Ainu education and was instrumental in providing medical and other welfare assistance to the Ainu. He was a consistent and fearless advocate of Ainu rights. He remained a tee-totaller all his life and fought hard against the debilitating effects of alcohol on the Ainu with whom he came in contact. His behaviour as a firm Christian believer had thus a much wider influence than an unknown number of conversions.

Dr John Batchelor no doubt, like every human being, had his weaknesses. It seems possible that he was, probably sub-consciously, proud of his achievements among the Ainu and somewhat resented the efforts of others in their work on the Ainu language and customs. But this must be largely surmise. However true or false this may be, it should not be allowed to belittle his achievements as a student of the Ainu language and folk-lore and as a Christian missionary. He is rightly revered in Hokkaido where his house in Sapporo has been preserved as a Batchelor museum. With his long snow-white beard, he was seen in his final years almost as a biblical patriarch. His autobiographical sketch 'Steps by the Way' shows that he had a sense of humour as well as humility. It was sad that because of the war he had to return to England to die.

Yoshida Shigeru and Mme Yoshida at the London Embassy

IAN NISH

YOSHIDA SHIGERU and his wife, Yukiko, occupied the Japanese Embassy at 10 Grosvenor Square for two significant years – 1936-8. These were unhappy and difficult years for Anglo-Japanese relations; but the affection for Britain which they both felt from previous postings in London stayed with them in these disheartening times. These feelings seem to have remained with him when he rose to great distinction as prime minister of several cabinets between 1948 and 1954.

Yoshida was born in Tokyo on 22 September 1878 as fifth son of a Tosa samurai family. He was adopted into the family of Yoshida Kenzo who had stayed in London for two years in the 1860s and later became Yokohama manager for Jardine, Matheson.[1] A wealthy banker and financier, he died prematurely, leaving Shigeru with a good sufficiency at the age of ten. After many changes of schooling, he finally entered Gakushuin Middle School, though it was soon closed with the death of the principal, Konoe Atsumaro (father of Konoe Fumimaro). In 1906 he graduated in politics from Tokyo Imperial University and, after sitting the entrance examination, was admitted to the Gaimusho. One commentator has observed that 'among eleven persons who joined the Foreign Ministry in that year, including Hirota, Mushakoji, Hayashi Kyujiro, Yoshida appeared to be the least likely to stand out.'[2]

After a preliminary posting in China at Shenyang(Mukden), he joined the London embassy under Ambassador Kato Takaaki in 1908-9. On his return to Tokyo he married Yukiko, the eldest daughter of Count Makino Nobuaki (Shinken). Makino was the son of Okubo Toshimichi, the great statesman of Satsuma and Meiji Japan. He had accompanied his father, a member of the Iwakura mission, to the United States in 1872 and stayed on for further study. He was assigned to the London legation and spent over three years there. He had a varied career as a diplomat, ending up as foreign minister in 1911-12 and 1916-18. Hence Yoshida, the adopted son of a prosperous business background, had married into one of the influential families of Meiji and become a Meiji gentleman. While Makino had been minister in Italy and Austria, Yukiko had gone to English-speaking schools and become an expert in the English language and literature.[3]

Yoshida was appointed consul first at Antung and later, more significantly, at Tsinan, the capital of Shantung province. He was lucky to be invited by his father-in-law to accompany him to Paris as his personal assistant at the Peace Conference in 1919. The other senior delegates were Chinda, the ambassador in London, and (later) Prince Saionji. After he returned home, Yoshida was posted to London in 1920 as first secretary, a position he held for two years, serving for part of the time as honorary secretary of the Japan Society of London. Yoshida and his wife accordingly had a prominent role to play in receiving the Crown Prince (later to be the Showa Emperor) on his visit to Britain in May 1921.

Yoshida returned to China service as consul-general, first at Tianjin and later at Shenyang. In 1928 he successfully lobbied the new Seiyukai leader, General Tanaka Giichi, to become vice-minister for foreign affairs under Tanaka himself. During his years in China, he had not liked the non-interventionist policy of Foreign Minister Shidehara and his party towards that country. He therefore claimed Seiyukai membership and offered his services. In 1930 he was appointed to his first ambassadorial post in Italy; but, because Japan was embroiled in the dispute over Manchuria during his tenure there, he found himself spending most of his time attending sessions of the League of Nations. After his return he was sent on a tour of inspection of Manchuria and China in 1933. In 1934-5 he made a lengthy tour as inspector-general of legations which took him round Europe and the United States. He resigned from the ministry (*taikan*) in October 1935.

His appointment as ambassador to London was connected with the Incident of 26 February 1936 in which the army tried to take possession of the central districts of Tokyo and to assassinate key political leaders. While it was primarily an example of military insubordination by younger officers which their seniors were unable to control, it still had implications for diplomacy. The attacks on statesmen included that on Count Makino, formerly the Lord Keeper of the Privy Seal and therefore a close adviser to the Showa emperor. Insofar as the army officers involved believed that the emperor was being misled by his civilian advisers, they were gunning for Makino especially. Fortunately, he escaped from the inn where he was staying in Yugawara by the rear entrance, with the help of his grand-daughter. This left the attackers so furious that they set the building on fire.[4]

The mutiny was crushed following an outright rejection of the cause by the emperor who called on loyal troops to suppress it. It nonetheless caused the collapse of the cabinet. The mandate passed first to Prince Konoe Fumimaro and, when he declined it on grounds of ill-health, was re-directed to Hirota Koki, a former ambassador to the Soviet Union. Yoshida commented: 'I had never taken any active interest in politics and always avoided being mixed up in such matters, but on this occasion was asked by Konoe President of the House of Peers to prevail upon Hirota to accept the Premiership and assisted in the selection for various posts in the Cabinet.'[5] The genro's invitation was accepted by Hirota. In the formation of Hirota's government, Yoshida Shigeru was in effect his chef de cabinet (*sokaku sosambo*). It was widely speculated in the press that Yoshida would become a member of the new ministry, probably in the role of foreign minister. But the army staged an unequivocal piece of interference in cabinet-making. General Count Terauchi Juichi, who had been nominated by the army for the post of war minister, led a delegation of senior officers including General Yamashita Tomoyuki which declared that the army would not serve in a cabinet containing Yoshida (among others) on the ground that he had offended the military. Perhaps the fact that Yoshida was the son-in-law of Makino may have contributed to his unpopularity with the army. The puzzle for the historian is why the army which should have been in disgrace after the mutiny came out of the incident strong enough to lay down the law in this way.

AMBASSADOR TO BRITAIN

It took four days for Hirota to announce his cabinet on 9 March.

He decided to appoint as foreign minister Arita Hachiro who had been minister to China and to look for another outlet for Yoshida's energies. Fortunately, Matsudaira Tsuneo, the ambassador to Britain then on leave in Tokyo, was appointed on that day to the imperial household and would not be returning to London. Though he was reluctant, Hirota eventually decided to send Yoshida as ambassador to London after the issue had passed over. In his writings Yoshida dismisses the issue casually as though the offer of the foreign ministership had not been made but it was public knowledge and clearly was to affect his tenure in London. On 20 March newspapers reported the possibility of Yoshida becoming ambassador though it was not officially announced until three weeks later.[7]

Yoshida departed for London on 21 May via Washington. He had encouraging conversations before he left with the British ambassador, Sir Robert Clive. He also met the representatives of British newspapers to present his thinking on his new mission. Thus, the reputation that he was 'intensely pro-British and believes that the only solution of the Far Eastern problem is cooperation between Japan and ourselves' reached London before him.[8] The three issues on which he would be concentrating were apparently leaked to the press who reported them as: 'The situation in China, the British Empire and naval policy'. Yoshida, however, made the point that: 'Many influential Japanese dislike the present isolation of their country, and his efforts to revive the former friendship with Britain have military as well as official and popular support.'[9]

When Yoshida arrived at Waterloo Station on 25 June, he was entering a complicated area in British foreign policy. Officials and ministers in Whitehall and outsiders differed widely among themselves in their prescriptions for the most desirable course for Britain to take on the Far Eastern scene. To simplify greatly, there was a Treasury group associated with the names of Neville Chamberlain, the chancellor of the exchequer, and Sir Warren Fisher, the head of the Civil Service, which was in the ascendant in 1936. Their attitude towards Japan was one of Realpolitik, that is, Britain's prime enemy was Germany and, being unprepared for that, she must seek accommodation with Japan which might entail offering concessions connected with naval matters or with China. In the end Britain alone could not, the group believed, be successful in any Far Eastern war. The group's first ventures – the Barnby mission to Japan (1934) and the mission of Sir Frederick Leith-Ross to China (1935-6) – had, however, been failures. The Foreign Office who had scarcely been consulted in these ventures was by contrast more inclined to be sympathetic to China and distrustful of Japan. Its position was reinforced by the return from the legation in Peking of Sir Alexander Cadogan who became deputy under-secretary in the Foreign Office in 1936 and then permanent under-secretary on the retirement of Vansittart in December 1937. These divisions were well-known to the Japanese and to Yoshida in particular.

Another lobby which was non-official included A.H.F. Edwardes, an adviser to the Japanese embassy in London, Howell Gwynne, the editor of the *Morning Post* and others with access to the corridors of power. These already had connections with Yoshida from his earlier official tour of diplomatic missions overseas in 1934-5. A Japanese official writing of Edwardes described him as always close to the Japanese embassy. Gwynne, for his part, was one of the old-style editors who occupied the editorial chair for a long period (1911-37). Gwynne was one of the first hosts of Yoshida at an influential dinner party. Edwardes, writing about the event, told Gwynne: 'As you know, he was the "fons et origo" of the conversation [at] your dinner party. Although this fact is manifestly unpublishable, I think it would be an excellent idea to refer to Yoshida's definite policy as expressed by him on his departure from Tokyo.'[10] The *Morning Post* not unexpectedly carried articles about Yoshida's views.

Perhaps with a view to preparing the atmosphere, Shigemitsu Mamoru who had been vice-minister until May entered the lists. He prepared the way for Yoshida by sending a conciliatory letter in English to Edwardes which appears to have reached London on 11 July so it must have been written about three weeks earlier. Its theme was:

> In the commercial field, the conflicts of interest are certainly visible as they are real – in India, in Canada, in Egypt, in Australia and practically in all parts of the globe. The Japanese are extremely irritated under the pressure of British policy against the legitimate expansion of their trade, which is of vital necessity to their national existence and growth, and which, despite the alarm so loudly sounded, constitutes only 3 or 4 per cent of world trade. Here our grievances are justified, I believe, to a large extent. . .A general conversation between the two Governments on the subject of the Anglo-Japanese relations as a whole may be

quite valuable; it may help pave the way for an amicable solution of individual questions as these are more or less inter-related.'[11]

Edwardes passed on Shigemitsu's letter to Gwynne: 'I think much valuable use can be made of it if it is shown to the select few.' Gwynne replied that he could 'make good use of it quietly and confidentially'. Fisher, though he was anxious to prevent tensions from developing with Japan, wrote on 31 July:

> While we must accept a larger degree of Japanese interest [in China], it is quite a different thing to acquiesce in Japanese monopoly or to accept the view that China can for all time be dragooned into 'brotherhood', i.e. subordination by Japan against China's wishes.[12]

Yoshida for his part must have drawn much satisfaction from the views contained in *The Times*' editorial of 8 August:

> A renewal in some form of the Anglo-Japanese Alliance would be a development welcome to Japan. It is true that Japan is very far from being inherently pro-British. Granted the expediency, however, there is nothing in the temper of the country to prevent an Anglo-Japanese rapprochement; and there is much in the traditions of both parties to forward . . ..[There are serious though not insuperable obstacles], nevertheless *this country would welcome the friendship of Japan, a proud and gallant young nation for whom we have always had respect.*[13](My italics)

Whether this guarded reaction was an early response to Yoshida's new broom or the cumulative effect of his predecessors like Matsudaira Tsuneo and Fujii Zennosuke is impossible to tell. But Yoshida, having met a cross-section of British opinion, wrote to his father-in-law that the atmosphere on his arrival was more friendly than he expected. But everyone was out of town and so the Yoshidas set off to Scotland to stay at Marchmont.[14]

OLYMPIC AND HIGHER DIPLOMACY

The initial issue to which Yoshida had to turn his attention was what in the annals of history may seem an unimportant one but which in national terms was politically vital: where would the Olympic Games be held in 1940? Following the Oslo meeting of the International Olympic Committee in February 1935 there had been intense competition between Helsinki and Tokyo to host the event. In June 1936, London threw its hat into the ring also – though belatedly. It became a triangular contest; and a truly Olympian struggle between the three cities began.

Like the Japanese Olympic delegation under the leadership of Count Soejima, Yoshida in London had to do formidable lobbying. He met not only government ministers but also the Lord Mayor of London to urge his case. Whether his special pleas struck a responsive chord we cannot say; but England voluntarily withdrew her application on 30 July. This facilitated Japan's success. By 36 votes to 27 it was decided by the IOC meeting in Berlin on the occasion of the Olympic Games there, to award the event in 1940 to Tokyo. When the crucial decision was announced, the Japanese press and athletes were over-whelmed with joy. Some said: 'The Japanese people's ambitions have finally succeeded. . . In Olympic history a significant "new epoch" is opening up. . . In 1940 the sacred flame will come for the first time to the East.' As an additional guarantee of success it was stated that the army authorities would help the organizing body (*soshiki iinkai*) from the outside though they would not want to take a prominent part.[15]

These preliminary efforts of Yoshida and his colleagues had secured tangible results. His embassy had started with a triumph. But, alas, the Tokyo government on 15 July 1938 announced that, because of the 'extension' of the China Incident, it would be inappropriate to hold the Olympics in Tokyo under wartime conditions.

Yoshida is often accused of using unofficial channels for influencing the British government. This was true and was resented by the Foreign Office. But it was a style pursued by his predecessor, Matsudaira, and his successor, Shigemitsu, also.[16] In any case it was not unnatural for the Japanese ambassador to get his message over in whatever way possible in the knowledge that Britain was pursuing a dual diplomacy at this time. As long as the Foreign Office was at loggerheads with the Treasury group, the ambassador had in effect a choice of routes by which to exert influence over British elite opinion. Naturally, the Treasury group praised Yoshida, while the Foreign Office was caustic in describing him. Indeed, the Foreign Office records include a minute criticizing his suitability as ambassador to London and his handling of Anglo-Japanese relations. Another condemned his 'inefficiency' in handling affairs.[17] Surely a very extreme reaction by officials at the end of their tether!

Despite this, Yoshida persisted in putting forward his views on reconciling Anglo-Japanese differences which were of course considerable. From Yoshida's point of view there was considerable urgency because of European developments. When he reached London, Japan's negotiations for an agreement with Germany were reaching their final stages. The Foreign Ministry had taken over the negotiations from the army general staff. Under the Hirota cabinet it was decided to carry on these talks during the summer, even if the majority of Kasumigaseki officials disapproved of them. It was clearly pressure from the army which made the cabinet come down in favour of the anti-comintern pact. As a compromise, however, it decided to consult Japan's diplomatic representatives overseas. This was the special task of Colonel Tatsumi who had just arrived as military attaché. Later, his pleas were reinforced by those of Colonel Oshima, the military attaché in Berlin who paid a special visit to London. Yoshida records: 'I replied that I was opposed to the idea: an opinion I repeated when, later, both Eiichi Tatsumi and Hiroshi Oshima visited me in an effort to prevail on me to change my views.'[18] The pact with its accompanying documents was signed on 25 November.

Yoshida embarked on the first phase of his overtures to Britain through the Conservative party in October and they continued in dilatory fashion well into the new year. But Neville Chamberlain very properly passed his rough draft of an Anglo-Japanese agreement to the Foreign Office for consideration.[19]

Japanese scholars have made clear that Yoshida's overtures were not authorized from Tokyo and were made on his own initiative. He was careful to say that they were personal. Yoshida did not clear his actions with Tokyo because he knew that he was *persona non grata* with the military and, therefore, wanted to go as far as possible on his own. This is not unknown in diplomatic history but is a risky course. So convinced was Yoshida of the need and the opportunity that he was prepared to take the risk. But Britain by her enquiries in Tokyo and by intercepts was baffled by his actions and was privately highly critical of his tactics. There were more hopeful signs when a change of ministry took place in Tokyo in January; and both the prime minister, General Hayashi, and the foreign minister, Sato Naotake, gave pro-British speeches. During their brief tenure of office, Yoshida felt that his views were commanding support, as he wrote in his letter to Makino.[20] It seemed a good omen also when Neville Chamberlain with whom Yoshida had good relations took over as prime minister in May 1937.

Yoshida frequently spoke of the need for him to return to Japan to talk the matter over with his government. As late as 1 May the press was giving publicity to a report of Yoshida's negotiations with 'a high official' of the Foreign Office for a settlement of Anglo-Japanese differences and misunderstandings.[21] But when war broke out between China and Japan in July, Yoshida's mission (as he saw it) became impossible. Once the Japanese army in China intruded into Shanghai and the Yangtse valley, it was inevitable that many issues of difference with Britain would come to the fore and many complaints would be registered. A sustained campaign from some organs of the press in favour of China resulted. Left-wing demonstrations outside the ambassador's residence was reported from 24 September – the strongest since Matsuoka's visit to London in 1933. But embassies do not invariably report such indications of national unpopularity. Commenting on this change, Mme Yoshida wrote poignantly: 'British feeling naturally went with the Chinese.'[22]

GROSVENOR SQUARE

Domestic affairs are not often mentioned in diplomatic history. Yukiko Yoshida, gives us an account of these in her memoir of these years in English, entitled *Whispering Leaves in Grosvenor Square*. She had come to London for the first time as 'a young attaché's wife' of 19 with some excitement because her father was an Anglophil and often wrote letters to his daughter in English. The embassy had then moved to 10 Grosvenor Square. When she came as the ambassador's lady, she was, she writes, delighted with London but the embassy in Grosvenor Square 'was a disappointment to us as it was so neglected, having been vacant for ten months. We had to spend over a month among cleaners and painters before the house was habitable, and even now we are gradually improving it when our Government allows us the expense'. Yoshida was not partial to golf like the rest of his embassy colleagues. Instead, he took exercise during the week from horse-riding in Hyde Park. The only other sport recorded was salmon fishing. The Yoshidas travelled most weekends, either to political country-house parties or for independent sightseeing. From 1 July 1937 they rented a country cottage called Little Fishery at Maidenhead for two months. Sometimes, Mme Yoshida went her own way and had her own entertainments.

She seems to have had an especially cordial relationship with Mrs Neville Chamberlain. Her interests were literary and she wrote a good deal of poetry in English about London.

The ambassador and his wife had to be observers and reporters on the British scene. They had to describe the distress felt by the people over the abdication crisis. Mme Yoshida writes: 'On the morning of 11 December I heard the sad news of the Abdication. . . I listened with emotion to the King's last speech on the radio which moved me greatly.'[23] The crisis had relevance to Japan in two respects: Edward VIII as prince of Wales had visited Japan in 1922; and Japan was also a monarchy.

The agony of the abdication was dispelled by the anticipation of the coronation. The Yoshidas were also deeply involved with the preparations for the coronation of King George VI and Queen Elizabeth. As representatives of the Japanese Emperor, Prince and Princess Chichibu arrived on 13 April and stayed at Hove for a month. The Yoshidas were partially their host, especially at the Emperor's birthday reception on 29 April. At the main ceremony at Westminster Abbey on 12 May, Prince and Princess Chichibu, representatives of one of the world's monarchies, were given precedence over the other foreign royalties. Although a farewell dinner in honour of the Chichibus was given on 24 June, the Princess suffered from the first of a series of illnesses which prevented their departure before 18 September.[24]

Mme Yoshida's health was always delicate and took a turn for the worse in August. Suddenly, she was taken to the London Clinic and operated on for hernia. During the long period of her convalescence Yoshida had to rely on his daughter Kazuko to act as hostess at embassy functions.[25] Thus, Kazuko addressed the Japan Society on 26 May 1938 on the subject of the Japanese Woman.

DEPARTURE

In August 1938, Mme Yoshida left with her daughter for Japan. Yoshida who had now come to the age of 60 was recalled from his post in London on 3 September and returned to Japan on 19 October. It is not easy to discover whether he left at his own request or whether he found it opportune to go when policies that he disliked were being followed. It certainly suited him to return at this time because it enabled him to attend the wedding of Kazuko to Aso Takakichi in November. He had appeared to get on well initially with General Ugaki who occupied the portfolio of foreign minister for four crucial months. But it was ultimately he who was responsible for his recall. Moreover, it was Ugaki who thought that his diplomatic career should be ended when he returned from London, regardless of his connections with Makino and Saionji. It may have been a factor that Yoshida had written some 60 letters to the *jushin* which may have been resented at an official level.[26]

The Foreign Office considered the question of conferring some decoration on Yoshida on the occasion of his departure. But the consensus was against doing so. He eventually retired from the foreign service a second time in March 1939, London having been his final post. Yoshida's departure led to a general post among diplomats. Konoe, by now prime minister, promoted Military Attaché Oshima Hiroshi as ambassador to Berlin, while the controversial Shiratori was sent to Rome. Whatever gloss is put on these appointments, they were anathema to Yoshida who was clearly anti-fascist and a member of the Anglo-American group in the Foreign Ministry. They were clearly concessions to military opinion. This was not the scene on which Yoshida wanted to operate.

What impression did Yoshida have of his years in London? Yoshida's biographer, Professor Inoki, says that he appreciated especially the attitudes and style of Sir Robert Craigie and Neville Chamberlain. Yoshida highly valued what he regarded as Chamberlain's policy of reconciliation with Japan as also his tactic of reconciliation with Germany by the Munich settlement. As a student of diplomatic style, he found Japan's diplomatic style too rigid and unyielding, but found England's to be flexible and pragmatic.[27]

John Dower writes that Yoshida was more Anglophil than pro-American. He was not put at his ease during visits to the United States either in 1934 or in 1936. It is hard to reach either a contemporary assessment of his thinking because of the rhetoric in which an ambassador has to indulge. It is also hard to believe all that was said after 1945. Dower goes on to say what is unquestionably true: Yoshida belonged to the 'Ei Bei riyoha', the group which believed in using Britain and America for the solution of Japan's problems. He was opposed to Japan's German leanings and opposed the suggestion of a full alliance. He was in touch in his retirement in Tokyo with both Joseph Grew and Craigie and was in favour of peace and against the continuation of the war.[28] It is probably true that Yoshida was greatly impressed by the aristocratic style of the upper levels of British politics.

Yoshida was notoriously inconsistent and opinionated. He was a man of action rather than a political philosopher. We need not be too swayed by the vindictive and savage criticisms made of his personality by Foreign Office bureaucrats. In a sense Yoshida was a businessman in diplomatic garb. He had assumed the clothes of his father-in-law Makino happily enough but he did not really fit into the pinstripes or at least the conventions and courtesies of diplomatic protocol as practised in Europe.

It was Yoshida's misfortune to be ambassador at the Court of St. James for two years and four months at a time when relations were deteriorating. When Yoshida was in London, as he later wrote in his autobiography: 'Japan reversed its stance, making enemies of Britain and the United States and forging ties with the more distant Germany and Italy. This was not only inept strategically but truly deplorable in that it lost Japan the good faith of the international community.'[29] Yoshida Shigeru was to live on until happier days and to become prime minister, the highest officer of state under the post-war constitution. In his contacts with General MacArthur he looked a sort of English figure from the past with his spats and his outsize cigar. When the general was planning reform of the police system, Yoshida argued unsuccessfully for the adoption of the system of London bobbies on the beat.

Yukiko, whose memoir of London, was full of prayers for peace with China, was not to survive beyond 1941. Touchingly, Yoshida who remarried dedicates his memoirs to Yukiko: 'the memory of whose constant faith in her country and her people strengthened me during the years of crisis'.

Shigemitsu Mamoru and Anglo-Japanese Relations

ANTONY BEST

SHIGEMITSU MAMORU, 1887-1957, was Ambassador to Britain in the critical period from 1938 to 1941 but his earlier career had many British connections. He is known to those interested in Japan's foreign relations in the twentieth century as one of the most influential diplomats of the Showa era and possibly as the most difficult to categorize. To some Shigemitsu is a figure to be vilified as an expansionist and a collaborator with the Imperial Japanese Army; to others he emerges as an enlightened figure keen to expand Japan's links with the West and fighting a rearguard action against the army's excesses.[1] Part of the difficulty in coming to any understanding of Shigemitsu is that his career was so long and varied: he was the Minister to China (1931-2), the Vice Minister for Foreign Affairs (1933-6), the Ambassador to the Soviet Union (1936-8). Following his embassy in London, he became the Ambassador to the Nanking regime (1942-3), and Foreign Minister on three separate occasions (1943-5, 1945, 1954-6). In addition, one might note that he was the hobbling, almost anachronistic figure (dressed in top hat and tails) who signed the surrender document on the USS *Missouri* on 2 September 1945 and that, at the end of the Tokyo War Crimes Trial in 1948, he was sentenced to a seven-year term in prison.

The wide range of Shigemitsu's responsibilities means that it is difficult to follow the continuities in his thinking, but an assessment of his role in Japanese diplomacy is important because his continued proximity to the decision-making process allows us to illuminate some of the motivations behind Japan's actions.

This is particularly the case in terms of the development of Anglo-Japanese relations from 1934 to 1941. In analyzing Shigemitsu's impact on this relationship it is important to bear in mind a number of constant themes in his thinking. It is clear, for example, that he considered relations with China to be the most significant axis in Japan's foreign relations, and that he consistently sought to find a means of reconciling the rise of Chinese nationalism with Japan's domination over East Asia. In addition, like many of his peers he was profoundly suspicious of the Soviet Union and wanted to form bonds with other countries in order to contain communism. Indeed, one may go further and state that he was uneasy with any of the new 'progressive' thinking that affected international relations in the inter-war period. He was opposed to the League of Nations and had little time for American moralizing.

One of the major problems that Shigemitsu faced in his diplomacy was how to reconcile his desire for a strong Japanese influence in Asia with the need for Japan to remain on good terms with a global power such as Britain. Clearly, Japan could not afford to alienate Britain, which was the world's leading financial and naval power and a major trading partner. The problem was, however, whether Britain would be willing to accept an expanded role for Japan in China. If Anglo-Japanese relations had remained as cordial as they had been at the height of the Alliance, this might have been possible but, as far as Shigemitsu was concerned, British attitudes had changed for the worse after the end of World War I. Indeed, a central element in Shigemitsu's thinking towards Britain from the time of the Washington Conference onwards was that it was Britain, not Japan, which had changed the nature of the bilateral relationship. Like others of his generation he regretted the ending of the Anglo-Japanese Alliance, but his disquiet with British policy was greatly exacerbated by the famous memorandum issued by Austen Chamberlain, the then Foreign Secretary, in December 1926 which announced that Britain would pursue a more liberal line towards Chinese nationalism. As far as Shigemitsu was concerned, Britain in this memorandum changed from its previous policy of seeing Japan as a collaborator to viewing it instead as a competitor; this justified Japan's move towards a more forthright policy in East Asia in order to defend its own interests.[2] The problem facing Shigemitsu in his dealings with Britain in the 1930s was whether it was possible to reverse this emergence of competition and return to a more convivial relationship.

Both as Vice-Minister for Foreign Affairs and as Ambassador to London, Shigemitsu contended that such a change was feasible, and he was encouraged in this belief by some of his British contacts who expressed both their dismay at the decline in Anglo-Japanese friendship and their lack of faith in the pro-Chinese and pro-American policy favoured by Britain since 1926. The most important contact Shigemitsu had was Arthur Edwardes, whom Shigemitsu had known in China when the former had worked as Acting Inspector-General of the Chinese Maritime Customs in 1927, and who in 1932 became the London-based adviser to the Manchukuo government, and later the adviser on world affairs to the Japanese embassy in London.[3] Edwardes was well-connected; he had friends in the media such as the pro-Japanese editor of the *Morning Post*, H.A. Gwynne, and contacts in Whitehall like Sir Warren Fisher, the Permanent Secretary at the Treasury, Sir Maurice Hankey, the Chief Secretary to the Cabinet, and Sir Horace Wilson, the Chief Industrial Adviser to the Government. Through these channels Edwardes was able to communicate his own and Shigemitsu's views to the very highest levels. The problem was, however, that, while it was relatively easy to influence the Treasury, the Foreign Office tended to remain impervious to these unofficial blandishments; indeed Edwardes was virtually *persona non grata* as far as the latter ministry was concerned.[4]

The opposition of the Foreign Office to an improvement of relations with Japan was seen by those like Shigemitsu as a result of its being steeped in enthusiasm for the new thinking in international relations epitomized by the League of Nations. As far as Shigemitsu was concerned, this interest in the League was evidence of a disturbing tilt leftwards in British politics under the influence of pro-American internationalists, such as Winston Churchill, allied with radical left-wing groups who favoured the Soviet Union. Disturbingly, this leftist influence, he believed, was even felt in the Conservative party due to the prominence of Winston Churchill and younger politicians such as Alfred Duff-Cooper and Anthony Eden.[5] The problem facing Shigemitsu was how to outflank this radical group. The obvious answer was that Japan should attempt to appeal to the British government not through the Foreign Office, but through sympathetic mandarins such as Fisher and Wilson, and by appealing directly to the 'orthodox faction' within the Conservative party, led by figures such as Neville Chamberlain, Sir Samuel Hoare and Lord Halifax, who, it was hoped, would welcome a return to the traditional Tory policy of friendship with Japan. This was the motive for the myriad unofficial contacts made by Shigemitsu and his predecessor, Yoshida Shigeru, which so antagonized the Foreign Office during this period, although it is worth noting that, increasingly, Edwardes was able to find one sympathetic contact at the Foreign Office, the Parliamentary Under-Secretary, R.A. Butler, who was a protégé of Chamberlain's.[6]

Shigemitsu's superficial perspective on British politics raises a number of problems; in particular by painting pro- and anti-Japanese sentiment as a simple right-left divide it greatly underestimated the sense of genuine outrage in Britain towards Japan which was apparent across the whole political spectrum. For example, Shigemitsu noted in 1952 in his book *Gaikō Kaisōroku* (Diplomatic Memoirs) that at the time of the Tientsin Crisis in the summer of 1939 anti-Japanese feeling in Britain had been provoked by the activities of the pro-American faction and by left-wing propaganda; in reality it was simply abhorrence at the Japanese army's treatment of British civilians which caused a wave of protests to be sent to the press and to the Foreign Office – it did not need to be stirred up by the left.[7] Again, it is significant that in 1940, when Britain proposed a temporary solution to the Burma Road crisis which met Japan's wishes, Shigemitsu's interpretation of this decision was that it was the traditionalist high Tory, Lord Halifax, who had persuaded the pro-American Prime Minister, Winston Churchill, to accept this measure of appeasement, when in fact it had been the other way round. Indeed, Halifax was consistently from the start of the Sino-Japanese War one of the figures in the Cabinet who argued for tougher measures against Japan, a stance which appears to have been influenced by his disgust at Japan's propensity for bombing civilians in China.[8]

Another, perhaps even more significant, problem was that, putting the moral issues aside, the belief that a traditional Conservative government free of pro-American and pro-Soviet influences would necessarily try to establish a new relationship with Japan which would be acceptable to both sides was clearly misplaced. The fact is that during this period neither Britain nor Japan was willing to allow the other a dominant position in East Asia, it was rather the opposite as each sought to expand its own influence. Shigemitsu was, in fact, one of the key figures on the Japanese side who was pushing for the diminution of the Western stake in China and the establishment of a new Sino-Japanese understanding which would enhance Japan's standing. Obviously, it was extremely unlikely that a British government would enter into a new arrangement with Japan in which it would agree to any such sacrifice of its own position in China, and therefore the result was that Shigemitsu's policy towards China directly contradicted the aim of achieving better relations with Britain.

PROBLEMS AS FOREIGN VICE-MINISTER

A clear example of this disparity of interests came during 1934–5 when Shigemitsu was Vice-Minister at the Gaimushō. As Vice-Minister Shigemitsu was aware of the advantages that could accrue to Japan from an improvement of diplomatic relations with Britain, since this would allow Japan to escape from diplomatic isolation and to avoid a major crisis over the collapse of naval limitation. He was not, however, prepared to see any *rapprochement* which would impinge upon Japan's interests in East Asia and instead wanted British recognition of Japan's paramount position in China. This essential qualification was not clear in the vague overtures that Shigemitsu and the Foreign Minister, Hirota Kōki, made to Britain during this period, with the result that those in Britain who sought a *rapprochement*, such as the Chancellor of the Exchequer, Neville Chamberlain, and Sir Warren Fisher, felt that the Gaimushō's soothing words were sincere and augured well for Anglo-Japanese cooperation in China.[9]

The problems which led to this misunderstanding began in the autumn of 1934 when Shigemitsu created much interest in the British Treasury by enthusiastically welcoming to Tokyo the Federation of British Industry mission led by Lord Barnby which was due to visit Manchukuo to assess the possibilities for British trade. Even more significant was the series of talks he held with Arthur Edwardes, who travelled to Tokyo with the FBI mission. Edwardes informed Fisher on his return to London that Shigemitsu had informed him that the Japanese people were 'pro-British' and that the 'Japanese Government would greatly welcome a gesture of friendship from this country'.[10] These hints encouraged Chamberlain and Fisher to believe that an understanding could be reached if only the right means could be found, and they hoped that better relations with Japan would allow for the recovery or even expansion of Britain's economic position in China. Such thinking could not have been further from Shigemitsu's intentions. In a memorandum of 20 November 1934 Shigemitsu recorded his view that, if Japan was to accomplish its aims in East Asia, this meant 'the expelling of politically influential countries and foreigners from China' and specifically the withdrawal of Western garrisons and the destruction of the British-dominated Chinese Maritime Customs Service.[11]

The British Treasury's misinterpretation of the Gaimushō's thinking helped to lead to the plan in 1935 to send Sir Frederick Leith-Ross, the Chief Economic Adviser to the Government, to East Asia to try to arrange a Sino-Japanese settlement through the medium of a joint Anglo-Japanese loan to China in return for Chinese recognition of the independence of Manchukuo, a development which, it was hoped, would ease Anglo-Japanese tensions and advance the cause of British trade in the region. Leith-Ross arrived in Tokyo in September 1935 and held a number of talks with Shigemitsu and other prominent figures, but found little enthusiasm for his ideas. Shigemitsu later claimed in *Gaikō Kaisōroku* that the Gaimushō's response had been lacklustre because they had been caught offguard by Leith-Ross's proposals having failed to receive any forewarning of his plans through Sir Robert Clive, the British Ambassador in Tokyo, or Matsudaira Tsuneo, the Japanese Ambassador in London.[12] Such an explanation seems at best disingenuous, for in reality Shigemitsu stood opposed to any plan that would have involved Anglo-Japanese political cooperation in China; the most he was willing to tolerate was a British economic presence. At the very time that Leith-Ross arrived in Tokyo the Gaimushō was involved in the formulation of Hirota's 'Three Principles' for relations with China which, it was hoped, would reassert Hirota's control over Japanese foreign policy in the face of army activism and which dealt with China solely in terms of the Sino-Japanese relationship. The proposals brought by Leith-Ross were an unwelcome diversion.[13]

The failure of the Leith-Ross mission to elicit a positive response from the Japanese government was a severe blow to Anglo-Japanese relations, for even though Shigemitsu and Hirota had decided by December 1935 that it was necessary to restore Britain's trust in order to avoid alienating the Treasury, it blunted the cause of the pro-Japanese lobby in London and strengthened the scepticism of the Foreign Office.[14] It is significant, however, not just for its short-term effects but also for the light it sheds on the fundamental incompatibility of Anglo-Japanese interests in China. Unfortunately, Shigemitsu was never able fully to come to terms with this. Later, as Ambassador to London, he continued to press Britain to accept only an economic role for itself in China and to accept Japanese political domination. In December 1938, just after his arrival in London, Shigemitsu approached the Conservative MP, Sir John Wardlaw-Milne, who was chairman of the House of Commons China Committee, to suggest a scheme that would break the deadlock in relations, a central element in this plan being recognition by Britain of 'Japan's unique position in China'.[15] The proposal did not prosper. Later, in October 1939, he again pressed for Britain to change its stance towards war in China, convinced with the start of the war in Europe 'that there were the conditions for an appropriately fair settlement of the China problem, and that Britain would exhibit its traditional statesmanship and recognize Japan's position in East Asia and China'.[16] For a brief moment he believed that he had made a breakthrough when he reported to the Gaimushō that the Foreign Secretary, Lord Halifax, had informed him that 'His Majesty's Government had no intention of pursuing political designs in China, their interests being limited to commercial and financial considerations'.[17] This was, however, a misreading of the British position; the Foreign Office had no intention of starting a British retreat from China. It was only at the end of his time in London that Shigemitsu admitted that perhaps Japanese policy and he himself had been misguided, when he noted in a conversation recorded by Leith-Ross that:

> [Japan] had made many mistakes in her policy towards China, but now both the civilians and the military were agreed that peace should be made without territorial gains and without indemnities. . . . [H]e regretted that collaboration with us had not been arranged at the time that I went out to China.[18]

This was, however, too little and too late.

China was not the only area of policy in which Shigemitsu felt that progress could be made; he was also keen to see a settlement of commercial tensions, but believed that here, too, it was for Britain to make concessions and allow Japan greater access to markets within the British Empire. The importance of these commercial issues was one of the reasons why Leith-Ross was invited for a second visit to Japan in June 1936. In addition, in a letter that Shigemitsu sent to Edwardes at this time he argued that this was one of the major areas of concern and observed that:

> The Japanese are extremely irritated under the pressure of British policy against the legitimate expansion of their trade, which is of vital necessity to their national existence and growth, and which, despite the alarm so loudly sounded, constitutes only 3 or 4 per cent of world trade. Here our grievances are justified, I believe, to a great extent.[19]

His stress on this area of relations was, however, not so great when he was in London, as the start of the Sino-Japanese War had the initial effect of lessening trade tensions outside East Asia, although over the longer term the issue was to re-emerge in the different form of protest against British sanctions towards Japan.

A more significant policy area which Shigemitsu, both as Vice-Minister and Ambassador to London, hoped could be used to construct a new Anglo-Japanese understanding was to stress the advantage of Anglo-Japanese cooperation against Soviet activities in East Asia, in the hope that this strategy would appeal to those on the traditional wing of the Conservative party who were deeply antagonistic towards the Soviet Union. The effort to play on British fears began shortly after Leith-Ross's visit to Tokyo in September 1935 and can be seen in part as an effort to repair the damage: it was, however, also an element in a wider attempt by the Gaimushō to construct a 'Defence against Communism' policy which would help to rein in the Japanese Army in north China and push them from anti-Chinese into an anti-Soviet direction. In January 1936 Shigemitsu informed the British Ambassador in Tokyo that recent events in north China had to be seen in the light of Soviet machinations and that it was necessary for Japan to construct a barrier against communism.[20]

AMBASSADOR TO LONDON

In London, after two years of service in Moscow from November 1936 to October 1938, Shigemitsu's willingness to use the anti-Soviet card became much more marked, as his animosity towards Soviet communism had grown with acquaintance. In his talks with Halifax and Butler he consistently emphasized the threat that the Soviet Union posed to other states and that Stalin would be the only one to gain from the differences that existed among the non-communist countries. This line of attack became particularly noticeable following the conclusion of the Nazi-Soviet Pact in August 1939 and the subsequent opening of hostilities in Europe. Clearly, Shigemitsu hoped that Britain's experience of Soviet duplicity after the Anglo-French-Russian talks of the summer of 1939 had been a bitter lesson and would lay the basis for Anglo-Japanese collaboration. In the spring of 1940 he informed Butler that 'the determination of Japan to keep on terms with us against Russia was undiminished' and warned that 'the ardent desire of the . . . Soviet Union was to keep everyone in trouble and gradually getting weaker'.[21] Here again, however, he was misjudging the climate of British opinion, for while there was little love for Russia there was even less for Japan.

Although his efforts to engineer an overall improvement of relations with Britain came to nought, Shigemitsu was able as Ambassador in London to ease some of the tensions in relations. He worked well, for example, in the first six months of 1940 to deal with some of the economic problems that arose from the start of the European war, and was able to lay a basis for a policy of 'gradual cooperation', a policy aided by the relationship between Butler and Edwardes.[22] All of this began to change with the Burma Road crisis in the summer of 1940.

Shigemitsu first became aware of this crisis when he called on the Foreign Office on 21 June 1940 to explain the demand made to the British Military Attaché in Tokyo by a representative of the Japanese Army that Britain close the Burma Road or face war. Shigemitsu was initially taken aback by this news, but soon recovered his composure to argue that Britain was wrong to take seriously warnings emanating from unofficial channels. This approach was, however, quickly undermined when two days later the demand for the closure of the Burma Road became official policy. Despite this setback, Shigemitsu tried to turn the crisis in relations to Japan's advantage so that Japan could gain the dominant position in East Asia but without risking war with Britain.[23] As with other prominent Japanese policy-makers, Shigemitsu realized that the conditions in South-East Asia following the defeats suffered by Britain, France and Holland in Europe favoured an increase in Japan's political and economic influence in the region, but in addition he believed that Britain's insecurity could lead it to back a Sino-Japanese peace settlement. He was therefore enthusiastic about the settlement of the Burma

Road issue negotiated by Foreign Minister Arita Hachirō and the British Ambassador in Tokyo, Sir Robert Craigie, which stated that the Burma Road would be closed for three months while Japan sought a 'fair and equitable' solution to the China problem.

In London, Shigemitsu did his utmost to try to forward what he saw as this 'great opportunity', as he believed that there had been 'a major conversion of its [Britain's] policy towards Japan and the obstacles to the East Asian problem'.[24] He visited the Foreign Office frequently for talks with Halifax and Butler and once again used Edwardes as a vital but unofficial conduit of information. Shigemitsu also sought to persuade the Gaimushō to adhere to his policy and take a firm line towards Britain designed to push the latter towards a recognition of Japan's interests. On 25 July he explained that at this time:

> . . . it was necessary for Japan to consolidate her position in East Asia. As a result Japan should encourage England to get herself out of the position she has got herself into, & help her towards her policy of promoting peace in China, in the hope that the U.S. will follow suit.[25]

In a further telegram to Tokyo on 5 August Shigemitsu observed that Japan should proceed with 'scrupulous consideration and prudence in our relations with Britain' and noted that, if Japan carried out its 'Greater East Asian policy with a responsible, fair and square attitude, we may properly expect Anglo-American obstacles to be removed in the natural course of events'.[26]

By this time, however, Shigemitsu's cautious policy for expanding Japanese influence was being undermined by the incoming Konoe government with Matsuoka Yosuke as Foreign Minister. The first act of the new administration in regard to relations with Britain was at the end of July to arrest over twenty British civilians in Japan and Korea on charges of spying. Shigemitsu was furious at this flagrant insult to Britain which he believed would undermine all he had been trying to achieve. Worse was to follow, for within a month Matsuoka initiated a drastic purge of the Gaimushō which included orders for Shigemitsu's trusted deputy, Okamoto Suemasa, to return to Tokyo. Shigemitsu began to fear that the diplomatic service was being handed over from mature, cautious professionals like himself to young, inexperienced and hot-headed reformers, and confirmation that this was so came on 27 September when news arrived at the Embassy in London that Japan had signed a Tripartite Pact with Germany and Italy.[27]

For Shigemitsu the conclusion of the Tripartite Pact was a mistake of the greatest magnitude, and in hindsight he declared that it set Japan 'on the road to the death of the nation'. His opposition to any anti-Anglo-Saxon combination with the Axis powers was longstanding, as in the winter of 1939, he had mobilized opinion among the majority of the Japanese ambassadors in Europe to any strengthening of the Anti-Comintern Pact. In the early autumn of 1940, he was still of the same opinion, despite the series of German victories since April of that year which had convinced most Japanese observers that Britain was on the verge of defeat. Shigemitsu believed by late September that Germany had missed its chance for victory over Britain; it had failed to defeat the Royal Air Force and could not launch an invasion. Britain, meanwhile, was increasing its production of armaments and Churchill was manoeuvring to win over American opinion. Moreover, Shigemitsu was struck by Britain's resolve in the face of the shock fall of France and the German bombing of British cities. This was not merely an abstract observation as Shigemitsu himself had personal experience of the Blitz; he had remained in London in September and thus witnessed at first-hand how Britain had coped with the German onslaught without buckling. The experience, one might postulate, did not endear Germany to Shigemitsu, as during this period the Embassy buildings in Portman Square were half-destroyed and the farewell party for Okamoto was disturbed by an air-raid.[28]

Following the arrival of this new pro-German line in Japanese foreign policy, Shigemitsu was tempted to resign, but after reflection he decided to remain in London to do what he could to mitigate its effects and avoid direct Anglo-Japanese confrontation. In *Gaikō Kaisōroku* Shigemitsu noted of this period that:

> Tokyo's position was simply to persist in an extreme way with the destruction of Britain, but I thought privately, that in their moves in international relations they were virtually blind to the course of the war in Europe. I felt I had no choice but to become a pillar and support the nation. That is to say that, to make sure a sudden break in relations did not occur, it was necessary to support Anglo-American relations in London. This was the first point, next was also to give accurate reports about the outlook for the course of the war in Europe, this point would show that Tokyo had made a mistake (it was in vain, they did not take this news

255

into consideration at all). I decided to be as resolute as I was when I did not flinch in the middle of a bombing raid, I would harden my determination to fight alone in this extremely difficult period.[29]

It was, however, very difficult for Shigemitsu to make any positive impact on Anglo-Japanese relations. By the autumn of 1940 many of the pro-Japanese figures of the mid-1930s were marginalized and those such as R.A. Butler that did remain were now much cooler. In his conversations with Butler, Shigemitsu's argument that the Tripartite Pact was analogous to British support for China cut little ice and his efforts to revitalize talks about a payments agreement met with little enthusiasm. Shigemitsu did try once to use unofficial channels to stem the tide and held a series of talks with Lord Hankey, the Chancellor of the Duchy of Lancaster, and Lord Lloyd, the Secretary of State for the Colonies, in an attempt to arrange a ministerial visit to Tokyo. These efforts were in vain, as the Foreign Office was now interested solely in the containment of Japan in league with the United States; the time for talking had ended.[30]

The seriousness of the situation was brought home to Shigemitsu when on 7 February 1941 he was called to the Foreign Office for a meeting with Eden who had recently replaced Halifax as Foreign Secretary. At this interview Shigemitsu was, without warning, faced with a tirade from Eden about Japan's ambitions in South-East Asia and its confrontational policy towards Britain. Shigemitsu tried to argue that the crisis in Anglo-Japanese relations had been exaggerated by Eden and that he was relying too much on inaccurate newspaper reporting. He also attempted to demonstrate that Japan's ambitions for East Asia were not any different to the spheres of influence controlled by the British Empire and the United States and asked, in the light of Japan's claim that 'it possesses the greatest economic and political interest in East Asia', whether Britain was opposed to the 'assertion of the United States that it has the greatest interest in the Western Hemisphere'.[31] Despite this bravado, Shigemitsu was deeply concerned at the appearance of the 'war-scare' in East Asia and his fears were not calmed by the subsequent correspondence that took place between Churchill and Matsuoka in which he acted as postman.

During Matsuoka's visit to Europe in March-April 1941 Shigemitsu tried to arrange a meeting with his Foreign Minister in Berne in order to bring to the latter's attention his own interpretation of the prospects for Anglo-Japanese relations and his own predictions for the future of the war in Europe. Shigemitsu worked through Butler and Hankey to arrange transport to continental Europe, but in the end the meeting never took place. It is, however, interesting to note that the British government was enthusiastic for Shigemitsu to make this trip and that the chartering of a plane for him was approved at the War Cabinet level. This interest in Shigemitsu resulted from the realization that the Japanese ambassador had what Butler referred to as 'a proper view of the British war effort and the state of Europe', that is, that Shigemitsu believed Britain would eventually win.[32]

This understanding of Shigemitsu's thinking came not only from his comments to British ministers and officials but also from the fact that since February 1941 (and possibly before) British codebreakers were regularly deciphering Shigemitsu's telegrams home. These revealed that, while the ambassador was not an outright Anglophile, he did perceive that Japan would be making a very rash move indeed if it should enter the war on Germany's side. In one of these telegrams Shigemitsu noted, as a comment on the last of the messages sent by Churchill to Matsuoka, in which the British Prime Minister declared that the United States was in effect already a combatant in the European war, that:

> If America enters the war the Tripartite Pact comes into operation whereby Japan may be involved. It is not, however, quite clear as to whether when the Pact has failed in its objective of preventing America's entry into the war, Japan is bound to come in immediately. The moment of Japan's entry must be very carefully chosen in the interests of the Axis & it might be best for Japan to remain neutral until she is able to clarify the situation by entering the war after Britain and America's strength is exhausted.
>
> In fact careful thought should be given to the point that those who enter the war precipitately will finally exhaust their national resources & will be unable to move if non-belligerents such as the U.S.S.R. then decide to establish themselves in advantageous positions.[33]

This carefully weighted message was clearly intended to play on the fears of Japan's policy-makers and reveals once again Shigemitsu's own concerns about Soviet ambitions. As such one can presume that it was read with interest in Whitehall.

With the failure of his plan to meet Matsuoka in Switzerland, Shigemitsu's time in Britain drew to a close. The exact circumstances of his return to Japan are not clear. Shigemitsu always claimed that it had been his decision to withdraw from London in order to report his views in Tokyo in person, but one of the intercepted telegrams from Matsuoka to Shigemitsu suggests that the Foreign Minister was behind this decision.[33] Whatever the case, it is clear that, before Shigemitsu left, he was feted by many members of the War Cabinet and by top Whitehall officials. The idea was to buttress his belief in British victory and to provide him with ammunition for his forthcoming struggle with Matsuoka. In fact, by the time of his return to Tokyo, Matsuoka had resigned; but this did not make Shigemitsu's task any easier as the army and navy were set on the path to war. Shigemitsu did try in September 1941 to put pressure on Craigie to push London into taking a role in the Washington talks, but once this effort failed he slipped into the background and played no further part in averting confrontation.

To assess Shigemitsu's impact on Anglo-Japanese relations in his time as Vice-Minister for Foreign Affairs and as Ambassador to London is not an easy task. It would clearly be a mistake to view him as an Anglophile, as contemporaries such as Lord Hankey, Major-General F.S.G. Piggott and even Shigemitsu's secretary, Kase Toshikazu, did in their memoirs, but it is also difficult to paint him as anti-British. What does emerge from a study of his career is that he was prepared to see Japanese cooperation with Britain as long as the latter was willing to accept a reduction of its influence in East Asia and recognize the economic and political paramountcy of Japan in the region. This, as far as Shigemitsu was concerned, was only accepting the reality of the situation, and he appears to have believed that, if Britain followed its traditional diplomatic practice, it would have recognized this. His diagnosis was that British opposition to Japan was due to its new 'left-inspired' adherence to the principles of the League of Nations, and that Britain would only see sense when the orthodox wing of the Conservative party asserted its control. To a degree, this assessment has the ring of truth, as it was quite clear in the 1930s that much of British public opinion objected to Japan for moral reasons, but it ignores the fact that this morality extended to both right and left. Even more, it also misunderstood the intentions of those in Whitehall and the Conservative party who favoured closer relations with

Japan, failing to acknowledge that their wish was for a revival of British interests in China rather than a retreat. Shigemitsu may have argued in his last year as ambassador for a cautious policy that would avoid a direct Anglo-Japanese clash, but it is difficult to escape the judgement that it was his earlier policies that had contributed to lay the roots for this confrontation.

Japanese Businessmen in the UK

SADAO OBA

ALTHOUGH BUSINESSMEN, including acrobats, magicians and housemaids, were to be found among the first group of Japanese who came to Britain in the period of the 1860s, most of them were not much more than peddlers or artisans. It took a decade before the settlement of 'businessmen' in the modern sense took place when WATANABE SENJIRO (1860-1916), 22 years old, was posted to the office of Mitsui & Co. in the City of London which had only been open for two years. This essay attempts to sketch some of the prominent businessmen who spent significant parts of their careers in Britain.

BIRTH OF JAPANESE BUSINESS COMMUNITY

Watanabe was one of the first graduates of the Shoho Koshujo (Commercial Laws Training School) which was the forerunner of the existing Hitotsubashi University. After nine years Watanabe was promoted to the manager of the London office and held that position for thirteen years until 1902. It covered an era of industrial expansion for Victorian Britain and light industrialization for Japan. Watanabe secured various fruitful agencies from companies like Platt Brothers & Co (spinning manufacturers), Joseph Sykes Brothers (card clothing), Babcock & Wilcocks (boilers), Clarke Chapman & Co (marine winches), John Hastie (marine engines) and other leading manufacturers to supply machinery and later to arrange technology transfers to Japan.

During his twenty years' stay in London, Watanabe contributed not only to his company but also to Anglo-Japanese relations. He was a founding member of the Japan

Society[1] and was married with Mrs Mary Ann Davison, widow of late Colonel Thomas Davison in 1893.[2] In Japan, he advanced in his company's hierarchy to become managing director but was unlucky enough to have died while swimming off Kamakura in 1916. He was 56 years old.

Another early arrival was KATO SHOZO, an antique dealer who settled in London in 1889. He is reported by Minakata Kumagusu as a son of a *karo* (minister) of a daimyo in Bushu (now Saitama prefecture).[3] For some unknown reason, Kato became eccentric, poor but the best friend of the encyclopaedic Minakata. Minakata reportedly borrowed several ukiyoe from Kato and sold them, with Minakata's explanatory notes, to buyers. Kato could utilize Minakata's knowledge and Minakata could earn commission. Minakata often visited Kato's house late in the evenings to wine and dine. For instance, in the month of December 1895 he paid eleven calls.[4] Most probably he was not much welcomed by Mrs Kato.

Kato gave a helping hand to the Japan Society when Lt-Colonel E.Z. Thornton delivered his lecture entitled 'Military Works in Old Japan' in January 1908 by supplying materials. He was a talented soloist of traditional Japanese ballads such as *naga-uta* (long epic songs) and *ha-uta* (short love songs) which were usually performed by him at the official dinners of the Japanese community.[5] He is supposed to have been the first Japanese civilian who took a seat on board a RAF Handley-Page Bomber 'at his own risk'.[6] He was so popular among the Japanese community that he was described as 'genro' (grand old man). In 1928, on the occasion of the Grand Ceremony of the Accession of Emperor Showa he represented the Japanese community in the UK by contributing a congratulatory message. He died unluckily in a traffic accident in 1930 and was sorely missed by many Japanese from the community.[7]

THE FIRST PHILANTHROPIST

Japan's victory in the Sino-Japanese War of 1894-5 raised Japan's international status as well as the number of the Japanese community in the UK. MATSUMOTO YONEKICHI, newly assigned manager of Kansai Trading Company, assumed his job in Manchester in 1898. In 1902, due to his company's bankruptcy, he established his own company of Matsumoto & Co. there.

Matsumoto was a rather unusual businessman. His business ethics were not only to seek profit but also to spend it for

Christianity, the UK and Japan. He taught Japanese manufacturers and exporters not to 'export cheap and shoddy goods'. During the Russo-Japanese War (1904-5) he worked for Japan and was popular as 'Matsumoto of Asia House'. In August 1914, when a moratorium was proclaimed just after Britain's declaration of war against the Austro-Hungarian Empire, he dumped all his stocks to pay his clients. The Manchester office was closed the following year and in London he established Nippon Shoko Kaisha (Japan Trading & Industry Co., hereafter abridged as JTI).[8]

JTI was the brainchild of Matsumoto and his collaborators such as Yoshimoto Kaoru. They defined the charter of the company as a programme of spending, realized through Anglo-Japanese trading, for the benefit of Christianity through such causes as social reform. In February 1917 he bought £5,000 of Government Bonds in Manchester to 'express his serious sympathy as an allied citizen'. According to the *Nichiei-Shinshi* journal, Matsumoto's fine deed seemed to have impressed citizens there and newspapers like the *Manchester Guardian* and the *Evening Chronicle*, which had often been anti-Japanese, praised Matsumoto's gesture in purchasing military bonds as an excellent example for patriotic Britons to follow.[9]

The London Japanese Christian Association was launched in August 1920 at the proposal of Matsumoto Yonekichi, Nagai Teiji, Kimura and others as a church as well as a social club. Japanese clergymen delivered good messages on Sunday afternoons at 28 Prince's Square, Queens Road, London W. A Social Club was attached to the JTI. JTI continued to gain sizeable profits which were spent for this purpose.

Matsumoto's mother, who was an ardent Christian, died and was buried in the Brookwood Cemetery, Surrey in 1922. He followed her in 1925 and was buried in the same cemetery. As a successful businessman he was generous in contributions for the welfare of the Japanese community. He gave a lot of his private money to the Kanto Earthquake Disaster Fund. He supported *Nichi-Ei Shinshi* so as to ensure that the newspaper be regularly published.[10] Under his will £1,000 was donated to it by his British wife. His aspirations for Christianity and social reform most probably originated from his mother and his study at Doshisha Primary School, Kyoto in 1889.[11] The Japanese business community are justifiably proud of having such a pioneer in philanthropy nearly eighty years ago in the UK.

A BANKER AND MITSUI MAN

KANO HISAAKIRA (1886-1963), son of Viscount Kano who used to be a daimyo in Chiba Prefecture, was posted in 1921 to the Yokohama Specie Bank in the City of London. The bank was the dominant foreign exchange and finance business in Japan. The Japanese business community in London increased substantially during the First World War because of the sudden increase of Anglo-Japanese trade, especially Japan's export to Britain; and the number of Japanese companies and banks increased to twenty-one.

Apart from his daily business the young Kano was active in Anglo-Japanese events. He chaired an ordinary meeting of the Japan Society in December 1922[12] and delivered a speech on the 'Social and Economic Situation in Post-War Japan' at Budo-kai, Japanese martial arts club, in the same month.[13]

ITO YOSABURO (1887-1978) was assigned to the Mitsui office in the City in 1910 where he spent a very busy and turbulent eleven years. He recalls the booming years of the First World War when 'although there have been various restrictions to our trade with Japan we could easily sell whatever products we imported from Japan. At the last stage of the war we even thought of selling *tofu* (soya cake) or *kairo* (portable body warmers) in Britain. As we had imported every possible product we could buy in Japan, we were at a loss, after the end of the war, how to dispose of the mountain of shoddy goods which we had failed to sell.'[14]

Ito returned to Japan in 1922 the same month that Yoshida Shigeru, First Secretary of the Embassy, returned home. Yoshida and Ito are supposed to have taken the same boat. Kano returned home in 1924. Consequently, the three were simultaneously living in London for a period of one or two years. Their encounter and the friendship that followed in London between the promising diplomat, the banker and the businessman bore fruit in the difficult decades to come.

As the post-war recession progressed to world-wide depression in the 1920s and 30s, Anglo-Japanese talks like the Cotton Conferences took place. In London, the first business association 'The Japanese Businessmen's Association' (London Shogyo Konwa-kai) was launched to discuss common problems and issues among Japanese businessmen. At an ordinary meeting on 15 May 1928 they discussed a) how to make a case list of untrustworthy non-Japanese businessmen, b) how to deal with unjustifiable claims from Japan, c) information on the Japan

Research Committee, d) issues on the Economic Advisory Committee of the League of Nations. Mukai Tadaharu, general manager of Mitsui & Co. and the chairman of the Association, emphasized at the meeting the importance of the Association and his determination to publicize it, after he was transferred home, so as to make a contribution to foreign trade.[15]

CRITICAL YEARS

Both VISCOUNT KANO and ITO YOSABURO coincidentally returned to London in 1934 as the general managers of Yokohama Specie Bank and Mitsui & Co. respectively. The Anglo-Japanese relationship had been gradually worsening as Japan's invasion of China intensified. On the one hand, Japan's 'cheap yen policy' in the international foreign exchange market increased her exports, causing trade friction in various products like cotton goods. Ito Yosaburo represented the Japanese Spinners Association at the World Spinners Conference held every other year. He made various social contacts and arranged nemawashi (groundwork meetings) with the British and European representatives so as to soften the anti-Japanese feelings among the delegates.[16] Viscount Kano rose to becomes vice-chairman of the Japan Society.

YOSHIDA SHIGERU became the ambassador to the Court of St James in 1936. The next year a Sino-Japanese clash at the Marco Polo Bridge near Peking developed into an overall confrontation and spread to the Yangtze river basin where Britain and the USA had large investments. In London the Chinese Embassy used the opportunity and launched campaigns against the Japanese invasion. Public hearings and lecture meetings were organized by the Chinese embassy when Japan was accused of what the Japanese army had been doing in China.

The Japanese Businessmen's Association launched a counter-attack against Chinese propaganda.[17] A brochure 'Some Facts about the Sino-Japanese Conflict'[18] was published and distributed. The brochure argues that 'If the question be asked, What has led to the present hostilities in China?, the answer is, emphatically, The persistent anti-Japanese campaign of the Chinese Government'. It attacks 'any economic manifestation of a hatred of Japan – through boycott. Seven times since 1915 Japan has suffered this form of planned dislocation of her most important market.' The six-page brochure continues by commenting on the history of foreign troops being stationed in China since the Boxer Rebellion, the necessity of manoeuvres for foreign troops there, the outbreak of the Marco Polo Bridge (Liukouchiao) Incident and, following that, the enlargement of the war and concludes that 'In stating the foregoing undeniable facts Japan is engaging in no special pleading, but wishes to place them on record, and asks all peoples to remember that there are two sides to every question, and that all war news comes, quite naturally, from China, and, equally naturally, gives the Chinese version of events.'

The above-mentioned campaign was most probably initiated by Ambassador Yoshida as Ito Yosaburo recalls that 'Yoshida disregarded the formality. He surprised me often by asking me, by telephone, to come to see him immediately. He asked for my comments on Britian's economic situation, Anglo-Japanese trade issues etc. I told the Ambassador that he is very clever to ask us businessmen from whom he could obtain up-to-date information. The reports from his ministers are supposed to be somewhat out-of-date. I advised him to call the general managers of Mitsui or Mitsubishi personally and try to find the best answer. It is free of charge'.[19] By the same token, Kano Hisaakira had frequent talks with Yoshida.[20] Ito returned home in 1938 and had very difficult negotiations, under the orders from the army and navy, with the Dutch East Indies authorities in 1940-1 to try to obtain a concession to explore oil in Borneo, Celebes and New Guinea. Because of his tenacious negotiations he succeeded in making a provisional contract. But on his return voyage to Japan he was surprised to receive a cable that the contract had been annulled due to the Japanese army's advance into Southern French Indochina.

THE SHIPPING MAN

ARIYOSHI YOSHIYA (1901-82) was another middle-class manager of Nippon Yusen Kaisha (NYK) who was assigned to the London branch in 1934. The world was still in recession. Then, according to his memoirs,[21] the British staff of the office did the main business by themselves and left the Japanese staff only 'the second front' routine work such as accounting and administration. Ariyoshi's frustration was intensified by another fact, namely that NYK's allowances to expatriate employees were the lowest among Japanese companies in the City. Ariyoshi made as many visits as possible to newly-built ships, shipyards and machine-building factories in Britain and Europe. Because of the value of 'NYK' as a good client, most of them welcomed him.

For recreation he enjoyed dog-racing, as horse-racing was too expensive, and playing mahjong with fellow Japanese.

In 1938, Ariyoshi was transferred to the Berlin branch. Japan's alliance with the Axis powers had become even closer. Japan, as well as Manchukuo, were drastically increasing the demand for weapons, explosives, FIAT bombers and machine tools to produce weapons. The transportation of these army cargoes were ordered by military attachés as 'priority one cargoes'. For newly-assigned Ariyoshi there were too many cargoes for him to handle himself as those were 'secret army cargoes'. Moreover, there were other cargoes such as the coal-liquefaction plant for Mitsui Miike Coal Mine, Kyushu and a plant to treat poor ore mined in Manchukuo. Ariyoshi struggled to obtain ship space as NYK's shipping quota in the Euro-Far East Shipping Conference, the shipping tariff cartel of liner companies, was limited. The more space Ariyoshi obtained the less the London branch could get. Ariyoshi was put in a very awkward position between the demanding and pushing military attachés and his own frustrated London branch. In August 1939, Ariyoshi was suddenly ordered by Ambassador General Oshima to utilize the newly-arrived *Yasukuni-maru* to evacuate Japanese women, children, students and travellers as war was imminent. He made every effort to accommodate as many persons as possible and the ship sailed from Hamburg with a full load of Japanese evacuees on the evening of 26 August. The ship anchored one week in Bergen, Norway, in order to see how war was launched on 1 September, and then the *Yasukuni-maru* sailed direct to Japan. Ariyoshi returned home in January 1940 after six years' stay in Europe.

THE PACIFIC WAR

Soon after the outbreak of the Pacific War, Japanese citizens in the UK, including expatriates, were detained in the Isle of Man. VISCOUNT KANO was the unlucky one among them. The Japanese internees were described as follows:

> The earlier Japanese arrivals – 34 of them – were described by a Manx newspaper with something approaching respect. They were by far the most prosperous-looking members of the incoming contingent, many of them 'having an appearance of well-to-do business men'. The reportage was accurate, for that is precisely what they were. They came from the very small but flourishing Japanese business community in the City of London, and most of them were

seniors in the London branch of a Yokohama bank. It was believed that their top director was a member of the Japanese imperial family. Whether that was true or not, he was immediately made leader of the house which had been assigned to the party in the Palace Camp, and no unit in any of the camps was said to approach it for severe cleanliness. The main staircase had been scrubbed white by the first morning of their arrival, and the place was run on strict military lines. The same reporter wrote sniffily that the next consignment of the Japanese was very different. Yet, even so, the Japanese were the star internees.[22]

Kano did not belong to the Imperial family but his attitude and behaviour as the descendant of a daimyo might have convinced the islanders that he did. After about a half year's internment Japanese expatriates were repatriated, leaving only a few dozen Japanese who refused to return home. Kano was promoted to become a director of the bank but had to spend difficult and gloomy days in Tokyo as he was watched by the authorities as a member of the 'Eibei-ha' (Anglo-American sympathizers).

ARIYOSHI was seconded in 1942 to the Sempaku Un'ei Kai (Shipping Management Committee) which controlled the merchant marine of about 2,700 ships totalling 6.3 million gross tons in order to serve the war effort. The rivalry between the army and the navy to secure bottoms was so severe that the Committee had many difficulties in allocating the ever-decreasing tonnage, due to serious losses and poor shipbuilding capability.

ITO YOSABURO and the other management of Mitsui & Co. had to resign in 1943 because of the 'Taiyuan Incident'. The incident emerged suddenly as newspapers and radio in Japan reported that 'Mitsui had hindered the army's operations in Northern China' or 'Mitsui had done illegal business'. These reports, which were widely believed after the war, had been fabricated by the army in China to warn and tighten up control of the Japanese business community there. Ito became the chairman of Toyo Rayon (present day Toray) and was ordered by the army to try and build aeroplanes.[23]

IN 'OCCUPIED' AND POST-WAR JAPAN

ARIYOSHI heard with tears the Imperial broadcast on the very hot day of 15 August 1945 at the Shipping Management Committee. He found himself again in the feud between the army, which was hastening to repatriate its own three million soldiers from all over Asia and the navy, which was concerned to import foodstuffs for the starving nation. The Civilian Merchant Marine Committee (CMMC), the renamed Shipping Management Committee which reported to US Occupation Forces, began to operate transportation for the repatriation of Japanese from Korea, Taiwan, Karafuto (Sakhalin), China, South East Asia and the Pacific Islands. At the end of the war it was estimated that 3 million military personnel and 3.6 million civilians had been located in that vast area and it would take eight years, if the repatriation was limited only to such war-torn Japanese vessels as had survived, before the last Japanese could be repatriated. Very fortunately, the US government released, to expedite the repatriation, 215 of their War Standard Type vessels – 100 Libertys, 100 LSTs, 9 C1s, 6 Liberty-Type Hospital Ships totalling 1.4 million tonnes. Thanks to this the repatriation was finalized in a couple of years or so, except from Siberia where half a million Japanese were detained much longer in the labour camps.

The Civilian Merchant Marine Committee cooperated with the US Forces, during the Korean War from 1950, to transport personnel and goods. As the Japanese sailors were familiar with Korean waters, they were often praised by the US forces for their valuable cooperation.

After eleven years' secondment to the Merchant Marine Committee during the war and the Civil Merchant Marine Committee during the Occupation, Ariyoshi Yoshiya returned to NYK in May 1953. The shipping industry had been recovering from the damage during the war and competition was becoming even keener. In order to fight with non-conference ships, the Pacific conference abandoned fixed freight tariff between the USA and the Far East. The Mitsui Shipping Co., an outsider of the Far Eastern Freight Conference (FEFC), stormed into the Far East-Europe business which jeopardized the position of insider companies like NYK, Osaka Shosen Kaisha (OSK) and European shipping companies. Ariyoshi who was promoted as a Director and General Manager of the business department had to cope with those difficult issues and problems.

At the end of 1953, Ariyoshi made his first post-war tour of London where strong anti-Japanese feeling still persisted. He was very pleased, however, to be warmly welcomed by old colleagues and clients. He discussed with the top management of leading shipping companies like P&O and Blue Funnel lines how to cope with the rapidly changing shipping world.

After having ascended the company ladder he became president of NYK in 1965. The Japanese economy had been achieving hyper-growth and it required a vast tonnage of ships. He realized the coming requirements of specialized ships to import raw materials for the ever-expanding Japanese manufacturing industries and ordered in Japanese and foreign yards the manufacture of specialized cargo ships for woodchips, bauxite, coal and motor-cars. NYK was also the first operator of container-ships across the Pacific. He managed to merge with Mitsubishi Shipping.[24] As a result of Ariyoshi's excellent management NYK has grown to be the biggest shipping company in the world.

Ariyoshi was active not only in the shipping world but also in the wider international business community. He was the chairman of BIAC (Business and Industry Advisory Committee to OECD), a member of the Council of the Atlantic Committee and president of the Japan-Netherlands Association. He is remembered as a researcher on the 'Edo senryu' (short humorous verses which were made during the Tokugawa period) which includes many erotic ones. His collection of senryu was published.[25] He died from pneumonia in September 1982. He was decorated with the First Class Order of the Sacred Treasure by the Japanese Emperor, KBE by Queen Elizabeth II and medals from the Dutch and Norwegian governments.

KANO left the Yokohama Specie Bank after Japan's surrender and was assigned to the post of deputy director, Shusen Renraku Chuo Jimukyoku (Central Liaison Office) which was responsible for liaison between the Japanese Government and the Occupation Forces. He was also a member of the Shokuryo Taisaku Shingikai (Food Commission) which discussed emergency measures to secure food supplies. Undoubtedly, his expertise in finance and his worldwide network of acquaintances was a very important asset for the job. Soon after, however, he was purged by GHQ from official jobs as he had belonged to the management of the Yokohama Specie Bank which was regarded as closely connected to the Imperial Japanese government.

The GHQ's occupation policy was gradually eased in accordance with the intensifying cold war and Kano was released from the purge in 1950 when the Korean War broke out. He became the chairman of the Hakodate Dock Co., a shipbuilding company, and the president of Nippon Remington, subsidiary of Remington of USA which sold office equipment. He became popular, however, when he was assigned in 1955 as the first president of the newly-launched Japan Housing Agency, a governmental corporation which aimed to supply decent and good-quality housing at reasonable prices to accommodation-hungry Japanese.

Kano had had various 'dreams' since his youth.[26] The dreams reappeared and persuaded him to appeal to the nation with big plans. The mass media called him 'the greatest braggart since Goto Shimpei'[27] who had master-minded reconstruction of Tokyo after the Great Earthquake of 1923. In 1959, after his retirement from the Housing Agency, he made a round-the-world tour in order to inspect examples of town-planning in many countries. After the trip he revealed big projects such as redeveloping Tokyo by establishing networks of high-speed motorways, a large-scale excavation of Tokyo Bay, and developing flat lands for housing etc by transporting sand from the mountain areas. These dreams were realized in the hyper-growth era that followed.

In 1962 Kano was elected, as the recognized candidate of the Liberal Democratic Party, Governor of Chiba Prefecture where his daimyo ancestors governed during the Tokugawa period. He announced revolutionary plans such as 'developing water-supplies, roads and housing' and 'bi-weekly free Saturdays for prefectural employees'. The proposal for 'bi-weekly free Saturdays' was rejected by the Self-Government Ministry but Kano insisted on 'no intervention into my administration'. He was, however, finally obliged to obey the Ministry. He died suddenly in February 1963 after only three months in office. He was missed not only by the residents in the prefecture but also by many Japanese. He was decorated with the Second Order of Merit with the Sacred Treasure. He was a life-long supporter of Romanization of kanji (Chinese characters) and often signed as his name using katakana.

REESTABLISHING THE JAPANESE BUSINESS COMMUNITY IN THE UK

During the Pacific War the Japanese business community in the UK disappeared because of internment and the repatriation of Japanese expatriates to Japan. In the first half of the 1950s, however, Japanese businessmen returned to London one by one as the representatives of trading, shipping and insurance companies. Not surprisingly, they were often not welcomed by Britons. They had difficulty in finding lodgings. They were accused in pubs for what Japanese soldiers had done to the British POWs and internees. The expatriates endured these accusations in order to reestablish themselves among the local community.

Then, HOTTA NAOMICHI (1893-1981) helped those Japanese expatriates to fit in to the business community in London. Hotta, a Tokyo University graduate and then an employee of Suzuki & Co, received a cable from Tokyo head office while he was on board ship loading sugar at a port in Java in 1918 ordering him 'Hurry up to the West'. The ship sailed straight to London where he began work at the London branch of Suzuki & Co. In 1927, just after his English wife Ethel had produced her first son, his company went bankrupt. He decided to remain in Britain and work independently picking up any business which was not of interest to Mitsui or Mitsubishi and began to import lumber and butter from Hokkaido. He worked as the secretary to the Japan Committee of the International Chamber of Commerce (ICC) and also as the representative of Chicken Sexers Association in Nagoya. Because of his intelligence, business expertise and sincerity, he acquired a high reputation and obtained a reasonable income until the Pacific War. He was not repatriated to Japan as he had dual nationality and family in England. During the war he retired to Hampshire to raise chickens and produce milk.

In post-war Britain he resumed his work for Japanese companies and for the Japan Committee of ICC. He relaunched the pre-war 'Palmerston Kai', a monthly luncheon meeting of the general managers of Japanese companies. The meeting is still held regularly at the Great Eastern Hotel at Liverpool Street Station, London.[28]

The number of Japanese companies in London increased gradually. In July 1959, the Japanese Chamber of Commerce and Industry in the United Kingdom (JCCI/UK), a private company established under British law, was launched by more than thirty companies. In the next year the Nippon Club, successor to the pre-war Nihonjin-Kai, was established by 50 corporate and about 250 private members. In the following two decades many Japanese companies, banks and manufacturers set up their offices and manufacturing operations all over Britain. By the beginning of 1996 418 companies associated with JCCI/UK[29] and about

270 Japanese manufacturers were operating manufacturing plants and research institutes.[30]

According to the annual survey made by the Japanese Consulate-general, London, 43,527 Japanese were living in the UK on 1 October 1994, and 20,200 were registered as private company-related and their families.[31] The number of Japanese businessmen is estimated, therefore, at around 10,000 which is more than twenty times compared with the number in the 1930s. It will take another few decades before prominent businessmen like Watanabe Senjiro, Matsumoto Yonekichi, Kato Shozo, Kano Hisaakira, Ito Yosaburo, Ariyoshi Yoshiya and Hotta Naomichi who represented the Japanese business community in the past will emerge.

Christmas Humphreys and Japan

CARMEN BLACKER

CHRISTMAS HUMPHREYS, 1901-83, lived, and memorably moved, in several distinct walks of life. His profession was the Law, which he considered to be a high and honourable one, and he was proud to follow so closely in the footsteps of his eminent father that he rose to be a QC and eventually an Old Bailey Judge. As Crown Prosecutor he was involved in several notoriously sensational cases. The Towpath murders, the Craig and Bentley case, the trial of Donald Hume, 'who murdered Stanley Setty, cut up his body and dumped it in parcels from his plane into the Thames', ensured that his name hit the headlines forty years ago with a panache hardly possible today when such crimes are a daily occurrence.

By conviction he was a Buddhist. As an undergraduate at Cambridge he had first discovered the Theosophy of Madame Blavatsky, and then Buddhism. The two together seemed to give him the answer to the nagging question, 'What's it all about?' Here was his path, and for the rest of his life he continued to tread it, and to promote its truth by every means in his power.

Nor were his powers inconsiderable. He founded the Buddhist Society of London in 1922, and remained its President for the rest of his life. He was a dramatic and persuasive speaker, a gift which stood him in good stead both at the Bar and at Buddhist gatherings all over the country. He radiated and communicated a masterful energy and vitality. Problems which seemed daunting to everyone else were solved as soon as he entered the room. He was a natural leader. During the short term that I served on the Council of the Buddhist Society in the 1950s, I recall that it was only Miss I.B. Horner, the Pali scholar, who in her tart Cambridge voice dared to contradict him.

He was no mean poet. He had strong views on the authorship of Shakespeare. And he was a prolific writer. When he surveyed his life from the autobiography he wrote in 1978, he could claim to have written three books on law, five on poetry, one account of Buddhist travel and some fifteen on Buddhism and Oriental philosophy.[1]

His connections with Japan occurred in both Buddhism and the Law. It was the Law which took him to Japan in 1946 to act as junior to Arthur Comyns Carr K.C. during the International Military Tribunal for the Far East. It was from Japanese Buddhism that he discovered the path, Zen, which he believed to be specially his own, and the sage whom he always regarded as both his teacher and the greatest man alive, Dr D.T. Suzuki.

His one visit to Japan came as a bolt from the blue. In January 1946, with no warning at all, the Attorney General, Sir Hartley Shawcross, asked him, 'Would you like to go to Japan as junior to Comyns Carr in the International War Trial?' If so, he must leave in ten days.[2] He made up his mind at once. He would go, not only for the historic importance of the part he would play in the War Crimes Trial, but also for the opportunity of making direct contact, for the first time in his life, with Japanese Buddhists and Buddhism. Never before had he been out of Europe, much less to any Buddhist country.

He arrived in Tokyo on 3 February 1946, barely six months after the dropping of the atom bomb on Hiroshima and the extraordinary events which crowded the last twenty-four hours before the Emperor's surrender broadcast. The trial did not begin until 3 May, but the intervening three months were fully occupied with preparing the long indictment, deciding on who among the list of generals, admirals, ministers and diplomats should be prosecuted, ensuring that the Emperor did not number among them, and preserving agreement among the eleven prosecuting countries. His own commission was to compile and record the evidence for the attack by Japan on the British Empire.

During this preliminary period Toby, as he liked his friends to call him, was able to attend some of the interrogations of the prisoners in Sugamo gaol. He was surprised to note that many of them seemed only too anxious to confess a greater responsibility for the outbreak of the war than was warranted by the facts.

Though worried that 'men were being tried for their lives for the breaking of a law which did not exist at the time when they broke it', he nevertheless found the trial 'profoundly impressive'. Eleven judges, one from each of the prosecuting countries, faced twenty-six defendants who included fourteen generals as well as diplomats, ministers and admirals. The appalling difficulties of interpreting were well managed by Commander Denzel Carr, USN. The court-room was glaring and stiflingly hot, and the trial moved necessarily slowly and cumbersomely.

After two months his own commission was completed and, not being required to prolong his stay in Tokyo, he left Japan in July. He therefore witnessed only a small part of a trial which was to continue for two-and-a-half years. The verdicts, which condemned seven of the defendants to death, were not announced until November 1948.

But his duties in Tokyo during the six months of his stay did not prevent him from pursuing what to him were more important contacts in Japan. He lost no time in travelling to Kamakura, there to call on Dr Daisetsu Teitarō Suzuki.

Toby had first met Dr Suzuki at the meeting of the World Congress of Faiths in London in 1936. He was already familiar with the *Essays in Zen Buddhism*, which were published in 1927 and, though they attracted few general readers, had an impact on the few who did read them which Toby described as momentous. Hitherto, it was only Theravada Buddhism which was known in England. It was Dr Suzuki's *Essays* which first told the West of the 'glories of the Mahayana'. Here was 'the love of beauty, the laughter, the splendour of life' which the Pali canon had always discouraged, not to say banished. Now, thanks to Dr Suzuki, no longer could Buddhism be represented as an escape from life. And, of course, the *Essays* had revealed, too, that Dr Suzuki was the 'greatest living exponent of Zen Buddhism' who had given Zen to the Western world. For the rest of his life he referred to Dr Suzuki as the Master.[3]

Dr Suzuki, now aged 76, had spent the war quietly writing in one of the sub-temples of the great Zen monastery Engakuji. He welcomed Toby with warm courtesy, regaled him with a meal which for those stringent times must have been a notable feast, conferred on him all rights to reprint his collected works in England, and put him up for the night in his new house on the hill at Matsugaoka.

Toby was enchanted by the beauty of Engakuji, and

responded immediately and in poetry to what he saw as the Japanese secret of harmonizing art with the underlying patterns of nature. Before he left, Dr Suzuki dictated to him the lectures which subsequently became *The Essence of Mind*.

Toby's next Buddhist call was to the big Sōtō Zen temple, Sōjiji. His description of the early morning session of *zazen* there must be one of the first eyewitness accounts by a Westerner of a formal session of Zen meditation. A meeting was arranged with Buddhists of various sects, to whom Toby presented the Twelve Principles he had drawn up in the belief that they were common to all Buddhist sects and schools. This short charter, he told the group of Buddhists, might encourage the emergence of 'one tremendous Buddhism' capable of standing up to the menace of Western materialism and the decay of spiritual life sure to follow after a war.

Before he left Japan, Toby had the satisfaction of seeing his Twelve Principles accepted by representatives of 17 different sects in the Nishi Honganji in Kyoto. He left believing that his efforts to distill an essence of Buddhism would bear good fruit. These efforts deserve their record here, for alas, fifty years later few people in Japan recall them.[4]

Toby never returned to Japan in more peaceful or prosperous times. He attended the Buddha Jayanti celebrations in India in 1956, but the new, rebuilt, rich, mechanized, economically booming Japan he was never to witness.

Under his direction, however, the Buddhist Society in Gordon Square, London, prospered. Toby was the acknowledged leader of the 'Buddhist movement' in England. He would discourse effortlessly and notelessly on Karma and Rebirth, on Being Whole, on the interior causes of war. Often he would talk about Zen, expounding Dr Suzuki's writings, narrating the stories, encapsulated in the famous *kōans*, of old Chinese Zen Masters. There would be 'discussions' afterwards which I sometimes found irritating. People would utter easy 'Zen phrases', such as 'Everything is nothing', or 'I am you', which reminded me of the boy in the Mumonkan *kōan* who held up his finger. Toby never told them to shut up.

Sometimes, he would arrive in a dinner jacket, ready to move on to the Covent Garden ballet after he had finished what he had to say about the Four Noble Truths. His wife Puck wore the distinctive evening dress of the pre-war Theosophist and mystic. Or again, he would arrive from the Old Bailey, where he had spent the afternoon proving that the witness had not, as she had testified, been upstairs with the baby, but downstairs with the body, chopping and mopping.

He was courageous enough, in that conventional period, to espouse causes which were beyond the purview of most of his colleagues in the law. 'Fringe medicine', for example, was only minimally acceptable in the 50s. Toby took care to neutralize all the 'shots' he was required to have before his visit to the East, by 'herbal iodine' and other products of the Society of Herbalists. He reported miraculous cures from the Bates System of Natural Eyesight, spines straightened by Swedish osteopaths, and astounding prophesies from his astrologer friend, Phyllis Naylor.

His big house in St Johns Wood was full of rare and arcane books, golden Buddhas and other trophies of his journeys to the East, and memorabilia of the six great men whom he deemed himself lucky to have met. Among these was a large book of the paintings of the Russian explorer and mystic, Nicholas Roerich. This strange and spiritually gifted man had once, on a visit to London, rescued Toby from a condition of accidie and depression. He had simply pointed out of the window and uttered the words 'No, look!'

In 1956 the Buddhist Society, thanks to Toby's energy, business sense and private generosity, moved its premises to a bigger house in Eccleston Square. Under Toby's direction it soon became the focal point for any Buddhist visitors to England. From Japan came a particularly interesting succession. Dr Suzuki paid two visits to this country, in 1953 and 1958, and each time delivered notable lectures at the Society. Zen Masters from Kyoto, Kamakura and Mishima arrived, and lectured in Eccleston Square. The Prince Patriarchs of both the Higashi Honganji and the Nishi Honganji in Kyoto were also welcomed by Toby.[5]

Meanwhile, Toby's Pelican *Buddhism*, first published in 1951, continued to sell in remarkable numbers. Reprinted again and again, its sales reached the half-million mark during Toby's lifetime. In due course, he himself began a weekly Zen Class at the Society. Though he never abandoned his 'catholic' view of Buddhism as a whole truth, he now increasingly left the exposition of Theravada and Indian Mahayana to others, to concentrate himself on Zen.

Nor, however, did he ever abandon the Theosophy of

Madame Blavatsky which had been his creed before he discovered Buddhism. Zen and Theosophy were for him effortlessly reconciled. Some members of the Buddhist Society indeed were irritated by Toby's continued devotion to Madame Blavatsky, whose portrait, chin in hand, stared out from a prominent position in the Society's lecture room. I myself was in the doghouse for several months after he found on my desk, during a visit to Cambridge, a copy of Vladimir Solovyoff's book *A Modern Priestess of Isis*. This book gave a fascinating account of how the writer had caught Madame Blavatsky in her forgeries of the famous Theosophical classic *The Mahatma Letters to A.P. Sinnett*. The *Letters* purported to have been written by secret Masters in Tibet, materialized out of nothing and transmitted by astral post to the Theosophical Headquarters at Adyar in South India. Solovyoff claimed to have caught Madame Blavatsky virtually in the act of forging them herself, and had forced a confession. Toby's brief comment on seeing the book was 'Filth!' and, despite his legal training in the weighing of evidence, he continued to believe the *Letters* to have been written by Masters and sent by astral post.

★ ★ ★

From 1950 he began the important task of republishing Dr Suzuki's collected works. The *Essays*, in their stately and expensive edition of 1927, had attracted few readers and less sympathy. Unlike the Pali Buddhist canon which had long interested scholars on both linguistic and philosophical grounds, the texts of Zen had at that time made little appeal. The strange words and irrational actions of the old Zen Masters, as recounted by Dr Suzuki, appeared grotesque, irrelevant and brutal, a parody of Buddhism.

But for Toby Dr Suzuki had shown a kind of Buddhism which, 'without relying on words or scripture', could directly point to the disciple's mind and bring him to the experience of *kenshō-jōbutsu*, seeing his own nature and becoming a Buddha. By the methods of Zen, strange though they might seem, one could here and now in this very life realize one's innate Buddha nature, which we hold in common with all other sentient beings.

Dr Suzuki's forgotten works accordingly reappeared, under the imprint of Rider and Co. with the Buddhist Society, in seven modest brown volumes. For a year or two they had a steady sale among the members of Toby's Zen class. But towards the end of the 1950s there was a sudden and dramatic explosion, unforeseen either by Toby or by Dr Suzuki himself. 'Zen' was adopted by the hippies of San Francisco. It became the watchword of the counter-culture, the slogan of the Beat Generation and the Dharma Bums. Soon we began to hear that Zen promised you instant enlightenment if you simply Let Go, 'acted spontaneous', and did nothing except what happened to come into your head. Had not Dr Suzuki reported the old Zen Masters as saying that there was nothing to do and nowhere to go? Here at last was a way to enlightenment without tears, discipline or effort.

The responsibility for this strange, entirely Western phenom-enon cannot be laid at the door of either Toby or Dr Suzuki. Partly to blame, however, was undoubtedly Toby's old protégé, Alan Watts.

When Alan Watts was a schoolboy at Kings School, Canterbury, he wrote to Toby a letter on Buddhist matters of such mature wisdom that Toby was convinced it could only have come from one of the senior masters. When he realized that such insight came from a boy of seventeen, he was immensely impressed and, for the rest of Alan Watts's turbulent life, continued to give him every encouragement and support. It was Toby who helped him publish his little book *The Spirit of Zen*. It was Toby who gave him a platform when he came over from America in 1958 and lectured to large crowds at the Caxton Hall. Watts in his turn was fascinated by Toby's patrician panache, the arcane secrets with which he seemed familiar and the flattering attention heaped by both Toby and Puck on the then promising young man.

But Watts, now living in California, was soon shrewd enough to devise his own version of Zen that exactly fitted the needs of the new hippies. In books, lectures and broadcasts he insisted that the foolish Indians had always assumed that the spiritual life required effort. Yoga needed strenuous effort. But the wise Chinese knew better. They had said again and again that there was nothing to do, no need to try, nowhere to go. Simply 'let go' here and now and be spontaneous.[5]

Alan Watts had deftly gathered various quotations from Zen texts to prove his point. But what he never explained was that such remarks had always been made at the end of years of arduous and daunting discipline; the glorious freedom of which they spoke was only achieved after a hard struggle. To make such remarks at the beginning of your journey was unfortunately not the same thing at all.

It was several years, however, before Beat Zen was recognized to be a mere party game, which dismantled no neurosis, and led to no self-knowledge. It stood, on the contrary, all too often for 'the ultimate unsinkable Narrenschiff for many complacent egos'.

Alan Watts, to the end a cult figure with his own radio station in Sausalito, California, died in 1973 of a lethal mixture of drugs and alcoholic poisoning.[6] Toby, though he disclaimed Beat Zen, was always loyal to Alan Watts. Though he detested drugs, insisted that the Five Silas or Moral Principles should underlie Zen practice, and was careful to explain that the Five Silas forbade free love or drugs, nevertheless refused to allow a word of criticism of Watts and his 'lifestyle'. 'If he wants to practise free love why shouldn't he?' I vividly recall him shouting one evening when the subject was tactlessly broached.

But Toby never succumbed to the temptation to become a New Age Guru. He insisted sternly on the traditional moral basis of Zen practice, that there were no short-cuts through drugs, and that, though life was 'great fun', fashionable permissiveness was like removing the banks from the river; the force and direction of the water turned into a sludgy stagnant mess. I remember someone remarking, after one such lecture to the Cambridge Buddhist Society, that 'the Flower Power people are in complete disarray!'

Dr Suzuki likewise always deplored the strange Western misunderstanding of his republished works. What was reported to him from California seemed like a bizarre caricature of his intended meaning. But three years before his death in 1966, Toby's powers of initiative again asserted themselves. Hearing that I was to spend a few months in Japan in the summer of 1963, he said to me: 'Tell sensei that we'd all like to know how he first came to Zen. What was the appeal of Zen in the 1890s? Tell him from me to write his autobiography.'

Accordingly, at the first opportunity, I made my way up to the Matsugaoka Bunko in Kamakura, where sensei was living and writing, with Mihoko Okamura as indispensable companion, secretary, nurse and cook. I gave him Toby's message.

'Well,' he said 'I'm 93,and I'm tired, and I've promised to write several other things. . .'

Suddenly, I had a brainwave. 'Couldn't you dictate something? I could take it down, then type it out, and you could correct anything you didn't like.'

'All right,' he said. 'We'll start now!'

Mihoko and I seized pencil and paper, and for an hour every day for the next week wrote down what he told us. He told of his discovery of Zen, his two teachers Imakita Kōsen and Shaku Sōen, his struggles with an inappropriate kōan, his obsessional passion to solve the kōan, and the final moment during the winter *rōhatsu* retreat when the first *kenshō*, or 'seeing of his own nature', burst upon him. Each day I typed out what he told us, and the next day he made a few corrections. Sometimes judicious questions were necessary. 'How did you get from your house to the temple over the Kurikara Pass?' 'On an old bus.' 'What sort of an old bus?' 'Only one horse. . .'

But it was owing to Toby's initiative that we have this document, the only first-hand account of Dr Suzuki's early encounters with Zen. It was published in the special number of the *Middle Way*, issued to mark the Society's 40th anniversary in 1964.

Even after Toby rose to be an Old Bailey Judge, he continued his weekly Zen classes at the Buddhist Society. And when Dr Irmgard Schloegl, after twelve years gruelling training in traditional Rinzai Zen in Kyoto, came back to England to teach the authentic way, Toby made over his house in St Johns Wood to her and the Zen Centre which she founded. After Puck's death the house began to fill up with disciples, both men and women, wishing to receive the traditional teaching as might lay followers in a Japanese monastery. Toby was housefather, and continued to preside, in a yellow dressing-gown for breakfast, at the head of the table in the dining-room.

When he died in 1983 he left twenty-five books, at least 300 articles and a reputation in the Old Bailey for the very qualities he hoped to inherit from his father – strength tempered with justice, courtesy and humour, and a sound knowledge of the English Law. He was hopeful to the end that Zen would in due time find its feet in the West for those people who were suited to its special ways and means.

In his last years he wrote two books, *Zen Comes West* and *A Western Approach to Zen*, which were optimistic and unhurried. Beat Zen was a thing of the past. Few Japanese Zen Masters could be expected to come West, and even fewer English aspirants to go to Japan for the full training. So we shall have to produce our own line of teachers. Why not? The Truth is there for all who can develop the faculty of seeing it. Zen is simply a new presentation of the Truth, which will be understood in its own time by people who have stopped trying to search for it with their everyday apparatus of thought, who have arrived at the point where they started and know it for the first time.[6]

To the question, What is Zen, Toby always replied Walk on! One of his books indeed bears this title. He never returned to Japan to submit himself to the rigours of Zen training under a teacher. But it was his unique combination of qualities which set the Buddhist movement on course in England. He had begun to teach Buddhism at a time when its principal truths were scarcely understood. Even the notion that ultimate truth can only be known by a change in our mode of consciousness was in the 1950s unfamiliar to his audiences, still more to the general public. His eloquence, dash and courageous style of leadership, not to speak of his books which sold in their thousands, and in the case of the Pelican *Buddhism*, in their hundreds of thousands, set Buddhism in England on a proper course. Bhikkhus might come from Thailand and Ceylon and Lamas, later, from Tibet, but it was Toby who at the outset, enabled the Buddhism of Thailand, Tibet and especially of Japan to strike a root and steer a course that bears the vigorous validity of tradition.

21

Sir Vere Redman, 1901–1975

SIR HUGH CORTAZZI

VERE REDMAN was successively an English teacher and a press correspondent in Japan before World War II. Shortly before war broke out, he joined the British embassy as press attaché. During the war he served in the British Ministry of Information dealing with Japanese affairs. After the war he was appointed information counsellor in the British mission in Japan. He retired in 1961.

Vere Redman's life and career centred on Japan. He worked hard throughout to contribute to understanding between British and Japanese. He was always loyal to his home country and did his best to explain British policies to the Japanese even though, like many other diplomats, he had his personal doubts about aspects of British policy. He was left of centre in politics and found it hard, for instance, to defend the British role in the Suez debacle in 1956.

Redman also did all he could to explain Japanese attitudes and policies to British people. He knew that to be successful in Japan a diplomat needed to be able to like the Japanese although he must not go overboard in his feelings and should understand Japanese limitations and faults. He was an eccentric in the British tradition. In appearance he sometimes suggested Tweedledum and sometimes Humpty Dumpty. If he was Tweedledum, then Madeleine, his French wife, was Tweedledee. Both were short and dumpy. Despite the fact that Redman was a difficult character and despite occasional storms[1] they remained devoted to one another.

Vere Redman's informal and unstuffy attitude contrasted sharply with the popular image of the typical British diplomat. Both Vere and Madeleine were down to earth and practical people. Indeed, Vere's language was often distinctly colourful not to say crude. Sometimes he could be downright rude and he had a tendency to make personal comments which could be taken amiss. One colleague recalls inviting Vere to lunch in Osaka and placing him next to an exceptionally large woman, the wife of a member of the British community in the Kansai. As the guests sat down Vere asked her in a loud voice: 'How much do you weigh, Mrs So and So?'[2] Another colleague remembers a lecture meeting when Vere who was standing next to him, suddenly announced in a loud voice: 'You're going bald!'[3] He also had a quick wit. During the occupation of Japan (1945-1952) he was seated next to the wife of the Trade Commissioner in the headquarters of the Supreme Command Allied Powers (SCAP), an American lady who was often described as 'mutton dressed as lamb'. She had had a lot to drink. She regaled Vere with a story of how she had married her husband because he bought her a brand new evening gown after having spilt a bottle of champagne over the one she had been wearing. She then said: 'You must think me a loose woman.' To which Vere replied with a straight face: 'On the contrary, madam, on the contrary.' His witty reply was, of course, quite lost on her.[4]

Vere was very unpredictable and often talked in riddles. It infuriated him if his listeners were slow in grasping his meaning. He had a very short fuse and his temper tantrums were memorable, but they soon ended and he generally forgot all about them. Sometimes, however, he could be unforgiving if he felt that someone was trying to take advantage of him[5]. Like many other egoists he did not suffer fools gladly. Some said that he was not greatly interested in the views of others. Others found him a good listener especially outside office hours.[6]

Vere Redman was far from easy to work for. Meriel Boyd[7] who was for a short time his secretary in the late 1950s noted that a special technique was required. His tantrums and sometimes provocative behaviour had to be ignored. Lady Bouchier, when she worked for him in the early years after the end of the war, found him disconcerting and difficult, although she came to have great regard and affection for him.[8]

Vere suffered from severe diabetes and required regular injections of insulin[9]. Even so he would from time to time lapse into a diabetic coma. When this happened whoever was with him had to feed him quickly with chocolate, of which he was always supposed to carry a supply (often it had been forgotten).

This brought him round and once more he would make sense in his eccentric way.

In the post-war years at least he seemed to some of us to live primarily on gin with a little water and cigarettes (he was a chain smoker and his clothes were permeated with cigarette ash). But he and Madeleine always 'kept a good table' and gave 'wonderful parties'.[10] Vere also served excellent wines. Indeed, he was a member of the the Tokyo branch of the Wine and Food Society as well as of the Good Grub Club which was more populist in its membership. He also enjoyed and took a real interest in Japanese food.[11]

He enjoyed swimming which he recorded in *Who's Who* as his only hobby. After the war he and Madeleine rented a cottage at Hayama on the coast near Tokyo and went there at weekends, whenever they could so that he could relax and swim.[12] Despite his unhealthy life-style he had such vitality that he lived until he was 73 and might have continued longer if Madeleine had not died in 1970.

Sadly, the Redmans had no children.[13] Perhaps this was one factor in their love of animals. In post-war years at least they always kept dogs (poodles) which were allowed a free run of their house including the sofas and the chairs. They also kept budgerigars. Lady Gascoigne, the wife of Sir Alvary Gascoigne, the head of the United Kingdom Liaison Mission (UKLIM) to the Supreme Commander Allied Powers (SCAP) had the Redmans' help in establishing the Japan Society for the Prevention of Cruelty to Animals. This later gave way to the Japan Animal Welfare Society (JAWS) established by Eleanor Close, wife of the first British Council representative in Japan.

Despite his peculiar manners and occasionally offensive behaviour, Vere generally earned the respect and the affection of those who came in contact with him. He and Madeleine were renowned for their kindness, hospitality and help, which they lavished, if possible unobtrusively, on friends and colleagues as well as on the lame ducks, especially British, who found their way to Japan before and after the war. Lady Bouchier records that he did much to help people get 'out of trouble, (such as several cases of embezzlement), paying their debts himself, and even perjuring himself in one notorious case'.[14] He was essentially a kind man, and if he was vain about his knowledge of Japan, he generally hid it reasonably well.

Although Vere Redman lived most of his working life (just

over 31 years according to his own calculations) in Japan he was not a scholar of Japanese history and culture like Sir George Sansom whom he got to know well and to respect and like. While Vere spoke a limited amount of Japanese he could not read Japanese. Yet his long experience in Japan and his ability to empathise with other people gave him an almost unique understanding of Japanese feelings and thought processes. He was an active member and firm supporter of the Asiatic Society of Japan. He joined the society in 1928 on his arrival in Japan and was first elected a member of the council in 1936. In 1961 shortly before he left Japan on retirement he was elected President of the Society for that year. His friends and colleagues always found in him a fund of wisdom about Japan.

LANGUAGE TEACHING

Vere was born on 14 October 1901, the second son of Charles D. Redman of Brockley in London. He was christened Herbert Vere but never seems to have used the name Herbert. Apart from the fact that he was educated at St Dunstan's College, Catford, and London University, *Who was Who* tells us nothing about his upbringing or background. Vere was reticent about his early life probably more from the feeling that no one would be interested than from any wish to hide what some people might call his 'humble origins'. His mother was demanding and difficult. His home was small and the rooms full of knick-knacks.[15]

After graduation he went to France to study French and there met Madeleine Aline, the elder daughter of Colonel Francois Mathieu of Rouen, whom he married in 1925. She was a Catholic and Vere who had been an agnostic converted to Catholicism.[16] According to one story, Madeleine's mother was at first not in favour of the match and said Madeleine was not ready for marriage as she had not learnt how to cook. The colonel replied that this did not matter as Vere was an Englishman! In fact she soon learnt to cook.

Soon after they were married, while Vere was teaching English and French in London, one of his pupils was Nagaoka Hiroma, professor of English at the Tokyo University of Commerce (Shodai, now known as Hitotsubashi University). Professor Nagaoka asked Vere if he would like to go to Japan to teach English at his university. Vere accepted and he was soon given a three-year contract to sign.[17] Vere recorded that:

I always kid myself that I was 'picked out' by him for I was already a teacher with some experience of teaching English as a foreign language. But the whole business was quaintly personal and empirical when one thinks of the careful impersonal selections of modern times.'[18]

On arrival in Japan, Vere and Madeleine first had to live in two rather expensive and uncomfortable hotels, but they were soon found a Japanese-style house adapted for Western needs. He continued to work as a teacher at the university for some six years from 1927 to 1933. His duties,

> . . . communicated to him with engaging casualness were to teach the English language for fifteen hours a week in the preparatory department of the university by any method and with any text books I pleased, and without any coordination of my work with that of my Japanese colleagues on the English staff.'[19]

Vere found that his students were able to understand pretty well everything he said to them:

> Their difficulty was to *use* what they had learned. My job was to help them to do so. It was a fascinating job, involving the most intimate contact with the students both inside and outside the university. In the classroom, there was the constant effort to create 'natural' situations for the use of English and outside there were English plays to be rehearsed and oratorical contests in English to be coached. This was mainly done in our house which, in the evening, was frequently full of students, mine mostly, but there were also some of my French wife's after she had been enrolled [a year after they had arrived in Japan] as a teacher of her language at Tsuda college, then the most liberal girls' school in the capital. There can be nothing impersonal about this kind of tuition, and we often reflected in later years that it was in this early period that we formed those really close personal associations with Japanese people which were to help us so much in our subsequent work.[20]

His students at Shodai remember him as an excellent, if eccentric, teacher. One of his former pupils Kakitsubo Masayoshi wrote that 'his lectures, spiced with humour, were the ones I sought after most keenly. . .He was a most hospitable man, and was always inviting me to parties at his home in Aoyama. Maybe the lavishness of his entertaining was why he had no money in his account'.[21]. Vere recorded in 1958 that:

In post-war days, former students whose fortunes had not been all that good came along and naturally expected me to help them: others, who had been luckier were eminent and powerful and took it for granted that they must help me with anything they could; contacts, information, entertainment, etc.[22]

His time as an English language teacher provided him with the basis for his contribution to the book which he and H.E.Palmer published in 1934 entitled *This Language Learning Business*. Harold Palmer, who was in Japan between 1922 and 1936, was an expert on teaching foreign languages and produced a number of books on the subject, having been associated with Professor Daniel Jones of University College, London. Palmer was picked up by Matsukata Kojiro of the Matsukata family and appointed linguistic adviser to the Japanese Ministry of Education (Mombusho) 'with a view to modernizing English teaching'.[23] Vere recorded that he sought Palmer's help with his teaching. This 'he gave in good measure, while I was able to help him to some extent with his work by faithfully reporting my class-room and extra-curricular experience with my students. This association which lasted some seven years till Palmer finally left Japan. . .was of enormous benefit to me'.[24]

In 1928 Vere was active in forming the Association of Foreign Teachers in Japan. The idea of forming an association[25] came from Professor John Owen Clark while the Redmans and the Clarks were staying together near Sendai in the summer of 1928. The first planning meeting took place at the Rikkyo campus home of Dr Paul Rusch. This was followed by a wider meeting at the Imperial Hotel in December 1928. The association held its inaugural meeting in February 1929 and Vere Redman became the first secretary of the association. In 1954 Vere was instrumental in reviving the association after the war.

Vere recorded that there were three types of foreign teachers in Japan. These were: 'Those who put a lot into Japan, those who got a lot out of her and those who put out a lot about her.'[26] Vere Redman did all three.

His work as a journalist in Japan began in 1930 when he became an editorial associate to the *Japan Advertiser*, a post he held until 1935 when he became associate editor of the journal, From 1930 on he gradually wrote more and taught less, remaining in this post until 1938. He was the Tokyo correspondent of the London *Daily Mail* from 1933 to 1939 and for *The Sun* (Baltimore) from 1935 to 1939.

Vere recorded[27] that his new life as a journalist involved irregular hours and night work so that he '. . . got to know something of Tokyo night life. . .not only its playboy cafes although I saw something of these, but also its *soba* barrows in the streets where one took a sizzling snack while waiting for a story to break'. Writing brought him into contact with Japanese officials, members of the armed forces and businessmen as well as 'the man in the street':

> As a teacher I had been mainly concerned to put things into them; now I was mainly concerned to get things out of them. There was a sense of participation in the events of an eventful period with its assassinations. . .a full scale military rebellion at home and successive invasions of the continent. . .New, exciting, a little frightening but not unenjoyable, this second view of Japan.

JAPAN IN CRISIS

Examples of his work as a journalist were collected in his book *Japan in Crisis: An Englishman's Impressions* which was published by George Allen and Unwin in London in 1935. In the foreword written in London in March, Vere Redman thanked the editors of the *Quarterly Review, Contemporary Japan, Oversea Education, Fortnightly Review, The Times, The Manchester Guardian* and *The Japan Advertiser* for permission to incorporate the substance of articles published in these journals. The pieces in this 1935 volume are, of course, long out of date. But they demonstrate some important facets of Redman, the journalist and interpreter of Japan. We must note in particular Vere's efforts to try to explain to his fellow countrymen Japanese attitudes. We can also observe his percipient understanding of Japanese traits. Some of his remarks and portraits ring true even today.

In the foreword Vere also admitted that: 'A substantial part of my income is derived from Japanese sources. I am associated with a semi-official propaganda publication in the English language.' He noted that:

> In an age of propaganda, all writers proclaim impartiality and are suspect of venality. I should like to say that I am impartial in the sense that, if somebody asked me 'are you pro- or anti-Japanese' I should be stumped for an answer.

He added:

> Confronted as I constantly am with qualities of social urbanity and courtesy, qualities, too, of self-sacrifice and personal affection, I am constrained to think 'good people'. Confronted as I frequently am with outbursts of some patriotic scribe in the newspapers or even of some super-patriotic official, I am constrained to think 'good God'.

Like many of those foreigners whose life has brought them into the Japanese scene for any length of time there is an inevitable 'love-hate' relationship, but perhaps the same goes for foreigners who come in contact with the British!

Redman's explanation of why he liked Japan in his essay 'The Foreigner in Japan' (page 117) is worth repeating:

> For some people, among whom I count myself, whose gifts, such as they are, are not easily capitalized in the West, who dislike 'cadres' of any kind, national or social, who can live without the stimulus of emulation and an atmosphere stressing the importance of being earnest; and to whom astringent, unassertive beauty in nature, art, and life has a strong appeal, Japan is among the most pleasant countries in the world in which to be a foreigner.

He expanded on this aspect in a lecture to the Japan Society in September 1958 declaring that he he had 'learned a good many aesthetic enjoyments in Japan'. The basic architectural and aesthetic lesson was, he thought, that 'space in the house is more soothing than clutter. I now find that, when I go home in England, my first impulse, on entering my flat, is to put a few things away.'[28]

A good example of his efforts to explain some Japanese attitudes towards Britain is contained in his essay on 'Empires and Empires'. The Japanese found it particularly difficult to understand the relationships between the British Government and the governments of India and of the colonies. To the Japanese our attitudes on trade and tariffs affecting India and the colonies and on Commonwealth preference seemed at best hypocritical. After all, a Japanese colony did as it was told.

Sometimes, perhaps with the benefit of hind-sight, he seems to have gone a little too far in his advocacy of the Japanese point of view. He thought that Britain should have supported the Japanese in their demands for parity with America in naval ships.

On Manchukuo he noted (page 140) that the Japanese wanted 'the sort of tacit recognition which might incline the Nanking Government to give up animosity for Japan as a bad job. . . .Britain, or at least large sections of British opinion, wants to recognize Manchukuo but without incurring the manifest disadvantages of formal recognition. Surely we have the basis here for some sort of understanding. . .All that would be necessary is that some plain words should be spoken to leaders of the Nanking Government indicative of the British conviction that the political situation established by Japan cannot be changed by foreign indirect pressure.' To some this will seem a realistic statement, to others it smacks of appeasement although anyone temperamentally less of an appeaser it would be hard to find than Vere Redman.

Some of Vere's comments at this time are still apposite. He noted for instance in his essay on 'Anglo-Japanese Relations' the vital importance in business dealings of personal contacts and stressed that there was profitable business to be done with Japan if our businessmen approached Japan in the right way.

His essay on 'The Rise of Camp Government' about the growing power of the military is still of interest. He noted (page 191) that 'the active rank and file of the Army. . .and in a lesser degree of the Navy, has a dominantly rural and [a diplomatic euphemism] educationally economical complexion'. He concluded percipiently: 'The Japanese civil service lost its reverence by becoming political. In the long run, the combatant services may find they have done the same.' His essay entitled 'Looking Backward and Forward' contains the following comment which is worth pondering: 'Public opinion in Japan strikes the outside observer as being a sort of dynamic resignation, acceptance on the ramp.' I remember that Vere Redman used to say that leading articles in Japanese papers were all much the same. Before the war they used to end with praise for the government; after the war they invariably called for 'self-reflection' by the government. Vere noted in this same essay the Japanese lack of diplomatic skill (page 208): 'Japan, as "Jesus of Nazareth", crucified by a wicked world opinion, the analogy which Mr Matsuoka permitted himself at Geneva, left the West not only distressed, which mattered perhaps little, but also distrustful, which mattered very much. And the picture was a false one. The Japanese are neither particularly unscrupulous nor particularly hypocritical. They are above all resolute, industrious, and collectively ambitious.' On Japanese nationalism Vere had this to say:

> Nationalism represents here as elsewhere an attempt, and a successful one, to meet the economic malaise produced by misdirected capitalism. But I must insist that it is not essentially that. It is predominantly what Laski would call a 'prestige nationalism', and there lie some of its dangers.

I particularly enjoyed reading in this book Vere's portraits of some typical Japanese. For instance his pen portrait of 'Omura', a professor of economics, suggests some Japanese many of us have met (pages 147/148). Omura had studied abroad and speaks English and French. He reads vastly but what is his thought? 'It is hard to define. It is certainly the slave of an emotion, and that emotion seems to be an urgent and torturing desire for self-esteem. He is eager to despise people, and one feels that if he could experience one supreme orgasm of contempt, he would have achieved happiness.' And what about Sugimura (pages 149-152)? Sugimura is a bureau chief. 'At his job he is tolerably efficient; at keeping it, consolidating it, and so to say, fecunding it, he is super-efficient.' He has arranged seventeen marriages and at different times placed forty-nine young men in various departments. 'He has a vast circle of gift receivers. He seems to exude baskets of fruit, dried fish, edible seaweed, and other delicacies, which he distributes at appropriate times and seasons, to the uninitiated, in indiscriminate profusion.' Sugimura 'lives as it were in the middle kingdom, established there by a fine balance between his connections above, below, to the right and to the left'.

DETENTION AND AFTER

Redman's next change of job in 1939[29] 'was sudden and complete. I left Japan in July 1939 travelling by way of the United States, with a view to combining establishment of chosen contact with my American and British newspaper employers and a holiday in Britain and France. When my wife and I returned three months later I was an official of the British Ministry of Information. . .My job was to conduct official British propaganda in Japan. But the appointment had come about so quickly that there was no clear idea in anybody's mind of what I was up to.' The Japanese word for information (*joho*) meaning both information and intelligence caused speculation in the Japanese press that he was 'some new kind of spy...This was natural enough but not calculated to make me particularly welcome to the Ambassador, to whom I was "attached", or to the Japanese public whom I was to propagandise!'

According to Sir Norman Brain[30] who was working on Japanese material in the Embassy at the time 'Vere's contribution to the propaganda effort was chiefly through reports and articles in the English language press, where his skill at finding a biting phrase was most effective, and indeed it was the use of this against Germany (e.g. "the hooked and double-cross") that was ultimately...the gravamen of the charge brought against him by the Japanese.'[31]

Vere Redman was arrested by the *Kempeitai* in 1941 and incarcerated in solitary confinement in Sugamo prison in Tokyo for eight months. The facts were set out in a report to a Foreign Office committee dated 6 May 1943. Vere Redman, although he was the head of the Information Department of the Embassy at the time of his arrest 'had not been accepted by the Japanese Government as on the diplomatic list',[32] but this fact did not absolve the Japanese Government. Redman would, as the official report pointed out, at least have been entitled to the immunities prescribed in international law for the clerical staff of the embassy. International Law prescribes that clerical staff cannot 'be subjected to local jurisdiction in any matter arising out of their official duties'. In fact the Japanese Government never preferred charges against Redman which could have been used to justify their arrest and treatment of him.

The facts as stated in the report were: 'The Japanese Gendarmerie [i.e. the *Kempeitai*) forcibly entered Mr Redman's house and seized Mrs Redman as a hostage for her husband, who was temporarily absent, he being then, in fact, in the Embassy on the orders of the Ambassador.'[33] (It was his habit in those days to go to the Embassy very early in the morning and this had been overlooked by the Japanese gendarmerie) 'The Japanese authorities first asked for his surrender by Sir R. Craigie, not on any specific charge, but "for examination". This demand being refused, the gendarmerie proceeded to remove Mr Redman forcibly from the Embassy, in the presence of the Ambassador and against the Ambassador's protests. Incidentally one of the arresting party actually assaulted His Majesty's Ambassador.'[34] Craigie had placed his arms across the wall in front of Redman and the Japanese could only get at Redman by removing Craigie's protecting arm.[35]

> [Redman] was twice stripped naked; and he was confined for many months in wantonly cruel physical conditions and subjected in the course of that time to some 840 hours of severe examination, practically all of which related to his official duties or those of other members of the Embassy's staff and therefore to matters which on any view were privileged from disclosure. He was first told that the charge against him was 'collecting and sending abroad information detrimental to the interests of the Japanese empire' but eventually the formal charge brought against him was that of 'conspiring to prevent the execution of Japanese national policy' by propaganda designed to separate Japan from Germany after the conclusion of the Anti-Comintern Pact of 1936, the Tripartite Pact of 1938 and the Tripartite Alliance of 1940. In other words, Mr Redman was charged with having worked to prevent Japan from pursuing a policy of hostility to the country whose interests Mr Redman was employed to further.[36]

The British Government, by way of reprisal and to ensure that Redman was repatriated with the other members of the embassy staff, arrested Mr Kaoru Matsumoto of the Japanese Embassy 'whose duties corresponded most nearly to those of Mr Redman, and held him hostage' in Brixton prison. (Redman and Matsumoto became good friends after the war and used to meet annually to celebrate their release from prison).[37] Eventually, after daily interrogations by the *kempeitai* Redman was formally tried before a district court in Tokyo and to his astonishment acquitted. This led to his release and made possible the exchange in 1942 of diplomatic officials who had been interned in Japan and in Britain on the outbreak of war.[38] (This had been held up as the British refused to agree to an exchange until Redman and other detained officials had been released.)

The official report does not mention that for a time Vere was denied the insulin which he needed to survive, on the grounds that he was taking drugs.[39]

Redman's case was the worst example of the flouting of international law by the Japanese authorities in relation to diplomats. But other British officials were also severely maltreated by the Japanese police. One of these was Frank Hawley, who was then Director of the Library of Information and Culture. Three other consular officials were also arrested. British businessmen and journalists suffered equally if not more harshly. One man shot himself shortly after being released from prison in Yokohama and another in Manchuria was found shot. Bishop Heaslett, the senior British Anglican clergyman in Japan, was among those arrested and maltreated.

Vere Redman never allowed his appalling experiences to turn him against the Japanese people in general.[40] In his lecture to the Japan Society in London on 16 September 1958 on 'Things I have learned in and from Japan',[41] Vere referred to his experience as a prisoner in commenting on 'the bath as an instrument of pleasure':

> I always recall my experience when I was in Sugamo prison. We prisoners were taken to the bath usually once in anything from seven to ten days. All of us regarded this as the one great break in the drabness and suffering of our lives. I remember, too, that when I was being interrogated, the prospect of a hot bath was often placed before me as an inducement to answer in the manner required.

After his return to Britain Redman was employed in the Ministry of Information where he served as Director of the Far East Division. In this capacity he was for a time in India in 1944. In London he and Madeleine reoccupied the flat which they had used from time to time for some nineteen years in Great Ormond street near the children's hospital. Vere recorded[42] how happy they had been living in Bloomsbury where they got to know the famous economist J.M.Keynes 'pretty well' and Arthur Waley ('who worked with me, a wonderful experience, from 1942-1945'). He liked to visit the publishers and booksellers near the British Museum and frequented Olivelli's cellar restaurant in Store street.

It seems that one of his tasks was to brief senior officials, including Mountbatten, and others about Japan and the Japanese. For his services he was awarded the OBE in 1943. According to one story,[43] some of those he briefed were startled to see him change his false teeth after eating and before meetings. He had what he termed his 'eating teeth' and his 'meeting teeth'. He would often leave his 'eating teeth' to dry on a piece of blotting paper in his office.

EMBASSY PREOCCUPATIONS

Vere returned to Japan in 1946 as Information Counsellor in the United Kingdom Liaison Mission (UKLIM) to the Supreme

Commander Allied Powers (SCAP), in other words the embryo British Embassy. He was made a CMG in 1951 and stayed on in the Embassy in the same capacity after the Peace Treaty came into force in April 1952 until his retirement in 1961. He was then made a Knight Bachelor, an exceptional honour for a temporary civil servant of only medium rank, but it was well deserved. In 1964 his services to Anglo-Japanese relations were recognized by the Japanese Government in the award to him of the Order of the Rising Sun, 3rd class.

It is difficult to summarize all Vere did for Anglo-Japanese Relations in these years as much of this consisted in the development of personal relations. But some facts stand out.

Redman acted as a kind of Oriental counsellor to Sir Alvary Gascoigne during the occupation years and Gascoigne came to rely greatly on Redman's advice. When Gascoigne was succeeeded by Sir Esler Dening in late 1951 Redman's advice was less needed as Dening was a former member of the Japan Consular Service and was well informed about Japan. However, Dening and his successors as heads of mission in Tokyo up to Redman's retirement in 1961 all appreciated the work which Redman did and generally seem to have enjoyed their relationship with their eccentric colleague.

Redman attached great importance to trying to explain post-war Britain to the Japanese and he expended much time and energy on drafting his regular pieces in 'British Opinion' (*Eikoku wa ko kangaeru*) and amending contributions from his assistants. This was published on alternate Thursdays and Vere would decide the previous weekend what he would write. His assistant would have to check dates and details and attempt to decypher Vere's peculiar handwriting. They then had to check the typing and, in those days before word processors and photocopiers, help to run off the 'skins' on the Gestetner machine. This was a time-consuming and inky task.[44]

Vere worked hard to reactivate the Japan-British Society in Tokyo. In a lecture to the Japan Society[45] about the Japan-British Society on 7 October 1952 Vere said that it was the Japanese members who took the initiative in reviving the society in Tokyo, but it is clear that he was the driving force.

He was also the inspiration for the establishment of the Elizabeth-kai, the group within the Japan-British Society which brings British and Japanese ladies together to foster personal contacts and friendship. He was a firm supporter of equal rights for women and knew how much women could contribute to mutual understanding. He spoke to the Japan Society on 8 May 1962 about 'Modern Japanese Women'.[46] In this he declared his belief in the future prospects for Japanese women.

He recognized the value of cultural contacts and helped to arrange for Edmund Blunden to return to Japan as Cultural Adviser to the British Mission. In his lecture to the Society on 'Foreign Teachers in Japan'[47] he explained how this had come about: when in 1947 or thereabouts he had discussed with a representative group of Japanese professors of English the possibility of getting a teacher of English attached to the British Mission 'so that his services might be placed at the disposal of Japanese universities the unanimous request was: "Bring back Blunden".' Blunden was at that time on the staff of the *Times Literary Supplement* and his services were borrowed for a couple of years, during which 'he lectured in virtually every university in the country and to groups of teachers in all the leading cities'. 'It was that completely unreserved giving of himself to everybody interested in English literature which created and sustained the Blunden legend.' When George Fraser came out to carry on Blunden's work Redman did all he could to help them especially at a time when Fraser had a nervous breakdown and attempted suicide.[48]

Among other scholars whom Vere helped was W.G. Beasley, the professor of Japanese History at the School of Oriental and African Studies (SOAS). Redman had very wide university contacts and put Beasley in touch with many of his friends. Before Beasley returned to Britain the Redmans gave a dinner for him and his Japanese friends. When Beasley protested against the invitation specifying black tie on the grounds that the scholars would not have dinner jackets Vere told Beasley not to worry; 'When you have explained it [i.e. the reason why the scholars were being asked to put on dinner jackets] to them, they will be delighted.'[49]

Vere Redman pushed hard for the British Council to establish an office in Japan and did what he could to help the Council when the office was established.[50]

Vere was an enthusiast for all sorts of causes. I remember his storming into my office in the Chancery once to seek my views and help over an appeal for essential repairs to Westminster Abbey. As he started the conversation in the middle and I had to guess that it was about Westminster Abbey I fear that he may have found me rather thick! One of his hobbies was amateur dramatics. Indeed, some would say that he was always acting. His eccentricity may have been put on at first, but as with so many other eccentrics it became part of his nature and he was himself rather than an actor playing at being eccentric. Redman helped to revive the Tokyo Amateur Dramatic Club (TADC) and was its president for a number of years.[51]

On 30 April 1951, George Clutton, then chargé d'affaires in the British Mission, forwarded an interesting memorandum by Vere Redman consisting of 'Notes on The Entertainment of Japanese'. While some of Vere's comments are now out of date, much of what he had to say still applies, and the memorandum could still be read with advantage by diplomats going to work in Tokyo. A few extracts such as the following give the flavour:

> In entertaining Japanese, the line of least effort is all too often the line of least effect.
> Entertainment of Japanese should never be showy, but it should always be the best available. As a practical slogan, I would say: 'You cannot use up yesterday's scraps on the Japanese.'
> Like most human beings, the Japanese are snobs about food and it is generally worth taking account of the most general of their fidgets in planning entertainment of them.

This led him on to list, in order of their acceptability to Japanese guests, the Japanese preferences in fish. In those days salmon was definitely on the list of unacceptables.

> I should say that the Japanese have a greater appreciation of humour than of wit.
> By and large, the Japanese are reasonably loyal, simple, generous and gracious and. . .these qualities can be engaging.
> All foreigners posted here should be warned of the. . .peril of getting 'a Japanese heart' which obscures standards, clouds judgement and generally reduces one's usefulness to both self and country.
> There are few absolutes in this business except that we should do our best and, when in doubt, rely on our native good sense and good will to guide us.

Above all, Vere insisted that 'the best way to get on with the Japanese is to like them'.

This maxim was one which he repeated in his most interesting and valuable lecture to the Japan Society on 16 September 1958 on the theme 'Things I have learned in and from Japan'.[53] In this he stressed: 'You cannot successfully pretend to like the Japanese. . .If you like them they know it. If you don't, they know it too.' Anyone posted to Japan who finds he cannot like the Japanese should seek another posting as quickly as possible.

Some other maxims from this lecture help to explain Vere's attitude towards and understanding of Japan:

> Human relationships [in Japan] are in accordance with a system of reciprocal obligation which is economic up to a point but much more social and personal.
> Among the things I have learnt from Japan [is] the conception of what I would call agreement by emotional attunement.'

On the subject of 'sincerity' a concept to which the Japanese are devoted Vere noted that he had written in a diary in 1937 the following: 'The Japanese motto would seem to be: "He only is sincere who also agrees with me".' Vere added: 'It was the bitter reflection of a young man and, like most bitterness, I suppose, it was not altogether justified and arose, in part, from misunderstanding.' He commented that to many Japanese 'sincerity' was denoted by the 'willingness, even eagerness, to sacrifice his life'.

After noting the Japanese longing to be liked Vere wrote; 'Another aspect of this appeal for affection is the almost instinctive showmanship of the Japanese. They want to impress; they are always putting on an act. . .' (Perhaps he had learnt this trait from his years in Japan.)[54]

He mentioned in this context the Japanese anxiety to make a good impression and to know what you think of them: 'When I arrived in Kobe for the first time on April 12, 1927, I - a pimply, bespectacled intellectual of the kind who naturally knew everything without ever having learned anything and whose opinions were obviously not worth a damn - was asked earnestly: "What are your impressions of Japan?" as eagerly as were Einstein or Claudel who came a few years earlier. . .the enquiry was an appeal. I felt it then; I feel it now. The difference is simply that I have now no difficulty in responding.'

He concluded by once again reiterating that to succeed in Japan you must like the Japanese. But he also warned visitors to be on their guard against the solicitude with which the Japanese often enfold the foreigner and be ready for aspects of the Japanese character which can 'act like a very cold shower when least expected.'[55] He had no illusions about the alleged glamour of geisha parties and warned members of the staff: 'Remember the children's parties of your youth. Be prepared to play a number of foolish games and above all go with a party piece properly prepared.'[56]

After his retirement he went to live in Goult in Provence which he called 'Mon Village' and about which he wrote pieces in *The Japan Times*. He did his best to keep up with his friends, many of whom visited him there. His mother came to live with them and outlived Madeleine. Unfortunately, she hated France and the French and made Madeleine's life a misery.[57]

In one of the last letters which he wrote,[58] Vere Redman reiterated his continuing interest in Japan and his admiration for many others who were contributing to the understanding of Japan abroad and of Britain in Japan and who might help with a new journal devoted to Japan. Among those he praised highly were Sir John Pilcher ('for his knowledge and wit and humour'), Duncan MacFarlane, ('a businessman who is really literate, who could produce an informed article on any aspect of Japanese culture'), Father Peter Milward (who 'is about the best foreign Shakespearean scholar in Japan at the present time') and Dick Storry ('a very old friend of mine, since long before the war, we both were seeking to teach English as a foreign language to the world's most diligent but linguistically the least gifted students, the Japanese').

When Vere Redman died in 1973, Britain and Japan lost an eccentric friend who had played a valuable role in building bridges so necessary for mutual understanding. Despite his own sufferings at the hands of the *Kempeitai* he did like the Japanese and he did a great deal in an unobtrusive way for Anglo-Japanese understanding.

The Anglo-Japanese Commercial Treaty of 1962: A British Perspective

ROBIN GRAY

AFTER EIGHT YEARS of negotiation Japan and the United Kingdom concluded a full-scale Treaty of Commerce, Establishment and Navigation. It was signed in London on 14 November 1962 in the presence of the prime ministers of the two countries and was duly ratified and came into effect the following May.

The aim of this essay is to recall the circumstances in which the Treaty was made and to note some of the implications that the things then done had for trade relations between the two countries.

The author played no part in the final negotiations. But he was party to the early discussions between officials of the two countries when the main problems became evident. Also in the 30 or so years following, as he rose up the Board of Trade ladder, he had much to do with issues arising over Anglo-Japanese trade relations. And, in the end, with EC/Japan relations.

Some sources are included in a short bibliography in the Notes. In some cases, sources are mentioned in the main narrative, the principal source being the British Foreign Office files now open to public inspection. The Board of Trade files of the time have not been found. The available official records are thus of the Foreign Office view of a negotiation conducted mainly by the Board of Trade. The author's debt to present-day staff of the Department of Trade and Industry for finding papers and information is gratefully acknowledged. Some of the comments made stem from the general feelings and experience accumulated over a long career: they are the responsibility of the author alone.

WHY WAS THERE A TREATY AT ALL ?

By the time the treaty was concluded, bilateral deals of this kind were becoming an anachronism. They had over a long period been progressively displaced by multilateral arrangements. In the treaty about a dozen such arrangements were 'saved'. The two major treaties not supposedly affected were the International Monetary Fund (IMF) and the General Agreement on Tariffs and Trade (GATT). Between them these two post-war agreements were designed to provide world rules governing trade, payments and exchange rates so as to avoid the protectionism, competitive devaluations, unfair practices and so forth which were widely believed to have been a primary cause of World War II.

The British wanted a special bilateral arrangement with Japan in order to normalize trade relations between the two countries. This was because, when Japan joined the GATT in 1955, the UK was one of a number of countries that had invoked GATT Article XXXV. Put simply, this meant that the UK had declined to apply GATT rules to trade in goods between the two countries. The British, from the beginning felt uncomfortable – even guilty – about this. But, as in other countries, there were strong recollections of pre-war Japanese trading practices which included low-cost competition based on low wages and unscrupulous copying of Western designs.

It was in nobody's mind at the time that Japan was beginning to become a high-wage country and would in due course launch a technological, manufacturing revolution that would astonish the world with new standards of reliability and an immense capability for innovation. What the British needed was an assurance that their traditional industries, textiles and clothing in particular, could be safeguarded against unacceptably large rises in imports.

As it turned out, the choice of making a full-scale treaty would prove a contributory cause of the long delay in reaching final agreement. It is probable that the UK was following the example of the USA which, at the time when Japan joined GATT, had concluded such a Treaty on seemingly advantageous terms. The Australians who were faced with similar memories of, and difficulties in, their trade with Japan concluded a much more down-to-earth agreement with Japan as early as 1957. While there had to be some sort of Anglo-Japanese agreement, it did not need to be so grand. As we shall see, when it was conceived, it attempted to solve broad problems and put trade relations between the two countries, and certainly between their officials, on a surer and more confident footing.

WORLD TRADE CONDITIONS AT THE TIME OF THE TREATY

Some of the essential background of world trade conditions at the time of the negotiation of the Treaty can be summarized as follows:

a. World trade was expanding fast. Tariffs on manufactured goods in the main industrialized countries had been reduced by about half in five rounds of GATT negotiations and more large cuts were in the offing. The 1951 Peace Treaty had guaranteed that Japanese goods would receive equal tariff treatment. This remained the case despite the invocations of Article XXXV. The safeguards (i.e. the protection) desired against the Japanese were non-tariff barriers – quotas and 'voluntary' restraints.

b. The recovery in the Japanese economy was beginning to take off and it was probably about 1960 when Japan regained her pre-war level of production. But she was again becoming a major exporter as the figures compiled at the time by the National Institute of Economic and Social Research display:

Percentage share of exports of manufacturers

	USA	UK	West Germany	France	Japan
1953	26	21	13	9	4
1963	20	15	20	9	8

Over a decade, the British and American share of world trade had declined from nearly a half to a little more than a third. These figures do not, however, tell the whole story. Apart from Japan, exports from Asian countries were excluded from the calculations but Hong Kong, India and others had become significant traders especially in the fields of textiles and clothing.

c. Indeed, world trade in textiles was in ferment; the old industries in Britain and the USA were under great pressure. And during the 1950s both of these countries sought shelter in a variety of restrictions which from 1960 had been 'legalized' by GATT arrangements on cotton textiles.

d. Japan certainly had serious balance of payments problems throughout the period of negotiation of the treaty and these weighed heavily on the Japanese team. Japan did not balance her current account until the mid-1960s and the persistent large surpluses that were to emerge later were not foreseen. Although Japan had been reducing her import controls, there were still a great many in place. But in 1962 Japan was cautiously preparing under GATT auspices to remove the bulk of her remaining controls on imports of industrial products.

THE NATURE OF COMMERCIAL TREATIES

To the uninitiated nothing is more baffling than the provisions of commercial treaties. It is not the purpose here to provide a manual on the subject but rather to outline some of the main concepts involved. This is done, not for its own sake, but because it helps to understand the differences between the two countries before the negotiating log-jam was cleared. Treaties between countries with market economies are not principally concerned with the ways in which private traders conduct their business. But they are greatly concerned with what governments may, and may not, do to regulate the flow of business intercourse.

There are essentially three kinds of control on Government behaviour that are employed: there are absolute standards and, in the jargon, 'national treatment' and 'most favoured nation treatment' (commonly abbreviated to 'mfn'). We look at each of these in turn, using examples from the treaty as it emerged in final form; and at the same time we identify some of the areas in which the views of the two parties on the appropriate standard to be used were very different and made for delay.

a. *Absolute standards*

One absolute standard, in Article 5(1) of the Treaty, reads:

'The nationals of one Contracting Party shall in any territory of the other be accorded liberty of conscience and freedom of worship.'

Then in Article 7:

'The nationals and companies of one Contracting Party shall

enjoy in the territory of the other constant and complete protection and security for their persons and property.'

We include these two quotations to illustrate how broad was the scope of a full-scale treaty.

In the Articles of the Treaty dealing with shipping (the 'Navigation' Articles), another absolute standard is found [Article 21(2)(b)]:

> If in any territory of one Contracting Party a vessel of the other is wrecked, runs aground, is under any distress, or requires services, it shall be entitled ... to call upon salvage or other vessels of whatever nationality to render such services as it may consider necessary.

A troubled Japanese tanker in the English Channel could thus call in a Dutch tug.

Even so, shipping was a major bone of contention. At the time of negotiation of the treaty, the United Kingdom's merchant fleet was of the order of 20 million gross tons. The Japanese merchant fleet was in the course of rapid expansion and by 1964 had reached 11 million tons. The British, with their established position, wanted free trade in ocean shipping; the Japanese did not. The Japanese argued that they were faced in Asian waters with countries with protective shipping regimes and that Japan must be able to defend herself. In the end the whole issue was fudged. An Agreed Minute on Shipping which was 'not to be published but could be quoted by either side' was set down:

> The Contracting Parties affirm the principle that there should be complete freedom of opportunity for ships of all flags and regard the general acceptance of this principle as a common objective. They recognise, however, that the need to negotiate arrangements with certain countries pursuing discriminatory policies may make it very difficult to observe this principle in all circumstances.

It may be added that the Japanese had IMF authority to restrict their use of foreign shipping because of their exchange, including sterling, problems. The Agreed Minute noted that these exchange controls would 'be used as far as possible in a manner consistent with this principle'.

We conclude this section on 'absolute standards' by recalling that from 1 January 1958 a general GATT ban on export subsidies (other than on agricultural and similar products) had been introduced. Japan gave tax advantages to exporters and, although the amounts were not, given Japanese price advantages, very significant, the British feared that opponents of the Treaty in Britain would focus on this subsidy.

National Treatment

The Treaty includes many standard 'national treatment' provisions as, for example, in Article 18(2):

> Products . . .of one Contracting Party. . .imported into. . . the other shall not be subject. . . to internal charges. . .in excess of those applied. . .to like products. . .of the latter Contracting Party.

This wording, taken like so much else from the GATT, means that, once goods have been imported and paid any import duty, no other special charge can be levied unless the same charge is imposed on home products. Thus, in those days the British could levy their purchase tax on imports and home products alike but it had to be at the same rate in each case.

National treatment provisions can also be found in those parts of the Treaty dealing with company activities. Thus in Article 7(4):

> The nationals and companies of one Contracting Party shall have access to the courts of justice, tribunals and administrative authorities. . .of the other for the declaration, prosecution or defence of their rights on terms not less favourable than those enjoyed by the nationals and companies of the (other) Contracting Party.

There was, accordingly, to be no discrimination against foreigners before the law.

But there were great difficulties about investment in Japan and the establishment of British companies there. In a memorandum of 13 May 1962, Mr Adrian Russell (the Foreign Office official who participated in the negotiations from beginning to end) records the main problem:

> Whereas the United Kingdom is willing to accord national treatment virtually without qualification, Japan, unfortunately, insists upon far-reaching qualifications. The effect of these would be . . . to exclude British companies from participation in a wide range of activities, banking, public utilities etc. . . Quite apart from the issue of substance, the existence of a large number of unilateral qualifications, nullifying so far as concerns the United Kingdom some of

the most important provisions in the Treaty, would provide a potential target for criticism in Parliament and elsewhere.

At the end of the long memorandum from which the above is taken, Russell generally urged a speed-up in the negotiations. He concluded by saying, 'The attitude of the Board of Trade towards the Treaty has always been somewhat equivocal and further delay might encourage the revival of positive opposition'. In this Russell had a point: when the author was in the treaty section, we 'experts' took the view that a treaty between two major industrial powers that lacked a substantial measure of national treatment in establishment matters was not only a bad thing in itself but also would set a bad example for the developing world.

The issue was further compounded in the minds of Board of Trade officials by the large amount of national treatment that appeared to be included in the 1954 Japan/US Treaty. So sensitive were the Japanese about what they had, or had not, agreed with the Americans that, when this subject was explored between Japanese and British officials in 1959, a British note states that 'to avoid embarrassing the Japanese their remarks are not included in the agreed record of discussions'. When asked why Japan could not concede to the UK what seemed to have been conceded to the Americans, one Japanese official told the author simply that 'this was a mistake'. The almost annual rows between the US and Japan about access to the Japanese market that became commonplace, suggest that the Japanese official was not far out in his assessment.

Nevertheless, the Japanese showed considerable ingenuity in defending their position. They could not breach their Alien Land Law. Control on royalty payments was needed in case Japanese firms made 'bad bargains'. They cast doubt on whether British policy on inward investment was as liberal as we said it was and probably had genuine doubts whether any country could be so ready to accept foreign manufacturing companies. Anyway they said the welcome afforded to American (and other) investment in Britain rested on no treaty foundation. To this the British replied that any change in their policy was unlikely in the extreme and that, in international law, it was practice as much as treaties that could be cited. And so it went on. The difference between the two countries' approach was enormous.

There was a similar problem on insurance well summarized in

the despatch of Sir Oscar Morland, the British ambassador in Tokyo, to the Foreign Office (31 August 1962):

> An attempt was made to secure for the members of Lloyds permission to employ agents in Japan who could secure and transmit business to London, particularly in the business of marine insurance. The Japanese side had little difficulty in showing that many other countries do not grant this permission and that their existing insurance legislation would not permit it, and they let it be understood that a great deal of the insurance or reinsurance business anyway goes to Lloyds.

The ambassador went on to record that the British hand was further undermined when British insurance companies in Tokyo, in an action subsequently repudiated by their head offices in London, publicly opposed Japan's recognition of Lloyds' special position.

Most-favoured-national (mfn) treatment

Unlike 'national treatment' the use of this old concept – which was already well developed by the 17th century and is fundamental to GATT – caused no problems and indeed was used to alleviate many. Mfn is based on the very human cry to another country – do what you like to protect your industry, trade and commerce but, in so doing, don't treat any foreigners better than us; we want to be like the most favoured nation.

THE FINAL NEGOTIATIONS

After an abortive attempt in 1959 to conclude the Treaty and enable the United Kingdom to disinvoke GATT Article XXXV, events so moved that serious negotiations were slowly resumed. The pace quickened and the whole Treaty and its Protocols were then finalized and signed in a few months in the second half of 1962. The main elements, quite suddenly impelling the two sides towards a compromise agreement, were:

a. The Japanese were most anxious that as many countries as possible should disinvoke Article XXXV of the GATT. They were anyway moving towards a 90 percent removal of their non-tariff controls on imports. In 1962 Britain was actively negotiating to join the Common Market and the Japanese clearly believed that a friendly Britain inside the EEC would be much to their advantage. The Japanese were engaged in talks with at least Benelux and France on trade matters and disinvocation of Article XXXV by Britain would, they believed, set a very good example for the Community as a whole.

b. The British who had always felt uncomfortable with their invocation of Article XXXV were increasingly finding the annual negotiations with Japan of short-term trading arrangements a burden. There was growing recognition that Japan was an export market with (it seemed) great potential. Last but not least the Japanese MITI was known to be putting pressure on the Foreign Ministry to confine some or all of their coming liberalization measures to those countries that did not invoke Article XXXV. Those who discriminated against Japan would themselves be discriminated against.

But it needed interventions by persons of authority in both countries to give the negotiations a new impetus. The flow of visits of important personages from each country, including exchange visits of Royal Princesses, increased. In the autumn of 1961 Sir Norman Kipping, the Director-general of the Federation of British Industries (now the CBI) visited Japan. Kipping was much respected and carried great authority; and his report underlined the potential of Japan as an export market and the fact that Japan was no longer a low-wage country. This gave focus to the interest of British industry and a large mission from the London and Birmingham Chambers of Commerce visited Japan in April 1962.

In the same month the President of the Board of Trade, Frederick (now Lord) Erroll, also visited Japan. He was the son of an engineer, trained as an engineer and had worked in industry before the war. He had been Minister of State at the Board of Trade since 1959 and became President in 1961. He was personally convinced of the opportunities of the Japanese market. In Japan the President met the Japanese prime minister and had two meetings with the Minister of Foreign Affairs, Mr Kosaka. He also met the MITI minister, Mr Sato.

In these meetings both sides expressed their wish to conclude negotiations quickly. Mr Kosaka hoped that this could be done in two to three months but equally rehearsed Japan's negotiating position. Mr Sato defended Japan's export subsidy and bemoaned the weak state of some sectors of Japanese industry. Mr Erroll pointed to the value of inward investment as a source of strength and mentioned earth-moving machinery in particular. In this he did not anticipate that British motorists crawling through motorway works thirty years later would be very familiar with the name 'Hitachi'. There was discussion about the initial duration of the Treaty – the Japanese preferred five and the British seven years. The Japanese saw possible difficulties with the Diet if the safeguard provisions lasted too long. The President equally foresaw difficulties with Parliament if the safeguards to British industry were of too short a duration. In response to Japanese questions, the President said the Treaty should be concluded before Britain entered the Common Market because it would then be free from EEC interference for at least some years.

Apart from these exchanges on broad issues, it was during the President's visit that key decisions were reached on practical arrangements. As Sir Oscar Morland reported:

> During the visit of Mr Erroll, Japanese Ministers had pressed for the transfer of the negotiations, particularly those concerning the Sensitive List and Safeguards Protocol from London to Tokyo. This proposal was strongly resisted by the President, on the grounds that discussions on these matters and consultations with industry could take place only in the country where the items under discussion were 'sensitive'. However, since on the Japanese side there seemed a real will to negotiations, as well as a tendency to accuse Her Majesty's Government of dilatoriness, it was decided that all issues other than the Sensitive List and Safeguards Protocol should be transferred to Tokyo.

In this connection it should be recalled that all the negotiations were conducted in the English language. Anyone who has negotiated in languages other than his own will know how difficult it is to handle detailed and often subtle nuances of wording. The Japanese acquitted themselves very capably indeed but in practice, as real decisions had to be taken, it was plainly sensible to move the discussions to Tokyo where the Japanese negotiators would not be separated from their departments by a long-distance telegraph and a time difference.

These practical procedures having been agreed, one other development became decisive. At about the time of the President's visit, there was a prospect that the Japanese prime minister would visit London and in due course the month of November was agreed. This meant that the negotiations had not only a settled machinery but also, that most important thing, a deadline.

There were lingering doubts in the Foreign Office about whether it would not be better after all if they took it over from the Board of Trade. The Japanese Embassy in London had themselves raised the question but more, it would appear, because their Foreign Ministry wished to stay in control, given some of the unwelcome ambitions of MITI. A Foreign Office official examined the whole issue in a lengthy minute which recalled that the BOT had run commersial treaties since the 1920s; that Sir Frank Lee, the BOT Permanent Secretary, had resisted a take-over bid in 1952; and that the Board remained jealous of their prerogatives in this connection.. The minute by Mr R.P. Heppel (2 February 1962) concluded:

> . . . any attempt . . . to supplant the Board of Trade would be unwise and counter-productive. . . The progress that has been made is to a large extent the result of a strong initiative taken by Mr Hughes, the Under-Secretary at the Board of Trade. An intervention by the Foreign Office might weaken his hand and revive opposition [inside the BOT].

Indeed, William Hughes (known as 'Bill') had in the winter of 1961 taken a grip on the situation. He had decided that an mfn Treaty was the only possible compromise – particularly on the establishment questions: whatever the Americans had secured on company matters could be claimed by Britain an an mfn basis. Something must be attempted for the shipping industry and Lloyds, and there must be some movement on Japanese export subsidies. Above all, there must be adequate safeguards for British industry. It seems probable, too, that it was on Hughes' advice that the President of the Board of Trade had agreed to the movement of the Treaty negotiations to Tokyo but leaving the Safeguard discussions in London. Hughes had taken a great interest in the meetings on the fifth round of discussions (in number 50 or more!) between Whitehall and the Japanese Embassy officials in London which had begun in November 1961. He knew the subjects, with all their pitfalls and technical difficulties, thoroughly.

And it came to pass that Bill Hughes with Leon Taylor from the Board of Trade Treaty Section and Adrian Russell of the Foreign Office Consular Department left for Tokyo. Between 19 July and 16 August 1962 they settled most of the Treaty. It is dangerous to do a pen-picture of someone whom the author still meets, but it should be said that Bill Hughes was tall, slim, erect – he could easily be taken for a Church of England vicar (or more) and would clearly have qualified for high position in the Foreign Office. He was absolutely straightforward, spoke his mind and actually believed, in common with many BOT staff, that expansion of trade, not protectionism, was the best way forward for Britain. No foreigner could meet Bill Hughes without recognizing him as the typical English gentleman. But he had steel. Taylor (always called LEM Taylor to distinguish him from other Taylors in the Board) was of the same general build as Hughes – tall, upright – and combined his good intellect with an engaging boyish manner and outgoing charm. But he too knew his treaty language. The Foreign Office member of the team, Adrian Russell, in contrast, was shorter in stature; he had been through all the original discussions. He was of Australian origin and had a hesitant way of speaking. But on paper he was excellent and his knowledge of treaty language on matters outside trade in goods was unsurpassed. He was a great connoisseur of wine.

To interject for a moment there was a story current in the Board of Trade which went like this. After their tasks in Tokyo were done, Hughes and Taylor (not Russell) went on a mountain walk properly equipped in shorts, climbing boots (and knobbly knees). The sight of these two tall Englishmen on their return to their hotel was too much for the Japanese lady staff. In place of their usual quiet giggles they were said to have burst into uncontrollable laughter.

In a month of negotiations, the British trio, accompanied by Embassy staff, met every two or three days Mr Morisaburo Seki (Director-general of the Economic Affairs Bureau), Mr Suzuki and Mr Sato of the MFA, accompanied by MITI officials. Taylor and Sato met almost every day on technical drafting points. By 1 August Hughes was able to telegraph to London the outline of the package deal that was emerging. He wanted the President to look at the package and added: 'If the best we can get falls substantially short of it, my advice is likely to be that I should return home without reaching agreement.' This threat of breaking off was quite sufficient. Within two days Hughes was told that the President had been through the proposed package and found it acceptable – but he still needed an assurance that Japanese export subsidies would lapse. Hughes and Taylor returned home in the middle of August.

The successful outcome was of great relief to the Foreign Office. An official there reporting to his seniors on the outcome said:

> I sometimes got the impression that Hughes . . .took a rather detached view and was not exerting himself unduly. I suggested to Sir O. Morland that when Hughes arrived in Tokyo he (Sir Oscar) might have a heart to heart talk with him in an effort to impress upon him the importance of getting on with the job.

Whether any such avuncular advice was proferred is unknown. What is certain is that Tokyo Embassy was delighted with the outcome of Hughes' negotiations. Colin Harris, Commercial Counsellor at the embassy, reported that he had been with Hughes during all the negotiating sessions and considered that he 'performed a most difficult task with the greatest patience, good humour, flexibility and determination'. But there was more. The FO official who had recorded his earlier doubts about Hughes was able to report that, in a private letter, Sir Oscar had written:

> Hughes has been absolutely first rate – he instinctively knows the right way to deal with the Japanese and he really sees their point of view – we have gained a lot from having him out here.

The Deputy Under-Secretary for Economic Affairs at the Foreign Office (Sir Patrick Reilly) wrote to the Permanent Secretary of the Board of Trade (Sir Richard Powell) to convey this very favourable report.

There were more issues to settle before the treaty could be signed. Japanese assurances about the lapsing of their export subsidies were given. The initial duration of the treaty was settled at six years – half-way between the positions of the two countries. And the safeguards issue was resolved after much haggling in two Protocols and some other exchanges. In essence:

a. In a formal letter to be attached to the treaty the British proposed to remove all their import controls on Japanese goods in most cases by 1965 but in some cases earlier and in others later, the whole process to be completed by 1968. These eight categories of goods included cutlery, sewing machines, fishing tackle, binoculars and certain toys and games and pottery. The Japanese formally accepted.

b. In a similar formal letter the Japanese proposed to take some of the 'liberalized' products under their system of voluntary export control and to apply this system to some other goods. The goods specified included a wide range of textiles and clothing, some radio apparatus and some pottery. The British formally accepted this – which they needed to placate determined opposition particularly in Lancashire and Yorkshire.

c. In a Protocol to the Treaty a general safeguard was established – and, though reciprocal in form, no one was in any doubt that this was for British use. What it did was to provide that, if particular imports from Japan came in such increased quantities and causing or threatening material injury, there would be consultations between the two countries. If no solution were found within thirty days (and in extremity sooner) the British could override the mfn parts of the treaty and impose restrictions. But (and this was very important to the Japanese) if the British could offer no compensation for their action, Japan would be free to retaliate.

The safeguard at c. in the previous paragraph was of much more international significance than it was for Anglo-Japanese trade. For the most part it used the language of GATT Article XIX which dealt with sudden surges of damaging imports and emergency action to deal with such situations. It so happened that nobody in GATT could ever agree whether Article XIX could be applied selectively, i.e. against one country, or whether, if imports from one country were causing difficulties, imports from all countries had to be restrained. Despite much research, it was never discovered what the 'founding fathers' of the GATT (i.e. those senior officials who negotiated it) intended.

So confused was the situation that both the British and the Americans, as it suited them (though at different times), had argued on the one side and then on the other. The important thing is that, in the treaty itself, Britain and Japan had agreed a selective safeguard and had also agreed in a confidential exchange of letters ('the very existence of which should be kept secret') that neither side would have recourse to the GATT if the safeguard was invoked. Quite why this was so 'secret' is not clear to the author. But, in accordance with what had also been agreed about what could be said publicly, the British White Paper in the Treaty (Cmd 1875) stated clearly that neither government intended to invoke the procedures of the GATT in respect of any action taken by the other in respect of the safeguard protocols. The GATT had been sidelined.

All was thus in place. Everything had been settled, given away or fudged. There was a full-scale treaty text agreed – with Protocols, Exchanges of Letters, Agreed Minutes etc. But who should sign for Britain? The Foreign Office wondered whether the Foreign Secretary alone should do so. But, after a short hesitation, the Foreign Secretary invited the President of the Board of Trade to be a party. Mr Erroll replied that he would be 'happy to join'. On the Japanese side, there was no doubt. Mr Katsumi Ohno, the Japanese Ambassador Extraordinary and Plenipotentiary, would affix Japan's signature. Mr Ohno may have been 'extraordinary' in the sense that, throughout all the negotiations, he had overseen a very successful mission to Britain (a point emphasized in the POBT's April visit to Tokyo). But as 'plenipotentiary' he had technically full authority to sign for Japan. Accordingly, in London on 14 November 1962, in the presence of the Japanese prime minister, Hayato Ikeda, and his British equivalent, Harold Macmillan, the treaty and surrounding documents were duly signed and exchanged by His Excellency Mr Ohno for Japan and, for Britain, by the Rt Hon Earl of Home and the Rt Hon Frederick Erroll. The treaty came into force, after being duly ratified, in May of the following year.

HINDSIGHT

It is worth taking a brief glance at a little of what followed in the decades after the conclusion of the treaty. The first obvious point is that, before it came into force, the negotiations for Britain's entry into the Common Market were stopped by France. The French had been kept informed of progress on the treaty. They were aware that it was being concluded at such time as would ensure that it could run without EEC approval – at least until the EEC's common commercial policy embraced Japan. How far this action served to add to the French reasoning that Britain was still unsuitable for EEC membership is unknown.

In practice, it was not until the early 1980s that the Community began to evolve anything like a coherent and common trade policy towards Japan. This followed the remarkable Japanese success in selling in Europe, not the old-fashioned products that consumed so much time in the 'safeguard' negotiations in 1962, but motor cars, televisions, copiers and the apparatus of information technology. In European (and American) markets they were setting new standards of reliability and showing great inventiveness in high technology products.

Motor cars provided one of the earliest signals of Japanese capability. Japanese penetration of the British car market rose from virtually nothing in 1967 to 11 per cent by 1977. There it was effectively frozen, not by the use of the safeguards so laboriously worked out some 15 years before, but by an inter-industry arrangement. This 'voluntary' restraint arrangement was preferred by the British to formal action partly because of a preference for sorting things out amicably but partly because, if formal action were taken, the British either had to provide compensation or face retaliation (perhaps on whisky where Japanese distillers would have welcomed even more protection from Scotch). The Japanese also had a predelection for sorting things out. First, safeguard action by the British could set a nasty example. Secondly, by controlling exports, the price premium accrued to the exporter rather than the importer or distributor. Moreover, since the limit on the Japanese was simply the *number* of cars, they were free and able to equip the cars more lavishly; the author recalls a British senior motor executive bemoaning the undeniably 'rich specifications' of Japanese vehicles.

The British encouraged other restraint arrangements and inter-industry agreements. These were primarily in products where the Japanese had made great technical advances; music centres, numerically controlled machine tools, colour television sets and fork-lift trucks are examples. We might also note that for all the blood spilled in the establishment provisions of the treaty the flow of manufacturing investment was predominantly from Japan to Europe, the U.K. in particular. The British welcome to foreign investment, so much doubted by the Japanese in 1962, proved real.

We might recall, in conclusion, that the 'voluntary' restraint arrangements (and inter-industry agreements) – devices employed not only by Japan but by many other countries – increasingly excited the interest and indignation of economists, consumer groups and politicians. The agreement for the establishment of the World Trade Organization (which replaces GATT) provides that all such measures must be phased out by 31 December 1999. Whether the new WTO with its panoply of

Codes, Committees and more judicial procedures will provide more assurance to consumers and offer greater harmony in trade relations remains to be seen.

23

Memories of the Anglo Japanese Commercial Treaty: A Japanese Perspective

SOSUKE HANAOKA

Translated by Ian Nish

I WAS TRANSFERRED from the Ministry of International Trade and Industry (MITI) to the Ministry of Foreign Affairs (MFA) and moved to a new appointment as secretary (*shokikan*) at the Japanese Embassy in London in November 1957. I worked there between the ages of 34 and 38 for about four years until I returned home in November 1963. During this period I took part in treaty negotiations, first in talks over trade arrangements lasting over half a year between December 1959 and June 1960 and again from November 1960 to the signature of the commercial treaty in November 1962.

In Britain trade liberalization came comparatively early. The rate of liberalization had by January 1960 reached 97 per cent; and the goods whose import from OEEC territories was restricted did not exceed 14 items. But Communist countries and Japan were excluded. In the case of Japan in particular, apart from the 14 items which applied to OEEC, the products restricted for discriminatory import amounted to 62 items and virtually all Japan's important exports were excluded.

Accordingly, the largest topic in the Japanese Government's economic foreign policy towards Britain at the time was to get rid of discriminatory import restrictions on Japan and to normalize trading relations between the two countries. Hence, the Japanese Government adopted two approaches: firstly, each time the Anglo-Japanese trade arrangements came up for annual re-negotiation, the discriminatory import restrictions should be reduced realistically; secondly, by concluding an Anglo-Japanese commercial treaty, we could settle the matter once and for all. The aforementioned trade arrangements had been made every year since 1951 and I took part in the negotiations twice, in 1958 and 1960. Negotiations for a new treaty were begun immediately after Japan's entry to GATT in October 1955 and, using the opportunity of the general meeting of GATT being held in Tokyo in 1959, the need for starting negotiations for a regular treaty was recognized by both countries.

My responsibility, which was concerned with trade matters, was generally limited to the section inside the Board of Trade concerned with treaty negotiations in London. I did not get involved in negotiations being conducted with the Foreign Office etc or in the final stages of the negotiations in Tokyo. At the embassy I served under Ambassador Ohno Katsumi for four years. The negotiating team leader at the start was Minister Nakagawa Toru (later ambassador to the Soviet Union) and, succeeding him, Minister Mori Haruki (later ambassador to the United Kingdom). The counsellor who was deputy leader was sent from MITI. At first this was Counsellor Matsumura Keiichi (later administrative vice-minister, Ministry of Economic Planning) and, following that, Ishimaru Tadatomi (later Board Member of the Japan Export and Import Bank). Among these Minister Mori and Counsellors Matsumura and Ishimaru have already passed away.

In December 1995, we held a reunion of embassy staff who had served under Ambassador Ohno, who is still hale and hearty at the age of 92 this year, with myself as one of the initiators. Over forty people attended. The large number attending included the present Foreign Ministry administrative vice-minister who had been studying in Britain at the time, the previous administrative vice-minister, a former ambassador to Britain and, apart from that, others who had had ambassadorial experience in major countries. Former staff (OB) from the Ministry of Finance, MITI, Ministry of Agriculture, Forestry and Fishery, Ministry of Transport and the Ministry of Science and Technology also attended and there was a most agreeable meeting as we expected. It was a further confirmation of how those in London in Ambassador Ohno's time were people of high quality in the Japanese Government.

When I was in London, the exchange rate was fixed at ¥1008

to one pound and ¥360 to one dollar, Japan's economic strength was still small and anti-Japanese feeling in one part of Britain continued to be deep-rooted. But, during the four years of my service in London, it was very pleasant that the Anglo-Japanese commercial treaty was concluded and Anglo-Japanese relations improved remarkably. At first the British side of the trade treaty negotiations was handled by Reginald Maudling, the President of the Board of Trade, A.E. Percival, the under-secretary (later the secretary of ECGD), Ms Reynolds, the assistant secretary, and J.H. MacPhail as principal. In the later treaty negotiations on the British side the foreign secretary was the Earl of Home, and the line-up at the Board of Trade consisted of Maudling and, when he became chancellor of the exchequer, F.J. Erroll. The under-secretary was W. Hughes (later second secretary); the assistant secretaries were E.L. Phillips and J.L. May; the principal was J.H. MacPhail and at the end C.A.F. Buysman. My counterpart was generally MacPhail, a man who was living proof of the excellence of the British bureaucracy.

It was a time when Japan's largest export to Britain was tinned salmon and, apart from that, transistor radios, cameras, motor cycles etc were coming into prominence as new export items. In order to maintain our quota for tinned salmon, we had to undertake negotiations with Japanese industry so as to establish a quota for ICI pharmaceuticals, woollen goods, whisky etc as British imports to Japan. I well remember the surprise and joy when tinned salmon was 'liberalized' in 1960, perhaps by the decision of Mr Percival.

At that time in Japan, the Ikeda cabinet was encouraging fast growth in the economy under the Double the National Income Plan. Under this MITI was embarking on the liberalization of trade and was promoting a fast liberalization of imports to which they were resigned. At the time Britain was in the middle of negotiations for entry to the EEC and was in the process of changing from her traditional imperialist principles of the past to a policy of sharpening her international competitiveness among the advanced countries of the EEC. The fact that the British government, industrial circles and the press recognized that Japan with her economic growth and trade liberalization might become a large export market for Britain was the reason why the conclusion of a treaty succeeded. On 5 December 1962 when Alan Green, the minister of state at the Board of Trade, in announcing the new Anglo-Japanese Commercial

Treaty to the House of Commons, spoke as follows:

The discrimination that we have practised against Japan has become increasingly undesirable on general grounds, and is no longer necessary on grounds of commercial policy. We have been willing to grant to almost every other country outside the Communist *bloc* firm guarantees of most-favoured nation treatment through the GATT. It would be wholly inconsistent with what we proclaim our general policy to be if we were to continue to discriminate in general terms against Japan and she against us.

Japan's wage levels have risen rapidly over recent years and in many production units are comparable with those ruling in some of the countries of Europe. The Japanese Government and the leaders of Japanese industry have made persistent and successful efforts to raise the trading standards of Japanese exporters.

In the cotton textiles and pottery industries, for instance, both of which were once notorious for the copying of foreign designs, there has been cooperation with British industry and control organizations have been set up which have virtually disposed of this nuisance. Japanese manufacturers cooperating with important British firms in joint ventures have won the firm respect and, indeed, admiration of their British partners.

The policy of discrimination has, in fact, become out of date. But there has also been a positive reason why we should get rid of it in our own economic interest. The growth of the Japanese economy over recent years has been phenomenal. It has brought with it a great upsurge in demand for industrial plant and for a constantly widening range of imports. With import liberalization also progressing rapidly according to plan this has opened great opportunities for countries, such as ours, which can supply an immensely wide range of goods.

Both the Director-General of the Federation of British Industries, who visited Japan last year [1961] and the London and Birmingham Chambers of Commerce Trade Mission, which toured Japan this year [1962], reported that it was essential to the full development of our export potential that the present trading arrangements should be superseded by a Commercial Treaty. Now that the Treaty has been concluded, it has, in general, been welcomed by the Press and industry.

It may be thought that Maudling's political determination as President of the Board of Trade over opening the final negotiations in 1960 for the conclusion of a treaty which would include the 'disinvocation' of Article XXXV of GATT. In connection with this, I asked Ambassador Ohno what he remembered about the circumstances of that time and he told me the following:

> In the 1950s Anglo-Japanese trade arrangements were being renewed every year. The fact that detailed negotiations over goods took over half a year to reach an arrangement which would only last for one year caused the business world trouble over cancellation of transactions. And government itself also felt great repugnance at the continuation of duplicated negotiations. But the hostility of the industrial circles to Japanese-made goods being imported as the result of a new treaty which would give Japan most favoured nation (mfn) treatment was very strong and government could not easily convince them otherwise. Ambassador Ohno and Minister Maudling were in agreement that the best policy would be to invite a representative of the British business world to Japan and get him to understand the real conditions there. Maudling examined the issue with appropriate colleagues after a cabinet meeting; and, having heard that the reaction was favourable, Ambassador Ohno returned to Japan early in spring 1961.
>
> As the result of preparatory arrangements with the Foreign Ministry, other ministries and with Keidanren (Federation of Economic Organizations) etc, Sir Norman Kipping, the director-general of the Federation of British Industry (FBI) was officially invited to Japan. During his visit in the autumn, Sir Norman examined the conditions of the Japanese economy minutely and was extremely impressed. Because he wanted to write his report without delay, he prepared the draft at Hakone before his return home and sent it to London. His account of his visit entitled *A Look at Japan* was widely read in Britain. It not only altered the perception of Japan in Britain, both among the government and the people, but it also had many readers in France, Germany etc. It is a valuable report which prepared the ground for the abandonment of Article XXXV of GATT by Britain and other countries. Ambassador Ohno states that, after Kipping returned home, he attacked in detail the anti-Japanese tone of British newspapers, magazines etc and denied their accuracy.

Again at this time there were visits by Princess Alexandra to Japan and Princess Chichibu to Britain. Chairman Ishizaka of

Keidanren led a delegation to Britain; and Foreign Minister Ohira and Mr Erroll of the Board of Trade also made visits. As a result, Anglo-Japanese rapprochement made great strides.

When Maudling became Chancellor of the Exchequer, Erroll succeeded him as President of the Board of Trade. Negotiations for the treaty proceeded smoothly until it was signed in the autumn of 1962. The treaty eventually came into force in May 1963. Regarding the 'Sophisticated products' of the new industries of Britain (i.e. those based on capital and technology) which had no worries if there was no sign of the market being 'churned up', Britain liberalized them in the trade talks and treaty negotiations. But mfn treatment for imports was not recognized unconditionally. In protocols attached to the treaty there were general safeguard clauses which would be applied between Britain and Japan. Again, Sensitive Items were specified. Among eight items in this category (knives, forks, sewing machines, toys etc) the British side set import quotas subject to a fixed period for liberalization. Again, over 14 items covering a range of textiles (cotton goods, woollen goods), radios, ceramics etc, the Japanese side undertook in a protocol to observe autonomous rules on export.

I was for about three years involved in negotiations on liberalized commodities , quota commodities and export-related commodities. According to a memorandum by Counsellor Ishimaru:

> When the remarks of British shipowners about the purchase of, or giving orders for, Japanese vessels based on liberalization in the trade talks were published in the newspapers, the powerful trade unions launched an opposition movement and it became the lead story in *The Times*. For a while we were inclined to fear the cancellation of liberalisation. But in *The Times* on the following day, Transport Minister Marples issued the following statement: 'Because there is no unfair competition on the part of Japan, we should like the trade unions to reconsider their position in order to develop the competitive power of British manufacturing industry.' We appreciated his toughness in adhering to what had once been agreed and not yielding to pressure from interest groups and now had the assurance that the treaty negotiations would succeed.

Five years later the British government withdrew the protocol on general safeguards between the two countries.

The predictions at the time of the British negotiating team led by Mr Hughes have now been borne out statistically. In 1962 Britain's exports to Japan did not exceed $146,000,000 but about thirty years later they had grown about 40 times to $5,900,000,000(1994) and $6,500,000,000(January-November 1995). Britain's total exports to the whole world amounted in 1962 to $11,000,000,000 while in 1994 they had grown 20 times to $2,040,000,000. This comparison shows that the rate of growth of exports to Japan was double that to the world as a whole. In this connection, Britain's main export items to Japan in 1993-4 were machinery, cars, pharmaceuticals etc; among Japan's export items to Britain in 1962 tinned salmon made up 45 per cent of the total, while in 1994 semi-conductors, electronic equipment etc take up about 30 per cent.

May I in conclusion make some remarks about the life-style of a Japanese negotiator? It was my good fortune to have cordial relations with many officials in London. Six years before I joined the London embassy, I had spent one year in Britain studying with a United Nations fellowship. I am left with an indelible impression of the very generous treatment accorded by the British Council to overseas students at the time. It is a pity that Japan has not yet set up an equivalent organization. On returning to Japan, I immediately joined the Japan-British Society and got to know many people, especially young officials at the British embassy who had entered the foreign service and intended to become specialists in Japanese. When I went to the Japanese embassy in London, I was invited by (Sir) Sydney Giffard (who was serving as private secretary to the permanent under-secretary) whom I had got to know through the Japan-British Society in Tokyo, to his flat in London. I remember affectionately nostalgic talks about Tokyo with Messrs Burges-Watson, Ellingworth and Bentley, who had all served in the British Embassy in Japan.

What I felt about the negotiations with the British Government was that the British appeared to be very tough negotiators. Especially at the beginning they were unapproachable. Once one could establish relations of mutual confidence, however, discussion became much easier. The fact that Britain became the first country in Europe to withdraw the invocation of Article XXXV of GATT is a manifestation of this. I learnt during the Anglo-Japanese negotiations how a relationship of confidence between the negotiators was important for success.

What amazed me was that, when it came to a holiday season like Easter, the summer, or Christmas, officials would stop work even in the very middle of discussions and negotiations would inevitably be suspended. We felt at the time that there was a radical difference of thinking between Britain and Japan over holidays. Another surprise was that the assistant secretary responsible for the trade talks was a talented lady; and women were quite numerous among departmental heads in Britain. Since women were still rare in administrative offices in Japan, we admired the way in which women in Britain had made progress in the workplace. Another point was that the section head responsible for imports had trouble with his eyes but the way in which he memorized all the minute quotas was astonishing.

On the Japanese side, whether it was the trade talks or the treaty negotiations, we had to return to the embassy when negotiations ended for the day. We reported on the negotiations, decided on policy to deal with them and took the views of the Counsellor, the Minister and the Ambassador in order to send a telegram to Tokyo seeking instructions. When you send a telegram of this sort during the night, it arrives, because of the time difference between Britain and Japan, in the morning. In Japan they would hold conferences in each ministry. By the time we arrived for duty in London the following morning, a telegraphic reply giving instructions had arrived. The amount of telegrams to Japan was so many that it was, I believe, a record.

At the time of the trade talks in 1959, the commercial section of the embassy was in an annex in Eaton Square, while the main embassy was at Belgrave Square. We had in the evening to take the telegrams by car to the main embassy. (I can remember that in Eaton Square there was the flat of Vivian Leigh and Laurence Olivier and there was a beautiful white Rolls Royce outside it.) Normally embassy staff had to help by rotation with Diet members and others visiting Britain (including weekends); but I remember that the commercial team engaged in treaty negotiations had the permission of Ambassador Ohno to be exempted from this duty; and this was very welcome. Immediately after the trade talks the embassy was transferred to Grosvenor Square; and the commercial department was integrated into the main building. In the new embassy the room occupied by the commercial staff was the ballroom which had paintings on the ceiling; it was said that Mozart had given a recital there.

Here is a story told me by Ambassador Ohno. The British prime minister at the time, Harold Macmillan, was the real owner of the famous publishing house, Macmillans. Maruzen was the exclusive purchaser in Japan of Macmillans' books. It seems that Prime Minister Macmillan said to Ambassador Ohno that Japan imported Macmillans' books almost comprehensively and that a studious people which read Macmillans' publications as widely as that could not be ignored from the standpoint of Britain's cultural policy. It was Ambassador Ohno's view that behind the success of the ultimate treaty was no doubt the fact that the prime minister gave it his personal backing.

Negotiations on the general clauses which were left over were held in Tokyo. Signature took place between Ambassador Ohno (for Japan) and President Erroll and the Earl of Home, the Foreign Secretary (for Britain), in November 1962 in London. Prime Minister Ikeda who was visiting Britain attended the signing ceremony. My wife and I were invited to a reception hosted by Macmillan to celebrate the signature of the treaty and shook the prime minister's hand.

In the autumn of 1963, a year after the signature of the treaty, we held a small party in our home in Holland Park on the occasion of our return to Japan; and we have the pleasant memory that Messrs Hughes, Phillips and MacPhail all attended.

24

The Impact in Britain of Japan's Post-war Novelists

SYDNEY GIFFARD

TO MAKE AN IMPACT in Britain, a Japanese novelist has first to be translated. That may usually be true also for a French, Spanish or Italian novelist. But the latter are writing within a broad historical and cultural context familiar to the British reader. A sympathetic translator is more easily found, even by a Greek or Russian novelist who writes from outside the Latin or Romance linguistic traditions. Japanese novelists have often been fortunate in finding translators who were more than competent, whose sympathy amounted in Arthur Waley's case even to genius – and we might say the same of Edward Seidensticker, but for our reluctance to admit the living into the hallowed precincts reserved for genius, once it has departed.

The Japanese language is deceptive. For all that it may seem, for example, to lack a certain flexibility, it displays (or conceals) a richness of connotation which, if only because it is partially visual, is necessarily diminished in translation. This may not remain true of some contemporary work, which has escaped into a global sub-culture, itself inaccessible to those brought up on nothing more exciting than alcohol or tobacco, and is largely devoid of reference to the Chinese classics; but the ability of the common reader abroad to penetrate below the surface of Japanese literature has been restricted, even for many of those acquainted with the Japanese language.

In these circumstances, Japanese novelists have generally had to wait for recognition abroad. It is different now for those in the new sub-culture, where Ryu Murakami and Banana Yoshimoto sell by the hundreds of thousand copies. We should not grudge them their success. It may mean that the time-lag is reduced, even for their more conventional successors. Whether it may also mean that a global cultural and literary tradition will tend to be thinner and shallower, less sustaining than the separate, local or regional components of our heritage from the past, is a question going far beyond the range of this essay. But it should be said here that one serious British critic has found Banana Yoshimoto's work 'uplifting'. She enjoys a literary inheritance, and writes with a pleasing optimism.

TANIZAKI JUNICHIRO

The immediately relevant point about the time-lag is that those Japanese novelists who made an impact in post-war Britain were, initially at any rate, writers of an earlier generation. Tanizaki Junichiro had made his literary debut as early as 1910 and, although Kawabata Yasunari was more than ten years his junior, he, too, was contemporary, not with most of those who first came to his work in translation in post-war Britain, but with their parents. Tanizaki's closest contemporary among writers of great stature in the British literary world was D.H. Lawrence, while Kawabata was born some years before George Orwell or Graham Greene. The European and American writers best known in Britain in the 'thirties were mostly younger than either of these great Japanese novelists, and this might seem to make the latter's post-war success with the British public the more remarkable. An explanation might be that Tanizaki, in particular, represented some reassurance that there was a certain continuity, not with the world of the 'thirties, which was associated with disaster, but precisely with an earlier tradition of civilized and cosmopolitan society. Younger Japanese novelists translated in early post-war years, such as Dazai Osamu or Ooka Shohei, tended to be too disturbing, for the general taste, though they were always highly regarded by discerning critics.

For those concerned to understand wartime Japan, and the effects of war on society and on individuals there, the appearance in 1954 of Brewster Horwitz's translation of *Kikyo* (Home-coming) by Osaragi Jiro was an event of great significance. Similarly, Ivan Morris' translation of the same author's *Tabiji* (The Journey) threw a brilliant light on life in Japan under the Occupation. Few British readers at the time were aware that Osaragi, whose real name was Nojiri Kiyohiko, had served under Prince Higashikuni immediately after the end of hostilities. But the depth of his insight, the quality of his characterization, the strength of his narrative and his sympathy with the most enduring of Japan's traditional values made an unmistakably important contribution, it is not too much to say, to the resumption of civilized international exchanges, and what might now be called cross-cultural dialogue.

In the same year, 1954, the publication of Edward Seidensticker's translation of Tanizaki's *Tade Kuu Mushi* (Some Prefer Nettles) illustrated the sophistication and subtlety of the greatest of Japan's established novelists, the greatest, that is to say, in cultural reach, in the breadth of his understanding of the human condition – for not even he could exceed Kawabata in subtlety, nor in his feeling for traditional Japan. Seidensticker's translation of Kawabata's *Yukiguni* (Snow Country) came out in 1956; translations of most of his other novels, rather later.

1957 was the year in which Tanizaki's marvellous novel *Sasame Yuki* appeared, in Seidensticker's wonderfully enjoyable translation, as *The Makioka Sisters*. Publication of the original, in serialized form, had been interfered with by the authorities in Tokyo during the war. At first sight, many British readers of the English version may have thought this seemed excessively sensitive, on the part of the authorities. On closer examination, touches could be found which might well have been considered subversive or defeatist. The political notes are, however, plainly incidental to the story of the four sisters and their families and friends. Living in the Kansai, they mix easily with members of the foreign community. The Kyrilenkos, émigrés from Czarist Russia, are convinced that Japan 'will fight longest against the Communists'. At the time of the Sian Incident, they express concern lest the Communists may come out on top in China. (This may have seemed in Tokyo, in the early 'forties, rather an exaggerated anxiety.) Later, young Mimaki designs expensive houses 'in the latest Western fashion, and orders fell off as the China Incident began to have effect'. Later still, the Kyrilenkos' daughter, Katharina, who has gone to Britain, is reported to be finding the war 'rather enjoyable'; but it is also believed that London is 'suffering terribly from German air raids'. Then the Stolz family goes home to Hamburg, and Mrs Stolz writes that 'We are both young nations fighting our way up, and it is not easy to win a place in the sun. Yet I do believe that we will win in the end.' She says she has to mend stockings which she would have thrown away before and, having reported that her son is leading a healthy, rural life with his class in Bavaria, she adds that 'Here in the city we all live in caves.' It is still only February 1941, so perhaps she does not mean this to be taken literally. As with the main events in the intricate domestic history of the Makioka sisters themselves, it is the exact and natural tone of the conversations, and the gentle irony of the narrative style which delight and remain with the reader.

Donald Keene was reported to have described *The Makioka Sisters* as 'the most important Japanese novel published in the years following the war'. It has retained a high place in the regard of the British reading public. Three years after the death of Tanizaki in 1965, the first award to a Japanese writer of the Nobel Prize for Literature was made to Kawabata Yasunari. For the wider public, throughout the world, this award ensured that the post-war Japanese novel would continue to command the attention it had already merited.

For, before this award was made, a generation of writers more properly regarded than Tanizaki or Kawabata as the representatives of post-war Japan had attained widespread recognition. The most famous of these was Mishima Yukio, in his youth a devoted admirer of Kawabata, and himself considered at the time by some foreign critics to be a strong contender for the greatest international literary prize. The senior members of this group of post-war writers in Japan included Ooka Shohei, whose wartime experiences in the Philippines as recorded in *Nobi* (Fires on the Plain) was now given in Britain, on the evidence of Ivan Morris' powerful translation, the respect already accorded to it in Japan, where it had won the Yomiuri Prize in 1951. Noma Hiroshi's *Shinku Chitai*, translated in 1956 by Bernard Frechtman as Zone of Emptiness, also dealt with the horror of war in the Philippines, and was also founded on first-hand experience. Shiina Rinzo's work attracted some attention abroad. He had suffered in Japan for his belief in Communism, of which he was said to have been cured by reading Dostoevsky. A man of the working class himself, he understood the world of the company office and the factory. His heroine in *Ai no Shogen* (The Flowers are Fallen) is remote from the OL, or office lady, of our acquaintance, but she is an authentic figure of her time.

ABE KOBO

Abe Kobo, who had grown up in Manchuria, was one of the most original and imaginative writers of this generation. His strange, somewhet surrealist work, best known in Britain in *Suna no Onna*, translated as The Woman of the Dunes in 1964, gained him a substantial reputation abroad. Despite the artifice and solipsism of his 'other' world, he is a creative artist and a seminal influence. He found a like-minded translator in E. Dale Saunders, who transposed his strange concepts with the greatest ingenuity into the English-speaking world.

DAZAI OSAMU

Dazai Osamu was a much older man, but he became a celebrity in Japan only after the Second World War. His novel *Shayo* (The Setting Sun), appearing in 1947, not merely captured but to some extent actually set the tone of the period preceding Japan's social and economic reconstruction. He took the I-novel (watakushi-shosetsu), always associated with Soseki, to a new pitch of tragic intensity (in keeping with his private life) and enjoyed a limited following abroad, especially for *Ningen Shikkaku*, translated into English in 1958, ten years after publication of the original in Japan, as No Longer Human. He was a writer's writer, immensely talented and sensitive, but whose work was sometimes found to be morbid, by the common reader.

Another survivor from a still earlier period, who is best known abroad for his post-war work was Ibuse Masuji, whose *Kuroi Ame* (Black Rain) has been taken to represent the reaction of Japanese writers to the atomic bomb. Its success led to the translation of some of Ibuse's substantial pre-war output, and of the satire on army life, *Yohai Taicho* (Lieutenant Lookeast), which was provoked by his conscription as a war correspondent.

The amoral hedonism of a section of the first genuinely post-war generation of Japanese youth has its memorial, and found its expression in Ishihara Shintaro's novel *Taiyo no Kisetsu*, which appeared in 1955 and was to be translated, as Season of Violence, ten years later. Meanwhile, it had been made into a film and had given rise to the naming as Taiyozoku (sun tribe) of the alienated young people whose uninhibited lifestyle had aroused much indignation and envy among Japanese cinema audiences. This was a social, rather than primarily a literary, phenomenon. It serves here as a reminder that the fertile literary activity of the early post-war years in Japan coincided with an outburst of achievement in the Japanese film-making industry.

KUROSAWA AKIRA

It might be supposed that this activity, in addition to making its own impact and establishing its own great reputations, might have accelerated and enhanced the growing interest shown abroad in the post-war Japanese novel. It seems doubtful if this was so. It was Kurosawa Akira and Kyo Machiko whose names caught the attention of Western audiences of *Rashomon*, – the former, certainly, to become one of the most highly respected figures ever to emerge from the entire, global film industry. Some literary foreigners were aware that the film of Rashomon was based on two short stories by Akutagawa Ryunosuke, and that he had committed suicide long before its production. But, although the short story had been a form highly cultivated by Japanese writers for generations, this was not the point taken by foreign cinema audiences. Nor did they have the chance, abroad, for many years, to see the cinema's brilliantly comic adaptation of Tanizaki's novella about *Shozo, a Cat, and Two Women* (Shozo to Neko to Futari no Onna).

MISHIMA YUKIO

The impact made abroad by Mishima Yukio's work did not need boosting by the cinema. It was direct and immediate, and remains unique in these respects, even if some doubts lurk now about the durability on British reading lists of his longest sustained work, the tetralogy known in English as *The Sea of Fertility*. The impact of this sequence might perhaps be fairly compared with that of Lawrence Durrell's *Alexandria Quartet*, which had come out not long before it. But it came late in Mishima's oeuvre, and translations, by various hands, appeared only after the author's sad, self-devised eclipse in 1970.

Many British readers were introduced to Mishima by his idyllic novel, *Shiosai*, translated by Meredith Weatherby as *The Sound of Waves*. This appeared in 1956, and was strongly influenced by Mishima's temporary, intense preoccupation with ideas of classical Greece, and its literature and mythology. It was a truly charming book, which did not foreshadow the darker development of Mishima's art, partly because its English translation appeared before that of *Kamen no Kokuhaku*, or *Confessions of a Mask*, though the latter had been the earlier composition. In 1957, the publication of Donald Keene's English translation of *Five Modern No Plays* stimulated the appreciation of

Mishima's versatility. The process was taken further when *Kinkakuji* appeared in English, as The Temple of the Golden Pavilion, in 1959, and reached a climax with the publication in 1963 of the translation of *Utage no Ato*, again by Donald Keene, as *After the Banquet*. Publicity surrounding the litigation which this book had provoked in Japan undoubtedly increased public interest in the author, abroad as well as among his own compatriots.

More important, however, was the critical admiration, in Western literary circles generally, of the dramatic sense and the narrative power of Mishima's writing. There was admiration, too, for the bold sophistication of his political and social comment. The frankness and worldly wisdom of it caused some amazement among British readers, who were not accustomed to hearing, for example, of a politician that, 'Corruption in an election or the victory of moneyed power did not in the least surprise him; they seemed as natural as stones and horse dung along a road', or from him, the novel's politician himself, that:

> I have been wallowing in the bog of politics for a long time, and I have in fact come to be quite fond of it. In it corruption cleanses people, hypocrisy reveals human character more than half-hearted honesty ... what we normally call human nature instantly disappears in the whirlpool of politics. I like its fierce operation. It doesn't necessarily purify, but it makes you forget what should be forgotten, and overlook what should be overlooked. It works a kind of inorganic intoxication.

The Sea of Fertility may have induced a kind of intoxication in some of Mishima's admirers, but it dealt with ideas and situations much further removed from ordinary, direct experience, and its mysterious attraction was not always strong enough to hold the common reader. Mishima was eventually lost to a peculiarly bitter intensity – an aspect perhaps of Ivan Morris' *Nobility of Failure*. But one of the things which should not be forgotten was the added impetus he helped to give to the development of mutual understanding between the literary enthusiasts of the West and the practitioners of post-war Japan. An outstanding example of this was his collaboration with Geoffrey Bownas in the editing (and in Bownas' case much of the translation) of the Penguin collection *New Writing in Japan*, which, as the latter had sadly to record in his brief Introduction, was brought out shortly after Mishima's death.

That collection of short stories (which included, among the most impressive, 'The Catch' by Oe Kenzaburo, winner of the Nobel Prize for Literature nearly a quarter of a century later) together with the earlier one of *Modern Japanese Stories* edited by Ivan Morris and put out by Tuttle in 1962, will serve fully to substantiate the mastery long demonstrated by Japanese writers of the short story as a form of literary art. All the contributors to both collections, including all the translators, some not yet mentioned here, such as John Bester and Geoffrey Sargent, would richly deserve to be studied at some length in any account more thorough and less cramped than the present one.

Mishima's work attracted many of the most able and distinguished translators of Japanese literature into English, and interpretations of his life were also offered, notably, for the British reader, by Henry Scott-Stokes. Japanese critics tended to stress Mishima's concern for the masculine traditions of the warrior, and to contrast this with Kawabata's concentration on the feminine aspects of Japanese culture. Their attitudes towards the world outside the Japanese tradition were certainly in complete mutual contrast.

Although Seidensticker's most accomplished translation of *Yukiguni (Snow Country)* had been available to the public as early as 1956, as mentioned above, the award of the Nobel Prize for Literature to Kawabata in 1968 came as rather a surprise to the common reader in Britain. In the Introduction to his translation, Seidensticker noted that Kawabata had adopted the haiku manner, 'notable for its terseness and austerity, so that his novel must rather be like a series of brief flashes in a void. In *Snow Country* Kawabata has chosen a theme that makes a meeting between haiku and the novel possible'. This was the angle from which Kawabata approached his acceptance speech. In Stockholm, and throughout the West, his brave attempt to explain the relationship of his work to Zen meditation, and to the poems of twelfth-century priests, was sometimes mistaken for deliberate mystification. It is not easy, in the long retrospective view, to see how such misunderstandings came about (though the work of the next Japanese novelist to win the Nobel Prize may have seemed equally difficult at first reading). What we remember now are the brilliant images of the snow country itself, the magical design of *Thousand Cranes*, the strength of the tea-ceremony bowls in *The Sound of the Mountain*, the economical beauty of Kawabata's landscapes, and the capacity of the characters in his novels, to convey in conversation so much more than they are permitted actually to say. British readers may have contrasted Kawabata's work, in this respect, with that of Ivy Compton-Burnett. She made her characters say what they would more naturally only have been thinking: he managed to show what his characters were thinking, although they maintained a most scrupulous and consistent reticence. Kawabata is now rightly regarded on all sides as having been a great craftsman among novelists. It took him no less than twelve years to achieve a version of *Yukiguni* which he was able to regard as finished. But the note of distinction in his writing was not limited to its meticulous craftsmanship. Ivan Morris described his novels as 'among the most affecting and original work of our time'.

ARIYOSHI & MARUYA

After the masterpieces of Tanizaki, Kawabata and Mishima, there might well have been something of a break, as it were for refreshment, among Japanese novelists. But we have noted that Oe Kenzaburo was already not only at work but attracting attention in translation. Mishima had once picked him out as 'the spokesperson for our 1960s'. In the 'seventies and 'eighties more and more Japanese writers were coming, through translation, to the notice of the common reader in Britain and throughout the West. Some, of whom Ariyoshi Sawako might be taken as an example, wrote in a conventional tradition, to use the expression respectfully: Ariyoshi dealt with serious social issues, as Enchi Fumiko and others had, before her. Some experimented with new forms or, like Maruya Saiichi, succeeded in exploring the deeper levels of human psychology in a notable humorous style. Maruya's best-known novel in translation in Singular Rebellion. He is a respected critic, and has himself translated into Japanese works by Graham Greene and James Joyce. He seems to care that it is a novelist's business to entertain the reader.

The same may be said of Murakami Haruki, whose novels (*A Wild Sheep Chase*, and *The Hard-Boiled Wonderland* and the *End of the World*) have been followed by *The Elephant Vanishes*, a collection of short stories cleverly translated by Alfred Birnbaum and Jay Rubin. Murakami Haruki has as strong a sense of dramatic fantasy as we saw in the work of Abe Kobo, but the disorienting effects are less tragically Kafkaesque, there is a social dimension, to counteract the isolation and alienation afflicting Abe's characters, and there is a sparkling spirit of comedy.

Murakami has translated work by Scott Fitzgerald and other distinguished American writers. His own novels in translation have achieved considerable popularity in the English-speaking world.

ENDO SHUSAKU

But, at least until the award of the Nobel Prize for Literature to Oe in 1994, the active Japanese novelist best known in Britain was undoubtedly Endo Shusaku. He had indeed been described by no less authoritative a critic than Anthony Thwaite precisely as 'the best living Japanese novelist'. In Japan, he is the most admired and widely read Christian writer, in any branch of the profession. His historical sense has been developed and sustained by his studies of Christians in Japan in the seventeenth century, and their persecution. Consideration of the place of religion in modern life has led him to make a searching examination of matters which are fundamental to the cultures of both East and West.

Examples of the range, which may serve also to indicate the depth of Endo's work, are his understanding of the Japanese student's loneliness in Paris, in *Foreign Studies*; of the psychology of guilt, in *Scandal*; of the wide variety of characters in *Deep River*, and of the pathos and heroism of *The Girl I left Behind*, – the latter so well brought out in Mark Williams' sensitive translation. Incidentally, the veteran Japanese infantry soldier in *Deep River*, which is also skilfully translated, by Van C. Gessel, gives the most vivid and telling account in Japanese literature of the horrors of the closing stages of the war in Burma. The focus of Endo's work, however, is on the future. Without loss of narrative power, he contrives to ask questions about the human condition which are as relevant to inhabitants of London or New York as they are to everyday life in Tokyo. This is, after all, a most proper task for the serious novelist of ideas, operating across the frontiers of cultural difference.

OE KENZABURO

If from the humanist rather than the religious point of reference, this is the challenge which Oe Kenzaburo is also consciously facing, and to which he brings an unmistakable and disturbing power. These qualities were already apparent in his short story, 'The Catch', mentioned above, for which he won the

Akutagawa prize in 1958. He became known in Japan for his scathing and aggressive social and political writing. Although Oe wrote always from a point of view on the political left, it was Mishima, from the other extreme of political standpoints, who was to say that Oe had 'reached a new pinnacle in post-war Japanese fiction', adding, as also noted above, that 'he stands alone as the spokesman for our 1960s'. Abroad, he became more widely known following the appearance in 1968 of John Nathan's translation, as *A Personal Matter*, of *Kojinteki na Taiken*, the account, written from the author's own experience, of a young man's response to the birth of his child with severe damage to the brain.

The award of the Nobel Prize for Literature to Oe, in 1994, was made with particular praise being given by the Committee to *Mannen Gannen no Futtoboru*, published in Japan in 1967, and in the English translation by John Bester, as *The Silent Cry*, in 1974. At the time of the Nobel award, this work was not well known to the British reader. It has since served to confirm earlier impressions of the sheer force of Oe's imaginative writing, and of his ability to disconcert the reader and to challenge the complacent or optimistic assumptions of a society preoccupied with material values, and with economic and technological advance. It has also greatly increased awareness of Oe's deep understanding of remote rural or insular communities, such as those of his native Shikoku or Okinawa; and of his concern for the local community in its relationship with the central power of the state.

In his acceptance speech in Stockholm, and in various public lectures, some of which were published with the Nobel Prize Speech, under the latter's title, 'Japan, the Ambiguous and Myself', Oe has offered a wider view of his work, and of his own approach to it. He distanced himself, in that speech, from his only Japanese predecessor as a Nobel laureate in the same field, though he did pay tribute to Kawabata's courage. Oe said he felt closer to Yeats. The ambiguity which he then attributed to Japan he described as 'a kind of chronic disease that has been prevalent thoughout the modern age'. This, in his own explanation, had to do with the modernization of Japan, with materialism, and with Japan's relations with the West, and also with the neighbouring countries of Asia. He placed great emphasis on the need for a quality of humanism, which he said he himself had come to regard as 'the quintessence of Europe'. On other occasions, Oe has expressed some pessimism about the future of writing in Japan. But he has also identified publicly a number of young novelists, including the daughter of Dazai Osamu, for whom he is able to envisage great achievement. Another thought from one of his public lectures is that connections formed with other Asian countries, and a sense of sympathy with suffering in the third world and with the victims of oppression, may provide a new direction for Japanese writers. Japanese writing on Vietnam, most notably that of Kaiko Ken, much of which is arresting, balanced and vividly observed, tends to endorse this supposition. The subject is not covered here, partly because the writing is on the border between reportage and fiction. But it amounts to a significant achievement, and touches on great questions of freedom and responsibility, themselves close to the enduring interests of middlebrow, Middle England.

Oe's faith in toleration and decency, in the renunciation of war, and in the healing power of art, are characteristics of the man which emerge in his work. The political context, which also remains a feature of it, raises the question whether, as has been famously suggested, all modern Japanese literature is really about relations between East and West. If the few writers considered in the present essay, and their impact on Britain, so far as this can be known, are to form the basis of judgement, it must surely be that this is much too restrictive a thesis. It is true that there has been space here only to cover a part of the field, the full scale of which may be guaged only most tentatively by the inclusion of John Lewell's biographical dictionary, *Modern Japanese Novelists*, of 57 entries, ranging back, however, at least as far as Akutagawa, whose suicide is now nearly seventy years in the past. (Nevertheless, the word modern still seems appropriate to his talent.)

While Oe's particular political concerns are naturally of interest in the immediate context of current events, we may note that they, and his humanism, will also come to form part of the longer term, historical perspective in which his foreign readers, even more than those in his own country, will look back at contemporary Japan. It was suggested earlier that the novels of Osaragi Jiro had considerable importance of this kind for British readers in the first post-war years. Equally, long ago, when we read Dazai's remark that 'it was not until about 1935, when the Japanese military clique was first beginning to rampage in the open', we not only learned something of a Japanese writer's stark view of a recent decade in his country's history, but our own view may also have been influenced by the knowledge that this was how he saw it.

OVERVIEW: AN ECONOMY OF STYLE

On an entirely different level, the impact in Britain of Japan's post-war novelists was a matter of strictly literary perception and assessment, not only for the professional writers and critics, but again for the common reader. The vivid economy of style, which had long been regarded as one of Japan's most highly valued contributions to enjoyment of the visual arts, was now seen more clearly to be an equally marked characteristic of the Japanese novel, evident in its structure and composition as well as in its typically sinewy narrative. It is already easier than it was in 1968 to grasp the significance of the points which Kawabata was most concerned to try to get over to his audience in Stockholm.

What is more, for the promotion of an educated, not to say learned, understanding of the modern Japanese writer's aims and methods, the work of distinguished Japanese critics and academic authorities is often now available in English, is indeed often written in English. For the present purpose it will be sufficient to mention Dr Yamanouchi Hisaaki's study, 'The Search for Authenticity in Modern Japanese Literature', which gives the background, as is proper, since the Meiji period, but includes also a mastery survey of the post-war foreground. There is a combination of brevity and depth here which is reminiscent of the essential qualities of the literature with which it deals. Since Dr Yamanouchi was himself the translator of Oe's Nobel Prize Speech, as Seidensticker was of Kabawata's, we may count him as a direct contributor to the impact now under discussion.

It must be evident already how much we owe to the translators, and especially, with due respect to the literary world beyond our own reach, how much, in particular, we laymen readers owe them. (One has only to substitute the words lay readers to see how easy it would be to go wrong – and how much easier still in cultural and social surroundings wholly different from one's own.) Tributes are also due both to the Japan Foundation and, if we may for once acknowledge its role, to UNESCO, which funded translations at a crucial period.

The layman reader in Britain has turned to the Japanese novelist first of all for enjoyment of the latter's skill and sense of humour: he has not been disappointed. But he has also wanted to learn about life in Japan, how it is lived in city and countryside, how it is varied by circumstance, and how it is changing. As to variety, we have glanced at some of it. There is much more: we think, for example, of Kita's *The House of Nire*; or Togawa Masako's mysteries, such as *Master Key*, in Simon Grove's translation; or of the humorous stories of Keita Genji, as translated by Hugh Cortazzi. And we should spare a thought for those many serious and highly talented Japanese novelists whose work has not yet found its way, through the matching interest of a translator, into our layman's library. Again, there are those Japanese writers who have made direct and most original contributions to English as well as to Japanese literature, among whom the laurels would surely be worn by Yoshida Kenichi. And then there are the contributions made by famous British writers in English who have lived in Japan — but that is another subject, not for this space.

Yoshida's name is resonant with quality, as he recognizes a sense of humour, across cultural boundaries. To take an example only quite recently made available, the British layman can see that there is as much to be learned about life in the midle of our century from any one of the exquisitely observed short stories of Koda Aya, as rendered by Alan Tansman, as there is to be learned about Tudor or Jacobean England from a single miniature painting by Nicholas Hilliard.

The quality of genius itself defies attempts at analysis. As laymen, we may have to be content, if shamefacedly, to admit that we know only what we like. It is not possible even to explain why, after all these years, we might remember with special pleasure the closing sentence of Tanizaki's masterpiece: 'Yukiko's diarrhoea persisted through the twenty-sixth, and was a problem on the train to Tokyo.' This sentence has been singled out before — probably it is immortal.

All this amounts, of course, only to a subjective view. It may be fair to raise the question, in conclusion, how many post-war novelists writing in any other single language have made a comparable impact on the common reader in Britain, either directly or in translation. The impact made by Japan's post-war novelists has certainly been such as to ensure that work of their successors will be awaited with expectations of enjoyment to be had from their technical skill, insight and vigour.

NOTES

Chapter 1 SIR HUGH CORTAZZI *Sir Rutherford Alcock [1809–1897]*

1. See *Transactions of the Asiatic Society of Japan* (TASJ), Vol. 9 (1994).
2. Alexander Michie, *The Englishman in China during the Victorian Era as Demonstrated in the Career of Sir Rutherford Alcock KCB DCL, Many Years Consul and Minister in China*, Edinburgh and London, 1900, Vol. I, p. 135.
3. Hugh Cortazzi, *Dr Willis in Japan, British Medical Pioneer, 1862-1877*, London, 1985, p. 33.
4. *Mitford's Japan*, edited by Hugh Cortazzi, London, 1985, p. 11.
5. Sir Rutherford Alcock, *The Capital of the Tycoon: A Narrative of Three Years' Residence in Japan*, London, 1863, Vol. I pp. 166-81.
6. *The Capital of the Tycoon*, I, 397 ff.
7. *The Capital of the Tycoon*, II, 64-150.
8. For detailed accounts of the first Tozenji incident, see, for instance, Laurence Oliphant, *Episodes in a Life of Adventure*, New York, 1887, and Hugh Cortazzi, *Victorians in Japan*, London 1987, p. 104. The British legation at Tozenji was again attacked almost exactly a year later, while Alcock was on home leave.
9. This recommendation was accepted and Laurence Oliphant was appointed to this post.
10. Dr William Willis was in due course appointed to fill the post of medical officer and legation assistant, but he did not arrive until after the first Tozenji incident. If Alcock had not himself had experience as a surgeon the legation would have suffered even more than it did in the 1861 attack.
11. Matsumai was the name of the Japanese fief which was responsible for the whole of Yezo, i.e. the present Hokkaido.
12. Alcock's 'imperialist' interests continued after his retirement from the post of minister at Peking. He became chairman of the British North Borneo company in 1881 and remained in this post until he resigned in 1893. K.G.Tregonning, *Under Chartered Rule (North Borneo 1881-1946)*, Singapore, 1958.
13. For details of Oliphant's experiences see *Episodes in a Life of Adventure*, New York, 1887, pp. 174-86. George Alexander Lensen in his book *The Russian Push towards Japan, Russo-Japanese Relations, 1697-1875*, New York, 1971 puts the episode in a different perspective. He asserted that (p. 448) 'The surveying of the Tsushima coast by an English warship in 1861 strengthened

the Russian conviction that the British, who had been prevented by the Russo-Chinese treaties of 1858 and 1860 from gaining a naval station on the Asian continent between the Amur River and Korea, might try to annex Tsushima and ultimately bottle up Russian expansion at this point. Consul Goshkevitch informed the Shogunate that the British had designs on the island, and urged the Japanese to make adequate defence preparations, offering Russian assistance in supplying Tsushima with cannons and in constructing suitable gun emplacements. The Japanese declined his offer. Nevertheless a Russian man-of-war soon arrived at Tsushima and the Russians appeared to be about to take over the island.'

14. Alcock, *Art and Art Industries in Japan*, London, 1878, pp. 15, 237 and 292.

Chapter 2 YUMIYO YAMAMOTO *Inoue Masaru – 'Father' of the Japanese Railways*

1. One of the 'pioneering' Choshu Five who went to England in 1863 and studied at UCL, on his return, Masaru Inoue took on the difficult roles of coordinating between Japanese bureaucrats and the '*oyatoi*' (foreign employees) and transplanting the seeds of scientific knowledge gleaned in the West to become the driving force and 'Father' of the Japanese Railways. His memory lives on in the 'Masaru Inoue Scholarship' set up at University College, London (UCL) from the private funds of his grandson, Katsuhide Inoue, for UK students wishing to study in Japan, to return in some small part the kindness shown to Masaru, and to continue the flow of knowledge and friendship between Britain and Japan.

2. '*Segai Inoue Kōden* I' (Hara shobō, 1968); '*Ito Hirobumi Den*, I' (Tōseisha 1940); W.G. Beasley, *Japan Encounters the Barbarian*, (Yale University Press 1995); 'White Adder' Official Log Book No. 4 O.N. 45052 (Crew Lists Holdings, Maritime History Archive, Memorial University of Newfoundland).

3. According to G.C. Foster's Obituary of Prof. Williamson in the *Journal of the Chemical Society* (87-1 Transactions of 1905), Williamson was chosen 'on the recommendation of Mr (now Sir Augustus) Prevost, who was a member of the Council of University College, London' but UCL Reports and Calendars show that he did not actually become an Auditor and member of the College Council until the 1864 Session, being but a Bank of England shareholder in 1863. E. Divers in his Obituary in the *Royal Society's Proceedings* (78A 1907) quotes Williamson as having received 'an offer to send him five young Japanese, to be boarded and looked after in matters concerning their education' from Hugh Matheson himself towards the end of 1863. Williamson's father having worked in the East India House and having had a hand in the original foundation of University College and the fact that Vice-Dean of the Faculty of Laws and Arts in 1863-64 was also his father-in-law, Prof. Thomas Hewitt Key, may also have had influence. At any rate, the Williamsons, who lived at 16 Provost Road, Haverstock Hill, in the early 1860s 'being very poor' (according to Prof. Williamson's daughter, Mrs Alice Maud Fison, in '*From Giessen to Gower Street*'; Harris and Brock), they moved to 12 Fellows Road, Hampstead, 'in 1864 or 1865'.

4. 'Segai Inoue Kōden, I' Hara shobō, 1968; 'Ito Hirobumi Den, I' Tōseisha, 1940; Minoru Ishizuki, *Kindai Nihon no Kaigairyūgakushi*, Kyoto, 1972 Chukoh Bunko, 1992, cites 'Mr Cooper' as a 'gako' artist, with (however) no clear authority.

5. Deprived of the use of his right eye at an early age and short-sighted in the other, he had also lost the use of his left arm through over-tight bandaging.

6. Obituary of Alexander William Williamson by G.C. Foster (*Journal of the Chemical Society* 87-1 Transactions 1905)

7. 'Ito Hirobumi Kankei Monjo' (Haniwa shobō)

8. *1863-64 College Fees Book*, Manuscripts Department, D.M.S. Watson Science Library, University College London (UCL)

9. UCL records show Masaru registered for Analytical Chemistry three times.

10. Possibly Russel Forbes Carpenter of London (matriculated 1863, having entered 1862-63; registered for Chemistry and French 1863-64; *1863-64 College Fees Book*, D.M.S. Watson Science Library, UCL)

11. *The Memorials of Hugh Mackay Matheson*, London: Hodder & Stoughton, 1899

12. *1864-65/1865-66 College Fees Book*, D.M.S. Watson Science Library, UCL; *1866-67 College Fees Book*, Records Office, UCL

13. Lay had publicly announced the sale of Japanese railway bonds at an interest rate of 4%; London *Times*, 23 April 1870

14. The two end stations of the Yokohama-Shinagawa line were in fact not the stations of Yokohama and Shinagawa as we know them today, but the current JR Sakuragicho station and the now non-existent Shiodome station. The first railway in Japan was actually the 600m track set along the Ohura coastline from Lot Nos. 1 to 10 of the foreign residents' quarters in Nagasaki by Thomas B. Glover in 1865, on which he ran the 'Iron Duke' for about a year. But this remains relatively unacknowledged, perhaps because it was a private line.

15. E.G. Holtham, *Eight Years in Japan, 1873-1881* (London: Kegan, Paul and French, 1883)

16. *Tokyo Nichinichi Shimbun*, 15 October 1872 (13 Sept. by lunar calendar)

17. Locomotive No. 1 of Vulcan Foundry Co. Built in England 1871, it however had a roof covering all the three classes of carriages.

18. *Japan Weekly Mail*, 19 October 1872

Acknowledgements

I wish to express my deepest and most sincere thanks in particular to Dr Carmen Blacker and Prof. W.G. Beasley; to Mr Jeremy J. Brown (Matheson & Co.), Mr John Wells (Manuscripts Department, Cambridge University Library); to Ms Pauline J. Ensor of University College London and Ms Gill Furlong (Archivist, Manuscripts Department, D.M.S. Watson Science Library, UCL); to Mr Michio Sato (Transport Museum, Kanda, Tokyo); to Ms Yoshie Kira (Yokohama Archives of History); Ms Roberta Thomas (Maritime History Archive, Memorial University of Newfoundland); to Mr

Ben Thorne, CMG MBE, Mr Alexander McKay, and to the kind support and encouragement of Sir Hugh and Lady Cortazzi, and to that of my maternal grandfather, Katsuhide Inoue, to whom I dedicate this humble chapter.

Chapter 3 CARMEN BLACKER *Laurence Oliphant and Japan [1858–88]*

1. There are two biographies of Laurence Oliphant: Margaret Oliphant, *Memoir of the Life of Laurence Oliphant and of Alice Oliphant his Wife*, 2 vols, 1891; Philip Henderson, *The Life of Laurence Oliphant, Traveller, Diplomat and Mystic*, 1956. His own *Episodes in a Life of Adventure*, 1887, vividly describes some of the principal dramas in his life.

2. Hannah Whittall Smith, *Religious Fanaticism*, ed. Ray Strachey 1928. Some of this book, daring because outspoken about the sexual basis for some of the spiritual delusions rampant in America in the 1880s, contains a chapter on Harris and his Brotherhood, and another on Oliphant himself.

3. Many of Mrs Margaret Oliphant's 125 books were 3-volume novels. In the same year that she produced the 2-volume life of her cousin Laurence, she wrote two 3-volume novels and a history of Jerusalem. See the *Autobiography and Letters of Mrs Margaret Oliphant*, introduction by Q.D. Leavis, 1974. She wrote to support her lazy sons and other parasites. That severe critic, Queenie Leavis, calls her 'an exemplary woman of letters'.

4. Oliphant, *Narrative of Lord Elgin's Mission to China and Japan*, 2 volumes, Edinburgh: Blackwood 1859-60

5. See Oliphant's own description in Vol. 2 of the *Narrative*. For the intimations of Japan as a fallen paradise, see Toshio Yokoyama, *Japan in the Victorian Mind; a Study of the Stereotyped Images of a Nation, 1850-80*, 1987

6. Oliphant's remark that these dogs may have been the progenitors of the King Charles spaniel rests on the theory that the Portuguese succeeded in bringing some home in the 16th century, that Katharine of Braganza, the Portuguese Queen of Charles II, brought a couple with her as part of her dowry, and hence that the 'little Dogges' which Evelyn describes as making 'free, and messes, in St James' Palace', were descended from Japanese forebears. See V.W.F. Collier, *Dogs of China and Japan in Nature and Art*. Also B.H. Chamberlain's *Things Japanese*, under the heading 'pup dogs'. The breed was officially recognized in 1895.

7. The following account is based on Oliphant's chapter 'The Attack on the British Legation in Japan in 1861', in his *Episodes in a Life of Adventure*, 1887. Sir Rutherford Alcock's eyewitness account of the attack is in his *Capital of the Tycoon*, 1863, Vol. 2, ch. 8

8. The drawing, entitled 'Outrage on the British Legation at Yeddo: Attack on Messrs Oliphant and Morrison', appeared in the *Illustrated London News*, 12 October 1861. It is reproduced in Philip Henderson's biography.

9. See the chapter 'A Visit to Tsushima', in *Episodes*.

10. Lord Redesdale, *Memories*, Vol. 1, p. 125. On p. 357 of the same work Lord Redesdale describes how he had seen the deep sword cuts in the beam which saved Oliphant from the assassin in 1861, but that by 1906 the beam had been removed.

11. The episode of the Satsuma students has been ignored by both of Oliphant's biographers. Accounts may be found of his services to the group, and of their subsequent fortunes in the Brocton Brotherhood, in W.G. Beasley, *Japan Encounters the Barbarian*, Yale, 1995, pp. 105-13, 129-38. Ivan Hall, *Mori Arinori*, Cambridge Mass., 1973, ch. 3. Also in the study of Thomas Lake Harris by H.W. Schneider and George Lawton, *A Prophet and a Pilgrim*, New York, 1942, pp. 194-9, 213-25. Also Inuzuka Kōmyō, *Satsuma-han Eikoku Ryūgakusei*, Tokyo, 1989, ch. 3. For generous help on the Japanese sources relevant to the Satsuma *ryūgakusei*, I am deeply grateful to Mr N. Koyama of the University Library, Cambridge.

12. Further examples of the later distinguished careers of this group are Yoshida Kiyonari, later to serve the Meiji Government as Vice-Foreign Minister and Minister to London; Samejima Naonobu, later Minister in London, Berlin and Paris; Matsumura Junzō, to be Admiral of the Imperial Fleet off Kagoshima during the Satsuma Rebellion of 1877. It should be noted that when the students left Japan they adopted assumed names to avoid detection by the Bakufu spies. Some, notably Matsumura and Nagasawa, continued to use these for the rest of their lives.

13. Oliphant conducted a voluminous correspondence with the wealthy evangelist William Cowper, and with Mrs Cowper. The correspondence is in Columbia University Library. Ivan Hall, *op. cit.*, p. 109. On 1 December 1867 Oliphant wrote that any financial help Cowper might give to Brocton would be a good work fraught with sublime results, 'helping to lay the foundation of a higher civilization than the world had seen since the decline of the Golden Age'. Schneider and Lawton, *op. cit.*, p. 225.

14. The discipline in the Gōjū and Zōshikan is described in Hall, *op. cit.*, pp. 37-40. It included some household chores.

15. Hall, pp. 114-28.

16. Another Japanese disciple who proved permanently devoted to Harris was Arai Ōsui, a young samurai from Sendai who joined the Brotherhood in 1871. He cheerfully performed what another disciple described as slave labour in the Brotherhood's printing press, uncomplainingly resetting the trivial changes which Harris constantly made to his verbose prose. He was forbidden to write to his family for nine years. He returned to Japan in 1899, after 28 years in the Brotherhood. There he lived until 1922 in abject poverty and chastity, producing his own version of Harris's teachings in five volumes, *Ōsui Kōroku*.

17. See Hannah Whittall Smith, *op. cit.*, ch. 8, 'The L.O. Fanaticism', especially pp. 220-3.

Chapter 4 YOSHIHIKO MORITA *Edmund Morel, a British Engineer in Japan*

1. Okuma Shigenobu (1838-1922), Hizen samurai. Student of Dutch, then English; held domain offices connected with finance and foreign trade before the Meiji Restoration (1868). Senior Hizen member of early Meiji government; leader of modernizing group. Later, political party leader, prime minister.

2. Ito Hirobumi (1841-1909) Also: Shunsuke. Choshu loyalist; son of farmer turned castle-town merchant. Made samurai, 1863. With Inoue Kaoru, studied in London, 1863-4. As 'Western' expert and colleague of Kido Koin, rose steadily in Meiji government, becoming first prime minister.

3. Morel was admitted as a member of the Institution of Civil Engineers on 23 May 1865. An entrance qualification in those days was that the candidate must be at least 25 years old, so, working back, this means that he should have been born before 23 May 1840. Although we cannot know the real background to Morel's admission to the Institution, there seems to have been some incongruity. Either the Institution overlooked his young age, or Morel lied about his age on his application.

4. The only article written by Morel that I could find in the British Library, dated 1863, concerned the graving docks at Hobson's Bay, Melbourne, Australia, with which he was involved.

5. According to the British Foreign Office records, Purcell's transfer to the service of the Japanese government was officially proposed by the War Office in a letter to the Foreign Office on 6 September 1871, following a request from the Japanese government.

6. Although the Americans lost the competition to construct the Yokohama-Shimbashi line, they were engaged in railway construction in Hokkaido.

7. Kido Koin (1833-77) – Earlier known as Katsura Kogoro, Choshu loyalist; son of official doctor; adopted by samurai. Official posts in Choshu from 1862. Effective leader of Choshu from 1865. With Saigo Takamori and Okubo Toshimichi he is regarded as one of the three heroes of the Meiji Restoration. Key member of early Meiji government.

8. Saigo Takamori (1828-77) – Satsuma samurai. With Okubo Toshimichi, leader of Satsuma after 1864. After Restoration, senior member of Meiji government. Broke with other leaders over Korea dispute, 1873; leader of samurai revolt, 1877. Committed suicide on battlefield.

9. Okubo Toshimichi (1830-78) Also: Ichizo – Satsuma samurai. Loyalist and domain bureaucrat; with Saigo Takamori, largely controlled domain politics after 1864. After Restoration, key figure in Meiji government; councillor; minister. Dominant figure after Korea dispute of 1873 until assassinated in 1878.

10. The *ryo* was replaced one-for-one with the yen under the New Currency Regulation later in 1871.

11. Goto Shojiro (1838-91) – Politician of the late Edo and early Meiji period. Born in the Tosa domain (Kochi Prefecture). He influenced the strong Tosa samurai Sakamoto Ryoma to a pro-imperial cause. After the Meiji Restoration he went on to serve in high posts but resigned in opposition to the government's decision to invade Korea.

12. Sanjo Sanetomi (1837-91) – Court noble and political leader of the Meiji Restoration. Appointed *Kokuji-Goyo-Gakari* (Commissioner of State Affairs) in Kyoto, then became *Dajodaijin* (Grand Minister of State) until 1885 when the cabinet system was introduced.

13. Yokohama kaiko shiryokan, containing a collection of Japanese and

foreign materials principally concerning the opening of Japan, and Yokohama port.

Chapter 5 OLIVE CHECKLAND & NORIO TAMAKI *Alexander Allan Shand [1844-1930] – a Banker the Japanese Could Trust*

1. Matsukata Masayoshi, *Report of the Adoption of the Gold Standard in Japan, Tokyo 1899*, gives a full account of the painstaking process by which the Japanese banking system was established.
2. See International Genealogical Index (Scottish Section) microfiche, Church of Jesus Christ of Latterday Saints (Batch C112476, Serial Sheet 0715), 1984.
3. Nishikawa Kojiro, *Nihon bokishidan* (Studies on the history of accountancy in Japan), (Tokyo 1971), p.129.
4. The manager of the Chartered Mercantile Bank at Hong Kong had been to Japan and had reported favourably on the prospects for business at Yokohama. See *The Bankers' Magazine*, 1863, p.455.
5. Takahashi, *Jiden*, (Tokyo, 1929), p.31. Takahashi was finance minister intermittently between 1913 and 1936 and prime minister, November 1921-June 1922.
6. N. Tamaki, *Japanese Banking*, (Cambridge, 1995), p.93.
7. Okurasho, *Okurasho hyakunenshi* (One hundred year history of the Ministry of Finance [MF], (Tokyo, 1969), Vol.1, pp.13-19. The Bank of Japan [BOJ], *Zuroku Nihon no kahei* (Pictorial history of Japanese coins), Tokyo, 1973, Vol.7, pp.161-4.
8. BOJ, *Nihon kinyushi shiryo (NKS) Meiji and Taisho*, Tokyo, 1955, has a complete set of materials of the eight exchange companies.
9. Okuma Ko Hachijugonenshikai (Ed.), *Okuma Ko hachijugonenshi* (Eighty-five years of Earl Okuma), Tokyo, 1970, Vol.1, p.287.
10. T. Kido, *Diary*, (translated by S.D. Brown and A. Hirota) (Tokyo, 1983), Vol.I, 18 October 1869.
11. T. Kido, *Diary*, (Tokyo, 1983), Vol.I, 13 December 1869
12. T. Kido, *Diary*, (Tokyo, 1983), Vol.I, 21 November 1870
13. T. Kido, *Diary*, (Tokyo, 1985), Vol.II, 11 November 1871.
14. Sawada Akira (Ed.), *Segai Ko jireki* (Careers of Segai Ko [Inoue Kaoru]), (Tokyo, 1978), pp.327-30.
15. Joseph Heco, *Diary*, Vol II, p.172, 20 August 1872.
16. The original drafts in English do not survive. The Japanese version is in BOJ, *NKS Meiji and Taisho*, (Tokyo, 1966), Vol.5.
17. Letters, Reports and Memoranda from Foreigners to S. Okuma and others (mostly in European languages), Okuma Collection, Waseda University, Letter No.726.
18. Koizumi Nobukichi and Nakamigawa Hikojiro were in London from October 1874 to 1878, studying at King's College, London, under Professor Leone Levi. Sonoda Kokichi was in London, between 1874 and 1879 as Consul. Soma Tanenaga was in London (or America) between 1874 and 1879.

19. Tsuchiya Takao's introduction to Shand *Detailed Accounts of Bank Book-keeping in ibid.*, MF, *Meiji zaiseishi* (Financial history of Meiji), (Tokyo, 1927), Vol.13, pp.626-8, see also N. Umetani, *The Role of Foreign Employees in the Meiji Era in Japan*, (Tokyo 1971), 'Alexander Allan Shand', pp.50-2.

20. H. Jones, *Live Machines*, (Tenterden, Kent, 1980), p.90.

21. Daiichiginko, *Daiichiginkoshi* (History of Daiichi Bank), (Tokyo, 1957-8), Vol.1, p.217.

22. The original drafts in English do not survive. The Japanese version is in BOJ, *NKS Meiji and Taisho*, Vol.5.

23. MF, *Meiji zaiseishi*, Vol.13, pp.113-41.

24. Parr's Bank Minute Books (National Westminster Bank Archives), 30 June 1892.

25. It was Koizumi Nobukichi (see Note 17) who brought Okuma's letter to S. Hihara requesting a bank account for the Yokohama Specie Bank with the Alliance Bank in London.

26. T. Suzuki, *Japanese Government Loan Issues on the London Money Market, 1870-1913*, (London, 1994), pp.69, 70.

27. T. Suzuki, *Japanese Government Loan Issues . . .*, (London, 1994), p.70.

28. N. Tamaki, *Japanese Banking*, (Cambridge, 1995), p.96, and T. Suzuki, *Japanese Government Loan Issues*, pp.70-3.

29. N. Tamaki, *Japanese Banking*, (Cambridge, 1995), p.96, and T. Suzuki, pp.70-3.

30. C. Adler, *Jacob H. Schiff, his life and letters*, (New York, n.d.),

31. *Gladstone Diaries*, ed. Colin Matthew, Vol. XIII, 1892-4, 18 August 1892, p.61.

32. Parr's Bank Minute Book No.2, Thursday, 17 August 1899.

33. T. Suzuki, p.70, the reference is to Japanese Ministry of Finance Archives, Tokyo, Matsuo Papers 4S-10, Kato to Inoue, 24 June 1898.

34. Parr's Bank Minute Books, 29 December 1904, 7 December 1905, 14 March 1907.

35. Sir Ewan Cameron served as manager of the London office of the Hong Kong and Shanghai Bank from 1893-1905, he had previously served the Bank in the Far East.

36. The executors to the Will of A.A. Shand were Norman Protheroe Shand, Major, H.M. Army, son; Helen Sidney Shand, spinster, daughter; Ida Mary Shand, spinster, daughter; Winifred Allan Shand, spinster, daughter.

37. Had Shand lost invested money in Japanese businesses following the industrial disaster of the Great Kanto earthquake of September 1923? 'Shand will be quite overwhelmed by the disaster but I hope he has no very serious financial commitments in Japan, beyond his interest in certain cotton mills', J.H. Gubbins to E. Satow, 5 September 1923, PRO 30/33, 11/9, with thanks to Ian Nish.

38. The emphasis in this chapter on the trustworthiness, honesty and integrity which characterized A.A. Shand, should be contrasted with the underhand behaviour of Horatio Nelson Lay who had earlier (1870) acted for the Japanese government in seeking a loan on the London Money Market. See

N. Tamaki, *Japanese Banking, a History*, (Cambridge 1995), p.23.

Chapter 6 SIR HUGH CORTAZZI *Royal Visits to Japan in the Meiji Period, 1868-1912*

1. *Mitford's Japan: The Memoirs and Recollections 1866-1906 of Algernon Bertram Mitford, the first Lord Redesdale*, edited by Hugh Cortazzi, London, 1985, pp. 163-8. Supplemented by extracts from despatches to the Foreign Office sent by Sir Harry Parkes, British minister at Tokyo.
2. At that time there were still British and French garrisons at Yokohama. These had been sent to protect British and French residents in the treaty port of Yokohama.
3. Mitford recorded this gift in the memorandum about the visit which he prepared for Sir Harry Parkes.
4. *Life of Sir Harry Parkes* by F.V.Dickens and S.Lane-Poole, London, 1894, Volume II, pp. 274-7. *Deutsche Botschafter in Japan 1860-1973*, Tokyo: Deutsche Gesellschaft fuer Natur und Voelkerkunde Ostasiens, 1974, pp. 29-30.
5. *The Cruise of Her Majesty's Ship 'Bacchante' 1879-1882*, compiled from the private journals, letters and note-books of the two Princes with additions by John N.Dalton, London, 1886. The visit to Japan is described in detail on pp. 17-137 of volume II.
6. Letter from Mr Isao Abe, Grand Master of the Ceremonies in the Imperial Household office, to Sir Hugh Cortazzi, dated 21 November 1986.
7. Leonard Moseley, *Hirohito Emperor of Japan*, New Jersey, 1966, p. 57, records the horror of the Japanese suite when the King, only half dressed, walked unannounced into Hirohito's rooms at breakfast time, slapped the Crown Prince on the back and said: 'I hope, me boy, that everyone is giving you everything you want. . .I'll never forget how your grandfather treated me and me brother when we were in Yokohama. I've always wanted to repay his kindness.' He chuckled. 'No geishas here though, I'm afraid. Her Majesty would never allow it.'
8. Mary Crawford Fraser, *A Diplomat's Wife in Japan* edited by Hugh Cortazzi, Tokyo, 1982, pp. 157-66.
9. The *soshi* were 'bullies' who were employed as agitators in support of treaty revision.
10. A. Henry Savage Landor, *Everywhere, The Memoirs of an Explorer*, London, 1924, pp. 80-1.
11. Douglas Sladen, *The Japs at home*, London, 1895.
12. Mary Fraser commented that the Duke and Duchess spent such a great deal 'on curios in both Tokyo and Kyoto that their visit will long be remembered by the curio dealers'.
13. Noble Frankland, *Witness of a Century*, gives an account of the life of the Duke of Connaught.
14. See Mary Fraser, *A Diplomat's Wife in Japan*, p. 282 et seq.
15. Lord Redesdale, *The Garter Mission to Japan*, London 1906. Extracts and a summary are contained in *Mitford's Japan* edited by Hugh Cortazzi, London,

1985. See also *'Mr Lampson's Private Diary of the Garter Mission to Japan, January 10-May, 1906.* Miles Lampson, later Sir Miles and then the first Lord Killearn, who was a member of the Diplomatic Service, was attached to the mission as acting secretary to the Order of the Garter.

Chapter 7 J.E. HOARE *Britain's Japan Consular Service, 1859-1941*

★ A version of this paper was given at St Anthony's College Oxford in February 1974. I am grateful to those who made comments, especially the late Professor D.C.M. Platt. The views expressed are my own and should not be taken as official British government policy.

1. F T Ashton-Gwatkin, *The British Foreign Service: A discussion of the development and function of the British Foreign Service*, (Syracuse, New York: Syracuse University Press, 1951), p.56. See also Peter Byrd, 'Regional and Functional Specialisation in the British Consular Service,' *Journal of Contemporary History*, vol. 7, nos. 1&2, p.128; and D.C.M. Platt, *Cinderella Service: British Consuls since 1825*, (London: Longman, 1971) pp. 5, 29-36.

2. Platt, *Cinderella Service*, pp. 125-6, 131-2.

3. Platt, *Cinderella Service*, pp.181-5; P D Coates, The China Consuls, (Hong Kong: Oxford University Press, 1988), pp.7-27.

4. Foreign Office, Embassy and Consular Records China (FO 233)/3, Circular from Sir John Bonham, 1 Sept. 1849; *General Instructions for His Majesty's Consular Officers*, (London: Foreign Office, 1907), p.367.

5. Coates, *China Consuls*, Chapter 4, 'The Infant Service.'

6. Platt, *Cinderella Service*, p.183.

7. Foreign Office, Japan (FO 46)/2, Malmesbury to Alcock, draft, no. 2, 1 March 1859; Coates, *China Consuls*, pp. 74-5, 502.

8. Alexander Michie, *The Englishman in China during the Victorian Era*, (Edinburgh and London: William Blackwood and Sons, 1900), vol.II, p. 14. See also FO 46/2, Lord John Russell to Alcock, draft. no. 44, 8 December 1859; FO 46/2, Malmesbury to Alcock, draft no.2, 1 March 1859.

9. Grace Fox, *Britain and Japan 1858-1883*, (Oxford: Clarendon Press, 1969), pp.54-5; Platt, Cinderella Service, pp.195 et seq; Foreign Office, Supplement to General Correspondence (FO 97)/ 269, Treasury to Foreign Office, no.11596 2/8 of 5 August 1862.

10. FO 46/2, Malmesbury to Alcock, draft no. 51, 22 December 1859; FO 46/51, Memorandum 6 November 1863 and related papers.

11. FO 97/269, Hodgson to Lord Russell, 11 March 1861; Alcock to Russell, no. 71, 16 September 1861; Russell to Hodgson, draft, 14 January 1862, and related papers.

12. J.E. Hoare, 'Mr Enslie's Grievances', Japan Society of London *Bulletin*, no.78, (1976), pp.14-19.

13. Foreign Office, Embassy and Consular Archives, Japan (FO 262)/ 161, Lord Clarendon to Sir Harry Parkes, no.25, 26 February 1869; FO 262/257, Parkes to Lord Derby, no. 29 consular, draft, 28 October 1874; FO 46/254, 'Mr Enslie's Grievances'; *Japan Weekly Mail*, 25 February 1882; *London and China Express*, 13 May 1887; E M Satow, *A Diplomat in Japan*, (London:

Seeley Service, 1921), p. 30; Sir Harry Parkes, Minutes of Evidence, *Report from the Select Committee on Diplomatic and Consular Services*, PPHC 1872 (314), VII, p.63.

14. J.E. Hoare, Japan's *Treaty Ports and Foreign Settlements*, (Folkestone, Kent: Japan Library, 1994), pp. 56-8; Platt, *Cinderella Service*, pp.189-90.

15. Satow, *Diplomat in Japan*, pp. 30-1.

16. Satow, *Diplomat in Japan*, pp. 17-21. Jamieson's defection led to the introduction of a bond to cover the cost of passage money: FO 17/617, E H Hammond to the Treasury, draft, 21 March 1865.

17. Satow, *Diplomat in Japan*, pp.55-6.

18. Satow, *Diplomat in Japan*, pp.57-9; *Minutes of Evidence, Report of the Committee on Oriental Studies in London*, PPHC 1909 (Cd 4561), Q.1914.

19. Allen, *Ernest Satow*, pp. 35, 60-1; Redesdale, *Memories*, I, 377.

20. Frank Ashton-Gwatkin, 'The meeting of John Paris and Japan', *Tsuru*, vol.3, no.1, p.3; Arthur de la Mare, *Perverse and Foolish: A Jersey farmer's son in the British Diplomatic Service*, (Jersey, Channel Islands: La Haule Books, 1994), p.71.

21. FO 262/256, Tenterden to Parkes, no.25 consular, 4 September 1874.

22. FO 97/582, Plunkett to Salisbury, no.25 consular, 24 July 1885.

23. Minutes of Evidence, *Fifth Report of the Royal Commission on the Civil Service*, PPHC 1914-1916, (Cd 7749) Q. 41,229; FO 262/191, Parkes to Clarendon, consular no. 50 draft, 21 July 1870; FO 262/ 227, Watkins to Granville, no 24 draft consular, 6 September 1872.

24. Foreign Office, Chief Clerk's Department (FO 369)/2152/K9097/6874/223, Sir John Tilley to A. Henderson, no.322, 25 June 1930.

25. FO 83/1486, Regulations for the Joint Examination 1896.

26. *Report from the Select Committee on Diplomatic and Consular Services*, Parliamentary Papers House of Commons (PPHC), 1870 (382), vii, pp. 300-301; S Leathes, Minutes of Evidence, *Fifth Report of the Royal Commission on the Civil Service*, PPHC 1914-1916, (Cd 7749), Q.38,820.

27. There is not a great deal of personal information available. Much of what is given here comes from volumes in the FO 17 series. See also *Japan Weekly Mail*, 15 December 1888; *London and China Express* 5 February 1897 for Quinn; P.F. Kornicki, 'William George Aston', in Sir Hugh Cortazzi and Gordon Daniels, editors, *Britain and Japan 1859-1991: Themes and Personalities*, (London: Routledge, 1991), pp. 64-75;

28. The FO/17 series contain some application papers and correspondence. See also Allen, *Satow*, pp.1-3 and P.F. Kornicki, 'Ernest Mason Satow', in Cortazzi and Daniels, *Britain and Japan*, pp.76-85; and *Japan Weekly Mail* 14 April 1888 and F.V. Dickins and S. Lane-Poole, *Life of Sir Harry Parkes*, (London: Macmillan, 1894), II, 114, footnote 1.

29. FO 262/191, Parkes to Lord Granville, draft number 69 consular, 5 November 1870.

30. *Who's who in the Far East*, 1906-7.

31. FO 97/582, Plunkett to Salisbury, no. 25 consular, 24 July 1885; FO 262/415, Plunkett to Granville, no. 156 confid., draft, 13 September 1884 and FO

262/412, Granville to Plunkett, no.97, 30 October 1884.

32. Obituary, Russell Robertson, *Japan Weekly Mail*, 14 April 1888; obituary, J.J. Quinn, *London and China Express*, 5 February 1897.

33. Hoare, *Japan's Treaty Ports*, pp. 18-20, 72.

34. FO 262/333, Parkes to Lord Salisbury, no.55, draft, 15 March 1879; FO 97/582, Plunkett to Salisbury, no.25 consular, 24 July 1885; *Japan Weekly Mail*, 5 August 1882.

35. Satow Papers (PRO 30/33)5/7, Bonar to Satow, 24 June 1896.

36. Minutes of Evidence, *Fifth Report of the Royal Commission on the Civil Service*, PPHC 1914-1916, (Cd 7749), Q. 38912; D C M Platt, 'The Role of the British Consular Service in Overseas Trade, 1825-1914', *Economic History Review*, second series, Vol. XV, No. 3, (1963), p.495. See also *Correspondence respecting the question of Diplomatic and Consular Assistance to Trade*, PPHC 1886, Commercial No.16 Parts I and II (C.4779 and 4779-1).

37. *Japan Gazette*, 15 September 1880.

38. *Japan Mail*, 27 September 1881.

39. J.H. Longford, 'England's Record in Japan', Japan Society of London, *Proceedings and Transactions*, Vol. VII (1905-07), p.93; PRO 30/33/11/6, Satow to F V Dickins, 24 July 1893.

40. PRO 30/33/15/2, Satow to Dickins, 22 August 1880.

41. FO 262/167, Parkes to Clarendon, no.66 draft consular, 5 November 1869, enclosing Sir E Hornby to Parkes, 23 October 1869.

42. *Japan Weekly Mail*, 25 May 1878; *Tokio Times*, 5 October 1878; *London and China Express*, 13 July and 9 November 1888

43. Hoare, *Japan's Treaty Ports*, pp.66-105; Richard T Chang, *The Justice of the Western Consular Courts in Nineteenth Century Japan*, (Westport Conn. and London: Greenwood Press, 1984).

44. *Far East*, 17 July 1871; FO 262/655, J. Troup to H. Fraser, no. 18, 22 May 1891.

45. FO 262/209, F. Adams to Granville, draft consular nos. 49 and 52, 16 and 30 December 1871.

46. Hoare, *Japan's Treaty Ports*, pp. 31-3; Minutes of Evidence, *Fifth Report of the Royal Commission on the Civil Service*, PPHC 1914-1916 (Cd 7749), Q. 42858

47. See the papers in FO 369/87; *General Instructions for HM Consular Officers*, (1863), enclosure no.15; Platt, *Cinderella Service*, pp.29-30.

48. *Japan Daily Herald* 13 September 1880.

49. E.g. FO 798/20, Dohmen to Hornby, draft no. 6, 19 June 1875.

50. See the annual *Foreign Office List*; *General Instructions*, 1907, pp.53-61.

51. Minutes of Evidence, *Fifth Report of the Royal Commission on the Civil Service*, PPHC 1914-1916, (Cd 7749), Q.42,741-4.

52. Ashton-Gwatkin, 'Meeting of John Paris and Japan', p.3; Minutes of Evidence, *Report of the Committee on Oriental Studies in London*, PPHC 1909, (Cd 4561), XXXV, Q.470; de la Mare, *Perverse and Foolish*, pp.64-5; FO 369/308, Sir C MacDonald to Lord Grey, no. 4 consular, 5 January 1910; FO 369/595/42565, Sir C Greene to Consular Dept, semi-off., 19 August 1913;

Japan Chronicle, 19 June 1930; FO 369/2151/K2207, minutes 3 February 1930; FO 369/2323/K4122, correspondence and minutes, 1933.

53. F O 797/1, Circular to all firms, 13 September 1901; FO 369/484/15974, Treasury to the FO, 15 April 1912; FO 369/735/6584, Green to Grey, no.8 consular, 27 January 1914; FO 369/1003/20363, Greene to A. Balfour, consular no 79, 17 December 1917.

54. See the extensive papers in FO 369/595.

55. See, for example, FO 369/595/42565, Greene to FO, semi-off., 19 August 1913.

56. FO 369/1167/18585, War Office to FO 1 February 1919, and minuting.

57. FO 369/2413/K7412, Sir R. Clive to Sir John Simon, no.294, 5 June 1935; de la Mare, *Perverse and Foolish*, pp.68-9.

58. E.g., FO. 369/1885/K11255, Sir C Eliot to Lord Curzon, no.308, 20 June 1921; FO 369/1978, Sir J. Tilley to Sir A. Chamberlain, no.596, 22 November 1927.

59. Platt, *Cinderella Service*, pp. 221 et seq; Byrd, 'Regional and Functional Specialisation', p.138.

Chapter 8 IAN NISH *John Harrington Gubbins, 1852-1929*

1. F.S.G. Piggott, *Broken Thread: An Autobiography*, Aldershot, 1950, p. 6

2. Mary Fraser, *Diplomat's Wife in Japan*, Tokyo, 1899, p. 13

3. 'Notes on a journey from Aomori to Niigata and of a visit to the Mines of Sada' in *Transactions of the Asiatic Society of Japan*, III(1875), pp. 74-91. (Hereafter cited as '*TASJ*') Also 'Review of the Introduction of Christianity into China and Japan', *TASJ*, VI(1878), 1-62, and 'Hideyoshi and the Satsuma Clan in the sixteenth century', *TASJ*, VIII(1880), 92-144.

4. K. Bourne and D.C. Watt (eds), *British Documents on Foreign Affairs*, part I, series E,'Asia, 1860-1914', vol 3, Washington, 1989, doc. 111, Fraser to Salisbury, 26 May 1892. (Hereafter cited as '*BDOFA*') Good accounts of Treaty revision are given in J.H. Gubbins, *Japan*, London: HMSO, 1920, pp. 64-7; and A. Fraser, R.H.P. Mason and P. Mitchell, *Japan's Early Parliaments, 1890-1905*, London, 1995, chs. 5-6

5. P. Wilkinson and Joan B. Astley, *Gubbins and SOE*, London, 1993, pp. 4-5. Also H. Cortazzi(ed.), R.H.Brunton, *Building Japan, 1869-76*, Folkestone, 1991, p. 26.

6. Sakane Yoshihisa (ed.). *Aoki Shuzo jiden*, Tokyo: Toyo bunko, 1970, pp. 117-227 is the most detailed account from the Japanese side. References to 1892-3 are found on p. 190ff.

7. Cabinet approves treaty proposals, 13 and 22 Nov. 1893, *Nihon gaiko nempyo narabini shuyo bunsho*. For Aoki's reluctance, see Sakane, *Aoki*, p. 218-19

8. Gubbins to Foreign Office, 26 Feb. 1894 in *BDOFA*, doc. 173. Reference to Gubbins' role is found on Sakane, p.222

9. *BDOFA*, doc. 173

10. *BDOFA*, doc. 173. Sakane, *Aoki*, p. 227. Gubbins' memoranda are to be found in *BDOFA*, docs 177, 180, 202, 205, 236, 238.

11. Gubbins, *Japan*, p. 67

12. Outside Tokyo Gubbins had only served at Yokohama.

13. J.H. Gubbins, *The Making of Modern Japan*, London, 1922, p. 215.

14. Gubbins to Satow, 5 Oct. 1900 in Satow Papers (Public Record Office, Kew, PRO 30/33) 9/14

15. Gubbins to Satow, 22 Feb. 1916 in Satow Papers 11/8

16. Wilkinson and Astley, *Gubbins and SOE*, p. 6

17. *TASJ*, 1875 and 1897. In Yasui's article, *bemmo* was a refutation of certain Christian arguments.

18. J.H. Gubbins, *The Progress of Japan, 1853-71*, Oxford, 1911, p. 3

19. Chamberlain was staying for the time being at 12 Rue de l'Athenee, Geneva.

20. Gubbins(Tudor House, Worplesdon) to Satow, 18 Dec. 1912 in Satow papers, 11/8

21. Gubbins to Satow, 29 Dec. 1915 in Satow Papers, 11/8

22. Gubbins to Satow, 28 Aug. 1916 in Satow Papers, 11/8

23. Gubbins to Satow, 12 June 1917 in Satow Papers, 11/8

24. Wilkinson and Astley, *Gubbins and SOE*, p. 23

25. Gubbins to Satow, 15 April 1918 in Satow Papers, 11/8

26. J.H. Gubbins, *Japan*, London, 1920 (Foreign Office Historical Section Handbook 73, RO 42) [They were in fact joint War Office/Foreign Office/ Admiralty handbooks.]

27. 'The "Hundred Articles" and the Tokugawa government' in *Transactions of the Japan Society of London*, XVII (1918-20), pp. 128-84, delivered at the meeting on 17 Dec. 1919.

28. Gubbins to Satow, 4 and 27 Oct. 1922 in Satow Papers, 11/9

29. Gubbins to Satow, 17 Jan. 1923 in Satow Papers, 11/9

30. Gubbins to Satow, 29 April 1925 and 17 Feb. 1926, in Satow Papers, 11/ 9. His pamphlet was entitled *Socialism and the Socialist Press: an address*, 20 pages, Edinburgh: W.M. Urquhart & Sons, 1926

Chapter 9 JULIA BOYD *Hannah Riddell, 1855-1932*

Acknowledgements

I have already acknowledged the help I received from many quarters in my book *Hannah Riddell: An Englishwoman in Japan* (Tuttle 1996). For help with the present essay I should like to express my special thanks to The Riddell-Wright Society, The Church Missionary Society, The Society for the Propagation of the Gospel, Romaine Bamford, Lia Beretta, Christopher Gotto, Mrs Mirohiro Hosokawa, Atsuko Kashiwagi, Rosemary Keen, Jerry Matsumura, Christopher Penn and Momoko Williams.

1. *Dictionary of National Biography*, Oxford: University Press, 1973

2. *The Mumbles Chronicle*, 1888

3. Church Missionary Society archives, GI J 1892/194 (hereafter cited as CMS)

4. Aoki Keisai, *Mission to Okinawa*, Hongkong: Christian Reading Room, no date

5. CMS, 'Miss M. Gollock', G1/J1902/348

6. H. Riddell in *Japan Christian Quarterly*, 1930

7. Aoki, *Mission to Okinawa*

8. Aoki, ibid

9. Aoyama Shigeru, 'Flowers along a Mud Wall' in *Aisei* journal, May 1994 – Jan. 1995

10. Tobimatsu Jingo, *Hannah Riddell*, Kumamoto, 1934 (Japanese) and 1937 (English)

12. Aoki, *Mission to Okinawa*

13. Aoki, ibid

14. Aoki, ibid

15. Tobimatsu, *Hannah Riddell*

Chapter 10 PAUL MURRAY *Lafcadio Hearn, 1850-1904*

1. Paul Murray, 'Lafcadio Hearn's Interpretation of Japan', *Proceedings of the Japan Society*, London, 124 (1994), 50-64.

2. Unpublished memorandum entitled 'Lafcadio Hearn', almost certainly by Edward Stephens, an Irish cousin of Lafcadio's, provided by family sources after publication of my biography of Hearn; a rough draft, it nevertheless gives a most illuminating account of the social and religious background to Lafcadio's period in Dublin.

3. Paul Murray, 'Lafcadio Hearn and the Irish Tradition of Literary Horror', Bram Stoker Summer School, Dublin, 30 June 1994.

4. Paul Murray, *A Fantastic Journey: The Life and Literature of Lafcadio Hearn*, Japan Library, 1993, 20.

5. Murray, 'Hearn's Interpretation of Japan'.

6. Ibid.

7. The most widely available anthology, Francis King, *Lafcadio Hearn: Writings from Japan*, Penguin Books, 1984, does not contain any of the major interpretative essays referred to here.

8. Basil Hall Chamberlain, *Things Japanese*, Fifth Revised Edition, London, J. Murray; Yokohama, Kelly and Walsh, 1905; reprinted in paperback as *Japanese Things*, by Charles E Tuttle, Co., Rutland, Vermont and Tokyo, 1971. (This edition is hereafter referred to as *Things Japanese*), 4-5.

9. Ibid. 4-5.

10. Murray, 'Lafcadio Hearn's Interpretation of Japan'.

11. For an in-depth study of Parkes, see Gordon Daniels, *Sir Harry Parkes – British Representative in Japan 1865-83*, Japan Library 1996; also, see Sir Hugh Cortazzi, 'Sir Harry Parkes, 1828-1885', in Ian Nish (ed), *Britain and Japan, Biographical Portraits*, Japan Library, 1994.

12. Nigel Brailey, 'Sir Ernest Satow, Japan and Asia: The Trials of a Diplomat in the Age of High Imperialism', in *The Historical Journal*, 35(1992), 115-50.

13. Chamberlain, *Things Japanese*, 489-97.

14. Brailey, 'Satow'; Murray, 'Lafcadio Hearn's Interpretation of Japan'; Chamberlain, *Things Japanese*, 360-3; 488-97.

15. Satow's pioneering studies included: 'The Shintō shrines of Ise', in

Transactions of the Asiatic Society of Japan, 1 (1874), 99-121; 'The Mythology and Religious Worship of the Ancient Japanese', in *The Westminster Review*, New Series, Vol. LIV (1878), 27-57; 'Ancient Japanese Rituals' in *Transactions of the Asiatic Society of Japan*, Vol. VII (1879), 96-126 and 393-434; and 'The Revival of Pure Shin-tau', Appendix to the *Transactions of the Asiatic Society of Japan*, Vol. III (1875).

16. The threat posed to Japanese development by Christianity, in Satow's view, lay in the authoritarian nature of Roman Catholicism, which could be countered by healthy Protestant constitutionalism: Satow, 'Vicissitudes of the Church at Yamaguchi from 1550 to 1586', *Transactions of the Asiatic Society of Japan*, Vol. VII (1879), 131-56.

17. See, for example, Joseph M. Kitagawa, *Religion in Japanese History*, New York: Columbia University Press, 1990, ix-xvii.

18. (Sir) George Sansom, *A History of Japan*, 1958; paperback version, Folkestone: Dawson, 1978.

19. P.F. Kornicki, 'Ernest Mason Satow (1843-1929)', in Sir Hugh Cortazzi and Gordon Daniels (ed), *Britain and Japan 1859-1991, Themes and Personalities*, London: Routledge, 1991, 85.

20. Murray, 'Hearn's Interpretation of Japan'.

21. W.G. Aston, *Shintō: The Way of the Gods*, London, 1905, and *Shintō: The most Ancient Religion of Japan*, London, 1907.

22. Aston, *Shintō/Way*, 44.

23. Ibid., 23-4, 40, 211.

24. Ibid., 44-7; see also 374.

25. Aston, *Shintō/Ancient*, 9.

26. Ibid., 8-9; Kitagawa, *Religion in Japanese History*, 13.

27. Lafcadio Hearn, *Japan: an Attempt at Interpretation*, New York: Macmillan, 1904, Reprinted by Charles E. Tuttle Company, Inc. Rutland, Vermont and Tokyo, 1956, 74.

28. Aston, *Shintō/Way*, 376-7.

29. W.G. Aston, *A History of Japanese Literature*, 1899; Reprinted by Charles E. Tuttle Company, Inc. Rutland, Vermont and Tokyo, 1972, 398-9.

30. Lafcadio Hearn, *Glimpses of Unfamiliar Japan*, Boston: Houghton Mifflin Company, 1894; reprinted by Charles E. Tuttle Company, Inc., Rutland, Vermont, and Tokyo, 1976, 209-10.

31. Kornicki, 'Aston', in Cortazzi and Daniels, 73.

32. Aston, *A History of Japanese Literature*, 4.

33. Hugh Cortazzi and George Webb (eds), *Kipling's Japan Collected Writings*, London: Athlone Press, 1988, 166.

34. Ibid. 74.

35. Chamberlain, *Things Japanese*, 257-8.

36. Aston, *A History of Japanese Literature*, 116-17.

37. Ibid. 384.

38. Lafcadio Hearn, 'Jiujutsu', *Out of the East*, Boston: Houghton Mifflin, 1897; Reprinted by Charles E. Tuttle Company, Inc. Rutland, Vermont, and Tokyo, 1972, 183-242.

NOTES

39. *The Kojiki (Records of Ancient Matters)*, translated by Basil Hall Chamberlain, in *Transactions of the Asiatic Society of Japan*, Vol. X (1882); paperback by Charles E.Tuttle Company, Vermont, and Tokyo, 1982, introduction, LXXIV.
40. Murray, 'Hearn's Interpretation of Japan'.
41. Lafcadio Hearn, 'About Faces in Japanese Art' in *Gleanings in Buddha Fields*, Houghton Mifflin Company, Boston 1897; Reprinted by Charles E. Tuttle Company, Inc. Rutland, Vermont, and Tokyo, 1971, 97-123.
42. Basil Hall Chamberlain, *Japanese Poetry*, London, 1911, 208-9.
43. Basil Hall Chamberlain, 'The Invention of a New Religion', The Rationalist Press Association of London, 1912; reprinted in *Things Japanese*, 531-44.
44. Ernest Mason Satow and Lt A.G.S. Hawes, *A Handbook for Travellers in Central and Northern Japan*, second edition, revised, London, 1884, 70; Basil Hall Chamberlain and W.B. Mason, *A Handbook for Travellers in Japan*, third edition, London, 1891, 22-3.
45. Hearn, 'The Household Shrine' in *Glimpses of Unfamiliar Japan*, 386.
46. Hearn. *Japan: an Attempt at Interpretation*, 301-2.
47. Kitagawa, *Religion in Japanese History*, 30-8; and Sansom, *A History of Japan*, Vol. 1, 62.
48. Chamberlain, *Things Japanese*, 538.
49. Paul Murray, 'The Dream of a Summer Day: Lafcadio Hearn's Japanese Memories of Ireland', paper given to the Irish Heritage Society, London, 2 October 1995.
50. Paul Murray, 'Lafcadio Hearn and the Irish Tradition', Edinburgh University, 21 February 1996.
51. This is especially evident in Hearn's letters to his half-sister, Minnie Atkinson, which have recently been made available to me by Hearn family sources.
52. Murray, *A Fantastic Journey*, 286; and London School of Economics, *Annual Report*, 1904.
53. Sukehiro Hirakawa, 'Who Was the Great Japan Interpreter, Chamberlain or Hearn?', *Perspectives on Japonisme: The Japanese Influence on America*, paper read to an International Conference at Rutgers, 13-14 May 1988.

Chapter 12 NAKAMI MARI *J.W. Robertson Scott and his Japanese Friends*

1. Nish, 'Ichi Japanorojisuto no mita Nihonjin', in *Sekai no Naka no Nihonjin* (Kansai-daigaku Hyaku-nen Kinen Kaikan Rakusei Kinen Kokusai Shinpojiumu Hōkoku-sho), Kansai University Press, 1990. I am indebted to Prof. Kakegawa Tomiko, Kansai University, for providing me with this article.
2. This section is based upon Scott's autobiography, *The Day Before Yesterday: Memories of an Uneducated Man* (hereafter *The Day*), London, 1951.
3. Ibid., p. 21.
4. Ibid., p. 86.
5. Ibid., p. pp. 82-3.

357

6. Scott, 'Sayonara: A Speech Before Seppuku', in *The New East*, vol. III, no. 4 (hereafter, 'Sayonara'), p. 320.

7. *The People of China*, London, 1900, pp. v-vi.

8. *The Day*, p. 278.

9. Scott, *The Foundations of Japan* (hereafter, *Foundations*), London, 1922, p. ix.

10. *Foundations*, p. 27.

11. 'Sayonara', p. 320.

12. *Foundations*, p. vii; 'Sayonara', p. 320.

13. 'Sayonara', p. 321.

14. *Foundations*, p. xi.

15. 'Sayonara', p. 321.

16. *Foundations*, p. xii; see also Ian Nish, *Alliance in Decline* (hereafter *Alliance*), London, 1972, p. 170.

17. Scott, *We and Me*, 1956, p. 187.

18. Scott, *Faith and Works in Fleet Street* (hereafter *Faith and Works*), London, 1947, p. xvi.

19. *Foundations* p. viii.

20. Ibid., p. xiv.

21. Ibid., p. ix.

22. Ibid..

23. Ibid..

24. Ibid., p. 51; see also p. 38.

25. Ibid., p. 53.

26. D.C.S. Sissons, 'James Murdoch, 1856-1921', in *The Transactions of the Asiatic Society of Japan*, fourth series, vol. 2, 1987, p. 45. Dr Nish kindly drew my attention to this article.

27. Scott to Mr Thring, 22 Nov. 1915, in file no. 56801 (Society of Authors), Dept. of MSS, British Library.

28. *The Countryman*, vol. 1, no. 1, p. 58; quotation also in *Foundations*, p. 92.

29. *Foundations*, p. 90.

30. *Faith and Works*, p. 100; see also Nish, *Alliance*, p. 169-70.

31. *Faith and Works*, p. 101.

32. 'Sayonara', p. 322.

33. *Faith and Works*, p. 101; *The New East*, vol. 1, no. 2, p. 30; more in detail, see Nish, *Alliance*, p. 230.

34. *Faith and Works*, p. 103.

35. 'Sayonara', p. 324.

36. On the process of its decision, see Nish, *Alliance*, pp. 232, 250-3.

37. 'Sayonara', p. 323; Nish, *Alliance*, p. 230.

38. Nish, 'Ashton-Gwatkin', in Nish ed., *Britain & Japan: Biographical Portraits*, Folkestone: Japan Library, 1994, p. 160.

39. Nish, *Alliance*, p. 230.

40. Nish, *Alliance*, pp. 252-3.

41. Scott, *Japan, Great Britain and the World* (hereafter *Japan, Great Britain*), Tokyo, 1916, p. 1.

42. Ibid., p. 2.

43. Ibid., p. 38.

44. *Foundations* p. xi.

45. *Japan, Great Britain*, p. 35.

46. Ibid., p. p. 26.

47. Ibid., p. 28.

48. *Foundations*, p. xi.

49. Nish, *Alliance*, pp. 169-70.

50. Sissons, *op. cit.*; see also, Nish, *Alliance*, p. 191.

51. *Faith and Works*, p. 104.

52. On this aspect of Yanagi, see Nakami Mari, 'Yanagi Muneyoshi no Heiwa-ron', 1-2, *Mingei*, Sept. and Oct., 1988; 'Chōwa-sha to shite no Yanagi Muneyoshi', 1-3, *Mingei*, Nov., 1989, Jan. and Feb. 1990.

53. *Yanagi Muneyoshi Zenshu* (hereafter *Yanagi Zenshu*), vol. 21-1, Tokyo, 1989, p. 186.

54. Ibid., p. 677.

55. *Shiga Naoya Zenshu*, vol. 8, Tokyo, 1974, p. 80; see also, Ibid., vol. 3, 1973, p. 119.

56 *The Day*, pp. 52, 62.

57. *Yanagi Zenshu*, vol. 21-1, p. 669.

58. Ibid., p. 661.

59. *Yanagi Zenshu*, vol. 21-1, pp. 646-52.

60. Ibid., p. 653.

61. Ibid., pp. 652-3. Underline by Yanagi.

62. Ibid., p. 645. Underline by Yanagi.

63. Scott pointed out that the slow progress in the development of Hokkaido supplied arguments for criticizing Japan's expansion beyond her own territory as an outlet for surplus population. See, *Foundations*, pp. 332(n.4), 360.

64. *Foundations*, p. 371.

65. Yanagi Muneyoshi, 'Ōbei Tsūshin', in *Yanagi Zenshu*, vol. 5, 1981, p. 365.

66. *Faith and Works*, p. xv.

67. *The Day*, p. 272.

68. 'Sayonara', p. 322.

69. *Japan, Great Britain*, p. 39.

70. *Yanagi Zenshu*, vol. 21-1, pp. 650-651. Parentheses by Yanagi.

71. *Foundations*, p. 254.

Chapter 13 HAMISH ION *Lionel Berners Cholmondeley: A Chaplain in Tokyo, 1887-1921*

1. *Japan Times*, 17 November 1914 quoted in Cyril Hamilton Powles, *Victorian Missionaries in Meiji Japan The Shiba Sect: 1873-1900*, Toronto: University of Toronto-York University Joint Centre on Modern East Asia, 1987, p. 159.

2. For brief biographical sketches of Cholmondeley see Shunjiro Kurita, *Who's Who in Japan 1914*, Tokyo: The Who's Who in Japan Office, 1914, p. 1254; and *Nihon Kirisutokyo Rekishi Dai Jiten*, Tokyo: Kyobunkwan, 1987, p.

868. The chief source of information about Cholmondeley's activities in Japan are the L.B. Cholmondeley diaries [hereafter cited as LBC diaries]. There is almost a complete set of diaries covering the years from 1888 to 1921. The earlier diaries until 1913 are held in the Nippon Seikokai Kantoku Shiryokan, Tokyo, Japan, and the later diaries are in the United Society for the Propagation of the Gospel in Foreign Parts Archives [hereafter cited as USPGA] in England. At USPGA, there is also a four box collection of L.B. Cholmondeley Papers [hereafter cited LBC Papers] as well as Cholmondeley's missionary annual reports located in the general South Tokyo diocese correspondence. Included in the LBC Papers are a number of letters from Hugh Byas, the *Times* correspondent in Tokyo, to Cholmondeley between 1932 and 1942. The USPGA were located on Tufton Street, Westminster when they were consulted, subsequently they have been moved to Rhodes House, Oxford. Also in Oxford is the correspondence of L.B. Cholmondeley, Ms Eng. lett.d. 99 (1914-1920), Duke Humfrey Room, Bodleian Library, Oxford University [hereafter cited as Bodleian Library] consisting of some 238 pages of letters to and from Cholmondeley and his friends and family concerning the first world war. There are a good number of letters from Cholmondeley to Sir Ernest Satow, the former British minister in Japan, covering the years 1907 to 1921 in the Satow Papers in the Public Records Office, London, PRO 30/33 [hereafter cited Satow Papers]. There are also occasional references to Cholmondeley in the microfilmed Satow Diaries 1861-1926 [hereafter cited as Satow Diaries] PRO 30, 11 reels.
3. There was some justification for this. His father, Canon H.P. Cholmondeley (1820-1905) was third son of Thomas Cholmondeley, 1st Baron Delamere. His mother was a daughter of the 1st Baron Leigh of Stoneleigh Abbey, Kenilworth, Warwickshire. One of his aunts married C.H. Adderley, 1st Baron Norton (1814-1905), and another the 6th Baron Berners. An older cousin married Victor Villiers, Lord Jersey (1845-1915). A younger cousin was Hugh Cholmondeley, 3rd Baron Delamere (1870-1931) of Kenya fame. One of his sisters was the second wife of Sir Charles Mordaunt, Bart. (1836-1897). Cholmondeley had four brothers, two of whom were also priests, and four sisters.
4. For a recent study of the British missionary movement in Japan, see A. Hamish Ion, *The Cross and the Rising Sun, Volume 2: The British Missionary Movement in Japan, Korea and Taiwan, 1865-1945* Waterloo: Wilfrid Laurier University Press, 1993. The standard history of the Japanese Anglican Church is Nippon Seikokai Rekishi Henshu Iinkai Hen, *Nippon Seikokai Hyakunen Shi*, Tokyo: Nippon Seikokai Kyomuin Bunsho Kyoku, 1959. Also of interest for the early history of the Nippon Seikokai is Tsuda Osamu, *Shoki Nippon Seikokai no Keisei to Imai Judo*, Tokyo: Seikokyo Shuppan, 1992. for Edward Bickersteth, see Rev. Samuel Bickersteth, *Life and Letters of Edward Bickersteth, Bishop of South Tokyo*, London: S. Low, Marston, 1899. For a brief biographical sketch, see *Nihon Kirisutokyo Rekishi Dai Jiten*, p. 1154.
5. *Letters of Edward Bickersteth*, p. 216. St. Andrew's Mission was modelled on the Cambridge Mission to Delhi of which Bickersteth had been a member,

and attempted to combine the intellectual stimulation of the senior Common Room at a Cambridge College with the mutual spiritual stimulation of a community of clerics, and the practical work of being a missionary in a foreign land. St. Andrew's aims were to train through a divinity school Japanese for the ministry, to organize other classes and lectures, particularly night schools for enquirers and younger baptized church members, and to evangelize in or near Tokyo. For a description of the work of St. Andrew's Mission at the beginning of the twentieth century see Alfreda Arnold, *Church Work in Japan*, London: Society for the Propagation of the Gospel in Foreign Parts, 1905, pp. 62-74. While a celibate St. Andrew's Missionary Brotherhood was formed by members of the mission, they did not live as a community. Nevertheless, St. Andrew's Mission House and its activities provided a unique spiritual and intellectual focus to the missionary activities of the diocese of South Tokyo. For a rather delightful fictional account which describes the atmosphere surrounding St. Andrew's, its High Anglican missionaries and Japanese student enquirers at the time of the Russo-Japanese War see Herbert Moore, *In Peace and War in Japan*, Westminster: The Society for the Propagation of the Gospel in Foreign Parts, 1915.

6. A steady stream of peripatetic English tourists, clutches of young midshipmen and shambles of other ranks from visiting warships arrived on Cholmondeley's doorstep. It also fell to Cholmondeley to visit those unfortunate Englishmen who, for one reason or another, landed in Ichigaya Prison. Fortunately for them, Cholmondeley also had the ear of the British ambassador, and did, on occasion, intercede with him for diplomatic help on behalf of a prisoner. See, for instance, LBC Diaries, 1908; entry for 11 November 1908.

7. For a description of the role of St. Andrew's Mission House in the life of the British community in Tokyo, see C. Kenneth Sansbury, *St. Andrew's Church, Tokyo (English Congregation)*, Tokyo: St. Andrew's Church, 1939, pp. 12-13. It should also be remembered that the financial contribution from the English-speaking congregations in Tokyo, Yokohama, Osaka and Kobe benefited the mission's Japanese work.

8. Lionel Berners Cholmondeley, *The History of the Bonin Islands from the year 1827 to the year 1876 and of Nathaniel Savory one of the original settlers to which as added a short supplement dealing with the islands after their occupation by the Japanese.* London: Constable & Co., 1915.

9. It was usual practice for SPG missionaries in Tokyo to teach in secular Japanese schools, most notably at Keio Gijuku. A.C. Shaw, Arthur Lloyd, Herbert Moore and William Gemmill were among the SPG missionaries who taught at Keio Gijuku at one time or another during this period.

10. St Barnabas' Church, Ushigome, was designed by Cholmondeley's friend, Sir Josiah Conder. It opened in May 1897, and subsequently enlarged again under Conder's design and reopened in June 1907. *South Tokyo Diocesan Magazine* [hereafter cited as *STDM*], XI, 33, July 1907, pp. 43-4. The church buildings of a classic English type were destroyed during the Pacific War, but a St Barnabas Church still exists on the same site which it shares with the

Provincial Headquarters of the Nippon Seikokai. The money for the building of this church, and later St George's, Bonin Islands, which Cholmondeley was also responsible for building and Conder designing, came from subscriptions raised in England as well as from SPG mission funds. Indeed, in both cases much of the money came from Cholmondeley himself and his many relations.
11. The house was furnished in Western style, and Cholmondeley was looked after by a Japanese housekeeper and her husband. He normally ate Western meals, but he was not averse to Japanese food.
12. For brief biographical sketches of the Hatoyamas see *Konsaisu Nihon Jinmei Jiten*, Tokyo: Sanseido, 1990 edition, p. 895. Cholmondeley baptized Philip Hatoyama on May 31 1903, LBC Diaries, 1903, entry for 31 May. From 1903 until 1908, when Hatoyama graduated top in the Civil Law List at Tokyo Imperial University and subsequently went to Europe to study, he was often mentioned in Cholmondeley's diaries. Indeed, in 1910 Cholmondeley conducted the service in St Barnabas' when Hatoyama married a daughter of Baron Kikuchi Dairoku. Hatoyama later became a professor in the Law Faculty of Tokyo Imperial University.
13. For brief biographical sketches of Saeki Yoshiro see Shunjiro Kurita, *Who's Who in Japan 1914*, p. 764-5, *Nihon Kirisutokyo Rekishi Dai Jiten*, p. 560. During the Pacific War, Saeki became a very controversial figure within the Nippon Seikokai. However, during Cholmondeley's time at St Barnabas', Saeki was very highly regarded and a prominent lay member of the Nippon Seikokai. Saeki was a lecturer at the Senmon Gakko, and later became Dean of the Law Faculty of Meiji University.
14. It is clear that he spoke some Japanese, and there are postcards to him from Japanese students in katakana which indicates that he could read Japanese at least to that extent.
15. He served as Vicar of the Edge, Painswick, Gloucestershire.
16. For a description of the consecration of St George's Church, Bonin Islands in October 1909 see *STDM*, XIII, 40, November 1909, pp. 84-92. Like St Barnabas', Sir Josiah Conder designed the church and Cholmondeley's relations liberally supported the building fund. St George's was a wooden structure on a solid concrete foundation with a thatched cabbage palm roof.
17. L.B. Cholmondeley, 'Importance of the Bonin Islands to the Seikokai', *STDM*, XIII, 38, March 1909, pp. 11-16.
18. For a brief biographical sketch of Joseph Gonzales see *Nihon Kirisutokyo Rekishi Dai Jiten*, pp. 546-7.
19. Lionel Berners Cholmondeley, *The History of the Bonin Islands*, p. 176. Interestingly, one of the critics of this book was Cholmondeley's own young soldier brother, who with justification noted that 'may I confess I was rather disappointed with your Bonin book, I don't think you had enough material to work on, and it must have been a difficult business to complete. A book of the recollections of the various people you have met would be really interesting and I wish you would see your way to it.' H.R. Cholmondeley to LBC, 17 May 1917, Lionel Berners Cholmondeley Correspondence 1914-20, Ms. Eng. lett. 99.

20. For Walter Weston, see A.H. Ion, 'Mountain High and Valley Low: Walter Weston (1861-1940) and Japan', in Sir Hugh Cortazzi and Gordon Daniels, eds., *Britain and Japan 1859-1991: Themes and Personalities*, London: Routledge, 1991, pp. 94-106. For John Batchelor's views as well as those of other British missionaries, see Ion, *The Cross and the Rising Sun*, Volume 2, pp. 109-13. The search to find the pristine and unspoilt in obscure places was not restricted to British missionaries in Japan, Bishop Mark Napier Trollope and his High Anglican missionaries in Korea devoted much effort in attempting to Christianize isolated Kanghwa Island at the expense of extending their work on the mainland.

21. See, for instance, Tsukada Osamu, *Tennosei shita no Kirisutokyo: Nippon Seikokai no tatakai to kunan*. Tokyo: Shinkyo Shuppansha, 1981, 54-65.

22. Tsukada Osamu, *Shochi Tennosei to Kirisutokyo*. Tokyo: Shinkyo Shuppansha, 1990, pp. 121-3.

23. In late 1905, on his return to Japan from furlough in England, Cholmondeley noted that 'there was a disposition [in Britain] to regard Japan as a very model for our imitation; there was an exalting of the Japanese to the depreciation of ourselves; and I was hardly prepared to find that even clergymen should believe that the "Bushido" of "*The Times*" was so permeating the nation that it had almost lifted it onto a higher plane than Christianity had lifted England. such ideas are as mistaken as they are subtly and far reachingly harmful.' L.B. Cholmondeley, 'Experiences and Impressions', *STDM*, IX, December 1905, no. 28, pp. 73-7. The reference to the "Bushido" of "*The Times*" was clearly directed towards the views of Colonel Repington, *The Times* war correspondent. Nitobe's book on bushido was Nitobe Inazo, *Bushido: The Soul of Japan*. New York and London: Putnam's, 1905. For a recent discussion of contemporary reactions to Nitobe's book, see Cyril H. Powles, '*Bushido*: Its Admirers and Critics', in John F. Howes, *Nitobe Inazo: Japan's Bridge Across the Pacific*, Boulder: Westview Press, 1995, pp. 107-18.

24. See John Imai, 'Bushido', in *STDM* IX, December 1905, no. 28, pp. 78-84. P.Y. Saeki, 'The Sources of Bushido', in *STDM*, XII, March 1908, no. 35, pp. 5-12.

25. Imai Toshimichi, *Bushido: In the Past and in the Present*, Tokyo: Kanazashi, 1906. for a sympathetic review of this book, see "'Bushido in the Past and in the Present', by Rev. John Imai", in *STDM*, X, July 1906, no. 30, pp. 54-5. For Cholmondeley's help in getting Imai's published, see LBC Diaries, 1906, entry for 5 February 1906. For a detailed analysis of Imai Toshimichi's ideas including his own views on bushido, see Tsukada Osamu, *Shoki Nippon Seikokai no Kaisei to Imai Judo*. Tokyo: Seikokai Shuppansha, 1992, especially 80-4.

26. LBC to Satow, 13 June 1913, Satow Papers, Public Record Office (PRO) 30/33/12/8 2689.

27. L.B. Cholmondeley, 'A Review of Japan's Attitude Towards Christianity', *The Contemporary Review*, CV, January-June 1914, pp. 220-6.

28. Ibid., p. 220.

29. Ibid., p. 221.

30. Ibid., p. 222. Writing to Satow in May 1910, Cholmondeley noted, 'ever since Treaties on equal terms with the Christian powers, ever since alliance with Christian England, increasingly since the war with Russia, I notice – one cannot help noticing the determination to prove themselves to have a religion on a par with Christianity – a determination to bring us as allies to respect Japanese religion, and not allow us to look upon them as religiously inferior to themselves.' LBC to Satow, Satow Papers, 21 May 1910, PRO 30/33/12/5 2683.

31. Ibid., p. 223. Cholmondeley certainly disapproved when Sir Claude Macdonald, the British Ambassador, attended Buddhist memorial services for King Edward. Cholmondeley complained that 'more and more it seems to me the Japanese are determined when they pay any compliment, as they think, to us, by attending a church or Christian ceremony to bring us to return the compliment by making us attend or take part in some great religious ceremony of their own.' LBC to Satow, 21 May 1910, Satow Papers, PRO 30/33/12/5 2683.

32. Ibid., p. 224.

33. Ibid., p. 224.

34. B.H. Chamberlain, *The Invention of a New Religion*, London; Watts & Co., 1912.

35. He baptized both the brother and son of Major-General F.S.G. Piggott, see Major-General F.S.G. Piggott, *Broken Thread: An Autobiography*, Aldershot: Gale & Polden Limited, 1950, p. 64.

36. LBC Diaries, 1894, entries 23 May to 6 June 1894 inclusive. See also enclosed letter in 1894 Diary from Theodora Ozaki to LBC, 24 May 1894 indicating Fraser's liking for Cholmondeley and Mrs Fraser's desire that he helps the dying man.

37. Letter from MacDonald to LBC, 2 April 1902, enclosed in LBC Diaries, 1902.

38. MacDonald was at Uppingham between August 1865 and October 1866 leaving when he was only 14 years and 4 months presumably to go to a crammer for the Sandhurst entrance examination. Cholmondeley came to the school in August 1872 and left in July 1878. Although on one occasion he won a prize for French and seems to have been a regular speaker at School Debates, his school career was generally undistinguished. Headmaster's Secretary, Uppingham School to A.H. Ion, 25 March 1974, in possession of author. Cholmondeley went from Uppingham to Oriel College, Oxford where he took Greats and got a fourth class degree.

39. Cholmondeley noted about Parlett who came out to Tokyo as a Student Interpreter in 1890 that he was 'very capable, but quiet and unassuming – something of an Artist. Fondness of fishing and shooting took him much into the country and added much to his knowledge of Japanese. Served for some years in Korea. My intimacy with him dated from our spending 3 weeks together as guests of Sir Ernest Satow in his summer villa on Lake Chusenji beyond Nikko. Sir Charles Eliot had a high opinion of him and

recommended him for a Knighthood. He and I were both close friends of Hugh Byas "Times Correspondent" in Tokyo.' Cholmondeley note among SPG Series E Annual Reports Individual, USPGA.

40. For Calthrop see A. Hamish Ion, 'Something New Under the Sun: E.F. Calthrop and the Art of War', *Japan Forum*, vol. 2, no. 1, April 1990, pp. 29-41.

41. It would seem that Cholmondeley first met Sir Ernest on 2 August 1895, shortly after Satow's arrival in Tokyo as British minister in Japan. LBC Diaries, 2 August 1895.

42. At first glance, it might appear strange that Satow would pay any attention to a much younger Church of England missionary. However, some years prior to his return to Japan in 1895, Satow had become a convinced Christian. See P.F. Kornicki, 'Ernest Mason Satow (1843-1929)', in Sir High Cortazzi and Gordon Daniels, eds., *Britain and Japan 1859-1991: Themes and Personalities*, London and New York: Routledge, 1991, pp. 76-85.

43. Cholmondeley's reminiscences of Mrs Bishop and this holiday at Lake Chuzenji in Anna M. Stoddart, *The Life of Isabella Bird (Mrs Bishop)*, London: John Murray, 1908, pp. 327-9.

44. It is clear that Cholmondeley saw Takeda Hisayoshi (1883-1972), Satow's younger son, relatively frequently from 1900 onwards, just before Satow left Japan. While he was minister in Japan, it would appear that Satow looked to Archdeacon A.C. Shaw, the then Chaplain at the British Legation and a resident in Tokyo since 1873, for any help he might require. In March 1897, for instance, Satow noted in his diary: 'to Shaw & settled with him about Hisakichi [sic] going to live with him after Easter'. Entry for 23 March 1897, Satow Diaries microfilm PRO 30-005 (PRO 30/33/16/1). However, after Satow was translated to the Peking legation, the responsibility of keeping an eye of Takeda Hisayoshi and his mother fell to Cholmondeley. During the mid-1900s, Takeda Hisayoshi was studying in Sapporo (and was furnished by Cholmondeley with introductions to Archdeacon John Batchelor), but Takeda always made a point to have lunch with Cholmondeley or even, on occasion, apparently attend a service at St Barnabas' when he was back in Tokyo. Cholmondeley had less to do with Takeda Eitaro, the older son, because he emigrated to the United States, but it would seem that Cholmondeley thought quite highly of him. In July 1909 Cholmondeley wrote to Satow that 'I will be hoping to see Hisayoshi some time this summer. His mother is very constant Church [St Barnabas', Ushigome]. I feel sure that she finds help and pleasure in coming'. Cholmondeley to Satow, 23 July 1909, Satow Papers, PRO 30/33/12/4 2679. As a church member, Cholmondeley would see Takeda's mother every week. for a brief biographical sketch of Takeda Hisayoshi, who became a botanist and also a founding member of the Japan Alpine Club, see *Konsaisu Nihon Jinmei Jiten*, Tokyo: Sanseido 1990 edition, p. 756.

45. In 1907 Satow was elected one of the delegates to represent the South Tokyo diocese at the Pan Anglican Congress which took place that year at Lambeth Palace. *South Tokyo Diocesan Magazine*, XI, 34, November 1907. He

was the only lay patron of the Guild of Saint Paul which supported missions in the diocese of South Tokyo.

46. Satow to LBC, 20 October 1914, Lionel Berners Cholmondeley Correspondence, Ms.Eng. lett.d.99.
47. Ibid.
48. LBC to Gonzales, August 1919, LBC Correspondence.
49. Byas to LBC, 2 August 1932, LBC Papers USPGA.

Chapter 14 DOROTHY BRITTON *Richard Ponsonby-Fane: A Modern Scholarly William Adams*

1. Dr Thomas Baty, LL.D., adviser on international public law to the Gaimusho for over 30 years, in his tribute in 'Memoirs of Dr Richard Ponsonby'. Baty's works include *Alone in Japan*, Tokyo, 1959; 'The literary introduction of Japan to Europe', in *Monumenta Nipponica*, Vol. 7, (1951).
2. 'Orlando'
3. Letter from Sir John Pilcher to Mr Wada Jun of Japan Foundation, London. Sir John and I tried to get Brympton d'Evercy put on an itinerary for Japanese tourists.
4. 'An "outsider" working on the inside' by Kyōko Satō, *Japan Times*, 7 March 1996
5. From 'Tadori-koshi michi' (The road I have travelled) No. 10, an autobiography by Professor Emeritus Aida Yūji, serialized in the *Kyoto Shimbun*, ca. 1994
6. Ponsonby-Fane, 'The Imperial House of Japan', Kyoto: Ponsonby Memorial Society, (Kenkyusha), 1959, p. 359
7. Charles Clive-Ponsonby-Fane, 'We Started a Stately Home', Yeovil, 1980
8. 'East Coker'
9. Told to me by Charles Clive-Ponsonby-Fane
10. R.L. Arrowsmith & B.J.W. Hill, *The History of I Zingari*, London, 1982
11. Chronology and biographical details from *Ponsonbi hakase no shinmenmoku* by Satō Yoshijirō, Kyoto, 1958, and 'Brief outline of the life of Richard Ponsonby-Fane' from *Memoirs of Dr Ponsonby-Fane* edited by the Dr Ponsonby-Fane Memoir Publishing Association, 1939.
12. From 'Broken Thread' by F.S.G. Piggott, Gale & Polden, 1950, p. 48
13. 'The Imperial Family of Japan' has been incorporated, with six other papers on imperial subjects, in the Ponsonby Memorial Society volume entitled *The Imperial House of Japan*, published in 1959. It is a fine volume, beautifully illustrated with portraits of all the sovereigns and pictures of relevant places.
14. See 'Kyoto's British Eccentric, Richard Ponsonby-Fane', by Garry Evans, *Kansai Time Out*, August 1986.
15. From Baty's tribute in *Memoirs of Dr Ponsonby-Fane*
16. Clive Ponsonby-Fane, 'Stately Home'
17. Told to me by the above.
18. *Sovereign and Subject*, Kyoto: Ponsonby Memorial Society, 1962, p. 182

19. Ibid., pp. 1, 2
20. Ibid., pp. 17, 18
21. Ibid., p. 334
22. Ibid., pp. 342-4
23. Ibid., p. 341
24. Ibid., p. 347
25. Ibid., p. 346
26. *The Imperial House of Japan* p. 359
27. Hope, however, is at hand, in the person of John Hamilton, a professor at Aichi University. His grandfather was a cousin and contemporary of Richard Ponsonby-Fane! Hamilton wishes to continue his cousin's work, and has already contributed three papers to Aichi University Literary Association's *Bungaku ronsō* (in Volumes 92, 94, and 104) in which he not only elucidates some Ponsonby writings on Shinto but offers sidelights on the man himself through a mass of letters to Sato Yoshijiro in the possession of Sato's brother-in-law, Mr Hiyama, who lives in a house on part of the Ponsonby-Fane property. It would be interesting to know the extent of Ponsonby-Fane's original holding, in view of the passage in the Introduction to his great-nephew's book saying that he was 'probably the first foreigner to own agricultural land of any quantity'.
28. Ponsonby-Fane's monthly articles on Shinto shrines contributed to NYK's *Travel Bulletin* may be found in *Studies in Shinto and Shrines*, Kyoto: Ponsonby Memorial Society, 1954, reprinted 1957 and *Visiting Famous Shrines in Japan*, Kyoto: Ponsonby Memorial Society, 1957
29. I visited the house in Minami Oji-cho in 1986. Mr Sato had died not long before. The present owner of the house is the widow of a lumber merchant, who appreciates its beauty and its history and has expressed a desire to leave it in her will to some British authority who could preserve it as a memorial. She had bought it in 1976 from the owner of the Bank of Taiwan, who had had it up for sale for a long time because it was thought to be haunted. I was told there had been a TV programme about Ponsonby-Fane and the house, based on Sato's book.
30. Pilcher letter to Wada
31. The six volumes are as follows:
1 *Studies in Shinto and Shrines* (1954, 1957)
2 *Kyoto, the Old Capital of Japan, 794-1869* (1956)
3 *The Imperial House of Japan* (1959)
4 *Sovereign and Subject* (1962)
5 *The Vicissitudes of Shinto* (1962)
6 *Visiting Famous Shrines in Japan* (1963)

Chapter 15 IAN NISH *Crown Prince Hirohito in Britain, May 1921*

1. Yoshinari Futara and Setsuzo Sawada, *Kotaishi denka gogaiyu-ki,* Osaka: Mainichi Press, 1925, 495 pp. Translated as *The Crown Prince's European Tour,* (revised by Harold E. Palmer, Linguistic Adviser to the Department of Education), Osaka, 1926 (hereafter cited as 'Futara'). *Eikoku kinen: a*

photographic record of the visit of Hirohito as Crown Prince, London, 1921. London *Times* Special Supplement, 28 May 1921. Recent books which cover aspects of the Crown Prince's visit are L. Mosley, *Hirohito: Emperor of Japan*, London: Weidenfeld, 1966; E. Behr, *Hirohito*, London: Hamish Hamilton, 1989

2. Futara, p. 9
3. *Hara Kei nikki*, vols 8 and 9, especially 9, p. 104 (hereafter cited as *Hara nikki*)
4. *Hara nikki*, vol. 9, p. 104. Matsukata to Yamagata, 16 Jan 1921 and reply, 18 Jan in Tokutomi Iichiro, *Koshaku Yamagata Aritomo-den*, Tokyo, 1933, vol 3, pp. 1016-21
5. *Hara nikki*, vol. 8, p. 556
6. Philip Ziegler, *The Diaries of Lord Louis Mountbatten, 1920-2*, London: Collins, 1987, pp. 9-12 and 165
7. *Times*, 30 Dec. 1920
8. *Hara nikki*, vol. 9, pp. 193-8
9. Sugiura in Iwao Seiichi (ed.), *Biographical Dictionary of Japanese History*, Tokyo: International Society for Educational Information, 1978
10. *Hara nikki*, vol.9, p. 226.
11. *Taisho news jiten*, vol. 5, Tokyo: Mainichi Communication, 1988, pp. 225-37; *Hara nikki*, vol. 9, pp. 225-6; *Times*, 1 March 1921
12. Futara, pp. 42-3
13. Inoki Masamichi, *Yoshida Shigeru*, 3 vols., vol. 3, Tokyo: Yomiuri, 1981, p. 217, quoting Tamura Kosaku
14. Futara, pp. 63-4. See H. Cortazzi, article on Royal Visits in this volume
15. Futara, pp. 79-80
16. *Times*, 7 and 9 May 1921. E.L. Woodward (ed.), *Documents on British Foreign Policy, 1919-39*, 1st series, London: HMSO, vol. 14, no. 287 (hereafter cited as *DBFP*)
17. Admiral Kobayashi to Ide in Inoki, pp. 357-8
18. Entry for 12 August 1945 in Trefor Evans (ed.), *The Killearn Diaries*, London, pp. 344-5
19. F.S.G. Piggott, *Broken Thread*, Aldershot: Gale and Polden, 1950, pp. 126-7
20. Ian Nish, 'The Prince and the Principal', in *International Studies* (LSE: STICERD), 177(1988), pp. 19-31; *Taisho news jiten*, 5, p. 233; Futara, p. 83
21. *Times*, 21 May 1921
22. Evans (ed.), *The Killearn Diaries*, p. 345.
23. Futara, p. 84
24. Katharine, Duchess of Atholl, *Working Partnership*, London: Barker, 1958, pp. 112-14; S.J. Hetherington, *Katharine Atholl, 1874-1960, Against the Tide*, Aberdeen: University Press, 1989, pp. 91-2
25. *Times*, 28 May 1921
26. *Hara nikki*, vol. 9, pp. 416-18; *Taisho news jiten*, 5, 237
27. Inoki, pp. 357-8; *DBFP*, 1st series, vol. 14, no. 287
28. *Times*, Trade Supplement, 16 April 1921. See also minutes by Lampson and Curzon, 16-17 March 1921, in [British] Foreign Office papers, FO 800/329

29. Futara, p. 10; *DBFP*, 1st series, vol 14, nos 277-83 passim
30. P. Ziegler, *Mountbatten Diaries*, pp. 276-300; P. Ziegler, *Mountbatten: The Official Biography*, London: Collins, 1985, pp. 64-5; *Yamagata-den*, III, 1022-6
31. Atholl, *Working Partnership*, p. 148
32. Princess Chichibu, *Ei-Bei seikatsu no omoide*, Tokyo: Bummeisha, 1947; *The Silver Drum*, Folkestone: Global Oriental, 1996
33. *Times*, 3 May 1929

Chapter 16 SIR HUGH CORTAZZI *John Batchelor, Missionary and Friend of the Ainu, 1855-1945*

1. Richard Siddle in his well researched essay 'The Ainu: Construction of an Image' in *Diversity in Japanese Culture and Language* edited by John C Maher and Gaynor Macdonald (Kegan Paul International, 1995) outlines the development of the prejudices and discrimination existing towards the Ainu today and declares that these are 'the result of the blending of pre-Meiji stereotypes with the nationalist racial ideology that accompanied Japanese colonial expansion. . . This racialisation of the Ainu resulted in a complex negative image of the *Ainu Minzoku* as an inferior racial group'. He begins his essay: 'For many Ainu prejudice and discrimination are facts of life'.
2. *Japan Times* weekly edition, 10-16 April 1995.
3. Published by Westview Press, Boulder, San Francisco and Oxford in 1994.
4. Gaynor Macdonald, 'The Politics of Diversity in the Nation State' in *Diversity in Japanese Language and Culture*.
5. This account is based on 'Steps by the Way', an autobiographical sketch dictated by Dr Batchelor in his final years in England. It has not been published in English but has been translated into Japanese by Professor Nitami Iwao, the Japanese expert on the life and works of John Batchelor and published under the title *Waga jinsei no kiseki* by the Hokkaido Shuppan Kikaku center in 1993. A fuller summary of this sketch was given in my lecture 'Dr John Batchelor, British Scholar and Friend of the Natives of Hokkaido' printed in Japan Society, *Proceedings* No 105 (December 1986). 'Steps by the Way' is broadly similar in content to '*Waga kioku wo tadorite*', an autobiographical account published in Japan in 1928.
6. 1924 is the date given in *Ainu Life and Lore* published in 1927. In 'Steps by the Way' Batchelor gave the date of his retirement as 1922. Professor Nitami Iwao gives it as 1923.
7. *Ainu of Japan*, pp. 19-20.
8. See Jane Wilkinson's essay 'Gordon Munro: Ventures in Japanese Archeology and Anthropology' in the Japan Society's *Britain and Japan: Biographical Portraits*, Japan Library, 1994, pp 218-37.
9. *Ainu Creed and Culture*', p. 13.
10. See also *Ainu Creed and Culture*, p. 154.
11. Nitami Iwao, *Ikyo no shito* Hokkaido Shimbunsha, 1991.
12. *Ikyo no shito*, pp. 146-7.
13. Josef Kreiner (ed.), *European Studies on Ainu Language and Culture* in

Monographien aus dem Deutschen Institut für Japanstudien der Philipp-Franz-von-Siebold Stiftung, 1993, pp. 137-150.
14. Vienna, 1883.
15. Kirsten Refsing, *The Ainu Language: The Morphology and Syntax of the Shizunai District*, Aarhus University Press, 1986, p. 19.
16. Kindaichi Kyosuke and Chiri Mashiho, *Ainu goho gaisetsu* Iwanami, Tokyo.
17. 'Bemerkungen zur Ainu Grammatik' in Kreiner, *European Studies on Ainu Language and Culture*.
18. See page 83 in Dettmer's essay.
19. Katarina Sjoeberg, *The Return of the Ainu: Cultural Mobilization and the Practice of Ethnicity in Japan* Harwood Academic Publishers, 1993.
20. In a letter to me dated 25 February 1995.
21. *John Batchelor no tegami*, published by Yamamoto Shoten, 1965.

Chapter 17 IAN NISH *Yoshida Shigeru and Mme Yoshida at the London Embassy*

1. Yoshida's period in London has been comprehensively covered in Inoki Masamichi, *Hyoden Yoshida Shigeru*, 4 vols., Tokyo: Yomiuri, 1981, vol. 3, pp.7-111; Hosoya Chihiro, *Nichi-Ei kankeishi, 1917-49*, Tokyo: Todai Shuppankai, 1986, pp.8-13; *Ningen Yoshida Shigeru*, Tokyo: Chuo Koron, 1991; Ono Katsumi, *Kasumigaseki gaiko*, Tokyo: Nihon Keizai, 1985; Haga Toru, 'Gaikokan no bunsho', in *Gaiko Forum, 82-4(1995)*. I have published some studies of the subject in 'Ambassador at Large: Yoshida and his Mission to Britain, 1932-7' in Sue Henny and J.P. Lehmann (eds.), *Themes and Theories in Modern Japanese History*, London: Athlone, 1988, pp.195-212; 'Mr Yoshida at the London Embassy, 1936-8' in Japan Society of London, *Bulletin*, 4(1979), pp. 1-7;
2. Watanabe Akio in *Nihon Gaikoshi Jiten*
3. Ian Nish, *Japan's Struggle with Internationalism*, London: KPI, 1993, p. 49
4. John Dower, *Empire and Aftermath*, Cambridge, Mass., 1979, ch. 5; Ben-ami Shillony, *Revolt in Japan*, Princeton, 1973, p. 132
5. Yoshida Shigeru, M*emoirs*, London: Heinemann,1962, p. 13; *Kaiso 10-nen*, 4 vols, Tokyo, 1957, vol. I
6. Yoshida, *Memoirs*, pp. 13-14
7. [London] *Times*, 20 March, 9 April 1936
8. Ian Nish in Saki Dockrill (ed.), *From Pearl Harbor to Hiroshima*, London: Macmillan, 1994, p. 21
9. [London] *Times*, 22 May 1936
10. Miyake Kijiro in *Kasumigasekikai kaiho*, 1968; Dockrill, p. 21; Inoki, III, 39
11. For the text of this letter, see Dockrill, pp. 19-20.
12. E. O'Halpin, *Head of the Civil Service: a biography of Sir Warren Fisher*, London, 1989, p. 237. Also Gill Bennett, 'British Policy in the Far East, 1933-6: Treasury and Foreign Office' in *Modern Asian Studies*, 26(1992), pp. 545-68
13. [London] *Times*, 8 Aug. 1936
14. Yoshida to Makino, 7 Aug 1936 in Inoki, III, 29

15. *Tokyo Nichi-nichi Shimbun*, 1 Aug. 1936
16. Miyake in *Kasumigasekikai kaiho*, 1969, p. 12
17. John Dower, *Japan in War and Peace: Selected Essays,* Cambridge 1995, p. 209
18. Yoshida, *Memoirs*, p. 15. Inoki, III, 17-20 quotes Tatsumi; III, p. 45
19. Bennett, p. 568
20. Yoshida to Makino, May 1937, in Inoki, III, 45
21. Inoki, III, 53
22. Arthur Clegg, *Aid China, 1937-49: A Memoir of a Forgotten Campaign*, Beijing, 1989, pp. 74, 81-2. Inoki, III, 64-5
23. Yuki Yoshida, *Whispering Leaves in Grosvenor Square, 1936-7*, private, 1938, p. 28
24. Yuki Yoshida, p. 55. Princess Chichibu, *The Silver Drum: A Japanese Imperial Memoir*, Folkestone: Global Oriental, 1996, pp. 129-37
25. Yuki Yoshida, p. 70
26. Inoki, III, 115
27. Yoshida, *Memoirs*, pp. 16-17, 118
28. Inoki, III, 111; Ono, *Kasumigaseki gaiko*, pp. 4-5; Dower, *Japan in War and Peace*, p. 216
29. Yoshida, *Kaiso 10-nen*, I, 34
30. Richard B. Finn, *Winners in Peace: MacArthur, Yoshida and Postwar Japan*, Berkeley: University of California Press, 1992

Chapter 18 ANTONY BEST *Shigemitsu Mamoru and Anglo-Japanese Relations, 1887-1957*

I would like to thank Saho Matsumoto and Philip Best for their help with this essay.

1. For favourable contemporary views of Shigemitsu, see Lord Hankey, *Politics, Trials and Errors*, (Oxford, Pen in Hand, 1950), F.S.G. Piggott, *Broken thread*, (Aldershot, Gale & Polden, 1950), and T. Kase, *The Eclipse of the Rising Sun*, (London, Jonathan Cape, 1951). For a more critical assessment of his career see K. Usui, 'The Role of the Foreign Ministry' in D. Borg & S. Okamoto (eds), *Pearl Harbor as History: Japanese-American Relations 1931-1941*, (New York, Columbia University Press, 1973) pp. 127-48, and K. Usui, 'Japanese Approaches to China in the 1930s: Two Alternatives' in A. Iriye & W. Cohen (eds.), *American, Chinese, and Japanese Perspectives on Wartime Asia, 1931-1949*, (Wilmington, Scholarly resources, 1990) pp. 93-115. For more neutral views, see A. Best, 'Shigemitsu Mamoru as Ambassador to Great Britain, 1938-1941' in I. Nish (ed.), *Shigemitsu Studies*, (LSE STICERD, International Studies Series, 1990), pp. 1-44, and T. Sakai, *Taishō Demokurashi Taisei no Hokai: Naisei to Gaiko* (The Collapse of the Taishō Democracy System: Domestic Politics and Diplomacy), (Tokyo, Tokyo University Press, 1992), passim.
2. M. Shigemitsu, *Gaiko Kaisoroku* (Diplomatic Memoirs), (Tokyo: Mainichi Shimbun, 1978), pp. 201-2.
3. On Edwardes, see ibid, pp. 190-3, and I. Nish, 'Anglo-Japanese

Alienation Revisited' in S. Dockrill, *From Peral Harbor to Hiroshima: The Second World War in Asia and the South Pacific, 1941-45*, (London: Macmillan, 1994), pp. 19-22.

4. Shigemitsu, op. cit., p. 192.

5. Ibid, pp. 203-7.

6. Ibid, p. 192.

7. Ibid, p. 205.

8. Ibid, p. 212.

9. On Treasury thinking, see G. Bennett, 'British Policy in the Far East 1933-1936: Treasury and Foreign Office', *Modern Asian Studies*, 26, (1992) pp. 545-68.

10. Public Record Office (PRO), T172/1831, Edwardes to Fisher, 26 November 1934.

11. Sakai, op. cit., p. 59.

12. Shigemitsu, op. cit., p. 159.

13. Sakai, op. cit., p. 128.

14. Ibid, p. 129.

15. PRO FO371/22052 F13642/12/10, Howe minute, 19 December 1938. See also Best, op. cit., pp. 5-8.

16. Shigemitsu, op. cit., p. 209.

17. PRO FO371/23534 F11827/6457/10, Craigie (Tokyo) to Halifax, 11 November 1939.

18. PRO CAB96/3 FE(41)111, Shigemitsu/Leith-Ross conversation, 11 June 1941.

19. Shigemitsu to Edwardes, 11 July 1936, in Gwynne Papers, Bodleian Library, Oxford, Ms. Gwynne 18.

20. PRO FO371/20227 F209/34/10, Clive (Tokyo) to Eden, 13 January 1936. On the 'Defence Against Communism' policy, see T. Sakai, 'Nichi-Bei Kaisen to Nichi-Soren Kankei' (Soviet-Japanese Relations and the Outbreak of War Between Japan and the United States) in C. Hosoya, N. Homma, A. Iriye and S. Hatano (eds.), *Taiheiyō Sensō* (The Pacific War), (Tokyo: Tokyo University Press, 1993), pp. 133-61.

21. PRO FO371/24724 F2072/23/23, Shigemitsu/Butler conversation, 18 March 1940, and FO371/24708 F3174/193/61, Shigemitsu/Butler conversation, 26 April 1940.

22. Shigemitsu, op. cit., p. 210.

23. Ibid, pp. 212-3. See also Best, op. cit., pp. 14-18.

24. Ibid, p. 212.

25. The contents of this telegram are taken from a British decrypt, see PRO WO208/862 BJ.082394 Shigemitsu to Matsuoka 25 July 1940, (no decryption date).

26. Shigemitsu to Matsuoka 5 August 1940, in R.J. Pritchard and S.M. Zaide (eds.), *The Tokyo War Crimes Trial*, Vol. IV, (New York: Garland, 1981), p. 9713.

27. Shigemitsu, op. cit., pp. 220-1.

28. Ibid, pp. 216-17 and p. 220.

29. Ibid, p. 222.
30. See A. Best, *Britain, Japan and Pearl Harbor: Avoiding War in East Asia, 1936-41*, London: Routledge, 1995, pp. 153-4.
31. Shigemitsu, op. cit., p. 230.
32. Best, *Britain, Japan and Pearl Harbor*, p. 155.
33. PRO WO208/862 BJ.090111, Shigemitsu to Matsuoka, 18 April 1941, decrypted 23 April 1941.
34. Best, *Britain, Japan and Pearl Harbor*, p. 157.

Chapter 19 SADAO OBA *Japanese Businessmen in the UK*

1. Japan Society of London, *Transactions & Proceedings*, Vol. 1 (1892)
2. Noboru Koyama, *Kokusai Kekkon Dai-ichi-go* (The first international marriage), Kodansha, 1995
3. *Minakata Kumagusu Chinji-hyoron*, edit. by Hasegawa/Takeuchi, Heibonsha, 1995
4. *Minakata Kumagusu Nikki* (diary), I 1885-1896, edit. by Hasegawa Yozo, Yasaka Shobo, 1987
5. *Nichi-Ei Shinshi* (Monthly Anglo-Japanese Journal), February 1916
6. *ditto* February 1916 & October 1918
7. *ditto*, July 1930
8. *ditto*, April 1922
9. *ditto*, February 1917
10. *ditto*, November 1924
11. Letter from Doshisha University, February 1996
12. Japan Society of London, *Transactions & Proceedings*, Vol. 20 (1922)
13. *Nichi-Ei Shinshi*, December 1922
14. Ito Yosaburo, *Kaikoroku* (Memoirs), Mitsui & Co., 1976
15. *Nichi-Ei Shinshi*, July 1928
16. Ito, *Kaikoroku*
17. *ditto*
18. The six page leaflet is kept by the British Library
19. *Kaikoroku*
20. Telephone talk with Mrs Hideko Ito, daughter of Kano Hisaakira, March 1996
21. Ariyoshi Yoshiya, *Kaiun 50 Nen* (50 years in the shipping business), Nippon Kaiji Shinbunsha, 1975
22. Connery Chappell, *Island of Barbed Wire*, 1984
23. Ito, *Kaikoroku*
24. Ariyoshi, *Kaiun 50 Nen*
25. Ariyoshi Yoshiya, *Hana to Yanagi to*, Kokusai Kaiun Shinbunsha 1963
26. Telephone talk with Mrs Hideko Ito
27. *Asahi Shimbun Gendai Jinbutsu Jiten* (Asahi Press Who's Who of Today), Asahi Shinbunsha 1990
28. *Journey*, (Monthly magazine) July 1993
29. Information from JCCI/UK, January 1996
30. Information from the British Embassy, Tokyo, February 1996

31. *Big Ben* (journal of Nippon Club, London), May 1995

Chapter 20 CARMEN BLACKER *Christmas Humphreys and Japan, 1901-83*

1. Toby left two volumes of autobiography, *Via Tokyo*, 1948, contains the account of his visit to Japan in 1946, the War Crimes Trial, his Buddhist encounters and his journey home through China, Siam, Burma and India. *Both Sides of the Circle*, 1978, is a full autobiography. His father was the eminent judge, Sir Travers Humphreys.
2. *Via Tokyo*, chapter 8.
3. See Toby's *Sixty Years of Buddhism in England (1907-1967): a History and a Survey*, 1968, pp. 41, 56, 75.
4. *Via Tokyo*, chapters 4-7.
5. *Sixty Years*, p. 56. The visitors included Professor Ogata Sōhaku from Shōkokuji, Asahina Sōgen Rōshi from Engakuji in Kamakura, and Mr Hori Masato.
6. A few of Alan Watts's titles give an idea of his message. *Beat Zen, Square Zen and Zen*, 1959; *Nature Man and Woman, a New Approach to Sexual Experience*, 1958; *This is It*, 1961; *Erotic Spirituality*, 1974. See also the interesting biography by Monica Furlong, *Genuine Fake*, 1986, which describes his mounting sense of unease in continuing to instruct people 'how to live' when he was dying of LSD and vodka.
7. Toby was awarded the Prize for 1975 of the Bukkyō Dendō Kyōkai, or Society for the Propagation of Buddhism, conferred on him in London. His friendly correspondence with the Reverend Shōjun Bandō, of the Jōdo Shin sect, during the 1970s, should not go unremembered. In the course of many letters he reported that 'our work in London flourishes exceedingly'.

I must record my grateful thanks to the Venerable Myōkyōni of the Zen Centre to which Toby left his old home in St John's Wood, for generous help in this recollection.

Chapter 21 SIR HUGH CORTAZZI *Sir Vere Redman, 1901-1975*

Acknowledgements. I am indebted to many of Vere Redman's friends and acquaintances for information and stories about him. I should like to thank in particular. Professor W.G. Beasley, Dr Antony Best, Dr Carmen Blacker, Lady Bouchier (Dorothy Britton), Meriel Boyd, Sir Norman Brain, Reginald Close, Professor Ronald Dore, Richard Ellingworth, Sir Sydney Giffard, Henry Hainworth, Dr Jim Hoare, Ambassador Masayoshi Kakitsubo, Dr Douglas Kenrick, Dr Peter Lowe, Father Peter Milward, Professor Ian Nish, Paul Norbury, Duncan MacFarlane, Lady Pilcher, Lady Spreckley, Dorothie Storry, Donald Warren Knott, Professor Hugh Wilkinson.

1. Masayoshi Kakitsubo in a note dated 16 November 1995 commented that: 'Mrs Redman was a lively and independent person and their marriage was by no means always tranquil. I recall once seeing them having a loud argument in the Tokyo Kaikan restaurant.' See also note 58.
2. Letter from Sir Sydney Giffard of 26 October 1995.

3. Letter from R.H.Ellingworth of 17 October 1995.

4. Letter from Lady Bouchier of 11 February 1996.

5. Letter from Meriel Boyd of 12 November 1995: 'He was appallingly unforgiving. My successor was a better secretary but he never liked her. She committed the unpardonable sin of being off sick in the day but being seen out at a party that evening. . .He was furious at my taking her part. . .and his implacable hostility to her never left him. . .I think he never changed his mind about people: there were goodies, baddies and the rest, to whom he was indifferent.' Letter from Lady Bouchier of 11 February 1996: He harboured a grudge against John Morris, author of *Traveller from Tokyo*, London, 1943, and *The Phoenix Cup*, London, 1947, for 'having, as Vere contended, published a book that consisted entirely of the pickings of Vere's brains. I remember one day Vere looking out of the Information Section window and seeing John Morris entering the gate, whereupon grunting: "I don't want to see that man", he tore down the stairs and out the side door of the Chancery, leaving me to fabricate something when John made his appearance. For my part, I was rather pleased to see him, having worked for him in the BBC.'

6. Letter from Lady Bouchier of 11 February 1996: 'Perhaps he was under too much stress in the office to pay too much attention, but I always found him an exceptionally good listener outside office hours. I found him far from egotistical in the long sea voyage home with Vere and Madeleine the year he retired when, since there were only four passengers, we were in close contact the whole time.'

7. In her letter of 12 November 1995 Meriel Boyd wrote that she seemed to have an instinct for dealing with him '(because I liked him, I suppose, and found him both warm and interested and also fun and stimulating), so we always got on well. . .One of the things I did was take no notice at all of either his bad temper and irritable remarks (fixing one with that ghastly stare) or of his , what would be called these days, sexual harrassment (which was simply a totally non-serious, non-lecherous even, way of caressing one). I think both were aimed at provocation and I sensed immediately that the worst possible response would be – well any response at all. So I ignored both. He used to have a little tuneless hum as he walked about the office, chain-smoking, of course. His jokes would be frequently repeated: "Er – spelt with a zed, dear, as in banana," plays with people's names. . .'

8. Letter from Lady Bouchier of 11 February 1996: 'the four-letter words, the bottom-pinching, and verbal abuse'.

9. Robert Boyd (note dated 12 November 1995) said that Vere had told him that 'on initial diagnosis he was sent off to die, as this was the only outcome. Suddenly, he was recalled to be given a chance with the new treatment – insulin. He was thus one of that special cohort of diabetics for whom insulin came just in time'.

10. Letter from Meriel Boyd of 12 November 1995 but confirmed by all who knew him. Donald Warren Knott in a letter dated 5 December 1995 drew attention to the imagination which Madeleine Redman displayed in the presentation of meals when they were entertaining after the war. These were

'always a delight for the eyes as well as a feast for the stomach'. He recalled that 'One summer evening Madeleine had set three shallow bowls of pale green pottery on the table. Each held a "fish path" ikebana arrangement by her of flowers and reeds appropriate to the occasion, but she had enhanced the "fish path" in each case with tiny real goldfish. The admiration excited by these gave way to consternation when, presumably because the oxygen in the shallow water had become low, the fish began to leap onto the table. The efforts of the guests and the maids to rescue the slippery suicides enlivened what was already, as usual, a lively party.'

11. Letter from Douglas Kenrick dated 1 November 1995.

12. He took the initiative in collecting funds to build the embassy's swimming pool.

13. Letter from Lady Bouchier of 11 February 1996: 'The reason they had no children was deliberate on account of Vere's diabetes. Fear of passing it on, perhaps? I can't remember why, but I remember he was telling me about his diabetes and then added, in his provocative way, "So don't ask me to give you any children"!'

14. Letter from Lady Bouchier of 11 February 1996: 'A constant stream of people with problems used to visit him at breakfast time in his house. I, myself, had occasion to ask his advice about a personal problem, and was extremely impressed with the way he gave me his full attention as if my problem was the most important thing in the world. I consider this a very rare ability indeed.'

15. In a lecture to the Japan Society on 16 September 1958 given by Redman on the theme 'Things I have learned in and from Japan' [Japan Society *Bulletin*, 27 (1959)] he referred to his small home and the cluttered rooms.

16. Meriel Boyd wrote: 'He was extremely sensitive about his Catholicism, I suspect because he broke all the rules but never admitted to himself how fundamentally uninterested he was in the whole thing. He used to wear a certain look and voice when speaking of his religion which I feel now, thinking about it, masked his possibly rather ashamed indifference.'

17. Unpublished article for *Tsuru*, a magazine to be published by Paul Norbury for Japan Air Lines, written apparently in 1973 shortly before he died.

18. Lecture given by Sir Vere Redman to The Japan Society on 11 October 1966 in *Bulletin*, 51 (1967) on the theme 'Foreign Teachers in Japan'.

19. Unpublished article for *Tsuru*.

20. Unpublished article for *Tsuru*.

21. Note by Masayoshi Kakitsubo dated 16 November 1995 who added: 'One day he proposed a wager on which party would win more votes in the upcoming UK General Election. I forget the amount, but I accepted the bet. In fact I won, but he paid me with a cheque – and it bounced.'

22. Lecture to the Japan Society on 'Things I have learned in and from Japan', 16 September 1958.

23. In his Lecture to the Japan Society on 11 October 1966 on 'Foreign Teachers in Japan' he told his audience a good deal more about Palmer.

24. Unpublished article for *Tsuru*.

25. Letter from Professor Hugh Wilkinson dated 18 October 1995.

26. Lecture on 'Foreign Teachers in Japan'. Carmen Blacker recalls Redman saying to her that 'Any foreign teacher coming to Japan, whatever he might profess, was always sooner or later reduced to one of two moulds. He could either be a teacher of English, or an "environer". The supreme example of an "environer" was Edmund Blunden. With such people it did not matter whether you understood a word they said. You simply had to sit in their presence to receive the beneficial effects of their character by osmosis.'

27. Unpublished article for *Tsuru*.

28. Lecture on 'Things I have learned in and from Japan', 16 September 1958.

29. Unpublished article for *Tsuru*.

30. Letter from Sir Norman Brain dated 17 October 1995.

31. In *The case of Richard Sorge* by F.W.Deakin and G.R.Storry, London 1966, page 297; 'It was Craigie's view that the Germans were the prime movers in this unpleasant affair, and there is no reason to doubt that this was so. But, affected by the current xenophobia, the police and judicial authorities – perceiving the range of Sorge's activities and knowing that Vukelic had contacts in the British Embassy – certainly suspected that Redman might have been in touch with the Sorge ring.' Dr Antony Best has pointed out in his letter of 30 November 1995 that 'By 1941, British propaganda had slightly changed its priorities and efforts were made to publish and disseminate material designed to cause problems for the German-Japanese alliance. In July 1941, Craigie and Redman approved an SOE plan for a news story to be planted within an American newspaper detailing German fifth column activities in Japan. This move helped in September 1941 to provoke a Japanese clampdown on all foreigners in Japan.

32. It was later alleged that this was because the embassy had not pressed the case for his inclusion on the grounds that he was not an established member of either the diplomatic or consular services and that he was not 'a gentleman'.

33. According to Sir Robert Craigie's autobiography *Behind the Japanese Mask*, London, 1946, Craigie sent his wife on the morning of 8 December 1941 to try to extricate Mrs Redman, but Lady Craigie was at first refused access and the police refused to release Mrs Redman. Her release was eventually arranged after the Chief of Protocol in the Ministry of Foreign Affairs agreed to intervene.

34. Craigie, in his autobiography, p. 143, makes it clear that the Chief of Protocol, Kiuchi, had threatened that, if Redman was not surrendered, this 'might cause a change in the attitude of the police authorities toward myself and my staff.' Just before the arrest, Kiuchi made a formal call in top-hat and tail-coat to inform Craigie that the police would make a forcible arrest. Craigie describes how the *Kempeitai* in full force invaded the residence and recorded that: 'Some sixty plain-clothes gendarmes, hands grasping revolvers inside their pockets in true gangster style, had taken up positions around the house and in the garden; they were even discovered in the trees! Apparently the *Kempei* had taken literally my warning that I intended to oppose Redman's

arrest and had anticipated a battle royal in the Embassy's grounds!'

35. Craigie insisted that the Redmans stay in the residence which he considered as safe a location as any; invasion of the residence would, he thought, be even more contrary to diplomatic practice than a move into the chancery building which was also used in those days to house language students in the consular service and which is nearer the embassy gate.

One story which I heard about the arrest must be apocryphal. This was that Vere Redman was smuggled between the Chancery building and the Ambassador's residence by crawling through the underground passage used for the central heating pipes. If he had done so I fear that like Pooh he might have had to stay there until he slimmed down, although he might well have been able to do this crawl after he was released as he had lost a great deal of weight as a result of his ordeal.

36. Craigie in his autobiography. p. 137 recorded: 'Although Mr Redman's activities had been confined to presenting-and presenting very ably-the British case in our war with Germany and Italy, and he had scrupulously avoided any action or propaganda directed against Japan, I knew that his barbed shafts had infuriated the Germans, who might now be relied upon to seek their revenge. I accordingly instructed Mr Redman to remain in the Embassy.'

37. Unpublished article for *Tsuru*.

38. Masayoshi Kakitsubo who was working in the Gaimusho in the summer of 1942 was ordered to escort the British party to Yokohama to board the ship which was to take them to Lourenzo Marques where the exchange was to be effected. 'Just when they were about to get into the Embassy cars at the Embassy compound, Mr Redman, a diabetic, who had been kept in custody by the Kempeitai, fainted for lack of insulin. After some delay we set out for Yokohama. It was hot but the cars had no air-conditioning. Lady Craigie, the Ambassador's American wife, grew impatient (as she often did) and wanted the cars to drive fast so that a cool breeze would come in through the open windows; but I reminded her that we had a sick man with us, and the convoy continued at a sedate pace. When we arrived at the dock, Redman was still pale and shaky, and I literally had to help him up the gangway and into the cabin. His wife, a French lady, was most grateful for my help and to my amazement (for it was war time), she produced a bottle of cognac and offered it to me. I replied politely that I did not drink.'

39. Sir Arthur de la Mare who was then a member of the embassy staff recorded in his autobiography 'Perverse and Foolish' Jersey, 1994, p. 80: 'We told them of his need for insulin, but they merely said that was just too bad.' Paul Gore Booth in his autobiography *With Great Truth and Respect*, London, 1974, (p. 111) wrote: 'Vere's captors, after letting him collapse by withholding his insulin in an effort to force him to talk, realized that dead he would be of no use to them. He survived his eight months' solitary, was evacuated with the rest of us, played a notable part in information work in India in the war, and returned to Japan later to become something of a legend as the foreigner with the most personal friends among the Japanese.'

40. Meriel Boyd in her letter of 12 November 1995 said that Vere never

forgot the loyalty of his Japanese friends, who must have risked a lot visiting him and supplying him, I think, with a few material comforts [during his imprisonment]. He used to tell how, although he was harshly treated (and perhaps even tortured?) by the Japanese, his only really bad moment was when two German Nazi officers came into the room. He realized that he could maintain some sort of relationship with and understanding of his Japanese captors – this was something else, far more frightening.'

41. Japan Society *Bulletin*, 27 (1959).

42. Letter from Sir Vere Redman to Paul Norbury dated 22 January 1973.

43. Lady Pilcher is the source for this story.

44. Donald Warren Knott in a letter of 5 December 1995 recorded that, as a junior and bachelor member of the Information Section, he was expected to be more or less at Vere Redman's disposal no matter how odd the hours. One of his tasks was to take male guests 'on the town'. These included Arthur Koestler when he was seeking material for his book *The Lotus and the Robot*. Donald added: 'After a Sunday night hearing about the pieces to go into EKK [Eikoku wa ko kangaeru i.e. British Opinion] the next week, both of us lubricated by gin and I half asphyxiated with his cigarette smoke, he would talk of some of his experiences. Life would have been much duller for me – and I suspect for many others – if I had not known Vere Redman.'

Lady Bouchier in her letter of 11 February 1996 wrote: 'I learned a lot from him, too, about how to write clear, unambiguous English.'

45. Japan Society *Bulletin*, 9 (1953).

46. Japan Society *Bulletin*, 37 (1962).

47. Japan Society *Bulletin*, 51 (1967).

48. Letter from R.H.Ellingworth dated 17 October 1995.

49. Letter from Professor W.G.Beasley dated 24 October 1995.

50. Reg Close in a letter dated 30 November 1995 commented that his relations with Vere Redman were professional and friendly. They were both academically interested in the teaching of English as a foreign language. They first came in contact in 1933 when Reg Close was in China and Redman in Tokyo. They met through Harold Palmer. When Close left Japan he was appointed to direct the British Council's 'Teaching of English Overseas' operation and Redman came to see him in London to discuss this with him. Reg and Eleanor Close visited the Redmans after their retirement to France. Following Madeleine Redman's death they again visited Vere who insisted that Eleanor Close should have a piece of Madeleine's jewellery. Reg Close added that he admired Vere very much. Madeleine and Vere had been very kind to him and his wife.

51. Donald Warren Knott in his letter of 5 December 1995 said that he only saw Vere Redman on stage once in Tokyo 'when he appeared as the priest at the end of "Twelfth Night" in 1957, but I remember his surprisingly good delivery and his obvious enjoyment of being in the play.'

52. Basil Greenhill,CB, CMG, became the Director of the National Maritime Museum at Greenwich (1967-1983). He has also written many works about maritime matters and has been an eminent public figure. Mrs Greenhill

referred to here was his first wife Gillian who died in 1959.

53. Japan Society *Bulletin*, 27 (1959).

54. Donald Warren Knott in his letter of 5 December 1995 said: '[Vere's] set piece before a lunch party at his house is an example. As the guests gathered in the drawing-room he, without abandoning his perpetual cigarette, his drink or his flow of conversation, would shed his jacket, roll up his sleeve, receive from Madeleine a jab of insulin, resume his jacket and sweep his guests into the meal.'

55. Donald Warren Knott said that he recalled this phrase of Vere's when he came across Arthur Koestler's comment in *The Lotus and the Robot* that for a foreigner life in Japan is like lying in a hot scented bath – and receiving the occasional sharp electric shock.

56. Donald Warren Knott in his letter of 5 December 1995 recorded this comment.

57. Meriel Boyd recorded that in Goult it was Vere 'who did the before-breakfast shopping for baguette, cigarettes and the newspaper, stomping along with a basket, humming his non-tune, black beret on his head, throwing remarks at shopkeepers and passers-by, making the same sort of jokes in French as he had in English. I think he was probably very happy in retirement, continuing to write a bit, visits to England perhaps twice a year, a good relationship with a semi-retired judge in the village. . .And lots of visitors of all kinds. . .Four of us arrived one day back from a holiday driving to Istanbul and back. We camped in the garden. My husband to be and another man also called Robert were of the party. Vere couldn't resist it. "So it's Robert and Robbie and Bob's your uncle!"'

Meriel Boyd found him more difficult to handle when he was the host. 'I couldn't so easily employ my technique of ignoring his bad moods and furious asides as when I was working for him. Occasionally, I got quite irritated back and tried to argue with him. Fatal – he always had the last word. When he was really angry he would put me in coventry. It was quite uncomfortable. But on the whole I had some extremely happy times there, year after year. The clouds never lasted long, and . . .I got very fond of Madeleine, a lovely gentle person who put up with a hell of a lot, much of the time, from Vere I suspect. Come to think of it, she ignored his more outrageous moods. The worst thing for him was that his mother in her late nineties had to come and live with them for her last few years. She hated France and everything French and spent her whole time when she wasn't watching television complaining and demanding the way old people so often do. When Madeleine died Vere was heartbroken, and he blamed his mother for it. Robert and I visited him in about 1971 and were rather taken aback one lunch-time, when his mother opened her mouth to say something, Vere turned on her furiously saying, "Let murderers keep silent!" It rather put a stop to further conversation. . .The last time I saw Vere was not very long before he died. He'd had one heart attack already and I decided to go out and pay him a visit. He wasn't at all well and stayed in bed most of the time on doctor's orders. A kind, American I think, friend was keeping house for him. She was no cook and the uninspiring meals drove

Vere into a frenzy of rage. He claimed she was giving him the wrong balance of food for his diabetes, but it was really, I feel sure, the flavour which was at fault. I think the poor woman was trying to economise – there was a lot of such dishes as cauliflower cheese – and it now occurs to me that quite possibly Vere was forgetting to give her any money. Anyway she came in for a lot of anger and irritation. He had a small heart attack while I was there but it settled down again. A few months later I heard he'd died. . .It seems he fell down in the street, and it was very quick.'
58. Letter to Paul Norbury dated 22 January 1973 about possible contributors to *Tsuru*.

Chapter 22 ROBIN GRAY *The Anglo-Japanese Commercial Treaty of 1963: A British Perspective*

SHORT BIBLIOGRAPHY:

Foreign and Commonwealth Office files (Public Record Office, Kew), FO 371/164994-165003
Treaty of Commerce, Establishment and Navigation between the United Kingdom of Great Britain and Northern Ireland and Japan, in Treaty Series no 53 (1963) (Cmd 2085)
Government Statement on the Anglo-Japanese Commercial Treaty, November 1962 (Cmd 1875)
David Greenaway and Brian Hindley, 'What Britain Pays for Voluntary Export Restraints' in Thames Essays no 43, Trade Policy Research Centre, 1985
John Jackson, *The World Trading System: Law and Policy of International Relations*, MIT Press, London, 1989
Ian Nish, 'The Economic Bases of Japan's Foreign Relations' in *Social Structures and Economic Dynamics in Japan*, Milan: Luigi Bocconi University, 1975, pp. 289-302

Index